Jane Hutcheon bec[...] [...]on's China corresponde[...] five years. Born and rais[...] nate observer of China, a family tradition since [...] and-uncle Phineas arrived on the China coast in the mid 1800s. Jane has travelled widely throughout Asia and speaks Cantonese and Mandarin. She is a former presenter of *World at Noon* on ABC television, and is currently the ABC's Middle East correspondent based in Jerusalem.

FROM RICE TO RICHES

A personal journey through a changing China

JANE HUTCHEON

MACMILLAN

Pan Macmillan Australia

Note on exchange rates:
At the time of writing, A$1 = 4 yuan and US$1 = 8.26 yuan.

First published 2003 in Macmillan by Pan Macmillan Australia Pty Limited
St Martins Tower, 31 Market Street, Sydney

National Library of Australia
Cataloguing-in-Publication data:

Hutcheon, Jane.
From rice to riches: a personal journey through a changing China.

ISBN 0 7329 1172 9.

1. Hutcheon, Jane – Journeys – China.
2. China – Description and travel. I. Title.

951.06

Set in 12/16 pt New Caledonia by Post Pre-press Group, Brisbane
Cover and text design by Antart
Maps by Laurie Whiddon
Front cover photographs by Peter John Cantrill and Jane Hutcheon
Back cover photograph by Stephen Hutcheon
Printed in Australia by McPherson's Printing Group

For my parents, Bea and Robin

CONTENTS

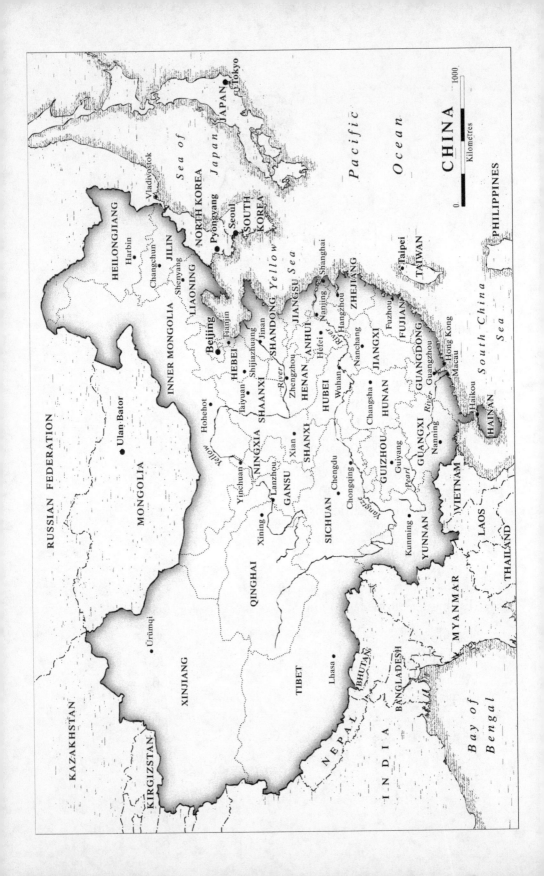

INTRODUCTION · CHOPSTICKS

'I don't want to sound paranoid – and please don't turn around – but I think we're being followed.'

Three heads immediately turned to peer out of the car's rear window.

'Not possible!' exclaimed our Chinese researcher, Zhang Lijia. She looked at me in such a way as to imply that I was clueless about how her country worked.

'You've lost it, Jane!' said Leon, the sound recordist.

'Who would follow us?' asked Sebastian Phua, the ABC's hippy cameraman.

I lowered my powder compact with the small mirror inside – I had used it to check what was going on behind me, like some 1960s Hollywood spy. Was I paranoid? Having been the ABC's China correspondent for six months, I thought I was just being vigilant.

'We've made four turns and there's a white car behind us that has done exactly the same thing,' I said, flustered. There was silence. 'Okay,' I reasoned, 'why don't we ask the driver to go around that roundabout twice and we'll see what happens.'

My colleagues agreed and the taxi-driver proved friendly and obliging. I held up my compact again to monitor the white car's movements, while the others tried nonchalantly to observe the tail. The big white car followed our taxi once around the roundabout.

Then twice. Doubt removed, we all sat quietly for a moment, unsure how to proceed.

'Where to now?' asked the taxi-driver, who must have decided that foreigners were indeed very strange creatures.

We were in the small, unwelcoming city of Clam Wharf (or, in Chinese, Bengbu), 1545 kilometres south-east of Beijing. A city of more than half a million people, it lies on the Huai River in central Anhui province. Bengbu had once been a famous centre for freshwater pearls because the fast-flowing waters of the 1000-kilometre-long river provided the perfect conditions for oyster cultivation. Throughout the 1980s, however, over-zealous industrialisation in what was once an agricultural heartland had polluted the water. Instead of pristine pearls, Bengbu and the surrounding towns began to produce more practical commodities like paper. By the mid 1990s, there was a paper mill every kilometre of the Huai River's length, and in several sections the river was literally dead. The anger – and in some cases despair – of local residents spilled out in front of our camera.

'The river can't be cleaned up even if they try for ten years. That's the truth!' said a woman among a crowd of people who had come to watch us film beside a stretch of the black river. It was unusual for someone to speak their mind so forthrightly to a foreign television crew. Apart from the fear of officials overhearing and seeking reprisal against the detractor, many Chinese people believe it is unpatriotic to be critical of their own country in front of foreigners. The outburst demonstrated the level of local frustration. Someone quietly chided the woman, but she immediately turned to her critic and retorted, 'What's the point in telling lies?'

Nearby, an elderly man in loose shorts and shirt and a floppy straw hat carefully stepped onto the bank to fill his buckets to water his crops. The water he scooped from the river was slimy and brown. 'This water is poisonous!' said the old farmer. 'It is killing my plants.'

The black river story was a wake-up call to me. Just a few weeks before in Beijing, the head of China's powerful Environmental

Protection Agency (EPA) had given his blessing for the Australian Broadcasting Corporation to film an investigative report on the pollution that caused grief to tens of millions of people and was a serious blight on one of China's major river systems. Despite the EPA chief welcoming the focus and assigning one of his colleagues to travel with us, on the ground in far-off Anhui province it was a different story. There, local officials arranged our schedule around meals rather than opportunities to film the environmental degradation.

On this assignment, I had sent Lijia, the ABC researcher, to the region one week before the official tour. When the rest of us arrived the officials contradicted most of what local residents had told her and refused to take us to the offending outfalls that she had located as the sources of pollution. When it became clear we were intent on filming what wasn't supposed to be revealed to foreign journalists, the surveillance team in the white car was dispatched to follow the camera crew and me as we attempted to film one evening before dinner.

To escape our tail, we changed taxis twice and eventually dived into a crowded street market. We managed to elude our followers and in the process film several highly critical interviews about the effect pollution was having on the population and the government's inadequate response to it.

While on one level the black river told the story of China's struggle to become a developed nation, it also taught me that Chinese officials did not like the way the foreign media viewed their country. They were extremely sensitive to criticism and unhappy about us filming areas that made China look poor or backward. As a correspondent I had to learn that there were various ways of going about my work. I could concentrate on non-controversial cultural stories or I could attempt to tell the wider account of a country struggling to modernise and regain its place in the world in the short space of half a century. To do this, I had to be resourceful and vigilant, and often had to check to see whether the crew and I were being followed. As well as being viewed with suspicion because I was a foreign journalist, I also learned that rules made in Beijing were ignored or side-stepped in the provinces, and the views of ordinary citizens were usually drowned in the pursuit of the government's 'greater good'.

In the new millennium China's catch-phrase is breakneck change. In 2003 a new generation of leadership took the reins, the fourth generation since the Communists came to power in 1949. The line-up will be in place in 2008 when Beijing will play host to the world at the Olympic Games. The country's accession to the World Trade Organisation is accelerating what has already been a remarkable quarter-century of economic transformation. When Mao Zedong died and the Gang of Four were toppled in the late 1970s, the vast majority of Chinese people could barely afford the rice in their bowls. Today rice is regarded as a belly-filler to supplement other more expensive and nourishing foods such as fish or lean meat. Not only does the population eat better, but now many can even afford diamonds, villas and fast cars. At the start of the 1980s, 220 million Chinese people lived in poverty. Today, albeit with much foreign assistance, the figure has dropped to less than 30 million. In the early eighties it was rare to find a telephone in a Chinese household. By 2005 the country will have 250 million mobile phone users, the highest usage in the world.

When I first visited Beijing in 1986 I travelled on a bumpy 'highway' where private cars – then a new phenomenon – competed with donkey-drawn carts laden with cabbages bound for the city markets. In 1993 I drove down the old airport highway and, on the same visit a few weeks later, returned to the airport on a brand-new six-lane tollway. And perhaps the most astonishing symbol of achievement, in 2003 or 2004 China will send an astronaut into space in its Shenzhou ('the divine land') rocket series.

Chinese people are getting richer by the day. Between one and two hundred million people now make up a class of consumers with enough purchasing power to buy anything from imported lipsticks to DVD players to apartments. A smaller number of people are as wealthy as millionaires in the rest of Asia or the Western world. Thirty or so Chinese people even own Porsches. At least one delegate to China's legislature, the National People's Congress, travels to meetings in Beijing in his private jet.

In many Chinese cities where tea or water was once the main beverage, you can drink cappuccino at one of the scores of Starbucks outlets. At Zhengzhou airport in central Henan province I was recently offered an 'Italy cappuccino' made with instant coffee topped by frothy milk, without chocolate powder. When I asked to see the frothing machine, the waitress proudly produced a coffee plunger from a refrigerator behind the counter. She poured milk into the plunger and pumped the handle until the cold milk turned to froth.

'New Beijing, Great Olympics' proclaim the slogans plastered around Beijing today. 'Without the Communist Party there is no New China,' goes a song taught to kindergarten children. Yet with all the progress a quarter-century after emerging from the isolation, tumult and squalor of Mao Zedong's Cultural Revolution, China's new facade hides a multitude of problems. Many have dogged the nation for centuries, others are the result of the unfinished economic transformation started by Deng Xiaoping and continued by Jiang Zemin and the new president Hu Jintao.

No longer an ideological and inward-looking nation, China's Fourth Generation leadership is less likely to stick to a stubborn world view which runs against internationally accepted norms. However its population remains deeply nationalistic and even well-educated Chinese who understand Western ways and work in foreign companies dislike the American domination of global politics. While the government has played a more predictable diplomatic role in recent years, it can also revert to outdated dogma when it comes to unresolved issues like reunification with an unwilling Taiwan.

The 'iron rice bowl' system of cradle-to-grave social security perfected by the Maoists has been shattered in order to give the economy and the current regime a chance of long-term survival. But the modern-day rice bowl isn't yet well defined, which creates social tensions and an undercurrent of uncertainty.

This book, then, is a journey through an ancient civilisation undergoing a rapid and radical facelift. It contains the thoughts and words of the Chinese people I met, interviewed and befriended before and during my five-year posting as the ABC's China correspondent. It is also a book about coming to grips with China and trying to reconcile my own past.

My link to China was forged before my birth. The youngest of three children, I was born in the former British colony of Hong Kong, which reverted to Chinese sovereignty in 1997 after 156 years of British rule. My Eurasian mother Beatrice had spent most of her life in Hong Kong, living there from the early 1930s until the 1980s. Both she and my Anglo-Celtic father Robin had been born in Shanghai during its heyday as Asia's financial capital and 'sin' city in the 1920s. Shanghai is now trying to reclaim its title as China's paramount city.

My father, who grew up in Shanghai and Sydney, returned to the China coast in 1953 to work for Hong Kong's English language newspaper, the *South China Morning Post*, becoming editor-in-chief in 1967. My brothers and I grew up in Hong Kong in the 1960s and 1970s, when China's relationship with the rest of the world was tortured and vitriolic, reflecting the turmoil taking place within the Maoist state, just a few kilometres to Hong Kong's north. I followed the family trade; four out of five are or were journalists. My eldest brother Stephen joined the *Sydney Morning Herald* shortly after I began studying journalism at Charles Sturt University (formerly Mitchell College of Advanced Education) in 1981, and my other brother Andrew is a lawyer. I initially chose to study journalism not because of any obvious influence from my parents, but because Mitchell College enabled me to major in drama, which I loved. However I soon discovered the joys of journalism: I could indulge my insatiable curiosity about the way people live, fight, survive, die, create and destroy. This curiosity was fuelled each time

I returned to Hong Kong during the semester breaks, when I worked as a radio reporter for Radio Television Hong Kong. It was during this time that Vietnamese boat people were flooding the territory and given refuge in squalid camps before being allocated a new country. I befriended a British medical intern who secured us passes to one of the closed camps where we spent a week interviewing and photographing the refugees without any official interference. Whether they had left for economic or political reasons, their dangerous voyages and desire for a better future left a deep impression on me.

After graduating, I decided to return to Hong Kong, where the stories seemed to me to be so much more exciting than anything that was happening elsewhere in the region. With officials already locked in negotiations over Hong Kong's return to China, the territory was in the world's focus and making the most of its economic links with southern China. The domestic Asia Television (ATV) channel offered me my first television reporting role and from that moment I was smitten with the medium. As a young television reporter in 1986, I covered two major news events that awakened my fascination for China and thrust before me the complexities of its sensitive relationship with Taiwan, which China viewed then and now as a renegade province. The first was an unusual hijacking, the second was the Queen's first visit to the People's Republic after Britain and China had reached agreement on the terms of Hong Kong's return.

On 3 May 1986 a China Airlines jetliner belonging to Taiwan, flying from Bangkok to Taipei via Hong Kong, made an unauthorised landing at Guangzhou's White Cloud Airport. The plane was piloted by 57-year-old Wang Hsi-chueh. With him were his co-pilot, an engineer and a cargo of 96 500 kilograms of fruit and rubber tyres.

Within minutes of the plane's unscheduled landing, it was surrounded by gun-wielding People's Liberation Army soldiers. Then, before any orders had been given, Commander Wang Hsi-chueh appeared at the doorway and asked for political asylum. The defection

7

shocked Taiwan as much as it did the mainland. At the time, the tiny island was under the autocratic rule of Chiang Ching-guo, while in China the early stages of reform were in the air, albeit under the firm control of Deng Xiaoping.

In the days following, Commander Wang was feted by the Chinese government and his story provided a windfall for the state media. He told reporters it had been his long-held desire to return to the Chinese motherland, which he had been forced to flee with other family members at the age of twelve. His disbelieving wife, watching events from Taiwan, insisted her husband must have been brainwashed.

While the defection made world headlines for days, little attention was paid to the thorny issue of the presence of the plane and the two crew members who were 'guests' of the Chinese government. Meanwhile the grainy Chinese television pictures showed Commander Wang's arrival in Beijing. Still wearing his navy and white CAL pilot's uniform, Commander Wang descended the stairs of a chartered Air China jet to be treated as a people's hero and welcomed by a bevy of beautiful young women waving bunches of flowers. Waiting at the airport was Captain Wang's ageing father, dressed in a blue Mao jacket. It appeared to be a strange, unemotional reunion.

Eleven days after the plane touched down, Taiwan and China began negotiations for the return of the aircraft and its crew. It was a momentous meeting – Taiwanese and Chinese officials hadn't sat down together since the Nationalists had fled China for Taiwan in defeat in 1949. Taiwan had banned communication with the mainland: no mail, no transportation and no trade. In fact the only talk between them for 35 years had been of war.

The two sides chose Hong Kong as the venue for the negotiations. As a reporter for Hong Kong-based Asia Television, I covered the negotiations and the plane's return, which eventually took place at Kai Tak airport on 24 May 1986, three weeks after the drama began.

For the first and probably last time in my life, I was given access to China's highly secretive, defacto embassy in Hong Kong, to report on the meetings. The embassy was actually the New China News Agency; China would never agree to build an official embassy on soil that had been torn from it. I was familiar with the exterior of the New China News Agency building with its red Communist insignia above the iron gates of the entrance, but until the discussions over the plane, those doors had not been thrown open for a press conference. It was like entering a scene from Charles Dickens' *Great Expectations*; a dark, cavernous meeting hall was lined with heavy curtains drawn tightly together to block out intruding eyes. A long table had been placed in the centre of the hall and there, sitting together, were the three Chinas – British Hong Kong, Communist China and renegade Taiwan. The representatives smiled a lot, but a pall of anxiety hung in the air as they conversed in Mandarin. It was China's national language yet reaching an understanding seemed painfully difficult.

After reporting on my first ever handover ceremony, the return of the Taiwanese plane, I visited China later in 1986 to cover the first visit of a British sovereign. Though I had visited Shenzhen and Guilin in southern China before, I had never been to Beijing, and the whirlwind seven-day, six-city tour awakened a new curiosity in me. This was where my ancestors had come from and been drawn to, and the combination of authoritarian control, human diligence, the spectacular landscape but desperate poverty, made me want to learn much more. At the same time, the place of my birth, Hong Kong, was evolving from a beautiful city full of myths and fables about its mountains and rocks, as well as the personalities who lived there, into a modern metropolis. When I returned to work there as an adult, I found myself trying to rediscover the magical place I had known as a child. Sadly, it was being demolished to make way for a richer, status-conscious city that would ultimately be handed on a plate to another country.

After the Taiwanese plane incident, I decided to make a second handover the object of my ambition. By the early 1990s I had moved to Australia, despondent that my childhood home had disappeared. But I wasn't sure where home was or should be. I also felt the quality of Hong Kong's English language broadcasting was beginning to slip and that would affect my career one way or another. Yet I was still intrigued by China's unfolding transformation. By the mid 1990s I had become the Australian Broadcasting Corporation's China correspondent, living in Beijing and travelling to virtually every province. Eventually I covered Hong Kong's return to China, just as I'd planned so many years before. I also covered the death of paramount leader Deng Xiaoping, the Tenth Anniversary of the Tiananmen Massacre, the rise of Falun Gong and the unfolding of a modern nation of 1.3 billion people struggling, not just to survive, but to be a developed and powerful nation as it was before the decline of dynastic rule in the late nineteenth century.

There is already a great wall of words on China's latest transformation as foreign businesses and governments rush to break down the door to its vast market. But too much is written about the big picture – how size equals greatness – or individuals writing about their family's plight. The lives of ordinary people told me more about the country than any book about China I have ever read. 'The Communist Party is not the Chinese People,' a Beijing taxi-driver once told me. This feeling that ordinary views rarely rate a mention, combined with the frequent 'struggle sessions' I encountered over trying to tell the stories of China's wrestle with modernity, made me want to write this book.

Many Western analysts, particularly from the United States, predict that the pressures facing China will cause the present regime to collapse. Others, particularly Western business leaders, believe China is on its way to becoming the largest and most powerful economy in the world. Both scenarios have their elements of truth and wishful thinking.

The use of food as a metaphor throughout this book is apposite – when I think of China I think of food. China is renowned for its unique cuisine and rice is the staple dish. Even China's social security system is defined in terms of a rice bowl. Today, however, most of the nation does not rely only on rice, noodles or bread to fill the stomach; there is also meat and fish, and plenty of it. Until I moved to China, I had never been to a country where time was measured by the distance between meals, and where people would become unproductive if work strayed too far into the lunch hour, which began at twelve noon sharp. I enjoyed this obsession with food and found that restaurants were wonderful places to hold secret meetings with controversial characters or 'enemies of the people'. Food and the preparation of it frequently formed the backdrop to many of my television stories, since I discovered that people were most relaxed and comfortable when cooking up a storm in a giant wok or just seated around the dinner table.

My chopsticks and bowl were never empty, and each story I was told over every meal revealed a new morsel about a vast and complicated country, a morsel that added another piece to my understanding of China and how it came to be a part of my life.

PIG'S FACE

Eating braised pig's face for the first time requires the desire for a challenge and a strong, adventurous stomach. A white oval plate arrives at the table with a steaming pig profile upon it, floppy ear and snout included. Lying beneath the rich skin is delicious meat made succulent after several hours stewing in a secret concoction. Annoyingly, this prize is hidden under a mountain of opaque, wobbly fat. The challenge is to end up with tender morsels of meat and not a mouthful of blubber.

Consuming pig's face without letting the prize slip through your chopsticks requires dedication and patience. So did working in China as a foreign correspondent. Like eating pig's face I had to learn the etiquette of reporting China without running into the myriad of official blockages or simply giving up in frustration.

To assist newly arrived correspondents, the information division of the Chinese Foreign Ministry issues a handy rule booklet. The division is like a host organisation to the international press corps and Australian journalists are under the watchful eye of the Department of the Americas and Oceania. The Foreign Ministry minder I was told to report to, Mr Lin, had a surprisingly relaxed and casual demeanour. This was probably due to the fact that he had just returned from a posting in the United States, where he had spent many years. 'I've run out of those books I'm supposed to give you,' he said nonchalantly, 'but you know the rules; you have to get permission before you interview.'

The rules, which were written in the 1980s, are such that almost everything that comes naturally to a reporter in an overseas posting is considered *buxing*, not okay. Spontaneity is firmly discouraged. Written applications are required to interview officials or visit state entities like a construction site. For reporting beyond Beijing, foreign journalists are asked to apply to the Foreign Affairs Office (FAO) of the province they intend to travel to. Correspondents often use the Chinese name for the Foreign Affairs Office, *Waiban* (pronounced 'Why Ban'), because officials could ban us, and frequently did. The role of the FAO was to set up interviews and liaise with potential interviewees on the foreign news bureau's behalf. The Office was the first point of contact and if the *Waiban* director didn't approve of the story idea, permission was denied. It was rare to be told directly why the story was unsuitable. It was more common to hear a face-saving excuse like, 'Our office is very busy and we are unable to entertain your request at this time,' or, 'That person really isn't so interesting, but I have a better idea!'

Newspaper and radio journalists have an easier time dispensing with their official chaperones than television crews because, without bulky equipment, they can move around without attracting undue attention or controversy. The FAO charged between US$20 and $40 a day per foreigner for its service, which ranged from unhelpful, obstructive, lazy and incompetent to friendly and hardworking. As a general rule, FAO officials had very little understanding of how foreign television teams worked, and their job was to ensure that we had the best spin on a story, from the point of view of the Chinese government.

Because of the camera equipment we carried around and the need for a one- or two-person crew, trying to slip quietly into small cities or towns without attracting attention was a constant challenge. Often, the FAO's invitation was the only ticket to filming a story. Despite being part Chinese, I have fair skin and brown hair so in China I am instantly recognisable as a foreigner. Likewise, sound-recordist Kate Wakeman (who later became my sister-in-law) is also fair and could never blend into a Chinese crowd. But other long-term television colleagues did blend in. Charles Li, an invaluable researcher, computer whiz and human archive, travelled with me on virtually every assignment from the time he joined the ABC in October 1996. He replaced the opinionated but extremely bright Zhang Lijia, who left the ABC to have children and pursue her own journalism career. In my final year, we took on a bureau producer who doubled as a sound recordist, Cleo Leung, a lively American Chinese who grew up in Hong Kong and spoke fluent Mandarin and Cantonese. On the other hand, most Chinese didn't know what to make of our Singaporean cameraman, Sebastian Phua. His shoulder-length hair, headbands and tie-dye T-shirts always attracted much attention.

I discovered early in the piece that in some remote locations, not only would the provincial Foreign Affairs Office staff accompany us, but county-level and township or village officials would tag along too. A large minibus would have to be hired to transport the TV crew together with the official entourage to each location. To cap it off, a local television news team would often pull up shortly after our arrival at the location, tipped off by the FAO. All visits to small towns by foreigners are regarded as newsworthy and on those occasions when I was trying to find an element of controversy amongst the carnival atmosphere surrounding an official visit, the hangers-on made filming a constant challenge.

Far more frustrating than official visits out of Beijing were Foreign Ministry news package tours. These were designed specifically for foreign journalists, and they sometimes gave us access to difficult or off-limits people and places such as Tibet or the far-west province of Xinjiang. But there is an unspoken apprehension about letting foreigners linger in any one place for too long so, like all tour groups in China, correspondent tours were exhausting exercises: too many locations, extraneous interviews and meals thrown in. On these trips it was also a challenge to keep other cameras out of our shots, and nearly impossible to get minders to stop the bus in order to film relevant roadside action. In short, official trips were taxing, but often there was no other option. If I wanted to obtain a controversial interview or filming location, it was necessary to find some 'free time' or 'dinner without the crowd'.

As a result of the restrictions placed on foreign TV crews, unauthorised filming placed an unspoken pressure on me and I often thought up excuses on the way to a location in case we were caught. For example, I could claim that filming poor migrant areas was necessary for a story on a clever policy aimed at alleviating pressure on the underworked rural population. Feigning ignorance was also handy.

However not all police attention was unwelcome. At midnight on 31 December 1999, the crew and I filmed the Beijing millennium celebrations as part of the ABC's Y2K watch. Thousands of young people were out in force on a swarming Wangfujing Avenue. Seeing our camera, they thrust 'V' signs at the lens. Others followed, excited by the prospect of being on TV in another country. Suddenly, we were carried away in the sea of humanity moving with the crowd up Beijing's answer to the Champs Elysées.

Then I saw the familiar khaki hats moving towards us. It was the police, known in China as the *Gong An* or Public Security Bureau. As the crowds weren't part of an organised event, I didn't bother to get filming permission but I wasn't expecting any hassles. However when I saw the throng I realised that the police would be sensitive. Large gatherings – such as the Tiananmen protests of 1989 – offer the potential for civil unrest.

The crew and I were unceremoniously yanked through the crowd to a nearby junction, and as the huffing policemen dragged us along I wondered what it would be like to spend the first hours of the new millennium in a police cell. As the ABC bureau chief, I would probably be forced to write a 'self-criticism' of my actions. Developing this dismal scenario in my head, I felt annoyed and a little anxious. Then gaps began to appear in the crowd and the policemen relaxed their grip on our coats and sat us down on the street.

'You should be more careful,' said an officer, 'there are too many people on the street tonight. You shouldn't go back into the crowd.'

'Thank you, thank you!' Sebastian the cameraman said, shaking the officer's hand gratefully.

When I realised we were not being arrested but had merely been taken aside for our own safety, I vigorously shook the hand of one of the policemen and thanked him profusely.

Sebastian used to describe any trouble involving the Chinese authorities as 'getting busted', as if we were recalcitrant teenagers rather than journalists in search of a story. On the night of the new millennium we were spared the indignity, but altogether I was detained on four occasions, including, symbolically, my first and last assignments.

On the first occasion, the crew and I, together with Madeleine O'Dea, a Sydney-based producer, had travelled to picturesque countryside in central Anhui province. I decided that for my first major report in China I would focus on a phenomenon known as the 'floating population', the internal migration from countryside to city of some 150 million farmers. These migrants, fed up with the poverty of the land, began seeking a future in China's cities from the late 1980s. Though I was aware of the rule requiring permission to film outside Beijing, I chose to ignore it. I had already pinpointed the main character for the story, a Beijing-based migrant worker, Xiao Liangyu. A rubbish collector in his late twenties, he had agreed to take me back to his ancestral village for the traditional Spring Festival celebrations. I weighed up the risks, believing that if I approached the provincial Foreign Affairs Office I would end up losing control of the story, as the *Waiban* would certainly veto my selection and instead choose the perfect migrant worker who would naturally come from the most pristine village in China. I didn't want the sanitised view of why millions were leaving the countryside, so I decided the crew, producer, researcher and myself would go to the village with Mr Xiao and his family – but no official.

The village of Xiao Cun was a delightful escape from China's urban chaos. Deep in the heart of Anhui, it wasn't a place you just happened upon. It had taken us at least three hours by train and minibus to get there from the provincial capital, Hefei. Xiao Cun was hidden down a winding path near a bumpy road off the main highway from the provincial capital. The village was charming. It had 'mountains and water' as the Chinese often like to say in affirmation of geographical and geomantic balance and harmony. In warm weather the villagers grew rice, and in winter, rapeseed, cotton and wheat were planted in the hard, undulating hills.

Our team stayed in the village, the five of us staying in two different homes. It felt like a feudal farmstay, only we didn't pay for anything – the villagers refused to take any money. I stayed in a house with Madeleine and Lijia, down the hill from the Xiaos' place and past a small lake that the women seemed to use for all their chores, from washing clothes to gutting freshly killed chickens. I'd noticed the house on the day we arrived because there was a woman squatting in the front courtyard, peeling beans and dropping them into a bucket. The bucket caught my eye. It was wooden, held together with an iron belt and made so that it could sit on a yoke. It looked very old and had lots of character – I later saw that the women in all the other houses used modern plastic buckets.

Inside the house there were just two rooms, one for sleeping and the other for living. There was no flooring, just dirt, a single light bulb in each room, a black and white television and grimy glass windows with wooden shutters. The 'toilet', a hole in the ground with two planks of wood for your feet, was at the back of the house. It was best not to look down. In the few days I stayed in the village I never saw anyone taking a bath or shower. In fact, in the Xiaos' house and in the house where I stayed, there was just a single cold water tap in the kitchen, which was basically a wok furnace in a little alcove beside the front doorway. In the bedroom there were two large double beds. Unfortunately, the family's two little girls had been booted out of their bed to make way for Madeleine, Lijia and me. They slept with their parents in the other big bed.

Each family kept an assortment of farm animals including ducks, geese, chickens and pigs. In the egalitarian spirit of socialism, the animals stayed in the farmhouses with their owners. When the single light bulb and the TV were switched off at night, human snores mingled with the grunts, chatters and farts of the beasts. Come dawn, the cock in the next room let out deafening crows. It was still pitch black but the crowing was a signal for someone to shoo the animals outside into the yard where they wandered about for the rest of the day. The freedom made them content – and succulent, was my bet.

The village was just as I had imagined rural China to be, quiet and sparsely populated, nestled in coffee-coloured hills crisscrossed by meandering paths. Like the farmhouses we stayed in, most of them – around eighty or so – had stood unchanged for a hundred years. But a surprising number were being modernised, having extra storeys added as well as flushing toilets and hot running water.

This was the tangible result of the mass migration from countryside to city; when people like Mr Xiao began to make money, it was sent home to the village to build better homes and lives. In Beijing, Mr Xiao earned 2000 yuan per month – what many in his village earned in an entire year. His life as a garbage collector in Beijing was the envy of others, including his sister, Yu Fang. She was in her thirties and had never been to school. While her husband worked in the fields, she did chores and cared for her two children – in the countryside, the One Child policy doesn't apply because farmers have traditionally had large families to help with labour. Since family planning came in during the late 1970s, rural families have been allowed two children if the firstborn is a girl. In the past, girls were rarely sent to school because they would eventually be married into someone else's family, and boys like Mr Xiao rarely stayed at school beyond fourteen because of the pressure to work on the farm. Nowadays there is a greater emphasis on education, though in poor, remote areas you can still find little girls who don't go to school.

I enjoyed Xiao Cun very much and despite the lack of a shower I could have stayed in the village for a week. It was so pristine and quiet and the villagers were so kind. But the good luck I'd had so far was about to run out. In hindsight I was naive to believe that I could travel with a team of five, including three foreigners, into the heart of rural China without attracting attention. We were in the middle of an interview, with Mr Xiao telling me of his dream to become a chauffeur to the new rich, when his father hobbled towards us looking more alert than at any other time during our stay.

'They are here!' said the old farmer, shouting as he navigated the terraces. 'They are here for you.'

'They' meant the local Public Security Bureau or police, who had travelled for nearly an hour down the highway and then down the rocky path to Xiao Cun. Old Mr Xiao had come to take us back down the hill to the police.

I snapped out of my daydream about the quaintness of the Chinese countryside. Someone in the village had objected to our presence and phoned the police. I was dismayed, but Madeleine acted quickly to save the interview by taking the tape out of the camera and inserting a fresh cassette. Sebastian began filming the rural scenery to present to the police if they demanded the tape, and Madeleine labelled the precious interview tape 'Scenery'. Then we followed the old farmer back down to the village and at the bottom of the path a large crowd waited: adults and children in a muddle of Western suit jackets, Mao jackets, bright colours, hats and scarves.

The farmers, or *nong min* (peasants) as China referred to them until recently, gaped at us and made us feel as though we had just stepped off a spaceship. They had watched us a lot since our arrival, but now their stares seemed to burrow into us as we faked jollity and sauntered into the farmhouse where the police were waiting. I stepped over the earth threshold and into the dark living room. The chickens and geese scattered out of my path.

At the square dining table in the middle of the room sat the policeman from the county. He wore a large, Soviet-style hat several sizes too big and which made him look as though he was a child who had dressed up in his father's clothes. The man sitting next to him introduced himself as being from the county's Foreign Affairs Office. They didn't seem friendly or amused and demanded our official accreditation. Not knowing exactly what it was like to 'get busted', I prayed that there were no prison farms, nuclear waste dumps, mental asylums, orphanages or reincarnated lamas in the vicinity of Xiao Cun. Linking us with any of these would surely have resulted in my instant expulsion from China.

After several minutes of uneasiness, the FAO official barked, 'Why didn't you register when you came here? Everyone knows. It's written at the back of your passport.'

I stared at him blankly. Registration? I thought it must have been a euphemism for something else. A frantic flip through my passport failed to reveal any such warning. I am not sure why the official believed foreigners had such an instruction in their passports, but it was the first time I had been made aware of the importance of registration, which China uses as a means of social control. It's usually done on behalf of the local police at hotels or guesthouses (there are approved guesthouses for foreigners all over the country), but Xiao Cun didn't have any guesthouses, just lots of farmhouses. Registration was in theory a means of keeping tabs on the population, including foreigners, and particularly journalists. By failing to register we had gotten someone into trouble, and it seemed that our unofficial trip was about to come to an end. Curiously, however, after several hours of questions, the policeman and the FAO official left us at the village and promised to return the next day. We crammed as much filming as possible into the time we had left. Our tapes were never even looked at. The next day, after several hours in the county police station, we were sent back to the provincial capital, Hefei, where there were more words from more senior provincial Foreign Affairs officials. After we returned to Beijing, my applications to travel outside the capital were knocked back for months. Some time later, a Foreign Ministry spokesman took me aside and asked why I had gone to Anhui unofficially when the Foreign Ministry could have easily arranged a trip for me. 'We could have taken you to a much better village!' exclaimed the perplexed official.

Despite the minor trouble, I didn't regret the decision for a moment. Spending three days and nights in a regular Chinese village in an ordinary peasant home – even with the farm animals – had been a fabulous experience. The villagers sent us off in taxis summoned from the nearest town, lighting firecrackers to ward off evil spirits as we drove away. As well as all our tapes, I left the village with the beautiful old wooden bucket, bought for 50 yuan (A$13) from the family I'd stayed with and which sits on a special shelf above my kitchen sink. To this day I adore the bucket, though I still feel guilty for asking the family to sell it to me. They, on the other hand, didn't seem at all perturbed and quickly replaced it with a plastic one. The trip had been well worth the short travel ban that had been placed on the bureau.

Getting busted wasn't always so painless, particularly when official mismanagement was the focus of our story. The optimistically named Blue Sea Sky Shopping Centre was one of many new glitzy department stores that began to open around Beijing in the late 1990s to cater to the growing numbers of new rich. Trouble was, the district government-owned shop set up right across the road from another very popular shopping centre called the Blue Island. The Blue Sea Sky had been open for less than a year when staff arrived one morning to find its doors barred shut. It had gone out of business due to a lack of customers. Sound-recordist Kate Wakeman, who cycled past the department store every day on her way to work, noticed the angry crowd assembled outside the main entrance. We headed out, armed with cameras and with ABC radio correspondent Michael Cavanagh in tow.

The sudden closure of the department store had left dozens of wholesalers out of pocket and they gathered outside the locked doors, demanding the return of their stock or payment for it. One of the protesters said she had invested her savings into the stock and was owed the equivalent of A$2000. While Sebastian filmed the protest with his large professional camera (which we nicknamed John, after the ABC's foreign editor, John Tulloh), I filmed with the small digital camera. (This one we called Little John. Later we used an even smaller, palm-sized digital camera, which became known as Baby John.)

The protesters – about one hundred of them – decided to block the road to draw attention to their plight. If the district government wouldn't heed them, they would make other Beijing residents sit up and listen. Soon buses and cars came to a standstill and sounded their horns. Commuters leaned out of the bus windows, shouting to the protesters to let the traffic through, and within minutes there was mayhem.

I could have pulled out at that point; we had plenty of video and protests in China are rarely captured on tape. I stayed, however, because I wanted to see how the action would be resolved. I didn't have to wait long before I heard shouting above the protest noise and saw Sebastian struggling with a policeman over his camera. Kate, too, was being dragged towards a side street. I handed Little John to Michael Cavanagh, and followed Sebastian and Kate. Then Michael, too, was nabbed and the four of us were escorted to the back entrance of the Blue Sea Sky and ushered in through the security door.

I had never been detained in this fashion before: virtually the entire bureau was held in a small room, and after requesting the use of a toilet, a policewoman accompanied me. While we waited for the police from the Foreign Visa Section to arrive, Michael filed radio reports from inside the 'cell' until he was told to turn off his phone. Sebastian's tapes were confiscated. I managed to slip my two small camera tapes down the front of my jeans. I got the idea from a documentary about correspondents working on hazardous assignments, in which a BBC journalist described how she often 'slipped tapes down her knickers'. I was confident that even if the Chinese police searched us, they wouldn't dare to search there.

After several hours of waiting, the four of us were taken through the security area and onto the shop floor. It was still full of stock, as if nothing out of the ordinary had happened. We were taken to different sections of the store so that we could be interviewed separately. My interrogation took place in the bedding section. I could see the crew: Sebastian in homewares and Kate still in the security area, a little further beyond. My interrogator woke a security guard sleeping on one of the luxury display beds and ordered him to bring over a table and two chairs for the interrogation. I surveyed the shelves of brightly coloured bedsheets that few Chinese consumers could afford. With the Blue Island Department Store offering a more affordable range of goods right across the road, the Blue Sea Sky centre had clearly been conceived when some high-level official's head was in the clouds.

During the interrogation I was accused of ordering my colleagues to conduct 'illegal filming' and causing a traffic disturbance. I suggested the disturbance was more likely caused by the scores of angry protesters, but this idea was dismissed. Officer Jiang dictated the self-confession to me, stating that the filming had been my idea and that I was wrong to have chosen to film the protest. I actually wrote that it had been a regrettable decision to film the protest, but I don't think Officer Jiang cared about subtleties.

I am not quite sure what would have happened if we hadn't agreed to write self-confessions. In all, I was detained four times, and on each occasion was pressured into writing a self-confession. Perhaps it would have been no more serious than a few extra hours in 'captivity' or an official rebuke. In the interests of saving time, however, I always consented. Though the process was usually amusing in hindsight, while it was under way it was extremely stressful. I didn't want to put undue pressure on the crew or the local staff if I didn't conform.

The Chinese government insists that foreign news bureaus use government employees or at least government-registered employees as news assistants and drivers. On one occasion, moments before I was due to transmit a story to Australia, the local translator suddenly got up from his desk and demanded to know why I and other Westerners did not accept that Tibet was part of China. I told him we'd have to discuss the issue after the deadline. To find assistants who did a good job, most bureaus chose to employ outside the government, but this came with its own hazards. Non-approved employees risked detention if the bureau was involved in politically sensitive interviews or filming. Chinese nationals exposing the dark side of their country are considered traitors. Over the years news assistants for Western crews have been jailed and even tortured. These stories are rarely publicised as their release agreements generally require an undertaking not to comment further.

While self-criticisms and their written equivalent, the self-confession, have been around for hundreds of years as a tool of intimidation, they were perfected in the Soviet Union and exported to China under Mao.

After proclaiming the People's Republic on 1 October 1949, Mao quickly set about eliminating every major source of influence that wasn't already under party control. In 1956, he unleashed the Hundred Flowers Campaign, inviting thousands of writers, artists and scientists to express fresh ideas on the state of the country and the direction of the party, even to the point of criticism. 'Dust will accumulate if a room is not cleaned regularly, our faces will get dirty if they are not washed regularly,' Mao once said, somewhat ironically for someone who apparently bathed sparingly.

Several months after calling for 'One Hundred Flowers to bloom and one hundred schools of thought [to] contend', Mao cracked down on the detractors who had so readily voiced criticism. One Hundred Flowers was turned from a campaign promoting free expression into an 'anti-Rightist struggle'. Some of China's brightest minds were forced to swallow the contents of their criticism, sometimes quite literally, as the purge spread through the party ranks. At least half a million people are believed to have perished. This happened ten years before the start of what the Chinese call the Great Proletarian Cultural Revolution, which was Mao's final attempt to transform Chinese society spiritually and structurally. He did this by pursuing 'closet capitalists' hiding within the government and within the Communist Party itself. The result was widespread cruelty and oppression and an untold number of deaths.

Mr Lei is typical of millions of Chinese whose personal experience during the Cultural Revolution (1966–1976), a period of violent suppression of traditions and spiritual belief, remains with him to this day. Mr Lei works as a night watchman and makes a meagre wage of a few hundred yuan a month. He lives down a narrow alley close to the Beijing Zoo and rides a red motorised tricycle, made specially for China's disabled. There was a time when Communism was like a religion for Mr Lei.

'Communism still tries to teach people to be good, but it fails to inspire them,' said Mr Lei. The result, he believes, is a selfish society. 'I think life has been too unfair to me. I am a human being living with other humans in the same motherland, but really, as a disabled person, there's too little warmth,' he said.

Like many teenagers, Mr Lei had been caught up in the revolutionary zeal of the Cultural Revolution. One day, he accidentally gashed his leg and went to a Beijing hospital for treatment. On arrival, he found the qualified doctors had been taken off their rounds and given menial tasks like scrubbing floors and cleaning toilets. Overconfident, undertrained students had replaced experienced surgeons. Without the aid of anaesthetic and with only a piece of wood to bite down on, Mr Lei was taken to the operating theatre. The pain knocked him unconscious and when he woke his slightly injured leg had been amputated.

When the Cultural Revolution ended and China reopened to the outside world and its influences, Mr Lei was one of millions of

Chinese who became a ready convert to Protestantism and flocked to state-controlled churches. It helped him accept his fate. 'After joining the Church, I began to love life more. I became more determined to live.'

Massaging his leg just above the knee, Mr Lei rolled up his trousers to reveal a wooden prosthesis. He gave it three sharp knocks as if to dispel any doubt that it was artificial.

Today, belief is flourishing – China has five official religions, as well as fortune-tellers, shamans and cults. Others say half-seriously that China's new religion is money. For this theology, the Chinese have supreme patriarch Deng Xiaoping to thank. China is what it is today because of Deng.

I first glimpsed the diminutive leader when he emerged from a pavilion to greet Queen Elizabeth during her state visit to China in 1986. Deng was short, rotund and like many Chinese leaders was already an octogenarian. It was hard to believe that this shuffling, old figure was responsible for bringing much-needed market reforms to a creaking socialist system.

By the time I arrived in China in November 1995, Deng's life was in its closing stages and correspondents were on what was known as the 'Deng Deathwatch'. Leaving Beijing for an assignment or holiday became a risky enterprise. My correspondent colleagues and I were gripped by the fear that Deng would pass away while we were out of the country, and that we would miss the story of the decade. It nearly happened to me.

In early February 1997 the crew and I went to Hong Kong to film a series of stories on preparations for the July 1997 Handover. While we were in Hong Kong, strong rumours trickled out that Deng was close to death. Hong Kong-based newspapers reported the rumours, and it later emerged that Deng had been declared brain-dead five days before his death was officially announced, to give the leadership time to prepare for a suitable transition and commemoration, one that would acknowledge Deng's achievements without making him a cult figure, like Mao.

As the rumours continued to circulate, the crew and I took the three-hour flight back to Beijing. It was the longest three hours I had ever spent, but I tried to use the time productively, planning the coverage in my head in case the rumours turned out to be true. I arrived back on the evening of Wednesday 19 February 1997, and a few hours later news of Deng's death broke while the Chinese nation lay in a wintry sleep.

At home in Beijing in the early hours of the following morning I received three phone calls attempting to alert me to the news. But I was so tired after the Hong Kong trip that the ringing phone failed to rouse me. Eventually, I struggled out of bed to hear three messages on my answering machine: the first message was from, of all people, the ABC's London cameraman, Andrew Taylor, telling me that he'd heard Deng had died. His call beat one from my colleague, Kate, and another from a diplomat friend.

To mark Deng's passing, there were to be six days of mourning. On the fourth, the day of his cremation, tiny white paper flowers had been pinned to the branches of the trees along the wide avenues. Tens of thousands of mourners from all walks of life lined the footpaths. Many of them had been brought from around Beijing to pay their respects by their government work units: schools, universities and hospitals. But thousands, too, came without urging. What seemed the strangest thing about that morning was the silence. Chinese streets are rarely silent. Noise rolls up and down the alleys and avenues from morning till night. On this day, however, the breeze carried no sound.

I had witnessed several Chinese funeral processions before this. The public procession was always sombre and controlled. However, on one occasion, a family gave us permission to film the private funeral for an old man if I would give them a videotape of what we filmed. The family tearfully paid their respects around the open casket; the dead body in full view. As the funeral centre staff arrived to remove the coffin, the guests became hysterical. There was much screaming and wailing as the widow and children of the deceased tried to haul the casket back, as if toward the land of the living. A mini-riot ensued until the staff managed to move the casket behind two large steel doors, leaving the grief-stricken family empty-handed and distraught. The family didn't ask for more time, perhaps because the funeral parlour was one of Shanghai's busiest. I had never seen an outpouring of emotion like it and withdrew to the back of the chamber, unable to hold back my own tears. It was an awkward feeling sharing the private anguish of people I had only just met.

Deng's funeral, on the other hand, was not an intimate affair. As the procession turned the corner onto the street in front of me, my sombre mood was quickly shattered when I saw the hearse. Instead of a long black vehicle, the Little Man was taken to the crematorium in a pragmatic Toyota transporter, draped with a yellow and black ribbon and bearing a number plate ending in three 4s. In Chinese, the number four sounds like the word 'death' and Chinese people superstitiously avoid it on their car plates. On Deng's practical hearse the numbers said fittingly, 'Death, death, death.'

Several elderly mourners around me began to weep. 'Deng Xiaoping is the greatest man in the twentieth century,' shouted one woman. 'If it wasn't for him, China wouldn't have gained the respect of the world!'

On the street that cold, grey day, there was respect for the architect of the economic reforms, as well as uncertainty about the future, but very little emotional outpouring. Perhaps it was the heavy military presence, which hung like a cloud of ominous authoritarianism, or perhaps, as one commentator put it, 'We don't have any more artificial gods like the cult of Mao, and not much to believe in beyond the money we try to earn.'

Deng hadn't held any official posts since the end of 1989 and yet the reformist zeal he fostered continued up to and beyond his death. Deng's legacy put Communist China on the path towards a market economy – 'socialism with Chinese characteristics' as he called it. In the late 1970s he first freed the farmers from the shackles of the commune by allowing them, once they had fulfilled the state quotas, to sell excess produce and keep the profits. In the cities he removed the party from the day-to-day running of the factories and allowed private enterprise to grow alongside the state sector. By the second half of the 1980s, however, high inflation and rampant corruption dogged the economy and ignited the widespread dissatisfaction which led to the student protest movement in Tiananmen Square. On the night of 3–4 June the army, under orders from Deng, regained control of Beijing's centre by shooting down unarmed civilians around the square, with the loss of hundreds of lives. The event produced a kind of shock and paralysis both inside and outside the country so Deng travelled south, first to Shanghai in 1991 and then to Shenzhen in early 1992. In this southern city across the border from Hong Kong, Deng, by now an extremely frail man in his late eighties, embarked on a well-publicised trip during which he proclaimed to the country's leaders that, without development, China and the Communist Party were finished. He last appeared in public two years after the tour, when heavily edited television pictures showed an elderly man wearing the faint smile of senility, supported on the arm of his daughter and biographer, Deng Rong.

Prising open the command economy has seen China treble rural incomes, multiply foreign trade tenfold and boost economic growth to an average of 9 per cent a year. Since Deng's death, even greater changes have occurred in the lives of Chinese people. For example, in the 1980s urban Chinese consumed 145 kilograms of their staple food, grain, per person. By the late 1990s this had dropped to 88 kilograms as people increased their consumption of meat, seafood and vegetables. For farmers, however, grain is still a staple. Between the 1980s and 1990s per capita grain consumption dropped by just 10 kilograms from 260 kilograms per head to 250 kilograms. Apart from better diets, Chinese people are now frequent travellers, both at home and overseas. They have a longer lifespan than they did in the 1980s and urbanites earn seven times more than they used to. In 1989, Chinese banks held 500 billion yuan (US$60 billion) in savings; that figure has jumped to 8 trillion yuan (US$964 billion).

Despite the vast change, Deng didn't articulate an end goal other than to make China a moderately well-off country. Nor did he design a system of stable succession. Though Jiang Zemin relinquished the presidency to Hu Jintao at the National People's Congress in March 2003, Jiang retained the chair of the Central Military Commission, giving him ongoing control of the army. Hu Jintao represents the younger 'Fourth Generation' of leadership, with a promise to maintain the reformist momentum. Although China is now locked into a globalised trading system through its membership of the World Trade Organisation, there is still a deep ambivalence to foreigners.

Naively, my strong desire to go to China in the first place was because of my Chinese blood. I wanted to get in touch with my ancestry. No sooner had I arrived than I discovered that far more than a few genes were needed for me to be considered Chinese. As a foreign journalist, not only was I outside the circle, I was in a zone specially reserved for aliens. It wasn't just the officials who made me feel that way, it was the everyday people I met. I befriended a traditional Chinese medicine doctor by the name of Zhao Daifu who worked at a large Beijing hospital until 3 pm each day. She frequently gave me very vigorous Chinese massages, which some of my friends jokingly described as torture sessions. Apart from the massages, what I enjoyed were our conversations. Doctor Zhao, who is in her mid forties, earned 1200 yuan (US$150) a month from the hospital, spoke almost no English and wasn't internet savvy. But she was an avid television viewer (only of the domestic, state-run TV) and newspaper reader. Though I'd known her for several years, it never ceased to amaze her how different Westerners were from Chinese.

Once she brought her teenage daughter to my house so that she could see how foreigners live. Zhao Daifu often commented on how

curious it was that I liked antique and reproduction Chinese furniture. 'I like new things, like Ikea,' she once told me. 'The past is
past.' On another occasion, during a massage, she said out of the
blue, 'Isn't it sad how dirt poor the English are?'

'What?' I replied, thinking I must have misunderstood.

'The English. They were once such a great nation and now they
are so poor! In London, many people can't even afford leather shoes
and they wear rags!' I asked Zhao Daifu where she had heard such
things. It transpired that the *Beijing Evening News*, a tabloid newspaper, was running a series on Britain. One of the paper's reporters,
writing under the pen name Black Horse, had visited Britain and
was shocked to find that poor people were everywhere. 'They wear
simple clothes, old clothes, some even in rags. They can only afford
to shop in second-hand shops. For Chinese people who became rich
recently, we look down on these types of people,' he wrote. Black
Horse was able to penetrate 'grass roots' Britain, where he saw city
life which he believed resembled China in the 1980s.

The *Beijing Evening News* series astounded me. More than
forty-five million Chinese people regularly use the internet, and
although they are prevented from reading a plethora of political,
dissident or religious sites, they can at least access more information
than what the domestic Chinese newspapers and television offer.
They can argue with compatriots in Taiwan, Hong Kong or the
United States about attitudes and policies, and read the latest news
on trends, fashions, education. In short, the internet is a new world
for Chinese cyber-surfers. Yet an educated woman like Zhao Daifu
is just one of more than 1.2 billion people who do not have regular
internet access. She relies on newspapers like the *Beijing Evening
News* to tell her how people live on the other side of the world.

Despite the many bureaucratic restrictions, I wanted to be as
spontaneous as possible where my work was concerned. I decided to
take the camera outside the gates of the Workers' Stadium early one
morning to film ballroom dancers until they were comfortable
enough with the foreign television crew to let us focus in depth on

one couple. The middle-aged couples didn't seem to mind the camera, and the crew and I returned several days in a row. In those days, my Chinese wasn't good enough to have a lengthy conversation with local residents. Though I had studied Mandarin for two years prior to my arrival in China, it took me about six months before I gained the confidence to converse. After that I took more lessons and found that being immersed in the language improved my skills so that, eventually, I could comfortably converse with people. With a translator I approached the most charismatic dancer and asked whether I could interview him about why he liked ballroom dancing. I naively explained that I also wanted to learn about his life and how great a part dancing played in it.

Within moments a large crowd had gathered around us. Though our subject had appeared on the verge of agreeing to our request, the crowd quickly dissuaded him. His friends' views ranged from telling him to consider the request carefully before saying anything to asking for a filming fee, which I wasn't prepared to pay. Then someone shouted, 'Remember the Italian!' That did it. With the mention of this simple phrase the man shook his head and declared he didn't want to be filmed. Then he made a quick escape, unlocking his bicycle and slipping into the sea of people riding the wave of a morning rush-hour.

Remember the Italian? The Italian was film-maker Michelangelo Antonioni. In 1973 Antonioni made a documentary, *Zhongguo* (China), which was vilified by the Chinese government for presenting a cruel and backward picture of the country, while Antonioni had presented himself as a friend of China. The documentary was held up for ridicule and criticism in schools and government organisations throughout the country although the film was never actually shown. 'Remember the Italian' became embedded like a microchip in my brain. Every Chinese person, middle-aged and older, was going to 'Remember the Italian' before they opened their souls to me.

The theme of China being victimised or oppressed by foreigners resonated on many more occasions after the ballroom dancing episode. During the 78-day NATO bombing of Yugoslavia in 1999, China's state media, reflecting the view of the leadership, threw its weight behind the Milosevic regime. 'People now feel as if they have returned to the age of imperialism when the world was carved up,' said a commentary in the *People's Daily*, while the media generally reacted sceptically to Western claims of ethnic cleansing in Kosovo.

With anti-US and anti-NATO passions running high, on 7 May 1999 three missiles dropped by US B-2 planes struck the Chinese embassy in Belgrade, killing three Chinese journalists and wounding dozens of embassy staff. The CIA admitted responsibility for the mistaken attack, claiming outdated maps were used which labelled the Chinese embassy as a Yugoslav ministry.

I lived and worked in a compound for diplomats and journalists in central Beijing, guarded by khaki-clad People's Armed Police. In Beijing foreigners aren't permitted to live in housing provided for local residents. Foreign housing is much more expensive and ensures that, in the comfort of a compound, foreigners can be kept under surveillance. I lived in the Qijiayuan compound, a few hundred metres from the US embassy.

On the day the missiles struck the Chinese embassy in Belgrade, something also detonated in Beijing. Shopkeepers in the popular 'silk market', an outdoor bazaar consisting of rows of clothing and accessory stalls near my compound, began packing up even though it was only early afternoon on a busy Saturday in spring. They were in an obvious hurry, and so were Sebastian and I. With just fifteen minutes before we were due to send our story to Australia via satellite, we hadn't yet shot the 'piece to camera', in which I would speak directly to the camera for a few lines of commentary.

I delivered the closing words about how the domestic aftershocks of the bombing were unlikely to be short-lived and that the capital was gearing up for popular action. I signed off, 'Jane Hutcheon, ABC News, Beijing'. On hearing the words 'ABC News' and believing I was from the American ABC, not the Australian Broadcasting Corporation, the stallholders gathered around in a vaguely menacing way. They chatted loudly to each other and seemed to enjoy my discomfort.

'Let's go again,' said Sebastian, and more nervously than before I repeated my words and included the sign-off, 'ABC News . . .' Then my voice stumbled.

The vendors laughed and I turned to rebuke them in English: 'Please shut up!' Not a wise move.

'Why should we keep quiet?' retorted one of the vendors.

'I think you are very rude,' said another.

'Yes, you are very rude. You should apologise to us!'

Surprised at the response of the normally jovial stallholders, and sensing the situation might be getting out of hand, I flashed an inquiring look at Sebastian, who nodded and agreed that the first, less than perfect 'take' would be fine. We picked up the camera and tripod and virtually ran to the gates of the compound.

Shortly after the story had been transmitted to Australia via satellite that afternoon, a convoy of buses began to pull up in the narrow lanes leading to the silk market, which was located next to the commercial section of the US embassy. From the buses, young, bespectacled students spilled out, carrying hastily scrawled banners and placards painted in red to imitate blood. What was less obvious at the time was that they also carried projectiles – eggs, glass bottles and rocks. More buses arrived and more students joined the crowd already on the street in a march around the perimeter of the embassy, chanting, 'Down with American imperialism!' and, 'Repay blood debts with blood!'

By nightfall the marching had stopped, but a few thousand people had gathered outside the embassy's main gates. Many of them had been spurred into action by an extended and highly emotive evening news bulletin on Chinese Central Television, which slipped into passionate old-fashioned rhetoric about China as an innocent victim of foreign imperialist powers. The talk struck a chord with a population instilled by decades of education teaching them that foreign powers have conspired for centuries to keep China weak and downtrodden. The crowd swelled and began protesting around the British embassy as well, throwing rocks and paint-bombs at the buildings. Later, the composition of the crowd changed. Middle-aged louts, who had finished their Saturday evening meal and were clearly drunk, descended on the embassy district. Scuffles ensued and several foreign journalists and cameramen were injured by flying rocks as well as punches.

'Where are you from?' a man in a leather jacket shouted, breathing alcohol fumes over me.

'Australia. We are all Australian,' I said, indicating a British colleague and a nearby American journalist. Though Australia is considered part of the Western camp, back then it was looked upon much more favourably than the United States – the standard response whenever I told anyone I was from Australia was that Australia was a big country with a small population and a beautiful environment, whereas China was a big country with a big population and very polluted. By 2002, I noticed the attitude towards Australia had changed somewhat. A taxi-driver commented that Australia was becoming more like the United States by supporting a war against Iraq.

In May 1999 the Chinese government backed public protests for five days, before ordering people to cease. A televised address was delivered by Hu Jintao, then China's Vice President. As usual during a major crisis, none of the top-ranking officials made public comments in case the situation got out of hand and they were required to backtrack. The official party mouthpiece, the *People's Daily*, ran an editorial which both captured and inflamed the public mood and was entitled 'The Chinese People Are Not to be Humiliated'.

The 'National Humiliation' is revisited whenever a serious diplomatic row erupts with China on one side against another strong power, usually the United States. It serves the leadership in times of crisis because bringing up the sense of humiliation stirs patriotism, which deflects anger and resentment away from the party.

Modern Chinese nationalism has its roots in the later years of the Qing Dynasty (1644–1911). Western nations, Great Britain being the leading culprit, gained trading outposts in China after years of failed efforts, and were determined to exact equal trading terms from the Chinese. Natonalism grew as a reaction to these actions; foreign powers were viewed as imperialists whose intent was to divide and subjugate the Chinese Empire. Initially nationalism was an elite movement of students and scholars, but it picked up steam during the Sino–Japanese war in the 1930s and 1940s. The Japanese military, in a campaign to terrorise the Chinese population into submission, carried out systematic violence against the innocent and unarmed. Houses were burned down and civilians were raped and massacred. It affected the life of almost every Chinese, with civilian casualties in the tens of millions.

Around the same time, US support for the Nationalist or Kuomintang (KMT) regime during the Chinese Civil War of the 1930s and 1940s aroused unease. Many older Chinese also recall the Korean War of the 1950s. 'State propaganda in those days,' said a journalist friend, 'told us that American imperialists invaded our brotherly neighbours, killed innocent people and brought war to our gate. Chairman Mao ordered the People's Liberation Army to fight against Americans in North Korea, who were of course eventually defeated. Even now, Chinese people are fiercely proud of their role in the Korean War; they believe that the Chinese people defeated America.'

Even since the founding of the People's Republic of China in 1949, America has been perceived as having joined other capitalist countries to isolate China and stifle Communism. Today most ordinary Chinese believe that the West does not want to see China develop and will use all possible means to contain it. Ask many, particularly young, Chinese about the events surrounding the September 11 terrorist attacks in the US and they will tell you it was an understandable response to what they see as US arrogance and its attempts to dominate the world. While the official response offered sympathy and support to the United States, it masked what one diplomat described to me as 'the silent snicker of approval' felt by the public and witnessed on several occasions. International media outlets reported one such example. A group of Chinese journalists visiting Washington at the time of the attacks reportedly applauded and cheered on seeing television footage of the hijacked planes slamming into the World Trade Centre. The visit was subsequently cut short.

The real metaphor for the collision between the United States and China occurred in April 2001 when a Chinese fighter jet collided with a US surveillance plane in the international airspace near tropical Hainan Island in China's south. I watched the unfolding drama from the Hainan Peninsula Hotel after the damaged American surveillance plane was forced to make an emergency landing on a military airstrip on the island. Over a period of eleven days the Chinese delighted in bringing the United States to its knees, forcing an apology while a colourful myth was constructed out of the 'heroic' actions of the missing Chinese fighter pilot, Wang Wei.

I travelled with the crew to the coastal village where search efforts for the pilot were concentrated. In the distance we saw the Chinese naval base and, to my joy, discovered that a floating restaurant was located within a large bay about 500 metres from the base. A speedboat was sent to pick us up and take us to the restaurant, where we dined on beautiful fresh fish and filmed the exterior of the naval base without any problems. On board the floating restaurant we discovered that local residents had followed the events of the latest Sino–US crisis as closely as if they had been watching a television soap opera. The state media's message was that China was, yet again, a victim at the hands of an imperialist power.

'He was prepared for spending a long time in the water,' the restaurant owner told me of Wang Wei, the missing Chinese pilot. 'When his plane went down and he ejected, he was wearing a special suit which had food in it and kept him warm.'

The Chinese media portrayed Wang Wei as a patriotic hero, while the US described him as a hazardous pilot. He had once been photographed by US surveillance holding up a sheet of paper with his email – he had been so close to the US craft that the email address was legible. Alas, Wang Wei's body was never found in the warm currents of the South China Sea. The US crew was held on the island until the Bush administration issued the closest thing it could to an apology, despite insisting that the Chinese aircraft had caused the collision.

Another early challenge for me when I began working in China, though not such a politically charged one, was how to cope with the vexed issue of meals. On any official trip, three meals a day were usually included in the fee (of course, meals would be shared by officials too), with the host government providing a grand banquet at some stage. Whether or not it was intended, I soon began to notice that mealtimes had become the focal point of the day's activities.

The shoot would break at 11.30 am in order for us to be back at the guesthouse with hands washed ready for lunch at noon. Then it would be eight courses and another hour's 'rest' before filming would start again at 2 pm before the final wrap at 4 pm, the usual government knock-off time. Dinner was at 6 pm

In some poorer provinces, the size and quality of the banquet was embarrassing when local residents were clearly unable to eat as well. Officials would arrange sumptuous meals in the newest and most prestigious restaurants or hotels in town. Rarely would we dine in the public section of the restaurant; instead we would be shuffled into a private room (one was decorated to resemble a Tuscan villa) where we would be greeted by a young waitress in a tight red cheongsam or *qipao*, teetering on stilettos and with ankle-length stocking socks visible in the side-split, ruining the image of sophistication.

Where a sandwich or snack would have sufficed, a banquet fit for an emperor would glide through the door onto the Lazy Susan and into our undeserving stomachs. While such meals were prepared in deference to our visit, the drawn out etiquette of banquets scoffed up valuable research and filming time. As long as we were with local officials, I was powerless to change the system because our minders regarded free meals as a major perk. The topic of conversation, too, would usually be directed toward rearranging the shooting schedule to allow time to view the local silks or pottery, all at very good prices of course.

At the height of my banquet intolerance, I disgraced myself by challenging our host, the traffic police chief in Jinan city. In the mid 1990s cities around China began the 'Learn from Jinan Traffic Police' campaign and it became evident that a revolution had struck the until then haphazard world of traffic control.

Before the advent of the 'Jinan method', Beijing traffic police had been a sloppy lot. In the mid-1990s China's traffic police only had a few million cars to contend with. (A many as fifty million vehicles are expected to be using the roads by 2010.) But this was no excuse for their sloppy movements and listless swivels at the intersection. The head of traffic police in the small city of Jinan in Shandong province had devised the breakdance equivalent of traffic direction, first training his own force and then taking the method to practically every traffic police division in the country. Before long, traffic police from Lhasa to Luoyang, Xinjiang to Xian were practising precise hand gestures and neat swivels that would have made an American cheerleader green with envy. Supercop Li Dachen was the cream of them all, able to make more than two thousand arm movements and 1600 turns in a single two-hour shift. (It was equally impressive that someone had bothered to record the number.)

For half an hour one day, the patient traffic police of Jinan tried to impart some of their secrets to me, eventually conceding that I wouldn't pass muster. To finish the trip on a note of goodwill, the crew was treated to a sumptuous banquet at the gleaming new traffic police headquarters.

The banquet began in upbeat form with the usual questions about how foreigners were able to use chopsticks so expertly. It was a constant source of surprise to my Chinese hosts that many Australians learn to use chopsticks from an early age. I explained that Australia had a large Asian population. In addition, the quality of the cuisine was really excellent.

We had finished the turtle soup and the steamed black-skinned chicken when the police chief began to wax lyrical about food Jinan was famous for. 'We are known throughout China for the quality of our leeks,' he said proudly. 'We produce the biggest, sweetest leeks in the whole of China.'

Tired of being diplomatic and feeling a little guilty for having drunk soup made from creatures I used to keep as pets, I replied, 'Well, we have pretty sweet leeks in Australia too.'

'Oh, but ours aren't only sweet, they are big!' he said, using his hands to hold an imaginary leek the size of a drainpipe.

'In Australia, we have leeks that are even bigger than that,' I said, as the crew looked on nervously. Fortunately we had already completed filming. But Sebastian, Kate and Xiao Li (Charles' nickname, meaning 'Little Li') looked at me as if I were about to bring calamity on all of us.

'Well, Jinan leeks are very big *and* sweet. Rarely can you find such sweet leeks as ours,' he said seriously.

'Australian leeks are very big and very sweet,' I said firmly.

Not to be outdone, the chief summoned the waitress and ordered her to bring a plate of raw leeks for us to sample. Regardless of how big and sweet the leeks might be, I wasn't particularly fond of eating raw onion. But the gauntlet had been thrown down and the chief would be waiting for my pronouncement, which of course would have to be good or else I would be considered very rude.

We sat and waited, but no leeks were forthcoming. The chief grew impatient and again called the waitress, who explained that they weren't really in season, but she would see what she could do.

A few minutes later she returned with a large plate of leeks and timidly placed them in front of the chief. He waved his hands dramatically.

'These aren't the big leeks! Bring me the BIG leeks!' he cried, clearly embarrassed after his claims.

'That's all we can find right now,' replied the waitress meekly.

The chief was flustered and his staff looked on helplessly. My colleagues looked at me beseechingly, desperately wanting lunch to be over, but no-one could move until the chief gave the signal, which he didn't. Here goes, I thought, and I reached forward, grabbed the biggest leek on the plate and crunched my teeth into it.

'Mmmm,' I lied through a mouthful of masticated leek. 'This is good! Captain, you are right, they are *so* sweet! We definitely don't have leeks as sweet as this in Australia.'

After that experience, I decided to minimise excessive feasting and devised a series of rules that I told officials were ABC regulations and which had to be obeyed by the entire bureau. The rules were that filming came before feasting. Breakfast and lunch were to last just half an hour and include only the simplest of dishes, and evenings were to be free. In addition, to stop a ridiculous trend in which officials would try to get us drunk at lunchtime with toasting, I included a rule that head office outlawed alcohol consumption during working hours. This policy enabled the crew and me to slip out of the official grasp and into the backstreets where we enjoyed the tastiest and cheapest meals of our many journeys, sitting in local restaurants with local people.

While such experiences made for some of the happiest memories I have of China, it was and still is a country split into several worlds: rich, poor, developing, underdeveloped, sophisticated and backward, often with several traits living side by side in the same city or town. I was struck by how hard life could be outside China's major cities, and I was particularly moved by the plight of the farmers. In Xiao Cun, where the crew and I were detained, we met the Sun family. Their retarded daughter sat outside the farmhouse among the animals, twisting hay into balls of string to earn the family a few extra cents a week. She was just a few years younger than me, but had the mental age of a nine-year-old. The Sun house was decrepit, and the family was clearly in financial difficulty. Above the door hung a tattered sign that had once read 'wealth arrived', only now the Chinese character was faded and the paper torn. By the looks of things wealth still hadn't arrived.

Inside the house, Mrs Sun sat at a spinning wheel. 'The burden increases one year after another. How can we possibly be satisfied? We've been to the production team and township government several times, but they just ignored us. No-one listens. If you know people, you get things done. Otherwise, you cannot get anywhere,' she said helplessly. Other families in the same village might have a son or daughter in Shanghai, sending back much-needed cash to make life more comfortable.

In China there is a hunger for money that I have not seen anywhere else. The advent of market reforms created uncertainty and fear among people who once expected to rely on the state for every need. So when Deng Xiaoping invented his famous maxim of 'Black cat, white cat, as long as it catches mice it's a good cat,' he virtually gave Chinese society carte blanche to use whatever means to make money. On several occasions the ABC was the target.

My news editor requested stories about China's preparations for their 2000 Olympics bid. After calls to dozens of sports bodies, one association agreed to interviews and filming and asked our local Chinese interpreter to visit their office to make the arrangements. When he returned he said the association had asked for a filming fee of US$1000 cash.

On another occasion the ABC was offered a rare opportunity to film pandas, housed in a reserve outside the city of Chengdu, including permission to film the artificial insemination of a female panda. I grabbed at the chance, having tried for months to film a story about Professor Pan, a Chinese David Attenborough who trekked deep into the Qinling Mountains between Shaanxi and

Sichuan provinces to study the habits of wild pandas, whose numbers had dwindled to just one hundred.

Professor Pan had told us it was possible to accompany him. *National Geographic* had made a documentary about pandas in the wild in 1993, but fees to various ministries as well as expenses put the budget at US$50 000, well beyond the ABC's reach.

It wasn't ABC practice to pay filming fees, so instead of filming pandas, I accompanied Professor Pan to Guangxi, where his latest venture was a conservation plan to protect the endangered white-headed monkey. The monkeys were naturally shy, but once they got used to the attention they would come lower and lower down the mountain to see what we were up to. Then, when the monkeys were close enough to film, the official accompanying us placed his hand across the camera lens.

'This is a protected Chinese creature,' he said. 'Foreigners are not allowed to film them.' After several late night conferences and much precious filming time wasted, Professor Pan convinced the local authorities to let us continue filming because it would create a good impression of China overseas.

There was just one occasion when I agreed to pay a fee, and that was to film dinosaur skeletons in a rundown museum in Zigong city, Sichuan. The officials in Zigong put many barriers in our way, trying to force us to cancel a trip they had initially approved, but we needed to be in Zigong because it had been the scene of massive worker unrest, which we needed to tap into for the story we were really there to cover.

During the Fifteenth Communist Party Congress in October 1997, President Jiang Zemin gave orders to speed up the reform and restructuring of the state sector, closing down hundreds of lumbering state-owned factories at the expense of hundreds of thousands of state jobs.

The city of Zigong is an industrial centre famous since ancient times for its salt production. In the 1980s, salt ceased to be centrally produced and the huge factories of Zigong became victims of the market economy. In 1997 there were at least five demonstrations in Zigong, one involving six thousand irate workers who had been laid off and weren't receiving any wages from their bankrupt factories. In China, a worker who has been 'laid off' is frequently known as an 'off-post' worker. His or her name remains on the factory books and they are usually given the benefits of the iron rice bowl security system, but a much smaller wage, usually around A$20 a month.

Unfortunately, when we arrived in Zigong and paid a fee to film the dinosaurs and moribund salt factories, the instigator of the protests had fled in fear. But the trip to Zigong was troublesome before it even began. The day before we were due to leave, and after the close of business, the Zigong Foreign Affairs Office phoned the ABC bureau and warned us that we might need to pay to film several venues. I think it was their way of saying they didn't want us to come. The banks had already closed and I didn't have enough cash, but I really needed to get to Zigong to fill in a vital part of the story on workers' unrest. It was one of those bad China days when everything seemed to be flowing smoothly one minute and the next you find yourself sprawled on the concrete, wondering what tripped you up.

But on bad China days there was always something that rescued me. As I walked along Jianguomenwai Avenue towards my apartment one chilly night, my thoughts focused on the problems in Zigong. I felt enraged, double-crossed. Then a curious noise started up beside me. It was a voice, high-pitched and throaty. I stole a quick glance at my companion, walking on a wall bordering the footpath. He was a dwarf, singing at the top of his voice with his eyes looking up into the night, seemingly oblivious of me. My frustration with the Foreign Affairs Office and my bad China day wilted away, replaced by pure joy at this unusual scene. I too looked up and noticed that the moon was full and bright.

I felt rejuvenated. I would deal with the Foreign Affairs Office when I arrived in Zigong. Somehow it would all work out. It wasn't such a bad China day after all.

PEKING DUCKS

Peking Duck as we know it – cooked in the same style since the Ming Dynasty (1368–1644) – may soon be facing extinction. As part of the environmental clean-up Beijing has promised the international community for the 2008 Olympics, a trial is under way to test a computer-controlled electric oven for the city's more than one thousand duck restaurants. Chefs and gourmands are outraged because for centuries Peking Duck has been slow-cooked in a furnace stacked with fragrant wood. If the modern method becomes the norm, will the famous duck taste the same? Does the method of roasting really matter or are other factors like feeding (the ducks are force fed on gruel every four hours) more important? Whatever the outcome of the electric oven debate, it goes to show that in the vast reconstruction of the Chinese capital, no duck will be left unturned.

Change is occurring all over Beijing. Around the city the signboards proclaim 'New Beijing, Great Olympics'. 'New' isn't just hype, it's a mantra. Soaring construction cranes jostle for space on a skyline which now dwarfs the few remnants of China's ancient civilisation. Beijing is a city of walls and mazes at its core, peppered with construction sites and skyscrapers made to look like elongated pagodas. You couldn't say that the new architecture is inspiring, and the construction is faulty in many parts. But the operative word is still 'new'.

In and around Tiananmen Square, the city's heart, old and new collide. Like the buildings to its east, west and south, the modern square – 880 metres from north to south and 500 metres from east to west – was built in Maoist times. Most Chinese cities have large socialist-style squares, but Tiananmen is the king of them all, big enough to hold half a million people, as the tour guides like to say. The square is named after Tiananmen, or Gate of Heavenly Peace, which stands opposite it. Built in 1417, it was originally the main entrance of the Imperial Palace. From the top of the gate, which opens into a rostrum, Mao Zedong proclaimed the founding of the People's Republic of China on 1 October 1949. During the Cultural Revolution it was where he rallied China's youth, who waved copies of his *Little Red Book* of quotations.

The expansive square was designed to command respect, to overwhelm the individual. On each side is a building of historical or political importance. To the west is the Great Hall of the People, to the east, the Museum of the Chinese Revolution. Standing between them, with their soaring columns and proud red flags, it is easy to feel overpowered. Tiananmen is like a giant concrete cell, although at various times over the last few years it has resembled a circus, with police vans regularly combing the square for Falun Gong pro-testers. Half the hawkers and kite-sellers catering to tourists are undercover agents ready to drop their trinkets and pounce at the first sign of civil disobedience. If a protest erupts and you are found carrying a camera, chances are that you will lose it or the film, whether you're a tourist or not.

Beijing's tree-lined boulevards are also wide, built for spectacu-lar military parades and, these days, for increasing volumes of traffic. The avenues accommodate four to six lanes of traffic both ways, and all have bicycle lanes. Whenever a leading foreign digni-tary visits town, two flags are unfurled from the ornate street lamps along Chang' an (Eternal Peace) Avenue beside Tiananmen Square. One is the Chinese flag, five yellow stars against a red background, and the other belongs to the foreign dignitary's country.

'Walls within walls, moats within moats,' is how journalist Tiziano Terzani described the city. 'Peking was a reflection in stone of the cosmic order. Each building was in a calculated position: the Temple of the Sun to the east, that of the Moon to the west, the Temple of Heaven in the south, balanced by that of Earth in the north. And in the middle of it all was the purple Forbidden City, the Great Within as it was called, the heart of China, the centre of the centre of the world, the seat of the emperor from whom all power emanated.'

On a steamy summer's day I followed the crowds through the northern gate, once the tradesmen's entrance to the Forbidden City, with one of the few remaining members of the imperial family, Gobru Runqi. Introduced to me by Daniel Kane, the Cultural Counsellor at the Australian embassy in Beijing, Runqi is a lively man with large spectacles, prominent ears and puppet-like hands. His vivacious temperament masked a life of repression – Runqi had been tried as a war criminal and collaborator during the 1930s Japanese invasion of China and for his sins spent more than ten years in labour camps. Though he was almost ninety when I met him in 1996, he was pursuing a new career as a traditional Chinese medicine practitioner and is still going strong.

Runqi was born in 1912 into nobility in Manchuria (in the northeast of China, where the Qing or Manchus came from) and lived through the final phase of China's last imperial dynasty. Runqi's sister Wanrong became the teenage bride of the Last Emperor, Henry Pu Yi. Consequently, Runqi and his mother moved into the palace with the young princess.

I nicknamed Runqi the Last Brother-in-Law because of his ties to the Last Emperor, and asked him to take me on a private tour of the Forbidden City to film a story for the ABC's *Foreign Correspondent* program. So began our tour around the Forbidden City, built by Emperor Yong Le in the fifteenth century. While a complex had stood on the site for about five hundred years, in 1664 a fire burned it to the ground. Most of the present buildings are post-eighteenth century.

Early twentieth-century travel writer Juliet Bredon called the Forbidden City 'a haunted city of loveliness peopled by the imperial ghosts of vanished emperors'. For almost five centuries, the most powerful men and women in China lived within these high vermilion walls, surrounded by royal luxuries that Bredon says included 100 000 pieces of jade, 10 000 hand-drawn maps, more than a million manuscripts and an unknown treasury of priceless porcelain. While much of it was looted by the defeated Nationalists who fled to Taiwan in 1949, a sizeable collection remains in the vaults of the Forbidden City, out of public view. Until recently only those with historic or academic connections were able to view the priceless works. But with the coming Olympics, new exhibition halls will soon display what has been off limits to the general public for centuries.

Runqi and I entered the palace with sound-recordist Kate Wakeman and cameraman Sebastian Phua, who carried an array of equipment. The Forbidden City Administration had asked for US$5000 to film in the hallowed halls of the emperors. As it was well beyond the budget of a public broadcaster I told them I would think it over. It wasn't the largest amount of money I had been asked for in China, but rather than pay a filming fee, I chose to buy ordinary tourist tickets and had Sebastian film Runqi's tour with a handheld video camera. We didn't stand out amongst the throngs of tourists, all of whom, like us, seemed to be shooting mini-documentaries.

In the crowded courtyards of the Forbidden City, it took Runqi a little while to gather his thoughts. Eventually he found a small rockery where he had played with boy emperor Pu Yi and the emperor's brother Pu Jie. In an official Forbidden City publication, we found an old snapshot of the location with an impish Runqi sitting on a brass elephant, surrounded by Pu Yi, Pu Jie and Reginald Johnston, the imperial tutor.

In ancient times, a commoner could not enter the Forbidden City on pain of death. Inside, emperors, eunuchs and concubines lived a life of opulence while the general population suffered in grinding poverty beyond the grand walls and the moats of the palace. 'All commoners knew was that the emperor's position was very esteemed,' Runqi said. 'They might have *imagined* all sorts of things, but they didn't know anything about the reality.'

My first encounter with the Forbidden City was in 1986 when I covered the Queen's tour of China. It came two years after the signing of the agreement between Britain and China over the terms of Hong Kong's return to Chinese sovereignty. The visit was described as historic because it was the first by a British monarch, but was memorable for another, disreputable reason, namely Prince Philip's racist remarks to British students. He told them they'd return home with 'slitty eyes' if they stayed in China too long. Apart from waiting for the prince to put his foot in his mouth again, my fellow journalists and I were amused to find that a tennis court with a wooden floor had been erected in one of the courtyards of the Forbidden City. Years later I saw *The Last Emperor*, directed by Bernardo Bertolucci, and I realised the epic had been shot during the Queen's visit.

I asked Runqi if he had seen the film and whether it gave an accurate account of life in the Forbidden City. He hadn't liked the film because it painted his sister, Empress Wanrong, in a poor light; though she did succumb to opium addiction, her life had been tragic, destroyed by the circumstances surrounding the emperor's downfall.

Runqi pointed out several factual inaccuracies in the film. Pu Yi's tutor, Reginald Johnston, was credited with teaching the young emperor to ride a bicycle, which Runqi said wasn't how it happened.

'My mother and I had learned to ride. So *we* taught Pu Yi. After that he bought many bicycles. And after he learned to ride, his brother Pu Jie learned and then the empress started cycling around the Palace!' Runqi laughed at the memory of the sombre palace compounds being turned into a cycleway.

'Then, amazingly, the imperial concubine also wanted to learn to ride,' he said. 'Her hair was all done up and her heels were so high. Two wheels were no good so a third wheel was added. She cycled around, two eunuchs running behind her for protection!'

Runqi and I finally came across the dusty chamber, part of a smaller 'palace' (like a grand courtyard home), where he and his mother lived for several years. Through grimy glass we could see cheap antique furniture in the living room. Naturally, it was vastly different to how he remembered it, but by now his impromptu recollections were flowing freely. Some of the other tourists gathered around to listen.

'My feelings aren't very different from the ordinary tourist, the only difference is I know the background and the visitors don't,' he said. Runqi and the imperial household remained in the Forbidden City until 1924, when troops of the devout Christian warlord Feng Yuxiang seized Beijing and drove the regal occupants out, closing the gates on imperial rule forever.

In recent years there has been little sense of the 'imperial ghosts and vanished emperors' described poetically by Juliet Bredon. The 580-year-old relic is now undergoing yet another expensive facelift for the 2008 Olympics.

By the time the Olympic opening ceremony bursts into action, Beijing will be two cities in effect: one part a shiny, surreal, orderly Olympic city with big parks, clean air, blue sky, five-star toilets, English road signs and even more of those ubiquitous global fast-food outlets. On another level, it will still be the home and workplace of nearly thirteen million people.

A multi-billion dollar makeover has begun in earnest; the budget so far is US$22 billion. Apart from all the new Olympic facilities and a grand urban park, the aim is to reduce air pollution to the same levels as Paris by moving all factories out of the urban centre and converting public transportation from diesel to natural gas. This is no easy feat as, according to the World Bank, Beijing air quality is nearly twenty times worse than that in Paris. Tree coverage will be increased by 50 per cent in an attempt to minimise the mountains of sand dumped on the city each spring from the Gobi Desert. In addition to beautification there are also big plans for high-tech communication. The city will spend nearly US$4 billion upgrading its telecommunications infrastructure, aimed not at ordinary residents but at several fledgling high-tech zones and business districts. All in all, it's an astonishing to-do list in a country where nearly half the urbanites still live in dilapidated low-rise apartment buildings and can't bathe regularly because of the dearth of facilities. Published statistics are difficult to find, but China's most advanced city, Shanghai, has just 600 000 households with flushing toilets out of a population of 12 million, while just one in eight farms has access to modern latrines, without necessarily implying active sewerage systems.

In the Chinese capital, a life and death battle between tradition and modernisation is under way. Millions of bicycles, the workers' transportation, compete with a growing array of vehicles from Jeep Cherokees to Volkswagens, Buicks and Citroën hatchbacks, all made in China. Steel and glass buildings stand beside concrete Soviet architecture along the western part of Chang' an Avenue. In Beijing's spacious airport, immigration details have been digitised on state-of-the-art computers, but other problems are dealt with in very traditional ways. A young man in a blue jumpsuit patrols the giant windows armed with only a flimsy plastic fly-swatter. There are inconsistencies in the modernisation drive but the momentum is full throttle.

Today, brick by brick, Beijing's past is being dismantled. The destruction of ancient parts of the city began during Mao's chaotic rule after the Beijing government deemed that preserving the city's historic centre would be both too costly and against the prevailing ideology. Preserving remnants of tradition and feudalism was anathema in Mao's China. In his book *Chinese Shadows*, published in 1972, Simon Leys (Sinologist Pierre Ryckmans' pen-name) describes the destruction of old Peking as sacrilege. 'For those who knew it in the past, Peking now appears to be a murdered town. The body is still there, the soul has gone.' Leys recounts how the wholesale destruction began with the removal of the graceful archways of the old city wall. Blocks of ancient homes followed to make way for the wide avenues and squares so admired by socialists. Then the old city walls themselves, which Leys says expressed cosmic geometry rather than defence needs, became the next architectural relics to be pulled down over a period of twelve years until the early 1970s. A reconstructed gate, the Front Gate or *Qianmen*, to the south of Mao's Mausoleum, a few watchtowers and an observatory are all that remain of Beijing's old city wall. There is also a very small original section still standing in the inner city district of Chongwenmen, close to the Beijing railway station.

Residents I spoke to recalled how they helped to dismantle the ancient city wall in the 1950s and 1960s, and used the material to build their homes, after being told the bricks were as unworthy as clods of earth. By the 1990s, however, Beijing authorities began to worry about the shortage of historical sites in the city. In 1999 the Beijing government issued regulations demarcating areas of historical relevance and nominating 5.58 square kilometres for preservation in the vicinity of the Forbidden City. All together only twenty-five sites were singled out for preservation, including fifteen ancient streets, four courtyard residences and four historical laneways or *hutongs*. 'The Cultural Revolution began to destroy all beautiful things in Beijing,' lamented one Chinese scholar, 'but the real-estate development of the 1990s will complete the destruction.'

To reverse the shortage of historic sites, the government initiated campaigns like 'Loving Ancient Beijing, Donating City Wall Bricks'. Residents who might have hoarded bricks from the old city wall were asked to come forward and, sure enough, in the space of twenty days 18 000 bricks were collected. In 2002, the city government obliterated 2000 residences and sixty businesses to rebuild a section of the wall and incorporate it into a park.

In early 2002 I walked through some of the condemned old lanes of Chongwenmen which ran parallel to the remnants of the former city wall. A laneway with rudimentary homes on either side had the stench of death about it. Residents told me that this was the first day of a month-long eviction. They were distraught about being forced out of their homes of forty years.

'Mao had told us to live here,' said one elderly lady. 'Now the leaders have changed their minds.' She explained that compensation of 6000 yuan per square metre, with the maximum claimable being 6 square metres for elderly residents, meant that the payment wouldn't cover the cost of buying a new apartment on the outskirts of the city. The average cost of one of those is about 300000 yuan.

Most of the Chongwenmen residents were former workers, once considered the vanguard of Mao's revolution, who'd been permitted to build their homes beside the old wall. But the Beijing authorities used a new law to expel them. The homes were all declared illegal dwellings and the residents were given twenty days to vacate. If they had been assessed under the usual demolition law, they would have received greater compensation.

The day I visited the area, garbage rotted in piles and dirt and polythene bags swirled above the paving stones. In one of the narrow lanes I came across a family paying its last respects to a dead mother. Outside their front entrance, a table had been erected as a makeshift shrine. On it stood a sombre black and white portrait of the dead woman and offerings of fruit and dried meat. Paper flowers covered the small shrine and a black banner was draped around the photograph. The dead woman's brother, Mr Li, came out of the house and into the lane. He wore a black armband, a sign of mourning, and slowly lit a cigarette. 'It will be difficult for the family,' he said when I asked him how he felt about moving. He didn't elaborate and I was beginning to feel like an intruder so I thanked him and left the lane.

In the 1950s Beijing's most eminent architect, Liang Sicheng, advised the government to build the new capital west of the old one in order to preserve the ancient city. However, at the time, Soviet-style ideology and architecture prevailed while old things were considered feudalistic. Add to that the huge population explosion during the first thirty years of the People's Republic and Beijing's heritage never stood a chance. Between 1949 and 1984 Beijing grew from 1.2 million to more than 9 million residents, a result of both internal migration and population growth.

A *hutong* is a traditional city alley lined by a series of courtyard homes. Many of them were built around the Forbidden City during the Yuan, Ming and Qing dynasties. The courtyard homes were typically made up of four small rectangular houses looking into a square courtyard. Homes originally housed one extended family, but after the Communists came to power, an influx of migrants seeking opportunities in the city and a lack of new housing led to overcrowding, with an average of five to ten families occupying each establishment.

*Hutong*s were the dominant form of traditional architecture in Beijing, an integral part of the city's history and a unique way of life. In 2002 I stayed in a modern Beijing courtyard home, which had the traditional structure but a modern interior and fixtures. Today, modern courtyard living is reserved for wealthy Chinese or foreigners as they are more expensive to build and maintain than other housing. When I stayed in the courtyard it was late spring, so a few steps across the courtyard from the bedroom to the kitchen was no problem weatherwise, and the notion of being closer to nature – feeling the breeze and hearing the rustling leaves – was very pleasant. In the narrow lane outside, barely wide enough to fit a small car, neighbourhood life was in full swing from early in the morning. Knife-sharpeners and rubbish collectors passed through the lanes on their converted tricycles, advertising their trades with a musical call. Residents in the *hutong* woke early to buy fresh produce from the noodle-maker, the travelling butcher and the vegetable seller. The lane remained alive with noises, smells and bicycle bells until around 9 pm. Then it fell silent, the only sound an electric hum coming from the streetlamps.

Elaine Sun's family owned a small house in a one-hundred-year-old *hutong*. Elaine is a vivacious, straight-talking, tall Beijinger, and

I hired her to do the ABC's bookkeeping after she produced a wad of accounting credentials. I later introduced her to my cousin Stan and now they are married and living in Sydney. Her family remains in Beijing.

Unlike traditional courtyard homes, *hutong*s built more recently, primarily for the nineteenth-century working class, housed around four or five families in a narrow compound fronted by a large gate. The area surrounding Elaine's *hutong* wasn't deemed historically significant, and in 2000 the developers moved in, eventually evicting Elaine's family and their neighbours in late 2001. Where the family home once stood there is now a road stretching from the Temple of Heaven to the shopping district of Wangfujing. Elaine recalls her old home with fondness. 'I really liked life in the *hutong*,' she said. 'Our neighbours were closer than relatives. You could just shout out, "Old Mother Guo, I'm going out now!" and you wouldn't even need to lock your front door.'

In the *hutong*, the space between the houses was so narrow that only one person could walk past at any time. Elaine's family – two adults and three children (all were conceived before the One Child policy came into force in the late 1970s) – lived in a room with an area of just 9 square metres. Later, Mr Sun, Elaine's father, extended the 'house' so that it reached to the *hutong* wall, adding an extra 6 square metres. Into that small space went three beds (two double, one single), two wardrobes, one study table, a sewing machine, washing machine, refrigerator, bookshelf, a very big television and a fold-up dining table.

In spring the lane filled with the aroma of flowers, planted lovingly by elderly neighbours. All year round, cooking smells from five households wafted through the small community every evening. But as well as the cramped space, there were other downsides to life in the *hutong*s. The nearest toilet was two or three minutes walk from home, the bath-house several blocks away. Elaine said there was never a good time to use the stinking public toilets, which were nothing more than holes in the ground connected by an open channel. 'In summer, you had to be quick, or the mosquitoes would bite your backside,' she recalled. 'Sometimes you'd have to take incense into the toilet or use a fan to shoo them away!'

Using the public toilet in midwinter was even more inconvenient. *Hutong* residents had to dress warmly for each trek to the toilet, and if you had a stomach problem it was a nightmare. 'That,' said Elaine without a hint of regret, 'was just how life was.'

Before 1990, the family didn't even have a telephone. Like other working class families, they used a very public telephone at the local corner shop. When the family received an incoming call, someone from the store would run over to the *hutong* and simply shout through the gate. Telephones were once a status symbol. In the sixties only senior officials had them in their homes and even in the 1980s it was considered a great privilege to own one – the installation fee was prohibitive and there was a six month waiting period, depending on the size of the bribe offered to the telephone bureau. In 1989, however, the installation fee dropped to 5000 yuan. By 1999 it was 1700 yuan, and in 2000 it was abolished altogether. Even today, there can be a long wait before a phone is installed, which accounts for the rapid growth in mobile phone usage. Elaine recalls that only through personal connections, or *guanxi*, was her father able to secure the phone's installation for a few thousand yuan.

Unlike the unfortunate residents of Chongwenmen, the Suns were handsomely compensated by Beijing standards – 30 000 yuan per person in the household – when the eviction notices arrived in 2001. This is two years salary for a worker. As a result, the family put a 150 000 yuan down-payment on a 500 000 yuan four-bedroom, two-bathroom 140 square metre apartment, more than ten times the size of their original home in the *hutong*.

I visited the Suns' new apartment in the Tongzhou district, half an hour to the east, almost in a straight line from the city centre. In Tongzhou, there were no foreign faces or fancy department stores. But there was no pollution or traffic congestion, either. Elaine's family had made new friends, and with their spacious new dining area and four bedrooms they were able to entertain old friends from the state ivory-carving factory where Mr and Mrs Sun once worked. Elaine's parents and younger brother, Sun Jian, seemed extremely content. The whole family admired the gardens around the apartment complex and the lack of heavy industry or traffic. Even Xing Xing, the family poodle, seemed pleased, scampering around the house in a woollen coat and a white disposable nappy.

After joining the family in a simple meal of offal and bean curd soup (I passed on the offal), Mr Sun went fishing with an old comrade from the factory. He took out a number of rods before deciding on the appropriate one, and then called a motorised tricycle taxi to take them to the fish farm – because Beijing is land-locked, fishing takes place in small dams stocked with fish such as trout. The farm operators are paid according to how many fish are caught. If the Suns had still lived in the *hutong*, a fishing expedition would have been extremely inconvenient. Apart from the traffic congestion in the city, Mr Sun would have had difficulty carrying his rod, and later his fish, on a crowded public bus. He gave me a wide smile as he left the apartment. 'Ten years ago, who would have thought that we could live like this?' he said.

Until recently, grass was a rare commodity in Beijing. That began to change during the Great Remodelling in the lead-up to the fiftieth anniversary of Communist Party rule on 1 October 1999. Inside the compound where I lived, I feared the construction of high-rise apartments was about to threaten my precious light and ruin my privacy. I watched with trepidation as workers knocked down rows of old dormitory-style blocks where many of the Third World diplomats and their families lived. The diplomats moved into other apartments in the compound while workers and a few bobcats took just half a day to flatten three five-storey buildings. A few weeks later the rubble was taken away during the middle of the night, to comply with the truck curfew on Beijing's main roads. Finally, there was a vast expanse in front of my apartment building. To my joy, workers began to unroll large squares of turf and carpeted a giant park about the size of a football field. Finally, trees that had survived the demolition were hosed down with water, and *voilà*! – an instant big, green garden.

Turf mania began to take hold all over Beijing. It started off in small patches along the main thoroughfares visible to visiting foreign dignitaries as they passed through Beijing on their all-encompassing day visits to the capital. Now, inner-city buildings are actually being demolished and replaced with parks. Of course, no-one is allowed to walk on the grass; that would be destructive. Some cities employ grass 'police' to stop recalcitrant residents trampling the soft green blades. Despite the authoritarian approach, for most residents grass is a welcome alternative to the grey Soviet temples that made Beijing's wide avenues seem like tunnels.

Though the love affair with grass is bound to grow with the government's pledge to improve the environment, an associated problem could become apparent long before the 2008 Olympics. Beijing is one of China's driest cities. It has less than one-eighth of the national average water supply, and already excessive ground-water extraction has caused the subsidence of 800 square kilometres of land. City officials have earmarked millions of litres of water to ensure the supply doesn't run out before 2008, but there is, not surprisingly, open talk of a water crisis by 2010. City workers are frequently seen turning on sprinklers in the middle of the day during Beijing's oppressively hot summer. With rainfall low year round and the city's busy sprinklers unable to keep pace, perhaps the solution is something tried several years ago. Drastic measures were called for prior to the arrival of the final International Olympic Committee visit to Beijing before it was named host city for the 2008 Olympics. Confronted with unsightly brown, dying grass, offi-cials decided that rather than uprooting thousands of hectares, a quick paint job would temporarily solve the problem. Battalions of soldiers armed with spray cans were dispatched one morning to create a simple but effective lie – that the grass is always greener in Beijing.

While grass, artificial or otherwise, is moving *in* to Beijing, over the next few years authorities plan to move *out* of the city at least a quarter of a million people. City planners say Beijing's density is twice that of a typical city in a developed country, and they aim to halve the density to around 400 people per hectare. Ten new suburbs will be built to accommodate the larger living environment for Beijing's nearly 13 million people, but what is less certain is how authorities will tackle what the 2000 Census confirmed: that 3 million out of 13 million Beijing residents are domestic migrants, giving Beijing the dubious honour of housing the largest migrant population in the country.

For the first thirty years of Communist rule, Chinese people basically stayed in the place where they were born, bound by their *hukou*, or residence permit. The aim was to maintain social order. The *hukou* was introduced in 1958 during the Great Leap Forward, a massive communal agricultural and industrial campaign designed to quickly increase China's wealth and output. The *hukou* contained the official history of a Chinese person: their place and date of birth, schools and universities attended, and details of their marriage, spouse and parents. Divided into agricultural or non-agricultural status, it's been described as a tool of institutionalised discrimination. It entitles China's 400 million urbanites to all the amenities provided at the state's expense, diminishing though they may be, such as health care, education and housing. Farmers get nothing other than the right to live in the countryside, though in the days of the communes they received free food.

The phenomenon of the so-called 'floating population' (touched on in chapter 1), involved the movement of people from farm to city, more than a decade after Deng Xiaoping ended the rural communes. After twenty years of planned agriculture, farmers contracted land from the state and after selling the state a proportion of their output were free to sell the excess in local markets. With the onset of Deng's reforms, control over the *hukou* registration system was relaxed so that peasants could travel to the cities when there was no work on the land. By the 1990s, millions of peasants had moved to the cities year round, and came in such vast numbers they were known pejoratively as the 'blind flow'.

The system copes by granting temporary residence permits to millions of migrants, while the cream of the labour market can afford to purchase its mobility. A coveted Beijing *hukou*, for example, costs between 10 000 yuan and 100 000 yuan. While this is out of the reach of most ordinary citizens, some companies provide a *hukou* as part of an employment package, but this is usually only at the top of the labour market. The government estimates there are 80 million migrants on the move, but most commentators believe the figure could be double that.

Soon after I first arrived in Beijing in late 1995, I began to notice differences in the appearance of people on the streets. A typical Beijing office worker might dress in a windcheater and trousers and ride an expensive bicycle with gears. The domestic migrant, on the other hand, is distinguished by his bad haircut and shabby Western-style suit, worn without a tie. He often carries his life's possessions in a large bundle perched on his shoulder. Most migrants you see wandering the streets are men in search of construction work. Beijing people look down on them, calling them bumpkins and blaming them for the city's rising crime rate.

During my first weeks in Beijing, one of the air-conditioners in my apartment fell off the wall and crashed onto the desk below. After I reported it to the management, the janitor appeared at my front door with two migrant workers. They were cheaper to employ than tradesmen, plus the job didn't need much skill, just muscle. The janitor told them to go inside and fix the air-conditioner. The migrant workers were covered in thick dust, as though they had just had a flour fight. One of them removed his canvas shoes, unleashing an unbearable stench that lingered for several days. I think it was the first time they had seen a foreigner at close quarters because they stared at me open-mouthed. Fifteen minutes later the air-conditioner was back on the wall and the strange threesome left.

Until the mid nineties, migrant workers lived in haphazard enclaves dotted around Beijing. Different ethnic or regional groups drew together, sometimes outnumbering local Beijing residents. The locals described the enclaves as villages and they were named after the provinces from which the migrants came: there was Zhejiang village which was known for its tailors, leather and clothing stalls; Anhui village where many of Beijing's domestic helpers lived; and Xinjiang village, the home of the Muslim Uighur minority in Beijing.

Xiao Liangyu, a 27-year-old migrant worker whose village in Anhui province I had visited for my first report from China, had come to Beijing three years before. He had a wife and a one-year-old son and made a living as a garbage collector, selling cardboard and refuse to one of dozens of recycling centres. Ten kilograms of waste earned him 1.20 yuan and he made around 1000–1800 yuan a month. That was one year's salary in the countryside and would have been considered a decent wage even by Beijing workers' standards. He paid around 100 yuan for a monthly permit giving him the privilege of collecting rubbish inside Beijing's prestigious Qinghua University. To many migrants, the permit was worth ten times its weight in gold. However, one afternoon when the university gate-keeper saw my camera crew filming the garbageman, Mr Xiao was beaten up, probably out of jealousy, and had his precious permit and cart confiscated for a short time.

The world of the migrant worker gave me my first glimpse into how China's rural population lived. While Mr Xiao was considered a hero in his village, in Beijing he was an outcast who was frequently exploited by others. He, his wife and child lived in a one-room shack where they cooked, washed and slept. Though it seemed a harsh and basic existence on the fringe of Beijing society, there was no turning back. Mr Xiao's cousin, who had recently arrived from the countryside, joined us for a bowl of steaming dumplings. 'I can develop myself here in Beijing,' explained the cousin. 'It's where I've always wanted to be.'

After years of tolerating the build-up of migrant enclaves, Beijing decided to crack down on them for fear they could become hotbeds of dissent, and between 1995 and 1996 ordered the villages to be completely flattened. As a measure of the government's sensitivity, while filming in the Zhejiang migrant village, the ABC's feisty researcher Zhang Lijia got involved in an argument with a shopkeeper who didn't like our presence and within minutes the police had arrived and surrounded us. I told them that if they detained us it would cause a nasty diplomatic incident. They seemed unimpressed so I frantically telephoned the ABC's Foreign Ministry minder. The official unhelpfully suggested we co-operate with the police. I refused and we all stood on the street unsure of the next step as a crowd of onlookers grew bigger and bigger. Eventually the commanding officer received a telephone call. He and his men had been told to leave immediately. We, too, decided to leave Zhejiang village and returned the following afternoon to try once again to speak to Beijing residents about why migrant workers were feared or disliked. It didn't take long for the venom to spill out.

'They're a fierce bunch. A while ago, my car was in their way. They bloody smashed the window. Damn them! If they beat you up, one person hits you, then the whole group beats you and then runs away. Fuck them!' a man told us, confirming the view of many Beijing residents that migrants are responsible for the city's increase in crime.

Though the migrant villages disappeared years ago, today, one by one, cheap dwellings on the edge of the city are also being demolished. The migrants, many of them without legal documents, are being forced to find accommodation beyond Beijing's Fourth Ring Road, the boundary between inner and outer city. New residential developments are sprouting on the outer rings, with pockets of undeveloped land rented out to migrant workers and the poor until the land is slated for development.

Migrant worker Mr Li lives in a shack with his wife and two children in a suburb called Fatou, east of the Fourth Ring Road. As his registered home is in the countryside, in keeping with China's family planning policy he and his wife were allowed a second child because his first was a daughter. (In the city only one child is allowed, whether boy or girl.) Every day Mr Li pedals his tricycle cart for two hours until he reaches downtown Beijing. There he visits two or three restaurants to collect their discarded food scraps, pouring them into large drums on top of his converted tricycle. You would think the restaurants would pay Mr Li to get rid of the waste, but even for food scraps there's competition and Mr Li pays the restaurants a total of 80 yuan a month to cart away the slops left by city folk who can afford to eat out three or four times a week.

At a restaurant one lunchtime, I noticed the waitress breaking used chopsticks in half before discarding them. I'd seen people eating out of lunchboxes doing the same thing. Months later, as I was leaving an American franchise restaurant, I noticed a woman crouched over a large manhole used to hold restaurant waste. The woman, who was poorly dressed, retrieved chopsticks out of the muck and it dawned on me that she intended to recycle them either for resale or personal use.

I'd watched long-suffering men like Mr Li for years, mistakenly believing they were nightsoil collectors. Though it wasn't nightsoil, it was disgusting work. He took the drums back to his home where he tipped them into a giant cauldron that sat on top of a fire. The 'soup' bubbled away while Mr Li picked out the cigarette butts, broken chopsticks and large bones. Then he tipped the cauldron into a trough for his four hungry pigs and a dozen chickens. On restaurant slops he could feed his livestock and then sell the pigs when he needed extra cash.

Because they don't have a Beijing *hukou*, the children of migrant workers are not allowed to attend regular schools. There are an estimated 1.8 million migrant kids in China, but no-one knows exactly how many live in the capital. Around Beijing at least a hundred private, illegal schools have sprung up to educate migrant kids because they've been denied access to the public system. The Xingzhi primary school has changed locations several times because its student numbers keep growing. When I visited, it had around 1200 students from 28 provinces crammed into little rooms surrounding a dusty playground. The school premises were probably once a bus station, and the tiny classrooms formerly Chinese fast-food stalls. Though the facilities were basic, the children seemed content.

The school was set up in 1994 by Ms Li Shumei and her husband, Li Benyao, themselves migrant workers from central Henan province. Mr Li, the school principal, wore a blue Mao jacket and cap and sleeve protectors like a good Communist cadre. He would look out of place in a regular Beijing school, but in the boondocks it seemed perfectly natural. Ms Li wore practical grey trousers and a padded jacket. She had a quiet, diligent air about her. When she first arrived in Beijing she worked in a clothing market until she realised the demand for education for migrant kids. She began classes in her home before setting up a school. There was always a waiting list and from the fees (600 yuan a semester) Mr Li paid the rent on the premises, bought basic furniture and took care of a large heating bill in winter. Yet it wasn't a scene that I'd place in China's capital city; the school looked more like an aid project in the remote, poor west of the country.

If the city's transformation during the past decade is anything to go by, migrant workers will continue work in the hardest, dirtiest jobs, face strict controls as well as a lack of access to services as they try to overturn the 'misfortune' of being born a peasant.

However talented the Chinese have proven to be at population control, infrastructure building and economic goal-setting, taming the environment will be the most pressing concern in the lead-up to the Olympics. Beijing plans to spend an incredible US$5.4 billion to solve the environmental problem, an enormous figure for a developing nation to spend on a single city that is home to just one-hundredth of the country's population.

In springtime, 27500 tonnes of dust are dumped on the city from encroaching deserts on the city's outskirts. The rapid desertification is due to soil erosion, a result of decades of environmental neglect and mismanagement. Inside the city itself there are 110 polluting factories within the city boundary of the Fourth Ring Road, and 1.17 million vehicles with questionable emission standards. In winter, 10–15 per cent of inner city residents still heat their homes using brown coal. I estimated that each year there were between 60 and 100 days when the sky in Beijing was clear enough to distinguish the sun. Most days the sky was an indeterminate grey, and occasionally the haze was so thick that visibility was cut to half a kilometre or less. There were days too when my eyes stung and watered for no obvious reason. (Ironically, my brother Stephen, the *Sydney Morning Herald*'s Beijing correspondent until 1997, found his asthma improved in China, probably because there was little in the air that was organic.) Beijing's ambitious Olympic charter pledges that the devastating sand storms will be eliminated by 2005, 45 per cent of the city will be covered in parkland by 2007 and 90 per cent of the city will be serviced by a modern sewerage system by 2010, up from 60 per cent today.

Perhaps overly idealistic is the Olympic committee's commitment to 'raise the citizens' awareness' to adopt 'an environment-friendly lifestyle'. In a country where there are still no qualms about winding down the car window and throwing out cartons or lunchboxes, and where spitting and hawking are common amongst the bulk of the population, instilling an 'environment-friendly lifestyle' would appear to be an ongoing challenge for future generations. Fines for spitting in public places were only imposed in 2002 and though environmental messages were posted on all the major signboards around the city, I hadn't detected a change in people's behaviour.

Do people approve of the changes taking place in the city? Publicly, yes, because they believe the Olympics will bring the country honour and make China's opening up irreversible. However while most people I spoke to privately enjoy the city's neater appearance they are extremely dissatisfied otherwise. The problem appears to be the pace of the development, adequacy of compensation and what will become of those who are tossed on the social scrap-heap. Workers in many sectors fear losing their jobs. For example, Beijing plans to completely modernise its fleet of taxis. At present, there are various tiers of taxi service, ranging from large cars that cater mainly to upmarket hotels, to cheaper vehicles that roam the streets. Very few drivers speak even a few words of English, driving skills are variable and though the present fleet is less than three or four years old, the cars are poorly maintained and deteriorate rapidly. Changes to be put in place before the Olympics mean drivers will have to pass an English test and polluting cars will switch to natural gas. A younger, savvier breed of taxi-drivers will replace the present operators, many of whom have already been abandoned once by the closure of state factories.

In the last few years there have been scores of small-scale protests. Groups of elderly people frequently gather outside the gates of the Beijing Municipal Government or the Beijing People's Congress to demonstrate over housing demolition and compensation. There has also been an outcry over the city's renovation by leading architects, planners and even artists.

Most Western cities don't escape the curse of graffiti but Chinese cities have remarkably little of it. In Beijing in the mid 1990s that changed. Unlike most Western graffiti, the scribblings appearing on Beijing walls were of an eye-catching symbol – a large bald head. Sometimes there were several heads in succession and often they were accompanied by the symbols 'AK-47', like the type of rifle. The graffiti was found under flyovers and on walls adjacent to condemned areas.

The man behind the graffiti turned out to be a former commercial artist named Zhang Dali, alias AK-47. One winter evening with snow still on the ground, I followed him on a raid, watching him take a can of black spray-paint from his bag and, with a single sweep, spray his signature bald head on a wall next to a row of restaurants that were about to be knocked down. He drew the head beside a large Chinese character, *chai,* the order to demolish, that officials had painted on the wall. Not content with one head, Zhang Dali painted three. Then he signed his trademark AK-47 before jumping back on his bike.

In daylight the heads seem to be fixed in an expression of disbelief, reflecting Zhang Dali's own feelings. 'Ancient things are disappearing and traditions are being lost,' he said of Beijing's transformation.

As in most countries where graffiti is regarded as vandalism or an act of anarchy, Zhang Dali goes about his illicit work incognito, his face covered by a balaclava. I asked him why he didn't object to being filmed committing a crime, and his response was that the police had never caught him in the act. Nor could they prove that the man wearing the balaclava in the video was him. The police had warned him, however, not to paint outside his studio. Zhang also mentioned he held an Italian passport by virtue of marrying an Italian, so perhaps that gave him a measure of protection.

Zhang called the bald heads a series of 'dialogues', an attempt to engage Beijing residents in a discussion about the destruction of their city. However, when I approached a district with its own Zhang Dali original, the director of the neighbourhood committee was not impressed.

'This isn't art,' he said, waving his arms at the graffiti. 'It's ugly! If they want real art, they should go paint in a gallery.' Soon a small crowd of residents had gathered, quite disgusted at the desecration of their wall. Attempts were made to scrub off the paint and I left them deep in discussion about how the culprit had managed to get his paintbrush into the cracks of the wall.

As Zhang Dali explained, it wasn't just the city's architecture that was changing; it was its soul. Occasionally you see glimpses of the crafts, music and charming pastimes that must have been a major part of life before the founding of the People's Republic in 1949 and before the wholesale destruction of society during the Cultural Revolution. These days you sometimes see old men taking their caged birds for a walk and hanging the cages on the branches of trees while they perform their daily *Tai Chi*, the slow flowing movements that are deceptively simple but demanding on the body. Elderly Beijingers love their hobbies, whether it's joining the neighbourhood Peking Opera troupe, carving intricate whistles for the legs of homing pigeons, or engaging in the sport of cricket fighting. But the replacement of horizontal neighbourhoods with vertical ones, together with the closure and demolition of outdoor markets, which the government believes are unsightly and uncivilised, is turning the city into a more sanitised, uninteresting version of its former self.

Mr Fu Zhende, a retired cadre in his early sixties, learned the art of rearing crickets from his father. In ancient times ladies and gentlemen of the court kept crickets – insects which on reaching maturity have a hundred-day life span – to hear them sing. Crickets were also reared to fight and this was a form of entertainment, with the fighting taking place just before the end of the cricket's life cycle. From the start of autumn, around mid August in Beijing, Mr Fu focuses almost to the point of obsession on raising his crickets. As he took me through each stage of the process I discovered that the art of cricket fighting wasn't confined to watching two little insects belting it out in a 'ring'; rather, it is an entire sub-culture, from creating the correct food mixture down to selecting the clay pots and the delicate porcelain utensils used to feed the insects.

'Crickets are inherently born to fight,' said Mr Fu. 'In the past it was a great leisure activity for common people. Everyone would be raising crickets and watching them fight. Cricket fighting became a sport enjoyed by citizens and emperors alike.'

Normally Master Fu rode a train to nearby Shandong province to collect wild crickets, but on this occasion he arranged to meet a young farmer at the Yu Ting Qiao market (which has recently been demolished). The young man arrived with several cardboard boxes full of tiny jars, each holding a single cricket fresh from Shandong province. Mr Fu carefully uncovered each jar and put crickets, two at a time, on a piece of white paper. After examining each cricket he selected around twenty, based on their colouring, the size of their mandibles and shape of their bodies. Ten of them were to form my team of fighters and though I couldn't yet appreciate what Master Fu was talking about, he enjoyed singling out each insect's winning feature. We gave them all names and so I became the proud owner of Mr Mandibles, Jaws Too and Green Monster, among others.

Before Yu Ting Qiao market was demolished, it had been full of stalls selling cricket paraphernalia, lined up beside the edge of a canal. Hawkers stood at the entrance to the market making *Jian Bing*, a popular Beijing snack consisting of a large egg pancake stuffed with chives and a crackly wafer. As you walked further inside the market, there were all kinds of birds for sale, from rare owls to regular sparrows, which were almost completely exterminated during the late 1950s when they were declared one of the Four Pests (along with flies, rats and mosquitoes). When the campaign had ravaged the sparrow population and upset the ecosystem, the fourth pest was changed from a sparrow to a bed bug. Traditional pastimes like cricket rearing were banned during the Cultural Revolution, but Mr Fu and his friends have made up for lost time since the ban was lifted.

On the night of the fight, Mr Fu produced a perspex arena slightly larger than a paperback book. He then dropped a female cricket into each clay pot and waited for the crickets to mate, which increases their aggression. Then he and his friends erected a miniature measuring station, weighing the crickets using a unit of measurement known as a *li,* placing the smallest aluminium Chinese coin called a half *fen* as a counterweight against the crickets. Each insect's weight was recorded to ensure the crickets fought only against others in the same weight class.

In the perspex ring, two crickets faced off. Sometimes they took a little egging on, being tickled with a feather until they were in the mood to fight. When ready, they rushed at each other, locked mandibles and tried to wrestle their opponent out of the ring. As soon as one insect was proven superior, the fight was stopped and the winner declared. Mr Mandibles turned out to be a good investment for me that evening, winning me the princely sum of US$5.

As Master Fu packed up the arena and the weighing station, I asked him whether he ever felt remorse about rearing crickets, knowing they would die either at the end of the fight or perish when their hundred days were up.

'I guess sometimes when an unexpectedly good fighter comes along, I do feel remorse. But when it comes down to it, it's a natural process. You see, life is measured and you have to be realistic,' he replied.

I couldn't help thinking that even though tradition was unravelling around us, the transformation of Beijing was also a natural process. For the city's thirteen million people, being realistic – like the hundred-day insect trainer – meant learning to take the good with the bad and enjoying the ride.

SHANGHAI STIR-FRY

When Zhang Baogen won a lottery, he believed he had struck gold. The farmer's prize was a brand-new apartment overlooking the Huangpu River in Shanghai, China's equivalent to New York. It was the stuff of dreams; a one-way ticket out of the poverty of the countryside and into the beautiful new world of China's urban middle class. However, claiming the prize wasn't so straightforward. Zhang Baogen set off for the Big Smoke where he tracked down a young aunt. She invited him to stay but demanded he pay rent. He found work as a security guard and was then beaten up by a customer. Other Shanghainese took him for a ride. Even the real-estate company cheated him – the apartment hadn't been built yet and the company tried to convince him to accept a token cash prize in its place.

Zhang Baogen wasn't a real person but a character in the film *Beautiful New World*, which portrayed the city worshipped by China's middle class as being awash with lies, greed, envy and cheats. While Zhang Baogen was fictitious, his experiences were based on a true story, reported in a local newspaper. In the closing scenes of the film, the affable farmer brings his aunt, whom he eventually befriends, to the construction site where his apartment is taking shape. The film ends with an optimistic flourish as the two stand amid the scaffolding and concrete that will one day be their 'beautiful new world'.

Newcomers to Shanghai always marvel at the city from the wide,

71

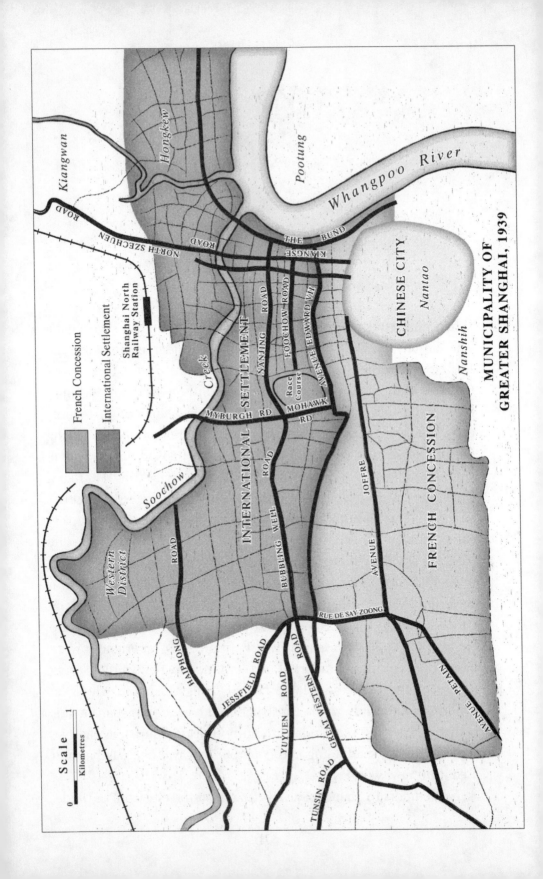

Scale

0 _____ 1
Kilometres

French Concession

International Settlement

Shanghai North
Railway Station

Kiangwan

KIANGWAN ROAD

NORTH SZECHUEN ROAD

Hongkew

Pootung

Whangpoo River

THE BUND

KIANGSE

CHINESE CITY
Nantao

Nanshih

Soochow Creek

NANJING ROAD

FOOCHOW ROAD

AVENUE EDWARD VII

Race
Course

MYBURGH RD

MOHAWK
RD

INTERNATIONAL
SETTLEMENT

JOFFRE

FRENCH CONCESSION

Western
District

ROAD

BUBBLING WELL ROAD

AVENUE

HAIPHONG
ROAD

JESSFIELD ROAD

YUYUEN ROAD

GREAT WESTERN ROAD

TUNSIN ROAD

RUE DE SAY ZOONG

AVENUE PETAIN

**MUNICIPALITY OF
GREATER SHANGHAI, 1939**

kilometre-long walkway called the Bund, on the west bank of the Huangpu River, a tributary of the Yangtze. The vista represents a kind of offbeat Chinese harmony: old Shanghai with its colonial facade on one side of the river, new Shanghai on the other – and the impossible dream always around the next bend. The Bund (an Anglo-Indian word pronounced like 'fund') is an audiovisual banquet. A cacophony of ghetto-blasters mingles traditional song with electronic foxtrot and insipid disco. Elderly men and women shadow-box holding swords and red fans. Nearby, couples do a slow, stately cha-cha while a tall thin man on rollerskates slaloms around a course of neatly placed soft-drink bottles filled with colourful milky liquids. It is 6 am and the sun rises behind the futuristic baubles and spires of New Shanghai, east of the river. The new, however, is challenged by the traditional: kites caught in the wind reach as high as the skyscrapers. Attached to nylon cord, they are launched by little old men, running a few dozen metres along the Bund until the kites take flight. Their time is precious; by 7.30 am the kites are packed away to make way for the steady stream of tourists.

In Shanghai, my favourite city in China, I like the locals' confidence and sense of purpose. They are passionate about life, whether they are kite-flyers, ballroom dancers or city planners. Nothing seems impossible: Shanghai aims to become Asia's financial capital, eventually overtaking Hong Kong. Even though it is not the Olympic host city in 2008, it wants to draw as much international attention to itself as possible. I find ordinary people in Shanghai to be more open and less suspicious of foreigners than any other city in China. Most of all, I like the way the history of its foreign enclave is now indelibly etched on the landscape.

In Shanghai I like to stay in the art deco 1930s building originally named Broadway Mansion, built by the famous Shanghai identity Sir Victor Sassoon. Sassoon was a Briton who built a number of apartment buildings and hotels in Shanghai, including the Cathay (now the Peace Hotel), where he lived in the penthouse and built a lavish nightclub beneath the roof. While the Peace Hotel is arguably Old Shanghai's most prominent landmark, Broadway Mansion, across the old Garden Bridge on the edge of Suzhou Creek, has a view down the length of the Bund. From the balconies of the former apartment building, now a government-run hotel renamed Shanghai Mansion, you can observe the city and the river spring to life. The river is a lifeline for farmers from kilometres around: a string of barges haul coal, timber and agricultural products such as rice. From a lower floor at Shanghai Mansion you can just make out the clothing of the barge drivers, grey and drab. Then cast your eyes to the people on the Bund and, at any time of the day, their clothes are full of colour.

Shanghai is known as the 'dragon's head' of the Chinese economy, because it's where the 'body', the Yangtze River, meets the ocean. The 'dragon' represents the river valley, a vast market of 400 million people. Many come to Shanghai to strike it rich and you can see them on the Bund, awestruck. Some mark the occasion with a photograph. It doesn't matter what the weather is like; a row of booths offers souvenir photographs with a choice of backgrounds. For a few dollars you can be digitally squeezed between colonial buildings or under fireworks in New Shanghai.

It's not just the Chinese who marvel at Shanghai; the rest of the world is here too, ensconced in the thrusting skyscrapers and sprawling factories of New Shanghai, which only ten years ago was farmland. Multinationals, lawyers, consultants and fools have all been lured by a market of 1.3 billion people and enticed by tax breaks, investment incentives and China's World Trade Organisation membership.

'There's a lot of interest here,' one Western banker told me, 'but it's hard to tell if anyone is making money.'

Shanghai lives for progress and so it was the city I went to for stories about advancement: the first city in China to achieve zero population growth, the first to build a state-of-the-art magnetic levitation train, and in keeping with its early twentieth-century reputation as a town of whores and hedonists, the first city to open a sex museum. The city loves a circus and every month plays host to the world's corporate or political elite. Hotels are never empty in this hard-working, confident, even arrogant city.

For the past decade economic growth has outpaced the rest of the nation – Shanghai attracts nearly one-third of China's pool of foreign investment. I paid my first visit to Shanghai in early 1993, when the city was waking up after four decades of neglect. Before the Communists seized power in 1949, Shanghai accounted for just 1 per cent of China's population but one-fifth of the country's industrial output and two-thirds of its foreign trade. The Communist takeover began Shanghai's conversion into a socialist industrial engine, forcing thousands of its entrepreneurs into exile in Hong Kong and Taiwan and over a million more to other parts of China. Wherever they made their homes outside the city, Shanghainese made their presence felt, setting up factories, welfare centres and residents' associations – the last of these were started mainly to ensure the continuation of the distinctive regional food, which falls under the category of Yangzhou cuisine and includes the cities of Hangzhou, Suzhou, and Nanjing, as well as the Yangtze River delta. Though influenced by cuisines from both the north and the south of the country, Shanghainese food tends to be a little sweeter than northern food, and is made with copious quantities of Shaoxing wine. When a dish isn't stewed or braised, it's usually 'drunken'. If I had to name my all-time favourite Chinese dish it would be the Shanghainese dumpling known as a *xiaolong bao*, or Little Dragon dumpling – steamed pork wrapped in soft pastry and sitting in a broth made with flavoursome crab roe.

During the first thirty years of Communist rule, the city's massive state sector churned out mountains of goods, turning Shanghai into the nation's cash cow. Ninety per cent of its revenue was handed over to the central government in Beijing. Very little was spent on the city itself, leaving it in a state of stagnation. Then Deng Xiaoping came to power. When he proposed to step up the modernisation drive in the 1980s he turned first to southern China where the quasi-capitalist Special Economic Zones were set up to experiment with foreign trade, investment and finance. Deng was at first reluctant to tamper with Shanghai, and as a result the city stalled for another decade. Then in 1990 approval was given for the city government to create a New Shanghai in the expansive rice paddies of Pudong, meaning 'East of the Huangpu River'. One year later, in January 1991, Deng paid a visit to Shanghai where he told the leaders, including an impressive English-speaking mayor called Zhu Rongji, that it was time to fire the starting gun on economic growth once again. It was the imprimatur for the city's leaders to do what had been done in Guangdong province and China's eastern coastal regions: make the city rich. Deng later declared that his 'biggest mistake' had been failing to include Shanghai among the Special Economic Zones set up in the 1980s.

Because of the city's stagnation, little of significance was constructed – or consequently demolished – before 1992, when the leadership eventually set about turning the rusting cogs of enterprise. Only a few years before, plans for new roads, bridges, apartments and hotels had been stuck in the bureaucratic pipeline; now they began to transform the appearance of China's former international city in a sustained building boom which continues today. In 1993 I remember looking out a window of the five-star Portman Hotel, which was then one of the tallest buildings in the city, and imagining how the city might have looked in the twenties and thirties. The hotel rose above the slum tenements and warehouses of old Shanghai and the smokestacks of its decrepit socialist industries. Several years later the skyline had altered – many of the stacks and the tenements had disappeared.

Across the river in new Pudong, a 523 square kilometre proposed industrial zone almost the size of Singapore was beginning to spring up from the paddy fields. An upbeat official from the Pudong Development Office told me, 'It's not possible to close our doors again. Closing the door would mean a death sentence for our economy.' Several years later, China's central planners allocated another huge cash injection to turn Pudong into the showcase industrial area for the whole country. The projects, including a new international airport, a subway, hotels, apartments and dozens of factories, are today up and running.

In 1993, cobwebs were dusted off and doors were opened everywhere in Shanghai, and residents rushed in to taste a new kind of freedom called consumption. The Sincere Department Store was once one of dozens of respected shops that had graced Shanghai's main artery, Nanjing Road, and later found sanctuary, survival and success in British Hong Kong after the Japanese invasion of Shanghai in the 1930s. It became the first foreign retailer to reopen since the Communist revolution. In 1993, unlike many of their Asian neighbours, the Chinese paid just 13 per cent of their total income on rent, medical expenses and education. At the start of a new consumer age, that left Shanghainese in the mood and with enough cash for shopping. In a single year they went on a US$186 billion retail binge as they tried to satisfy an insatiable appetite for goods once considered bourgeois affectations.

At the Sincere Department Store, one of the most popular counters offered instant ear-piercing. A newfangled ear-piercing gun was the centre of attention, being a huge advance on more traditional methods used around China. Even in Hong Kong in the 1970s I'd had my ears pierced by a jeweller using just the sharpened stem of an earring and plenty of ginger rubbed onto the ear lobes as an anaesthetic. At the earring counter of the Sincere Department Store, a factory worker arrived during the busy lunch-hour, still in her grey uniform but wearing bright red lipstick and a fussy hair-do. The gun stapled one ear – *kachoong!* – then the other. The worker examined herself in a hand-held mirror, thrilled with her dazzling new faux diamond earrings.

The state-run institutions were also changing. Further up Nanjing Road at the home of the famous Shanghai Acrobats, young performers sat glued to their newly acquired Walkmans and electronic games during rehearsals for the nightly acrobatic performance. Teenage girls looking like Communist gymnasts with their hair pulled tightly back, waited their turn to perform, slouching in the hard seats of the cold socialist-style auditorium, deep in concentration, frantically pressing buttons. Nearby, a young man balancing on a seesaw with a stack of bowls on his head suddenly lost his balance and the bowls clattered on top of him. These teenagers had spent years perfecting the art of focus but I wondered whether all the material diversions now available to them would cause them to lose interest. Today the Shanghai Acrobats are still tumbling and twisting in the same auditorium – these days mainly for the tourists. Yet, despite all the changes, the city manages to retain some of its old flavour. One of its special attractions for me is that it was the birthplace of my parents.

'Foreign Devils', as expatriates were known, began arriving in Shanghai and other Treaty Ports after China's defeat in the Opium War of 1839–1842. As the name suggests, the war was over the illegal opium trade but had its roots in a wider trade dispute. In the early nineteenth century, Chinese tea exports to Britain were in such vast quantities that the trade depleted Britain's supply of silver, China's only accepted form of payment. However, Chinese traders would and did accept large quantities of opium and soon the silver began flowing in the opposite direction. When China tried to put a stop to the trade, Britain resorted to arms, hence the outbreak of the Opium War.

After China's defeat it was forced to sign the Treaty of Nanjing in 1842, which allowed Britain and its allies, including the United States and France, to establish treaty ports where foreign nationals could live and work and where consulates and customs facilities could be set up. Prior to that the only place where China permitted trade with foreigners, and then only during the summer months, was in the port of Xiamen (formerly Amoy) in the southern city of Guangzhou (formerly Canton).

From the late 1800s Shanghai's population grew from around 500000 people, including fewer than 10000 foreigners, to three million in 1930, of which 36500 were foreigners. By then the city, because of its location, its status as a trading port and its entrepreneurial aptitude, had become one of Asia's most commercially successful and vibrant communities. My Scottish grandfather, Robert Rae Hutcheon, arrived on the China coast as a marine engineer during World War I when the city's wealth and decadence were at their height. A quiet, diligent man, he had left the sleepy village of Ellon in Aberdeenshire and eventually moved ashore to a comfortable expatriate position with the Asiatic Petroleum Company (North China), better known as Shell. His job was to manage fuel installations dotted along the Chinese coast and the Yangtze River at a time when ships were increasingly turning to oil instead of coal. Rae, as everyone called him, met Ethel, my grandmother, in the port of Hankou, now part of Wuhan city on the Yangtze. Ethel's father, Alfred Bryan, was an English army officer, part of the military contingent sent to safeguard the British and their possessions. Rae and Ethel's three boys, including my father Robin, were born in different parts of China: Ian in Kuling (1925), Robin in Shanghai (1928) and Patrick in Tianjin (1935).

The Shanghai Municipal Council, made up of foreign representatives from twelve nations, governed the expatriates living in the International Settlements. These settlements, or concessions, were not exclusive to foreigners but in them expatriates lived under a system known as 'extraterritoriality', meaning that foreigners were immune from Chinese law and could only be tried by their own consuls or courts. The British Concession and the American Concession eventually amalgamated to form the International Settlement. The French Concession remained a separate entity, preferring to keep its own identity. There were no restrictions on which concession foreigners could live in.

On the back of opium and, later, other commodities such as cotton, tea and silk, Shanghai with its class of Chinese traders became an international, affluent city. It was also a magnet to shysters, prostitutes, criminals of all nationalities and, because of its proximity to water, pirates. My father and his family had first-hand experience of them as they travelled from the port city of Tianjin to Shanghai in 1935. It was just one of many such attacks that occurred along the length of the Chinese coast, right up until the Communist takeover in 1949.

My father Robin was seven at the time of the incident but it remains as vivid in his mind as if it had happened yesterday. After boarding the steamer, the pirates engaged in a quick shoot-out on the bridge, seriously injuring a British officer. They then separated the male passengers from the women and children, locked them in cabins and then robbed them. My grandmother, my father and his brother Ian watched helplessly as the pirates searched through their belongings and selected a diamond engagement ring and several large items including a gramophone player. They escaped with their haul after dismantling the ship's radio. As soon as they left, the crew restored radio contact and a short time later help arrived. The Royal Navy dispatched an aircraft carrier, HMS *Eagle*, with a fleet of twin-winged fighter planes on deck, and gave chase after the pirates. Eventually, my father recalls, they located the pirates' junks making their way up the Yellow River. The fighter planes forced the pirates to beach, whereupon they fled, abandoning much of the bulkier loot including the family's portable gramophone. My grandmother's engagement ring was never found.

On the same trip another disturbing incident occurred. Third-class passengers aboard the vessel, fleeing civil war in other parts of the country, were driven by hunger to raid the ship's cargo and fell upon crates of fresh strawberries being transported to Shanghai. They gorged themselves on the unwashed fruit, which had been grown on Chinese farms with organic fertiliser. Tragically, they contracted cholera and many of them died. As they were at sea, their bodies were unceremoniously thrown overboard, in full view of the remaining passengers.

Foreigners in Shanghai, including my father and his family, were known as Shanghailanders, a play on Scottish Highlanders. There were lots of Scottish seafarers on the China coast and they turned the concessions into replicas of home. My grandmother Ethel's leather-bound photograph album reveals a glimpse of life in Shanghai's French Concession and China's other northern treaty ports. There was a cast of domestic helpers: cooks, drivers and amahs, who cleaned the home and cared for the children. One photograph shows my father holding hands with a neatly dressed amah, wearing a spotless white tunic, loose trousers and tiny black leather shoes on her bound feet. Whenever the family holidayed in the hills, sedan chairs carried by Chinese 'coolies' took them to the comfort of the mountain resorts where they escaped the summer humidity. The family ate English food and spoke very little Chinese, using, like the other Shanghailanders, pidgin English, which adapted English words to what foreigners regarded as Chinese pronunciation. For example, 'You no walkee this place' meant 'keep out', and 'Me no like-ee this thing' meant, 'I don't like this'. Most foreigners never bothered to learn Chinese, although my grandmother spoke a few words and my father could say 'How much does this cost?' During a scout camp on the edge of Shanghai, the scout master, on discovering the group had run out of eggs, asked if any of the boys spoke a few words of Chinese. My father reluctantly raised his hand and was immediately dispatched with one of the scout leaders to buy fresh eggs from a local store. The language gap mirrored the reality of the gulf between the worlds of foreigner and Chinese. In this supposedly international city the different nationalities rarely mingled, except in the colonial manner of master–servant relationships or through trade.

In Shanghai my father attended the Cathedral School. Though there were English-speaking schools up and down the China coast, the Cathedral School was an exclusive establishment run by the Anglican Church for British children. Robin studied Latin, French, English, maths and history, as he would have done in any school in the United Kingdom. He told me that it was not until years later that he realised how sensitive the issue of race was at the time, when he learned that some of his schoolmates had been Eurasian. The Gander brothers had skin darker than most of the fair and freckled British students, and their father always came to the school alone, my father said, because his wife was Chinese. Known Eurasians, like my mother, as well as other nationalities, attended the Shanghai Public School, a large institution run by the British-dominated Shanghai Municipal Council.

Twice a week, my father was taken to choir practice in a private rickshaw. It was on these journeys from the French Concession to the waterfront, a distance of about five kilometres, that he glimpsed the colourful and at times confronting world of ordinary Chinese street life. There were beggars with deformed limbs, and child beggars wearing an incredible assortment of rags. Sometimes his rickshaw would be halted by a funeral procession for one of the inhabitants of the old tenement dwellings. The heavy wooden coffin had to be lifted down from the window or roof of the house because the stairwells were too narrow. A procession of mourners dressed in white sack-cloth beat their drums and wailed to the ear-piercing strains of the mourning band.

Not far from the racket of street musicians, another musical style was making its mark. The twenties jazz boom that had begun in the United States caught on quickly in Shanghai and soon bands, mostly Filipino and Western, helped to turn the city into an all-night music hall. This led in turn to the blossoming of another Shanghai institution: tailored clothes. The city's most prestigious tailors set up large workshops on Nanjing Road to cater for a fashion craze that was sweeping liberated, outward-looking China, putting the skill of Shanghai craftsmen on the world map. 'The Shanghainese were inordinately proud of Nanjing Road,' writes Ling Pan in *In Search of Old Shanghai*, 'not only because of its shops overflowing with goods, but because there was truly nothing like it in the rest of China. It was so modern and nothing enthralled the Shanghainese more than modernity.'

One of the symbols of that modernity was the *qipao*, the body-hugging dress that evolved from a traditional Chinese Manchu (Qing Dynasty) garment. During the late 1920s when a dancing craze gripped Shanghai, the *qipao* with thigh-high splits became synonymous with oriental fashion as well as being *the* outfit for middle-class Chinese women in cities like Shanghai, Hong Kong and Beijing.

At the height of the *qipao* revolution in 1930, a teenaged apprentice named Zhu Hongsheng was sent from the outskirts of Shanghai to work for one of the city's leading tailors. His master provided lodgings and a weekly living allowance, and as per tradition the teenager began his apprenticeship performing menial tasks like cooking, cleaning and babysitting until he graduated to watching his master cut fabric, stitch and embroider. Apprenticeships lasted between three and five years until a tailor became an expert in his own right and was given the title *Shifu* or Master.

Zhu Hongsheng is only five feet tall (1.52 metres), but his clothes fit him immaculately. Even today, many Chinese, particularly the middle-aged and elderly, prefer to have their clothes tailored. Major urban department stores have resident tailors and made-to-measure garments are usually no more expensive than ready-to-wear items, taking only two or three days to complete.

Qipaos, which were considered bourgeois on the mainland and replaced by the utilitarian blue Mao suits during the fifties, sixties and seventies, were blessed with a revival in China in the 1990s due in part to oriental fashion coming into vogue worldwide. A Hong Kong shop called Shanghai Tang with the motto 'Made by Chinese' popularised Chinese-style clothing, using brightly coloured silks with a modern twist. A number of copycat stores, including one called Shanghai Xu, appeared on the mainland, further promoting the style. However the *qipao* or *cheongsam*, as it's called in Hong Kong, gained even more of an iconic status with the release in 2000 of a film by Hong Kong director Wong Kar-wai called *In the Mood for Love*. Set during a steamy Hong Kong summer in the 1960s, the film had popular Hong Kong actress Maggie Cheung appearing in a different eye-catching, body-hugging *qipao* in virtually every scene.

The revival brought Master Zhu and other old Shanghai *qipao* tailors out of retirement to cater for the new craze, this time not just among Chinese women but foreign women too. Modern tailoring workshops with electric sewing machines and air-conditioning are a far cry from the 1930s sweat shops. And the Shanghai of today is a kinder place, according to Master Zhu. 'When we were young, we didn't dare speak to the rich people. We were treated as flunkies and they looked down on us,' he said in his soft Shanghainese accent. He smoothed a bolt of red silk as he spoke, remembering the days when tailor shops filled entire streets, servicing fashionable Shanghainese ladies who would order several *qipaos* at a time. 'Nowadays we are equal and our rich clients are polite to us.'

If rich Chinese treated Master Zhu inconsiderately, coming face to face with a foreigner could be life-threatening. 'I was frightened whenever I saw foreigners on the street. Once one of their cars ran over my foot, but I didn't speak English, so I screamed, "Ouch, ouch, ouch!" And the foreign man didn't understand me either! Our country was bullied, but now the Chinese people have stood up.'

It's been sixty-five years since my father's family left Shanghai, after my grandfather reached the retirement age of fifty. The family was booked to return to the UK departing from Hong Kong via Canada, but the boat they were due to take, the *Empress of Russia*, had been commandeered as a troop ship. War was by this time raging in Europe. The only ship ready to leave Hong Kong in December 1940 was the MV *Neptuna*, which was bound for Sydney.

With the departure of the 'foreign devils' from Shanghai, many of their residences also disappeared. Miraculously, my father's former home is still standing. It was situated on Rue Ratard off Route de Say Zoong in the French Concession in a compound of about twenty houses with a large garden in the middle. Route de Say Zoong is now Changshu Road, Rue Ratard is Julu Road and the compound where Dad's family lived belongs to the Chinese Air Force. In recent years some of the mansions have been demolished to be replaced by a mirror-clad office tower. The rest of the houses have been remodelled into offices, luxury apartments and upmarket restaurants.

My mother Beatrice's parents were both half Chinese. Her father, a bookkeeper named Cecil Keat Greaves, was the son of a Scottish tea-taster who in the late nineteenth century was drawn to the China coast after the success of other family members. My great-grandfather the tea-taster, Alexander Ryrie Greaves, married Josephine Ng, a woman from southern Guandong province. On Beatrice's mother's side, her grandfather was half Chinese, and though he had Caucasian features he was usually seen in public wearing a silk cap and a long Chinese gown. He used his real surname, Mackenzie, when dealing with Western traders, and his Chinese name, Chan Hong Kuey, when dealing with the Chinese. His wife was part Chinese, part Portuguese.

In Shanghai, my mother's family lived in a large compound on the Route de Grouchy which was, like my father's house, in the French Concession. The mansion belonged to my mother's uncle, Henry Monsel Cumine. He was an architect by profession but later became interested in publishing. In 1928 he bought a prominent English language newspaper called the *Shanghai Mercury*. Beatrice, or Bea for short, recalls the whole family feeling terrorised by the larger-than-life H.M. Cumine, who also ruled his immediate family with an iron fist. 'He set the style,' Bea said. 'We all had to sing Scottish songs out of respect for Uncle's Scottish heritage, though he too was Eurasian.'

Despite Beatrice's mixed heritage, she went to a British school and had a very English upbringing. 'In Shanghai we all pretended to be Western,' Beatrice recalled. She lived in a Western house, the domestic help all wore uniforms and afternoon tea was taken every day. The family spoke English to each other but Cantonese or Shanghainese to the servants. Curiously, the family ate Chinese food only on Saturday, which was known as 'Chow Day'.

Anti-foreign sentiment in Shanghai reached a peak in 1925 after protests in several treaty ports against the Japanese occupation of Shandong province. This then led to industrial agitation by Chinese workers and the violent suppression by British police of a workers' movement in Shanghai. In 1927 Britain sent a strong military force to Shanghai to defend its concerns. Two years later, Hankou became the first treaty port to be returned to China as many foreign powers withdrew from the country. A few months later in April 1929, the fiftieth anniversary edition of the *Shanghai Mercury* underscored the tension of the times and the worsening relationship between foreigner and Chinese. A commentary penned by the Nationalist government's Foreign Affairs Minister, Dr Chengting T. Wang, refers to Shanghai as a 'unique emporium of the East'. Yet while 'its place on the world map cannot be denied', Dr Wang wrote, he respectfully drew attention to the 'Shanghai Mind', the international community's imperialist attitude and reluctance to relinquish administrative control over its settlements or enclaves.

'With their native genius for adapting themselves to a changed environment, the Chinese may be trusted to make good success of administering the ex-concessions or ex-settlements,' wrote Dr Wang. 'In the new China that is being built on the foundations of the old, foreign residents will have their proper place. This place will be doubly merited if they will meet the Chinese halfway . . . and clasp the hand of the Chinese in a true spirit of co-operation.'

On another page of the fiftieth anniversary edition, the drawbacks of the 'Shanghai Mind' become apparent in an article on 'Primitive Sanitation and the Vice of Comfort'. The British journalist noted, 'Whatever the foreigner has done to China . . . he may have been accused of introducing so deadly a narcotic as opium, but no-one has cursed him for introducing the railway, the motor-car . . .

the padded chair, the spring bed and, lastly, the convenient "convenience".'

As the 1930s progressed China became an increasingly dangerous place for foreigners, although many stayed believing war would never come.

Ironically, it was to be the Japanese who ended Shanghai's colonisation. The 1937 Sino–Japanese war battered Shanghai, causing tens of thousands of people, both Chinese and foreigners, to flee, although the International Settlement survived until December 1941. Shanghai was taken over by a Chinese puppet administration of the Japanese, followed by a brief Kuomintang interregnum after 1945, until the Communists descended on the city in the late 1940s, closing the iron door on the once great cosmopolitan city for nearly fifty years.

If the Shanghai Mind exists today, it would probably refer to the exceptional business acumen of the Shanghainese, a dogged determination and ability to drive a hard bargain. But until the early 1990s this entrepreneurial spirit was held back by political stagnation. After Mao's death in 1976, Jacky Cheung's mother decided the city had no more to offer the family. She applied for a permit to live in Hong Kong, and when it was granted Jacky and his brother Raymond followed her there. When Shanghai was in its heyday, Hong Kong had aspired to be as great. In the late 1970s the tables had turned.

Jacky, who had never finished school because of the Cultural Revolution, followed his elder brother in finding work in a factory and eventually ended up in the kitchens of the Hong Kong Hotel. After washing dishes for the first six months, Jacky began an apprenticeship in the pastry kitchen and quickly excelled. The boy from Shanghai spent the next decade as a pastry chef, working his way back to his home city in 1987 as the pastry chef for the newly opened Hilton Hotel. 'I had gone back every year and when I was earning HK$3000–4000 in Hong Kong my friends and family earned just 36 yuan in China. When I came back, I was like a king,' he said. At the Shanghai Hilton, his salary doubled and he was treated to all the expatriate benefits.

When the June 4 massacre took place in Tiananmen Square in 1989, Jacky hurriedly left Shanghai along with most of the city's diplomats and expatriates, after being offered a seat on a flight bound for Hong Kong chartered by the Australian government. Later he applied to emigrate to Australia with his Hong Kong born wife, Maria Chan, and their children, eventually settling in Melbourne and working as the head pastry chef at the Crown Casino. He loved Australia's good life and clean air, but it wasn't to last for long. A phone call from his brother Raymond in 1996 changed everything, and soon Jacky was on his way back to Shanghai to manage one of Raymond's investments. He has lived in Shanghai ever since.

In 1998, Jacky was looking for a location to open an upmarket restaurant, catering to foreigners and the growing numbers of wealthy Shanghainese. He was having a drink in a beer garden situated in a rundown compound of colonial houses in the former French Concession. He thought that if he could renovate one of the houses it would make the perfect setting for a modern Vietnamese restaurant. Four years later I had dinner with Jacky and his wife, Maria, in their stylish restaurant in the former French Concession compound, now owned by the Chinese Air Force.

'We were the first ones they rented to, so I signed a ten-year lease and I got a very good deal, because they really needed us,' Jacky said, showing me photographs of the crumbling house before its renovation. He smiled, remembering his good fortune at finding the compound. I was delighted too. We were sitting in the house where my father once lived.

For Jacky, Shanghai has brought wealth he never imagined. His US$500 000 investment in Cochin China, the Vietnamese restaurant, was returned in fifteen months. He now owns and manages two restaurants and a bar, and owns three apartments in Shanghai. 'I think Shanghai is the first good investment in China,' he said, grinning. 'The government wants Shanghai to be China's New York.'

Hurtling down an elevated road lit by bright neon tubes, Mary Gu recalls how she used to dream about Shanghai from her home in the nearby city of Wuxi. 'I loved its history and its excitement,' she says.

In 1990, a foreign businessman offered the 21-year-old English-speaker a job in his company's Shanghai office. He agreed to pay her US$250 per month, more than five times what she earned at the joint venture hotel where she worked in Wuxi. For Mary, that was a small fortune, and with her mother's grudging approval she packed two suitcases and took the two-hour train-ride from the grey industrial city to the place of her dreams. 'I've always been fascinated by the Shanghainese,' she says. 'They are smart and hardworking and they have a can-do mentality. They lead such busy lives, you know, everything is really fast. But they think Shanghai is the best place to live in the world.'

When Mary was a child, her mother, Teacher Gu, felt she was locked into a bad marriage, so she lived apart from her husband, eventually divorcing when Mary was fourteen. Teacher Gu and I – Mary was too busy working to come with us – visited the dilapidated rooms where the pair had lived, and incredibly some of the Gus' neighbours still resided in the rickety terrace. Teacher Gu told me how Mary was teased by her classmates for not having a father, a terrible stigma for a child growing up in a small city in the late 1970s. Despite the teasing, she was a good student and particularly loved English. By the time Mary graduated in business studies, Wuxi, like the rest of China, was beginning to change under Deng Xiaoping's early reforms. Wuxi's only joint venture hotel, where Mary worked, sent her to Singapore on her first overseas trip.

Now she calls herself a typical Shanghainese and she finds it impossible to do anything on a small scale. For her wedding in 2001 to Lawrence Chi, a Canadian–Chinese human resources manager, Mary organised the event of events. The banquet was a five-course Western meal with free-flowing French champagne. Her dress was designed by Shanghai's leading couturier, Chen Yifei; she used Shanghai's finest – and most expensive, she adds – make-up artist; and the location was the esteemed US$120 million French-designed Shanghai Grand Theatre. Personalities and brand names drop from her lips. Her shoes are Prada, the vase on her coffee table Baccarat. Yet she speaks without arrogance, as if naming brands is a way of adding precision. This is, after all, Shanghai.

Our conversation unfolds over pasta at Va Bene, a stylish Italian restaurant located in New Heaven and Earth, or *Xintiandi.* This is a US$3.5 billion urban redevelopment project spearheaded by Hong Kong developer Vincent Lo. Here, Shanghai yuppies – or shuppies – mingle with foreigners in a warren of fashionable eateries, chic boutiques and funky homeware shops. Prices are aimed at the ridiculously rich – and tourists. Bypass New Heaven and at the rear of the complex you come down to earth – the museum marking the first congress of the Chinese Communist Party in July 1921.

'Since the British invaders launched the Opium War in 1840, the Western capitalist powers came one after another to China, and China was thus reduced gradually to a semi-colonial, semi-feudal society,' reads a placard in the museum. Incongruously, less than one hundred metres away, foreigners, their money and their inventions bring pleasure to tens of thousands of Chinese visitors. Foreigners are accepted now, even feted. However the spirit of socialist sacrifice hasn't been completely trampled by the hordes: nearly 4000 working-class families were evicted to make way for New Heaven and Earth.

After dinner Mary and I take a taxi to the waterfront. As the driver presses down the meter a high-pitched recording greets us in Chinese and English. 'Hello Customer! This is Jinjiang Taxi. We will provide service to you with all my heart!' Unlike taxi-drivers in many parts of China, the Shanghainese are no-nonsense drivers who want to get to the destination as quickly as possible so that they can pick up their next fare. In Beijing, on the other hand, there seems to be an unstated speed limit of 40 km/h on a highway and 20 km/h in the city. Mary is proud of Shanghai's rapid development, speaking of it as if she and the city have developed in tandem. She tells the story of how, prior to the APEC meeting in 2001, she personally negotiated with the White House's travel director and succeeded in winning the business for her hotel to accommodate nine planeloads of American officials, including President George W. Bush. She proudly adds that she secured the top rate of US$290 per room from the White House.

The farsightedness and acumen of Shanghai's up and comers is shared by the city's leadership. When Zhu Rongji was Shanghai's mayor in the late 1980s he started a think tank known as the International Business Advisers' Council, an annual conference bringing together leading entrepreneurs to advise on how to take Shanghai forward. The government also realises the value of fresh blood. In 2002 the city introduced a new permanent residence permit or 'green card' system, aimed at attracting overseas talent and investment. Open to well-educated foreigners as well as Chinese (such as returned Chinese students with a foreign passport), the card gives the holder preferential tax treatment and the right to services including education for his or her children.

'They realise talent is the most important asset for the city to grow,' said Shanghai-born US businessman Tony Zhang. 'Most Shanghainese are not as hardworking as people from outside. Shanghai people like to enjoy life. People who are drawn here are more gutsy.' Mr Zhang said such is the lure of Shanghai, he frequently bumps into Chinese–American classmates and relatives on the streets. 'Overseas Chinese are taking a big interest in this place. Everyone is visiting,' he said.

For a roadmap to the future, the design of Shanghai's People's Square in the city's midst says it all. This expanse used to be Old Shanghai's racecourse, frequented only by the privileged. After the Communists came to power the square held giant portraits of Marx, Lenin and Mao. Today they've been swapped for ostentatious structures that include offices for the municipal government, the urn-shaped Shanghai Museum, the Grand Theatre and the clumsily named Urban Planning and Design Research Institute. The buildings are so magnificent, say local residents, they provoked instant jealousy in Beijing where construction is under way of an opera house to surpass Shanghai's Grand Theatre. In the centre of this opulence, there's a musical fountain where columns of water spurt in time to piped classical music. Not content to stand and watch, local visitors to the square have developed a game, waiting for a pause in the jets before jumping onto a marble plate in the centre of the fountain, all for a photograph. As I crossed the square a young woman holding her shoes jumped over what she hoped was a sleeping jet only to be caught out. In good humour, she smoothed her hair and struck a coy pose in her boyfriend's direction.

While the Shanghainese seem to embrace the rapid evolution of their city, through the doors of the Urban Planning and Design Research Institute just off the square you discover that there is, after all, a grand plan. A large golden replica of central Shanghai rotates on a rostrum, drawing gasps from scores of awestruck tourists from less affluent parts of the country. The Golden City aims to recapture the title of China's pre-eminent powerhouse, a title it held one hundred years ago. In the process of achieving this by 2020, the city is reaching for maximum exposure through a plethora of international conventions including the 2010 World Expo. 'Grant us this honour,' says a banner, 'and China will reward the world with more splendour.'

The propaganda entertains, but the real show begins on an upper floor of the Institute, where a space the size of a basketball court reveals a scale model of thoroughly modern Shanghai. It displays every significant hotel, public garden, lake, flyover, factory, apartment and commercial building that exists, is planned, or will be built before 2020.

Hundreds of people file past the model. Suddenly, there's a commotion as a large old man in an overcoat leans over the railings almost to the point of toppling into the display. If he'd fallen, the force would have shattered mini-Shanghai. But his family and security guards haul him to safety. Red-faced and excited, the man had located the apartment building where his family live. When the security guards were satisfied his actions were nothing more than exuberance, they left him in his wife's hands, posing for a photograph with his grandson in front of their 'home' in mini Shanghai.

Not everyone is lucky enough to find their home on the model. And, while the model is impressive, on the streets what often confronts you is a changing mess. Old Shanghai's colonial architecture along the length of the Bund has been saved from the wrecker's ball, but if you pull that backdrop to the side, Shanghai has few remaining heritage sights. The Shanghai government has factored in apartments for the rising middle class, a per capita greenery index and luxury shopping centres on virtually every intersection. Though there's a protection plan to safeguard 10 million square metres of what the government deems culturally significant buildings, the jackhammers and bulldozers nonetheless work around the clock.

Emerging from the Huangpi Road subway station I found myself in the middle of a large park with undulating hillocks and bubbling artificial streams. When I visited this area a year earlier there had been rows of Shanghai-style workers' homes with a single stylish, red-brick mansion in the corner of the block. Now everything was gone, replaced by the currently favoured urban oasis: a green belt.

The red-brick mansion had belonged to the family of internationally acclaimed, US-based architect I.M. Pei, who designed the

Bank of China building in Hong Kong, the Glass Pyramid at the Louvre and Boston's John F. Kennedy Library. I knew the mansion didn't stand much chance of survival. On the giant scale model at the planning institute, the area where the house once stood was covered in trees, just like the park I was looking at.

'A lot of traditional areas have been destroyed, because the government was in too much of a rush. They tore down lots of houses just to build the expressway! If they had done some research they could have changed the route and protected a lot of buildings,' Professor Ruan Yisan, a leading planner and conservationist, told me.

Though many Chinese officials don't consider 150-year-old buildings old, the problem with cities like Shanghai is that very little of heritage value apart from pagodas and temples remains. Ms Bei Nian-zheng greeted me at the front door of her mansion, and wasted no time in showing me to the back of the house where bull-dozers were busy in what used to be the family's garden. At one stage, like the home, the garden had been palatial in scale. It would have been the size of a football field, with an octagonal pavilion, a fishpond, flowing water, a small bridge and a rockery, all auspicious symbols designed to bring harmony to the household. The Chinese garden had long gone. In fact as Ms Bei and I stood on the balcony, the wreckers had already taken part of an adjoining wall that once separated the house from a school next door. She was afraid to leave the house for fear of it disappearing in her absence. I didn't dare tell her about the model of New Shanghai in People's Square, where her mansion had been replaced by a park.

Ms Bei (the *pinyin* or mainland Chinese spelling of Pei) was dis-tantly related to I.M. Pei. The family, once wealthy merchants from the nearby city of Suzhou, bought the nineteenth-century red-brick mansion in 1912, refurbishing it with the best materials available in Shanghai. The coloured glass in the windows was imported from France.

Like many homes belonging to capitalists, the house was confis-cated by the Communist Party during the anti-rightist campaign against intellectuals in the late 1950s. But after Mao Zedong's death in 1976, the mansion was returned to the family and according to Ms Bei granted national heritage status. 'I felt really distressed and sad when I heard this house was going to be torn down. This house represents the foundation of our family. All the Bei family, both overseas and at home, respect this house,' she said.

Ms Bei showed me the mahogany finishes and cavernous parlours, and pointed to where huge fireplaces once stood. Then she took me to a small, rickety annexe on the side of the home and introduced me to an old woman, an *ayi* or domestic helper, who quickly jumped up from her bed when we walked in. The annexe was where Ms Bei and her elder sister were confined during the Cultural Revolution, and it was their home for thirteen years. The old lady who'd been in bed when we entered was formerly Ms Bei's wet-nurse. Though she no longer had any domestic duties, she was cared for into old age by the family.

'We did everything in this room,' said Ms Bei, indicating the cramped surroundings. 'We used to eat, drink, shit, urinate and sleep in here.' And, though she didn't really need to say it, 'Life was really bitter,' she added.

Despite protestations by the family and a protection order, the municipal government refused to commute the mansion's death sentence and the courts refused to hear the case. The architects of New Shanghai spoke, and decreed the land where the red-brick mansion stood be remade as an urban green belt for the masses. Nothing was allowed to stand in the way of progress.

That went for factories too. Between 1992 and 2000, Shanghai's textile factories laid off 345 000 workers. Most were middle-aged, unskilled women. The problem was that labour costs in Shanghai were too high and for the city to recapture its position as the pre-eminent producer of high-end clothing, styles and equipment – and therefore people – had to change.

Wu Eryu was one of the lucky ones. In the mid 1990s she was about to be made redundant. Then, as part of a publicity stunt,

Shanghai Airlines took her from a nearly bankrupt factory, gave her a smart uniform and trained her as a flight attendant. In China's unequal opportunity airlines industry, it is usually only single women under thirty who are taken on. But Ms Wu, married and in her mid thirties, impressed the selection panel. She was also very attractive.

'I was self-confident and had a bright smile,' she said. 'The judge probably thought my character and appearance were very suitable, so I was chosen. It wasn't because I was very pretty.' She felt lucky to have found a new career when many women her age had been tossed onto the social scrap-heap.

Ms Wu took me to her home in one of Shanghai's old laneways. I was shocked to discover that this former state worker lived in what was virtually a slum. She was one of millions of workers who still lived in state-allocated housing. Most families stayed in the homes that were allocated in the 1950s, when China was much poorer. Ms Wu and her family hoped to move to a new apartment, as their home was little more than two dark, dank rooms, with the down-stairs room barely twice the size of my wardrobe (not a walk-in). The loft, constructed as an afterthought and accessible by a rudi-mentary ladder, wasn't much larger. The nearest public toilet was five minutes away, but Ms Wu was too embarrassed to take me there, so we walked to the nearest office building where she asked the janitor if I could use the bathroom.

In New Shanghai, this family used a chamberpot, cleared daily by a professional 'chamberpot aunty'. One Shanghai newspaper astutely commented, 'Even in the twenty-first century, the cham-berpot will still not be relegated to the museum. As long as the chamberpot exists, Shanghai cannot claim to be a completely modern and civilised city.'

Madam Chen also used a chamberpot, but unfortunately no-one in her family was being offered a cushy job with an airline; they were all former state workers who'd fallen through the cracks of the shattered rice bowl. Each of the five members of her family had worked in the great textile mills of Shanghai; all of them are now unemployed. Her house stands at the base of a tangled junction of new flyovers siphoning cars across the river to the booming industrial and financial zone of Pudong.

Shanghai's new commercial heartland boasts some of Asia's most unusual buildings, including the futuristic Oriental Pearl Television Tower and the Jinmao building, one of Asia's tallest. Madam Chen can almost see them from her yard, but rather than being impressed, she doesn't see why progress should trample a humble person like her. When the neighbours, who also worked at the textile mills, began to lose their jobs, Madam Chen rented out three shacks owned by her family and collected rubbish to sell to recyclers. Madam Chen says 94 families once lived in her neighbourhood. Now all the houses except hers have been demolished. The government wants to level the ground for development, but the old lady has refused to move until she is given a new three-bedroom apartment to compensate for the loss of her four 'homes'. The government refused her demand, saying it would only provide a two-bedroom apartment. As an added incentive for old Madam Chen to leave, the government cut off her water supply.

Madam Chen repeated something I'd heard from many Chinese people over the years. 'I blame Deng Xiaoping,' she said when I asked her who was responsible for her predicament. 'Under Chairman Mao's leadership, life wasn't so hard. It was affordable; vegetables and meat, all were very cheap. But now, everything needs to come from outside, the fields are wastelands.'

The lone shack has recently disappeared and the area is now a traffic interchange. More change, more mess. While those like Madam Chen with nothing to offer see their world growing smaller and poorer, city officials live it up in the futuristic hotels of Pudong, discussing the big question of how to ensure Shanghai regains its pre-1949 international supremacy and surpasses Hong Kong in the near future. The *Economist* magazine points out that however go-getting the Shanghainese are, it will still take up to fifteen years to reach the level of Hong Kong's wealth. Nonetheless, that is Shanghai's goal. Though Shanghai is ranked the easiest place to do business in China, it shares with the rest of the country the problem of poor financial regulation.

To 'stir-fry' stocks became a popular expression in 2000, after one of China's few hard-hitting financial magazines, *Caijing*, detailed widespread share price manipulation – the action of stir-frying is akin to whipping up sentiment – involving ten fund-management firms. Even one of the country's leading economists, Wu Jinglian, likened China's stock markets to casinos, plagued with corrupt practices. Apart from the lack of regulation in its stock markets, China and therefore Shanghai's legal system is insufficiently reformed, with limited accountability or transparency.

On my last assignment in Shanghai in 2001, something happened that made me question whether Shanghai's officials had enough knowledge and restraint to make the city a success in the way it was at the turn of the last century. In the middle of interviewing the master tailor Zhu Hongsheng, about three or four people burst into the second-floor *qipao* showroom. I thought they were noisy customers as they clattered about so I asked them to keep quiet.

'You will stop!' said a bespectacled man, shaking in anger. 'Public Security Bureau!' Sure enough, behind him was a uniformed policeman. The man in spectacles smirked. A terse woman asked for our passports. A client, according to the man in glasses, complained that a foreign film crew was on the premises and wasting the tailor's valuable time. I wasn't sure at first which part was the crime, though I knew I was technically supposed to get permission from Shanghai's Foreign Affairs Office, my friends the *Waiban*.

I hoped that after a few questions to ascertain the subject of the interview, the police would leave us alone. After all, what harm could be done interviewing an octogenarian tailor about life in the bad old days under foreign occupation? Unfortunately, and despite my protestations, it was clear that the bespectacled man and his flinty offsider were intent on making a big brouhaha out of my failure to seek permission for the interview. A quarter of an hour and some phone calls later, the section head of the Shanghai *Waiban* arrived, confirming that the incident wasn't going to be brushed aside. Our interview tape was confiscated (and later surprisingly returned), and I was ordered to write the fourth and final self-confession of my posting on my failure to obtain filming permission. Then the crew and I were told to re-book our flights and leave Shanghai the next morning.

For the rest of the day, we were kept under surveillance. Upon our return to our hotel, not-so-undercover agents with suspicious-looking handbags attempted to film us – through spyholes in the bags. We were even tailed to our favourite Japanese restaurant, where the agents notified the staff that we were being 'observed'. It was as if we had joined Shanghai's Most Wanted list. I felt extremely disappointed that my final assignment in China was ending in such a ridiculous fashion; this in my favourite Chinese city, the birthplace of my parents, China's most progressive metropolis. I succumbed to my anger and devised a devious yet juvenile trick. Pursued by two young female agents, I ducked behind a wall as they came around the corner, unaware of my prank. Then I leapt out and took a photograph of them. In the dimness of the street, the bright flash came as a huge shock and they stared at each other in amazement until one of them eventually shouted, 'Run!'

Though I'm not sure why, I ran too. I pursued them until they reached a big black car with a very large man sitting in the driver's seat.

'She took our photo!' one of the women yelled out to him.

His expression suddenly turned to anger and he began to get out of the car. I turned and ran in the opposite direction and this time nobody gave chase.

The following day the surveillance team accompanied the crew and me to the airport, cutting in and out of traffic behind, to the side and in front of our taxi. In the terminal building, I recognised some of the faces from the previous day, including a thin man in his fifties who was waiting at the boarding gate.

'Goodbye!' I said, approaching him. He ignored me so I repeated it in Chinese: *'Zaijian!'* Embarrassed, he laughed and replied in English, 'Goodbye, goodbye.'

The incident was disappointing confirmation that many of China's officials – even in Shanghai – still were not smart or flexible enough to discern the difference between damaging and harmless behaviour. A section chief had 'lost face' because a foreign journalist who should have been under his watchful eye had strayed, and his only response in front of his peers was to act harshly in an unbending fashion. Sebastian, Cleo, Charles and I boarded the Shanghai Airlines flight. Like everything new in Shanghai, the plane was clean and the service efficient all the way to Beijing. And in the true Shanghai spirit of cunning and perseverance, the next morning we boarded another plane and went straight back to my favourite city to finish filming the story. Sebastian and I stayed in different hotels and filmed on the streets with the small camera. This time we escaped hounding by the Foreign Affairs Office and, together with the interviews we filmed before getting detained, we eventually had enough material to complete the assignment. The story of Old and New Shanghai went to air a few weeks later.

SUBVERSIVE HOTPOT

As we slurped Beijing Zha Jiang noodles interspersed with mouthfuls of wine, Pang Meiqing's cold dark living room brightened. His wife poured me another glass of local red wine, topping it up with Sprite: a Chinese shandy. I promised to bring them a bottle of Australian red next time I saw them. 'No need,' said Mrs Pang. 'These days you can get everything in China, even red wine!'

We chatted and laughed for hours, munching on vegetables, tofu and my favourite noodles, although I expected the police to break down the door at any moment. It was a week before the Sixteenth Party Congress in November 2002 and the police had been here only days before. The Pangs' home was so small: a kitchen the size of a cupboard near the front door, a living room and a bedroom. If the police did burst in there would be nowhere to hide. Mr Pang was oblivious to my fear – he was too busy eating and talking. He loved to discuss the difference between Chinese people and Westerners and always peppered the conversation with new, disparaging theories about the way Chinese people think and live.

I had first come to Pang Meiqing's house near the Temple of Heaven almost three years earlier when he didn't know me and his living room was cold and uncomfortable, like his expression. The room was full of over-sized, grubby furniture; a shapeless sofa, chipped cupboards, an old television and, as people started to file in, collapsible stools and a small table were brought out, making the room very crowded but still cold. One window faced a brick wall, and the other faced a narrow lane, so that the only useful light came from a round neon tube on the ceiling. Back then, he had stared at me diffidently through large black-rimmed spectacles while he smoked a cheap cigarette. There were other people in the room, all of whom had harrowing stories to tell, but with his orthopaedic boots and a pair of crutches by his side, it was Mr Pang I wanted to listen to. I wanted to hear a story that for nearly ten years had only been told behind closed doors and among close friends.

Each person sitting in Mr Pang's dismal living room that afternoon in March 1999 was a survivor, somehow caught up in the massacre that took place in Beijing on the night of 3–4 June 1989. What began as a student-based movement calling for greater government accountability as well as swift action to curb spiralling inflation and endemic corruption ended with the People's Liberation Army shooting on crowds that had failed to leave the vicinity of Tiananmen Square. The sensitivity surrounding what the Chinese government calls an 'incident' means there was no official tally of the death toll from the June Fourth carnage. One individual, Professor Ding Zilin, has documented a list of 155 people who died. Human rights advocates believe the number may be far higher. On the Tiananmen massacre, there has been much debate: debate over what constitutes a massacre, debate over the government's handling of the crackdown, and debate about whether the student leaders had been overly ambitious. There will always be debate, but so far there is no conclusion except that it was a tragedy; that China's leaders turned their weapons on their own people.

On the night of 3 June 1989, Mr Pang, then a 25-year-old technician working in the state-owned railway industry, went to Tiananmen Square to look for his younger brother, who had joined the student ambulance corps. Near the northern entrance of Zheng Yi Road, just east of Tiananmen Square, Mr Pang was trapped between the crowds and a line of PLA soldiers when the firing began. Scores of injured young people dropped to the ground.

Mr Pang and other onlookers helped the injured onto carts which took them to Beijing's over-burdened hospitals. Unable to locate his brother, he turned to leave.

Looking over to the columns of the soldiers one hundred metres away, Mr Pang imagined them as po-faced terracotta warriors, like the famous army of Emperor Qin Shihuangdi entombed in a giant vault near the city of Xi'an. Suddenly more rounds of automatic gunfire punctured the night. He remembered dense crowds and lots of shouting, mainly cries for help. Then, in a second burst of shooting, Mr Pang was struck in the back, just above his waist. The bullet entered between the eleventh and twelfth vertebrae and he, too, fell to the ground. Now it was his turn to be lifted onto a cart, and in the panic of that warm June night he was rushed to hospital.

'After a big disaster, there are some innocent bystanders and some unlucky people. It can't be avoided. I'm just a symbol of that group,' he said quietly at our first meeting.

Several hours later, I left Mr Pang's dingy home with a heavy heart. He had been crippled for life because he was in the wrong place at the wrong time. Did that make him a dissident? He wasn't really one, or at least not in the beginning. As the tenth anniversary of June Fourth approached I was curious about how ordinary people dealt with the memory of the event, and indeed whether June Fourth mattered at all. A well-travelled Chinese academic once complained to me that the Western media continued to view China through the prism of June Fourth as if it was the only issue collectively pondered by the nation. I saw her point. China had moved on from the Tiananmen crackdown and on the surface many ordinary people didn't seem to think about it any more. To test that assertion one year, I sent the crew to interview some people on the street on the morning of June Fourth. An old man said with a straight face that the date was significant because it was the day he bought vegetables. Given that a large camera was pointed at him, he couldn't have said anything controversial and perhaps he really wasn't interested. However, several other conversations made me believe that there was far more beneath the surface.

A few years earlier an Australian friend living in China had been given several rolls of film and was asked to have them developed overseas. A Chinese journalist had taken the photos at a Beijing hospital on the night of 3–4 June 1989, but he had never dared to get them developed in China. The canisters had stayed in a drawer for nearly a decade, until the journalist found a foreigner he could trust. I soon understood why. The scenes showed mayhem in a makeshift emergency ward; I had never seen anything like them before. A night of carnage on the streets had caught the hospital unaware, with bodies piled up against a blood-smeared wall – the hospital staff didn't even have time to cover them with sheets. Bodies were also piled on the floor, in corridors and on carts outside the hospital gates.

A businessman who agreed to talk openly to me about June Fourth confirmed that it was a time of horror. Property consultant Frank Zhou (not his real name) was introduced to me by his cousin, a journalist working in Australia. Frank runs a real estate company and while outwardly he appears successful and content, privately the spectre of Tiananmen remains firmly in his mind. We spoke several times, on the first occasion at the upmarket Capital Club, fifty storeys high with a view of ever-changing Beijing. On another occasion we drove around Tiananmen Square and Frank pointed out how it had been transformed by the protestors in 1989.

In 1989 Frank had recently graduated from Qinghua, Beijing's most prestigious university. He'd been assigned a job in the design department of one of China's biggest and most influential state conglomerates. It was considered an excellent job for a young graduate and Frank was expected to work his way up the ladder, staying with the same company for the rest of his career. However after the protests began in the Square in April, he was quickly drawn to the students' cause. After all, many of them were his friends and former classmates. 'Towards the end of May 1989, every day I would go straight to the Square instead of going to work. During the last days,

I ate, slept and took part in all kinds of activities there,' Frank recalled. In the days before the crackdown, the massive protest movement on the Square created a sense of wellbeing throughout Beijing, as if major political change was in the air.

'I believe that the sense of humanity that emerged in 1989 had been buried. But once it came alive, that feeling of human dignity, you were no longer a slave,' is how student leader Li Lu described the atmosphere surrounding the protests. Ordinary workers brought food and supplies to the students and the city was gripped by a sense of peaceful revolution.

Until the crackdown, Frank's colleagues, including his superiors, sympathised with the students. 'They thought the students had good intentions because they wanted to fight corruption and government ineptitude,' he said. After the massacre, however, he returned to work to find that people's attitudes had done a 180-degree turn.

'After the incident nobody wanted to talk about it, or if they did, they totally took the official line,' he said. 'I had just graduated at the time and was very naive. I thought the truth should have been evident.' Frank's colleagues pressured him to write Communist-style self-criticisms, confessing his 'involvement' in what the government declared was an illegal 'revolt'. The pressure and change of attitudes around him proved deeply upsetting, and he felt he had no option but to leave his job and a promising future with the enterprise. The memory of the night left a deep and lasting impression on him. 'I was on Chang'an Avenue [the main thoroughfare which runs past Tiananmen Square] and I saw the whole incident,' he said, having great difficulty controlling the quiver in his voice. 'When I was a kid, I wanted to be a soldier. We Chinese regard them as members of the family, we never ever imagined that they would actually open fire. They opened fire on innocent people who weren't even putting up a fight.' Frank believes the event fundamentally changed him and his beliefs and he could no longer trust the Chinese government or work for one of its agencies. Not knowing where to turn, he found work well beneath his ability as a construction foreman.

In the post-Tiananmen economic boom instigated by Deng Xiaoping, Frank's thoughts turned to earning money. He worked his way up on the construction site until he was able to save enough money to start his own company. The pursuit of wealth, Frank discovered, was a way to dull his senses and his feelings of betrayal and dislocation. 'When we first came out of university, we didn't care too much about money. Then I learned that you can use money to make yourself numb,' he said.

Though on a practical level Frank frequently deals with the Chinese government in his business, he secretly hopes for its demise. 'I cannot forgive them,' he said of the leaders who ordered the June Fourth crackdown.

Li Na was a high school student in 1989, waiting to take her college entrance examinations when the students occupied Tiananmen Square. Li Na lived on a military compound. One of her neighbours was an official who was in charge of procurement. The official sympathised with the students and decided to offer them assistance. When weapons began to be removed from stores as the government prepared its military response, the official communicated the information on a piece of paper, sealed it in an envelope and told Li Na to take it to the student leaders in the Square. She cycled through the crowds until she approached the Monument, the large obelisk on the Square inscribed in Mao's 'handwriting', with the slogan, 'Eternal glory to the People's Heroes!' When she had located student leader Wang Dan, always deep in discussion, she gave the envelope to one of the student 'officials', asking for it to be delivered to him. Li Na waited until she saw Wang Dan take and open the letter before she left the Square, safe in the knowledge the information had been communicated.

The government's ongoing refusal to overturn the official verdict on the crackdown and rehabilitate those accused of inciting a counter-revolutionary rebellion created a festering wound out of the event. Though many of the student leaders from the movement sought refuge in the United States, Hong Kong or Taiwan, for those with insignificant roles, escape or exile wasn't an option. International human rights groups believe around two hundred people remain in prison for their part in the protest, and unofficially 155 deaths have been documented, numbers unlikely to pose a threat to the 66 million strong Communist Party.

I tried to cover the trial of former student leader Wang Dan. Wang had been one of the few dissidents who hadn't been exiled although he'd already served three and a half years for subversion for his role in the 1989 demonstrations. After his parole in 1993, he became politically active again. At the modern courthouse in the west of the city where the second trial took place in 1996, I arrived just as the police were cordoning off access to the court. The foreign journalists were moved more than 100 metres away from the building. The trial had been listed as a public one but in China, where great attention is paid to creative definitions, I didn't realise that 'public' meant a hand-picked public. There was no jury either, just a group of officials who considered the evidence and made a hasty deliberation. Not surprisingly, the trial took just four hours from the presentation of evidence to sentencing. Wang Dan was found guilty of plotting to overthrow the government and sentenced to eleven years in prison.

Outside the courtroom police tolerance was rapidly deteriorating. They decided that no cameras were to capture anything of the trial, including the arrival and departure of Wang Dan's family. Cameraman Sebastian Phua casually slung his camera over his shoulder, giving the impression he was about to leave the area, then he had me stand where I was shielded by a group of journalists to film a surreptitious 'piece-to-camera'. The police didn't realise we were filming and we left with at least part of the story of Wang Dan's 'open' trial, while most TV stations got nothing. As we finished, a policeman stormed past the group carrying a camera that had just been wrestled away from an agency cameraman. It was time to go.

Wang Dan served only a few years of his sentence before, like almost all of China's dissidents, he was deported to the United States. When a dissident leaves China it is like a disembodiment: he loses power over his countrymen because he can no longer influence the ideas of people around him and, from a human rights perspective, the imprisonment has been resolved. The Chinese government is well aware that exiled dissidents remain headline news for approximately one day, before becoming less significant feature material. For many dissidents – those who disagree with the prevalent political view – there is no prospect of high-profile expulsion. Minor dissidents remain in China, where they play a cat-and-mouse game with authorities if they choose to keep their cause alive. Anyone labelled a troublemaker faces regular harassment.

Mr Pang is only a minor troublemaker. After leaving hospital in the early 1990s he'd surprised doctors with his physical progress; he's now able to walk with crutches and a brace, but is often in pain. Emotionally, he has never completely recovered and is frequently depressed. He lives on a disability allowance and insurance payments of 600 yuan (A$150) a month, and has no fixed employment. His home belongs to his mother's work unit, the railways (where he was also employed before June Fourth). After his initial diffidence towards me, he opened up and became friendly and eager for the chance to talk about long-suppressed emotions. The victims' families and survivors of Tiananmen were never offered counselling or financial assistance for losing relatives or sustaining injuries. If they chose to speak out about their plight, they came under suspicion from the police or were detained.

Mr Pang told me that even those who donated blood for his operations after the shooting were investigated. The authorities wanted to know the donors' political position on the June Fourth incident and their relationship with Mr Pang. Because he was incapacitated, he couldn't return to work as a railway technician and no one dared to give him another job. Often he wondered whether being scarred by the bullet holes of the democracy movement was worse than being dead.

Mr Pang didn't put his name to any public protest until nearly ten years after the event. Then he signed a petition protesting against Chinese authorities freezing the bank account set up with overseas donations to help the Tiananmen survivors and families of the victims. After the incident, the Public Security Bureau (PSB), or police, paid frequent visits to his home. 'The PSB told me that I should co-operate and keep in contact with them and inform them if I know of any upcoming protests. They also said they would solve my wife's residence problem [as she wasn't from Beijing] and they could find jobs for both of us. It was very tempting,' he said.

As we spoke, the pain in his joints caused him to wince. 'I can tell you more precisely than a weather report when it's going to rain,' he joked.

Because Mr Pang's wife isn't a Han Chinese (the predominant race in China), but from the Korean ethnic minority without Beijing residency papers, which would entitle her to receive social benefits, she too is frequently harassed. But Mr Pang decided that however tempting the offer from the police might be, he couldn't turn into an informer. Instead he decided to make ends meet using his own wits.

'I'm creating, how should I say, positive opportunities for myself,' he said as he loaded up his motorised 'disabled persons' tricycle with paperbacks. Steering his tricycle on the bicycle lanes, he drove under flyovers and railway bridges on an almost clandestine tour of the capital that seemed to suit his purpose; a purveyor of controversial books and outlawed notions. Bringing his tricycle to a halt on a busy intersection south of the Third Ring Road, he unpacked his books, laying them out on a protective sheet on the pavement. For months he ran this pavement bookstore in Beijing's Fangzhuang district, where many white-collar migrants live. Later he serviced the growing queues forming in Beijing's embassy district, helping people fill out application forms for a small fee, using his rudimentary knowledge of English. Every so often the police would order him to stop his business, so he'd move on to another embassy. Eventually, however, he was halted by a group of thugs from China's north-east. Seeing an opportunity to prey on Mr Pang, they demanded one-third of his 60 yuan fee as 'protection' money. After that, he gave it up. Nowadays he's studying web design in the privacy of his home.

I asked Mr Pang who he blamed for his predicament.

'Chinese people and Chinese culture. Chinese history is a vicious circle; that's the fate of the majority of Chinese people.'

Curiously, he didn't blame the soldier who wounded him. 'Even if the man who shot me was sitting in front of me, even if I had a gun in my hand or his life was more miserable than mine, I wouldn't do anything. That would just be bringing one more disabled person into society.'

Yet for those who ordered the shooting he was less forgiving: 'Whenever I speak of them my teeth begin to itch.'

I visited post-Tiananmen Beijing twice in 1993. By then, most foreign trade and contacts between China and the West had been restored after the international outcry over the massacre. At home, Deng Xiaoping had come up with a brilliant diversion for the wide-spread popular dissatisfaction, rallying the Chinese toward an all-out 'get rich' assault during his tour of the south in 1992. Economic growth and ordinary livelihoods made rapid progress, but the spectre of Tiananmen just four years earlier loomed before the international community and when Beijing joined the running to host the 2000 Olympic Games, its human rights conduct was still viewed as highly contentious. Human rights organisations – backed by the US Congress – made highly critical statements on China's record culminating in the June 1993 resolution by an American foreign affairs sub-committee 'strongly opposing' Beijing's bid. The sub-committee quoted a State Department report that 'the Chinese government's human rights practices have remained repressive, falling far short of international norms'. Giving China the Games, said the sub-committee, was 'counterproductive for the Olympic movement'. In July 1993 the US House of Representatives voted overwhelmingly to oppose the Beijing bid.

Weeks before the International Olympic Committee was due to select the successful host city in Monte Carlo in September 1993, I made a documentary about the Beijing bid, interviewing Beijing's deputy mayor and chief executive of the bid committee, Zhang Baifa. I took an immediate liking to this plain-speaking, amiable party stalwart, who'd reportedly admitted himself to hospital during the June Fourth disturbances to distance himself from any potential backlash. He was unlike the usual official in both dress and demeanour. He wore a khaki suit with a tropical-coloured tie and sat patiently in a large conference room waiting for the crew and me to arrive. As we began the interview Mr Zhang was refreshingly relaxed and open in his approach, so much so he began to get quite annoyed when I brought up the question of human rights. Usually, Chinese officials would adroitly sidestep questions relating to the Tiananmen 'incident'.

'I don't want to talk about it! I get angry when I do . . . It's four years since the June Fourth incident! Why harp on it still? People don't ask about the Los Angeles riots or what's happening in Bosnia.'

He went on to describe the Americans as having the least regard for human rights, citing the example of the Panamanian dictator General Noriega. 'They seized Noriega and put him on trial. Is that human rights?'

Zhang Baifa was on a roll, and with little prompting went straight onto the issue of the resolution against the Beijing Olympics passed by the House of Representatives. 'If Congress can pass a resolution objecting to our bid for the 2000 Olympics, we could, frankly, boycott their Atlanta Games in 1996. If our bid fails, we could write to Congress to protest about their interference and justifying our revenge.'

At his mention of a boycott, I remember looking over my shoulder, raising my eyebrows at the cameraman, wondering whether I had heard Mr Zhang correctly. It was almost unheard of for a Chinese official to raise the issue of a boycott. In case I hadn't heard correctly or the interpretation was inaccurate, I asked him the question again, and he repeated his view that China should boycott the Atlanta Games. We concluded the interview on friendly terms, and a few days later I returned to Australia. The story was broadcast just a few days before the announcement of the 2000 Olympic host city. The program made international headlines and the Chinese delegation at Monte Carlo for the announcement was forced to deny adamantly that a boycott was on the cards. In hindsight, I feel that a boycott may have been contemplated at high levels but never acted upon. Mr Zhang had probably expressed a purely personal view to me, which, for such a senior official, was a rare thing to do on international television.

Today Beijing deflects criticism about human rights as dexterously as a top-seed tennis player. After a decade of rapid economic growth, China's economy is now the flavour of the month. No foreign government or global business believes it can truly succeed in the international trade game without a toehold in the vast Chinese market. The prevailing sentiment in the West is to avoid damaging potential opportunities by not upsetting the leadership of the most populous nation on earth. China has succeeded in forcing its trading partners to separate human rights from trade ties using the carrot and stick approach: the carrot being the promise of its giant market; and the stick, silence over human rights as a means of securing valuable trade. In 2002 Australia won a hard-fought, 25-year, A\$25 billion deal to supply southern China with liquefied natural gas. To ensure there's no hitch in the deal, due to begin in 2005 or 2006, it's likely the Australian government will go out of its way not to offend the Chinese government, particularly in the field of human rights.

In 1997 the contingent of Australian correspondents in Beijing was given an 'exclusive' (of other journalists) interview with then vice-premier Zhu Rongji, who was due to visit Australia with a seventy–person Chinese business delegation soon afterwards. In the usual highly controlled atmosphere of an interview with a

Chinese leader, we submitted questions for approval, but I wasn't allowed to ask mine which, if I remember correctly, was on unemployment. So I decided to be spontaneous. I asked Vice-Premier Zhu why he had cancelled a trip to Europe to visit Australia. He replied frankly that the scheduled trip was shelved because some European governments had backed a resolution attacking China's human rights record at the United Nations Human Rights Commission in Geneva. Australia had withheld its support for the resolution for the first time, after backing it the previous six years. The year 1997 marked a diplomatic coup for China's disarming of the resolution by also getting France, Italy, Germany, Spain, Greece and Japan to withdraw their backing for the condemnation. Each government would have put trade at the forefront of its foreign policy and each understood the drawbacks of being one of the handful of countries to continue public condemnation of China's human rights record.

The last time Australia significantly upset Chinese sensibilities was in 1996, after the newly elected Howard government backed US naval deployment in the Taiwan Strait during Taiwan's presidential elections. In the same year, John Howard met the Dalai Lama during his Australian tour, despite repeated warnings from China for the meeting to be cancelled. There was also a badly handled dumping of a soft-loan program, which funded small community projects around the country including sanitation and the provision of drinking water, and an unofficial ministerial visit to Taiwan. The symbol of the shift away from public criticism of China came in the form of a closed door 'human rights dialogue', the first of which took place in 1997, thereafter ensuring that human rights would play a backseat role in the Australia–China relationship. Then in 1999 Australian businessman James Peng was finally released from jail in China, removing the last sticking point. Mr Peng was kidnapped by Chinese agents from Macau and hauled back into China to stand trial for embezzlement after a bitter dispute with his former business partner, who was also a niece of late paramount leader Deng Xiaoping.

Since James Peng's release, Australia has shown itself to be a good friend of China, and Prime Minister John Howard has as much as admitted that. 'I try to focus on the things that can be productive for our two countries,' he said during his whirlwind visit in May 2002, meaning China's human rights conduct was yesterday's news.

The change has another element: it would be hypocritical for the international community to undermine China's Olympic bid and, crucially, the lucrative contracts that go with it for the sake of the 'high moral ground', which few nations can presently claim to stand on. In the meantime, a careful but ruthless campaign of suppression continues within China to silence, imprison or expel the voices of dissent. China has become the smart autocracy, though the dissident voices are becoming increasingly diversified due to the speed of economic reform. It's the call for political reform, however, which motivates the bulk of China's rebel voices.

If you speak to ordinary Chinese about the Western stance on China's human rights record, most believe that putting trade first ultimately benefits the country overall, and that it may some day flow into greater personal freedom. However most Chinese don't have a strong awareness of their rights and feel that they already have a significant amount of freedom – more than individuals have enjoyed for fifty years – and so they don't seem as dogmatic as many Westerners on the question of human rights. They get angry about corruption and ordinary people being ripped off by unscrupulous officials, criminals or shysters, but generally there is scant tradition of defying authority. For a thousand years the Chinese people have been taught to obey their government. Then came the Cultural Revolution of the 1960s, and millions were persecuted because they criticised Mao's regime. Those brought up during and after the Cultural Revolution were taught to never discuss politics in public.

Today the main preoccupation is with making money and improving your standard of living. Few people care about politics or state affairs because experience has taught them that no matter how concerned they are, they don't have the power to change anything. The only time I heard my friend Zhao Daifu mutter unsolicited criticism of the regime was over the celebrations for the fiftieth anniversary of the People's Republic in October 1999. Zhou Daifu's daughter had been selected, with thousands of other teenagers, to take part in the festivities in Tiananmen Square, which were to last several hours for a live telecast. Zhao Daifu didn't mind making a financial contribution for the costumes, even though the event was being staged by the top echelons of the national government. However, during rehearsals, which took place late at night or in the early hours of the morning in the week prior to the anniversary, she was horrified to learn that her daughter and the other young girls were given nappies to wear because no-one was allowed to leave the Square to go to the toilet. Generally, though, ordinary Chinese I knew rarely complained about their lack of rights.

Jiang Qisheng is a good-looking, softly spoken man in his mid fifties. I first met Mr Jiang with my colleagues over a fiery meal at a busy restaurant, where amid the chatter of a hungry crowd our conversation wasn't likely to be overheard. As a mature-age doctorate student at Qinghua University, Mr Jiang had been involved behind the scenes of the student movement in 1989. Initially, after the crackdown, the authorities didn't pursue him. Then, a month after the massacre, the vice-president of his university asked him to denounce other students who had been involved in the protests. Jiang Qisheng refused and in the face of the government's resolve to hunt down leading protesters and their allies, the university administration hardened its position. Like other state institutions it began a re-education campaign. Those targeted were threatened with losing their jobs if they failed to sign declarations or self-criticisms admitting their 'crimes'.

Three months after the massacre Jiang Qisheng was arrested and sentenced to prison where he spent seventeen months. On his release, he decided to abandon his lifelong devotion to aerodynamics and take up a more altruistic interest in human rights, living off the earnings of his newspaper and magazine articles.

Mr Jiang agreed to help me set up a story about the tenth anniversary of the Tiananmen crackdown. I wanted to interview Professor Ding Zilin, the spokesperson for the Tiananmen families, and I also wanted to see whether any survivors from the night of 3–4 June would be willing to speak publicly. There was an added difficulty. Being a nation strong on symbolism, the upcoming anniversary wasn't likely to pass without the capital being placed on a high state of alert for possible protests. The year 1999 also marked another important anniversary: fifty years since the founding of the People's Republic on 1 October. It was during politically stressful times like this that dissidents were encouraged to leave town 'on holiday' at the expense of the Public Security Bureau. Foreign journalists, on the other hand, found themselves the centre of attention, being tailed by large black cars.

To prevent any on the spot protest, Tiananmen Square was covered in scaffolding for six months for a major renovation. One month before the Tiananmen anniversary, extra People's Armed Police were posted at the gates of the foreign and diplomatic compound where journalists lived and worked, together with a contingent of plain-clothes agents. They might sound daunting, but we often glimpsed them napping at their desks, hence the nickname given them by our bureau producer, Cleo Leung: 'Bed-Heads'.

Mr Jiang arranged to accompany me to meet Professor Ding Zilin, the retired philosophy professor who lost her seventeen-year-old son, Jiang Jielian, in the June Fourth shootings. Professor Ding, formerly a Communist Party member for thirty years, broke her silence two years after the massacre, when she and Zhang Xianling, another mother whose son was shot dead, decided to take their story to the foreign media. No Chinese media would touch it; the topic is still taboo. The 'Tiananmen Mothers' demanded an investigation into the night of 3–4 June and called on the government to reverse its assessment of the incident, described by Deng Xiaoping as a 'counter-revolutionary rebellion' where the 'dregs of society' had sought to overthrow the party and the socialist system to establish 'a bourgeois republic entirely dependent on the West'.

Professor Ding decided to gather stories of as many victims as she could to establish a record of deaths, which the government had never attempted to do. She identified 155 victims, but believed, with many relatives too fearful of speaking out, the number could be far higher. Her attempts to locate the families of Tiananmen victims and raise funds to assist them brought her into frequent conflict with the authorities. At times, she's under virtual house arrest. Her phone has been bugged and she frequently receives abusive telephone calls. Because of the constant surveillance, she receives few visitors at her home situated on the grounds of the People's University. Despite all of this, I wanted to meet her in person rather than interview her over the phone.

So one chilly spring night in April 1999, I dressed in jeans and a bulky jacket and tucked my hair under a baseball cap. I grabbed a small backpack containing a digital camera, microphone and tripod. Because the start of the sensitive period before June Fourth was still a few weeks away, only a single guard was on duty at the gates of my compound. Careful not to draw his attention, I jumped into a taxi right outside the gate and asked the driver to take me to a nearby department store where I changed taxis in case I was being followed. I met Jiang Qisheng, waiting beside a streetlamp, and we continued to the gates of the People's University. With my baseball cap pulled down over my face and my heart pounding, I walked unnoticed past the guards and into the university grounds. Before reaching Professor Ding's apartment, Mr Jiang asked me to wait while he checked the vicinity for plain-clothes police at the entrance to Professor Ding's building. Minutes later, he returned saying the coast was clear.

Professor Ding and her husband, Professor Jiang Peikun, welcomed me into their large, comfortable apartment. Unlike many homes I'd visited, this one was very Westernised. It had new pine wooden furniture, pictures hung on fresh, white walls and it was immaculately clean – most housing allocated during socialist times isn't well-maintained or cleaned by its occupants.

I had already decided that I didn't want to get any of my colleagues into trouble over this interview. Sebastian's annual foreign journalist card was up for renewal, so I conducted it without a cameraman or an interpreter. I set up the small digital camera and took out a list of questions, written in pinyin, that I'd prepared earlier in the day with the help of researcher Charles Li.

Pinyin is a neat system of writing Chinese using the alphabet. It's really a guide to the pronunciation of the Chinese characters, which is useful for people like me who can only recognise around 500 characters. Though my Hong Kong upbringing meant that I already spoke Cantonese, I had never learned it formally, only speaking the language at home to my mother and our amah. Besides, the characters used in Hong Kong and Taiwan are more complicated than the simplified characters adopted by China many years ago. I had studied Mandarin Chinese twice a week for two years before I left for my posting, and though I was comfortable speaking everyday Chinese, my comprehension of the characters didn't get me much past road signs and menus – it's said you need to master 2000 characters before you can read a Chinese newspaper. Though I persisted with lessons in Beijing for several years, I eventually stopped because of the pressure of work. But as my spoken Chinese was quite good and I could master the four tones, Charles helped me phrase the questions phonetically, which was how I was able to conduct the interview with Professor Ding.

Professor Ding, who is in her mid to late sixties, has wavy grey hair and a tired face marked with lines of frustration. She smiled readily before the interview started, but once the camera started to roll her expression became as hard as steel. She began speaking in little more than a whisper, rising to a crescendo when she criticised the Chinese government. She talked of her duty, both as a mother and an intellectual, to speak out about her son's death. The harassment she received each time she spoke publicly made her firmer in her resolve to expose the truth behind the official lies surrounding the Tianenmen incident. Talking about it, she said, calmed her spiritually.

'About eighty million people have died during the Communist Party's regime [since 1949],' she told me. 'When I first read this figure, I was shocked. I suddenly realised my son's death was the result of the system; he was one of 155 people [who died in Tiananmen], which was just a small proportion of the 80 million.'

She called on international politicians not to be bought by the promise of China's market. 'China is a vast land with a big population, but please don't only think of our markets, don't only think of the orders the Chinese government can give you. More than one billion people need a life with their natural human rights. But these rights are being trampled on.'

The tearful professor took me into Jielian's bedroom, pointing out the artistic tributes to him, including a photograph of the seventeen-year-old taking part in a protest march. On the night of 3 June she had forbidden him to go out, but he disobeyed her and crawled out of the window.

I had expected to feel moved by the meeting with Professor Ding, because I'd known about her long struggle to reverse the official Tiananmen verdict. However, I left her apartment disappointed. She delivered a monologue that varied only slightly each time she gave it, and it was beginning to sound worn-out. When I interjected several times to bring her back to the point, she replied that she hadn't finished her answer. Then she continued her passionate diatribe, pausing several times to remove a crumpled tissue from her sweater sleeve to dry her teary eyes.

When the interview finally ended and the camera was packed away, Mr Jiang and I left the apartment, walking briskly through the darkened compound. I asked him how he thought ordinary people could commemorate the anniversary, and he said Tiananmen activists planned to write an open letter, calling on people to honour the occasion by turning off the lights in their homes and placing candles in the windows. Our steps quickened as we approached the gatehouse, and when we were safely out on the street Mr Jiang hailed a taxi for me. I never saw him again.

A month later a Hong Kong human rights group reported that Mr Jiang had been detained after distributing a leaflet entitled *Light of Myriad of Candles in Collective Commemoration of the Brave Spirits of June Fourth*. As he had said the night we visited Professor Ding, the open letter called on the public to pay tribute to the victims of Tiananmen by lighting candles.

Six months after his arrest, Jiang Qisheng's case went to court. The indictment document said that Jiang's leaflet 'slanderously referred to the June Fourth Incident' as 'an extremely tragic event that shocked the world and embodied injustice, falsehood and wrongfulness'. It incited people to 'denounce the atrocity that crushed human rights and to condemn the abrogation of justice in the name of "stability"'. He wasn't given access to a lawyer until a few days before his trial, and for the nineteen months between his detention and sentencing was refused family visits. After his trial in November 1999 another twelve months passed before a verdict – guilty of inciting subversion – and a jail sentence of four years was handed down, on 27 December 2000.

Jiang Qisheng's final court statement, obtained by overseas human rights groups, declared his innocence at a time in China's history when a trial of ideas was under way. He questioned why exercising free speech (a right upheld in the Chinese constitution) wasn't promoted and encouraged by the government.

'The future of China lies in great part on nurturing and uplifting this kind of civic quality,' he told the court. 'By contrast, those who attempt to fight against modern civilisation . . . are the real criminals among the Chinese people.'

By the time the tenth anniversary of the Tiananmen crackdown arrived in June 1999, most of China's leading dissidents had disappeared behind bars one by one, like Jiang Qisheng. All had fallen foul of an intellectual thaw known as a 'Beijing Spring' where authorities, for a period, tolerated different views on political reform. China had weathered several potential political storms including Deng Xiaoping's death, a smooth transition of power to Jiang Zemin, the Hong Kong Handover and a successful Communist Party Congress. The first sign of the thaw came in October 1997 when China signed the first of two key United Nations protocols, the International Covenant on Economic, Social and Cultural Rights, and a year later the covenant on Civil and Political Rights. Signing the protocols was seen as a major step towards bringing Chinese law in line with international human rights standards, though the covenants don't take effect until a country's parliament ratifies them. At the time of writing, Beijing hadn't endorsed the covenants.

With the arrival of the 'Beijing Spring', I too sensed a thaw and believed, naively, that the country was on the verge of change. For the first time ever I sat through an official news conference – Zhu Rongji's first as premier – in the Great Hall of the People without falling asleep. While the Chinese president has greater powers than the prime minister, including the power to appoint and remove the premier and all senior office-holders and proclaim martial law or a state of war, it's the prime minister who runs the day-to-day business of government. Zhu Rongji had the additional responsibility of reforming the state sector within the economy. Like Mr Zhang, who headed the Beijing 2000 Olympic bid committee, Mr Zhu has a casual, natural manner of talking, unlike the very formal jargon employed by most other senior Chinese officials. When Zhu Rongji began to answer questions from the international and domestic media, for ninety minutes I sat engrossed. It was the first time I'd been to a news conference given by a Chinese leader who hadn't read from a prepared script. Instead, Mr Zhu spoke off the cuff with charisma, charm and passion. Then he made a declaration that made him sound like a Western politician addressing an electorate, not an ageing Chinese leader: 'No matter what awaits me – whether it be landmines or an abyss – I will blaze my trail. I have no hesitations or misgivings.' However, in another similarity with Western politicians, many would later question whether he delivered on the promised reforms or simply left the glass half empty.

Though intellectuals and academics watched to see what would become of the 'Beijing Spring', I am not sure that ordinary people were aware of any real change. Several months after Zhu Rongji's 1998 press conference came another potentially groundbreaking event: a televised summit between President Jiang Zemin and the visiting US president, Bill Clinton. The US leader told his Chinese counterpart and a potential audience of 900 million people, 'I believe, and the American people believe, that the use of force [at Tiananmen Square] and the tragic loss of life was wrong. I believe, and the American people believe, that freedom of speech, association and religion . . . are the right of people everywhere and should be protected by their governments.' I never expected the Chinese government to agree to that broadcast, although it's unlikely many saw it, given that the live television summit took place unannounced and during the morning, when many people would have been at work.

Then, almost as suddenly as the 'Beijing Spring' appeared, it rapidly declined into a dark winter of political repression, claiming the freedom of China's leading dissidents.

Xu Wenli is a softly spoken man, aged nearly sixty, with wispy grey hair and high cheekbones. The former railway electrician made his reputation as the editor of a dissident magazine, *April Fifth Forum*. The publication was named after the April 1976 clashes between police and protesters, who had been commemorating the death of esteemed Prime Minister Zhou Enlai, and it was founded during the 1978–79 Democracy Wall period after the death of Mao and the overthrow of the Gang of Four.

In December 1978, another electrician, Wei Jingsheng, a former Beijing zoo employee, wrote a feisty manifesto in large Chinese characters and posted it on the Democracy Wall, located in the west of Beijing. (The wall no longer exists.) In the late 1970s, the wall and several others in Beijing became political bulletin boards, plastered with daring essays, petitions and passionate literature.

Deng Xiaoping's wide-ranging economic reforms were summarised by a blueprint known as the Four Modernisations: of industry, agriculture, defence and science. Wei Jingsheng believed four modernisations weren't sufficient so he added a fifth – democracy. He called his manifesto the Fifth Modernisation.

'Alas, the old political system so despised by the people remains unchanged, and the democracy and freedom they longed for has not even been mentioned . . . if we want to modernise our economy, sciences, military and other areas, then we must first modernise our people and our society,' the manifesto declared.

Wei's manifesto, together with a multitude of progressive magazines like the *April Fifth Forum* which sprang up at the time of the Democracy Wall, caught the attention of the public as well as the wrath of the leadership. Such a challenge to the government and a personal attack on Deng Xiaoping sealed Wei's fate. His arrest began a crackdown against the most outspoken activists and the closure of dozens of pro-democracy magazines. Wei was charged with writing counter-revolutionary propaganda with the aim of overthrowing the socialist system. He refused to plead, but the court found him guilty anyway and he was sentenced to fifteen years in jail.

Xu Wenli came under fire after writing a list of twenty suggestions to the Central Committee of the Chinese Communist Party, emphasising the need for democracy in a Marxist society. After publicly protesting against the arrest of fellow Democracy Wall activists, he was sentenced to fifteen years in prison for 'illegally organising a clique to overthrow the government'. He served twelve years, including long periods of solitary confinement. Like Wei

Jingsheng, he was released in 1993 as part of Beijing's attempt to win the 2000 Olympic Games.

During the 1997–98 'Beijing Spring', Xu Wenli and a handful of political activists began discussing the formation of a political party called the China Democracy Party. The Public Security Bureau began targeting Xu, visiting his apartment frequently and warning him to stop speaking with foreign journalists and publishing his ideas. On occasions, police were posted outside the gate of his apartment complex until well after nightfall.

Wherever Xu Wenli went, his wife He Xintong accompanied him. They were clearly devoted to one another and unusually openly affectionate for a Chinese couple of their generation. They always walked arm-in-arm. He held open doors for her and protectively ushered her out of elevators. She came to every interview, sitting out of camera shot, operating a tape recorder whenever he began talking. During television interviews, Mr Xu faced the camera but somehow kept his eye on Ms He's cup of tea. The moment it was half empty, he reached for the tea-pot to fill it up again.

Mr Xu was keen for me to film him in his home, but as with Professor Ding, the leader of the Tiananmen Mothers, there was a strong chance a foreign visitor would be detained trying to meet with a troublesome dissident. Instead of using a crew I decided to go alone, as I did with Professor Ding, taking a small digital camera with me. Mr Xu and Ms He picked me up near the ABC bureau, and in case the police were at the gates to their apartment complex I lay on the back seat of their Russian-style jeep. Years later Mr Xu's daughter, an arts teacher living in the United States, told me that the jeep was his pride and joy. He'd sat for his driver's licence when he came out of jail in 1993, only just qualifying because he was about to turn fifty and first-time licences are not issued to people over that age. He bought the jeep a short time afterwards, using the proceeds from the publication of his several books. Old Xu, as everyone referred to him, took life as an adventure and there was a twinkle in his eye as the jeep hurtled along the Second Ring Road with his wife in the front and me lying down on the back seat. When we arrived at the apartment compound, Old Xu drove the vehicle through the open gates and stopped in front of his building. Then with a scarf draped around my head to cover my light hair and pale skin, I was bundled into the building, supported by Old Xu and Ms He like a sick relative.

Neither Mr Xu nor Ms He were employed and they lived on Mr Xu's pension of about 1000 yuan (A$200) a month. The apartment was owned by Mr Xu's work unit, the railway corporation, though after Mr Xu's first conviction the corporation ceased to employ him and he and his wife were asked to pay full rent. The work unit even cut off its half of a measly five yuan (A$1) 'one-child award' payment made monthly to the Xus' daughter, Xu Jin. The apartment was so small that the kitchen was out in a corridor shared by Xu's neighbours, who could see the family's daily comings and goings. After Mr Xu's release from jail, the neighbours were paid to watch him.

The apartment was very cramped, with neat piles of books, papers and magazines on every surface. A photo of Mr Xu, Ms He and her daughter Xu Jin in graduation gown took pride of place on a bookshelf. On the other side of the room there was a double bed, desk, computer, fax machine, a foldaway dining table and a television, all of which Xu Jin helped to pay for by waiting tables and washing dishes between her studies. Behind the door Mr Xu kept a backpack containing pyjamas, clean clothes and a toothbrush in the event of his arrest.

While Ms He immersed dried noodles in a bowl of boiling water from a vacuum flask, I filmed Mr Xu showing me around his tiny apartment. Then he sat down at his desk and took a calligraphy brush and delicate writing paper and in long, confident strokes, penned a welcome message to me.

Like many thinkers, Xu Wenli was concerned about the massive layoffs taking place in the state sector. He felt the unemployment problem wasn't simply an economic issue but a political one because it had been mismanaged when the country was a centrally planned system. And because it was a political problem, it would have to be solved politically.

Mr Xu believed small-scale demonstrations around the country could help to focus attention on political reform. When he learned the Chinese government planned to sign a key protocol, the UN International Convention on Civil and Political Rights, he attempted to register a human rights organisation. That, he believed, was the first step toward registering a political party.

'They [the Chinese government] should give up one-party rule,' he said during a later interview, motioning his wife to turn her tape recorder on. 'They should let all kinds of political forces get together and solve the problem of laid-off workers and other social problems within China; this is very important. They should hasten the privatisation of the economy, and that way more and more working opportunities could be created.'

Outside China, this was hardly revolutionary or counter-revolutionary material. In fact Mr Xu was opposed to what he called 'violent revolution'. Democracy would be achieved gradually, and when people accepted this they wouldn't be impatient for a hasty resolution. However, in contrast to the Communist Party, many of the China Democracy Party members, including Xu Wenli, believed the only way to solve China's unemployment and other social problems was to remove the ban on free speech and free association. Mr Xu believed Chinese society had become increasingly polarised with the very rich living beside the utterly destitute. Many, including those who know China intimately, have warned that problems like unemployment have the potential to cause large-scale social unrest. But Xu disagreed.

'The masses in China possess tolerance. It's impossible for them to rashly go onto the street or cause large-scale riots simply by being laid off. Some foreigners don't have a realistic understanding of the current situation,' he told me during a long interview in my apartment, soon after I had visited his home. He was perhaps most realistic about the power of dissidents to change political life. He often spoke about whether people of his generation would live to see democracy in China, describing himself and other activists as 'cobblestones' on the road to democracy. Though his political ideas were conservative by dissident standards, the Communist Party considered them an affront.

Mr Xu pointed out that while he was opposed to the Communist Party's one-party autocracy, the way to achieve a pluralistic political environment wasn't by overthrowing the party.

'If the party does its job well, is not corrupt, represents the interests of the people, then there is no justification for any persons or political forces to overthrow it,' he said in his quiet, considered manner, still checking to see whether his wife had enough tea.

Throughout 1998, the state security apparatus was already mounting a case against the veteran dissident. After a thorough search of his home, the police took away most of his office equipment: the fax, computer, books and documents bought for him by his daughter. The police refused to return anything. They also took a number of items that had nothing to do with his activist work: a battery charger, a circuit breaker for the refrigerator, a CD player, tapes from his daughter and a Swiss army knife that had been sent by his cousin from overseas.

During my association with Old Xu and some of the other dissidents, I often wondered whether interviewing them had cost them their freedom. I still think about it. However, I wasn't the only correspondent who sought their views and Mr Xu, for one, never believed in hiding his political activities. The last time I saw him, I asked if he and his wife would take a walk in the grounds of the diplomatic compound so that the ABC would have some everyday shots of him. He and Ms He walked back and forth beside the basketball court several times, softly talking to each other. As I watched them, I wondered how they would cope without each other if he went to prison again.

The 'Beijing Spring' ended resolutely. One day, towards the end of 1998, Old Xu disappeared. In his case the wheels of Chinese justice moved rapidly, and in less than one month he was tried, convicted of subversion and sentenced to thirteen years in prison. His China Democracy Party colleagues disappeared one by one from the radar screen, going to trial and also receiving harsh sentences for subversion.

Xu Wenli stayed in prison, suffering from hepatitis B, until Christmas Eve 2002. Then, like Tiananmen dissident Wang Dan and Democracy Wall activist Wei Jingsheng, he and his devoted wife He Xintong were whisked away on a plane to the US after intense lobbying by US diplomats. The man who had spent more than sixteen of the last twenty-one years in prison for his support of democracy and free speech was finally released on medical parole to start a new life as a dissident-in-exile.

Like the freeways and tollways sprouting up all over the country, opening the way for a new type of adventure, the technology superhighway has also brought great promise to China. The government is pushing out 'the fastest, largest sustained communications network build-out the world has seen'. Dissidents and supporters of causes like Free Tibet and an independent Taiwan hope the spread of the World Wide Web in China will eventually crack the hold of the Communist Party. However the government, for all the resources it's pouring into its development, feels threatened by the potential of the internet, and wages an increasingly sophisticated campaign to restrict the content carried by the technology.

The internet's growth in China has been phenomenal. From 2.1 million users in January 1999, user numbers reached 45 million in July 2002. By the end of 2003 an estimated 80 million Chinese will be regular net users. While the penetration is still small compared to the size of China's population, and limited to mainly well-off urbanites, broad access is becoming easier, faster and cheaper. That presents the government with a challenge, according to China-based internet analyst Duncan Clarke: 'On the one hand you have desire for the economic benefits of the internet, to increase China's power. On the other hand, you have this very deep-seated fear of losing control. And unfortunately the two either come together, or there is a fundamental contradiction.'

That contradiction is emerging as a major headache for the government as the growing number of net users seeks to use the medium for the simple purpose it was intended for: spreading information. In the past few years, police have arrested several activists, including one who downloaded pro-democracy material from a friend's computer. Chi Shouzhu, who served a ten-year prison term for taking part in the 1989 pro-democracy protests, was picked up shortly after printing out the material, indicating Chinese authorities were able to trace the computer which accessed the offending web-site.

In August 2002, a prominent AIDS activist, Wan Yanhai, was detained by the high-level Ministry of State Security for publishing material on his web-site, www.aizhi.org, that the government deemed too sensitive, despite an official admission that AIDS has become a serious public health issue. China's Health Ministry expected one million people to be diagnosed with AIDS by the end of 2002, admitting that without adequate preventative measures the figure could reach 10 million by the end of the decade. Over the years, Dr Wan had revealed information relating to a massive cover-up by health officials in Henan province, now viewed as the epicentre of China's HIV explosion.

Dr Wan believed that commercial blood sales from the end of the 1970s until the middle of the 1990s contributed to 500 000–700 000 people becoming HIV-positive in Henan province. With the participation of the public health authorities, several hundred collection centres run by entrepreneurs known as 'blood heads' sent mobile units into Henan's poverty-stricken villages.

Peasants were encouraged to sell their blood to the units, a practice which is illegal. With no regard for protection, plasma was then extracted from the blood for sale to pharmaceutical firms and the blood then reinfused into the donors. Areas where blood plasma sales were most common have today become AIDS villages in which whole families are dying, off limits to the media.

Wan Yanhai was held for nearly a month after being picked up by state security and only released after a 'confession' that he illegally obtained classified documents and released them to others, including overseas media.

The struggle to control information disseminated over the internet – and through it the hearts and minds of China's millions – also saw a sweeping crackdown on internet cafes after a fire in June 2002 killed 24 people in the Lanjisu Cyber Cafe in Beijing. The cafe, or *wangba* as they are known in China, was one of thousands of unlicensed internet establishments. Yet in an exaggerated response to the tragedy, Beijing authorities closed all internet establishments, and other cities did the same, on the pretext of inadequate fire safety equipment. Chinese media launched a campaign criticising *wangba*s as virtual dens of iniquity, reporting stories of students who died of fatigue in the cafes, met sexual predators or dropped out of school after becoming addicted to the internet. The Lanjisu fire seemed to embody all the dangers of unregulated internet usage among the young. Six months after the fire many cafes reopened, subject to new laws restricting young people's use. The regulations banned minors from using cafes, required the establishments to close between midnight and 8 am, and prohibited illegal online material such as pornography, gambling sites and violent or 'superstitious' content.

The first person to be charged with a crime relating to the internet was a 30-year-old Shanghai computer technician named Lin Hai. In 1998 Lin Hai gave 30000 email addresses to a dissident e-magazine, *VIP Reference*, based in the United States. Convicted of 'incitement to undermine the government', he served eighteen months in jail. Half a year after his release the gentle, slightly nervous-looking man took part in a forum of internet professionals held in a club in Shanghai. The forum was, from my point of view, rather technical, but Lin Hai was looking for new work opportunities. Speaking quietly into the microphone, he introduced himself as China's 'first victim of the internet'.

Lin Hai was a graduate of the Beijing University of Aeronautics and Astronautics, where he had majored in computer science. In the early 1990s, before the general public knew much about the internet, he accessed the new technology through facilities in the Beijing Chemical University, where he was working, and opened the door to a type of freedom he had never even dreamed of.

'I was deeply attracted to the internet,' Lin Hai told me after the forum. He was nervous about our camera coming to his home so we did the interview in our hotel room. He was so softly spoken, I wondered how such a gentle man could have survived in jail. 'China was in a special situation then. We didn't have the latest technology and we never had such free access to information from the outside world. That's why Chinese people are attracted to the internet.'

When Lin Hai was freed from jail, he set up several web-sites including a job-search network. He still believed firmly in the benefits information technology could bring China, but after his experience agreed he would have to tread more carefully. 'Freedom is my perfect dream,' he said. 'I will not give it up. But I think what I've learned in the past few years is that I'll use more considered ways to achieve my final goal. If you can't grasp the tricks of survival, even if you have lofty ideals, you will accomplish nothing.'

Lin Hai soon found that his criminal record made it impossible to set up a company (it's illegal for anyone with a record in China) and potential employers stayed clear of him. 'There's a special system in China to forward your official personal record to all the human resources departments of state-run companies,' he told me recently by email. 'If you apply for a job in a joint venture [a partly foreign-owned enterprise] it's the duty of a government-run human resources centre to inform the joint venture about a candidate's background.' As a result, Lin Hai left China with his family in early 2001 for New York where he lives and works today, a free man, but one who still yearns to be on Chinese soil.

The ranks of dissident exiles grow larger as time passes. After spending a total of eighteen years in jail, Wei Jingsheng, the proponent of the Fifth Modernisation, was suddenly released on medical parole in 1997. It was clear that the post-Deng leadership had changed its view on dissidents and whether they should be imprisoned or forced into exile. I met Wei and his entourage of supporters at a hotel in Sydney's Chinatown in 2002. His minder told me we should find a place to talk where Mr Wei could smoke, because smoking helped him to think. The hotel we went to is favoured by scores of visiting Chinese because it is one of the few Australian hostelries which permits smoking in its public areas.

Wei Jingsheng's face looked just as it did in the photograph on the cover of his book *The Courage to Stand Alone*: part mischievous, part brooding. In freedom he has enjoyed more and better food than he consumed in captivity. He seemed impulsive and compulsive, lighting up his first cigarette as his heavy frame sank into a sofa. Then, like a typical Beijinger, he rolled his trousers up to his knees, revealing knobbly legs, ankle-length white socks and brown slip-on shoes. 'It's hot in here,' he said as if he needed to explain his actions.

As soon as he spoke, it became clear why he inspired activists and incensed his government and jailers. Wei's mind – despite the numbing experience of eighteen years in jail – was razor sharp, and his language witty and eloquent.

'Deng Xiaoping was very smart,' said Wei, stirring two sachets of sugar into his cappuccino. 'He understood that he had to trap people like me in his palm.' Yet after Deng died in 1997, the political atmosphere changed. Jiang Zemin believed dissidents were better out of the country, because then they lost their influence over the Chinese people.

Pouring more sugar into his cappuccino, another cigarette in hand, Wei said that five days after Jiang Zemin returned from his visit to the United States in September 1997, the guards at the Nanpu New Life Salt Works prison farm where Wei was held near the Bohai Gulf in Hebei had started to take photographs of him. He quickly guessed what was going on.

'They took photographs of me from the front and side. I told them they didn't need to deceive me and when was I getting my passport?' he said, laughing at the memory.

The following day, his captors confirmed preparations were being made for his departure and raised the issue of his possible expulsion. Wei asked to be sent to Germany where his younger sister lived. His captors told him if he was going anywhere it would be the United States.

Under President Clinton, the United States and China experienced warmer ties. The former American president is a powerful motivational speaker who made his message of global interdependence and integration seem an admirable and achievable goal. Behind the scenes he pushed to secure the release of China's leading prisoners of conscience like Wei Jingsheng. Events moved quickly. A mere eight days after Jiang Zemin returned from the United States, Wei was taken to Beijing in a police convoy, fit for the French president, he joked. The following day on 17 September, nine days after Jiang's return, China's most famous dissident was sitting on a plane bound for freedom and Detroit.

Despite his years of imprisonment during which he never wavered from his democratic ideals, Wei wasn't particularly supportive of the efforts of other Chinese democracy activists. When I asked him about Xu Wenli's abortive efforts to set up the China Democracy Party, he claimed the party never really existed.

'If it had been founded,' he said, 'the chairman would be me, not Wang Xizhe [another exiled dissident] or Xu Wenli.' When I pressed him further for his thoughts on Xu, Wei added, 'Xu Wenli did lots of wrong things and said lots of wrong words. We criticised him in the past and in the future some will still criticise him.' Without divulging what Xu's past wrongs were, Wei went on to talk about the splits and internal struggles that dogged the exiled dissident movement. To date, it seems that though united by a common belief in democratic theory, no-one is quite sure how to build a compassionate, fair or democratic process within the ranks of Chinese exiles. The movement might have had greater success had these rebels learned the simple art of cooperation, rather than vying with each other over who would be emperor.

Wei's visit to Sydney in 2002 coincided with the 'World Congress on the Peaceful Reunification of China and World Peace', a conference sponsored by what appeared to be a front company set up by the Chinese Communist Party. The congress smacked of Communist rhetoric and several speakers were sent from a think tank run by China's powerful State Council. The organisers denied the party or the Chinese leadership were behind the conference. They managed to rope in Bill Clinton and former Australian prime ministers Bob Hawke and Malcolm Fraser as speakers. In the end Bob Hawke pulled out and Malcolm Fraser only sent a speech. Bill Clinton was reportedly paid US$300 000 for his appearance, but to the disappointment of his hosts he didn't support the immediate reunification of China and Taiwan, preferring to leave the question to the vagaries of the future.

'There are some problems in the world that time will take care of and some that will get better right now . . . I believe the issue between Taiwan and China is an example of the first kind of problem,' he told his audience.

A few days before Clinton's appearance, Wei Jingsheng released an open letter to the former president warning him that his appearance may be seen to support the growing nationalism advocated by the Chinese government and obscure the debate around human rights and democracy. 'I guess you wouldn't know in detail what this conference is about,' wrote Wei, 'that's why I came to Sydney to join the "anti-autocracy, advance democracy" movement. I don't want to see my friend stand on the wrong side of history.' Wei signed the letter 'The prisoner you exchanged from Jiang Zemin's hand'.

After Bill Clinton's speech, I left the auditorium and found that the conference organisers had barred the main doors to the Sydney Convention and Exhibition Centre, located in the heart of the Darling Harbour tourist area. I soon discovered why. A noisy protest by members of Australia's Taiwanese community was in full swing while the pro-mainland lobby sat in plush seats inside. 'Taiwan is democratic and free!' shouted the Taiwanese, waving Nationalist flags high in the air. Wei Jingsheng was also present, taking questions from a local Chinese radio reporter.

I greeted Wei and as we chatted about seeing the two Chinas clash on foreign soil, suddenly two men, one wearing a white Mao jacket, broke through the ranks of the protesters. They were holding a banner which read 'Destroy Taiwan Independence. Reunify Now!' The protesters were caught off guard but passions quickly boiled over and in seconds the punches flew. The Taiwanese supporters tried to drag the offending banner from the hands of the Communists. It was high drama: the two sides of the Taiwan Strait meeting face to face, not in mortal combat as China so often threatened, but in a childish propaganda exercise, appropriately theatrical beside the jugglers and stilt-walkers entertaining nearby crowds gathered for the Lunar New Year dragon boat races. Wei disparaged the pro-Communist protesters as hooligans, as they ran up the stairs and into the safety of the conference centre.

I told Wei that his book held special significance for me, though probably not for obvious reasons. When my shipment of personal effects left China bound for Sydney, the moving company informed me that Chinese Customs had searched my belongings. I possessed a library of 'unsuitable' books about China, most of which officials would probably consider offensive, but as all of them were in

English I presumed I couldn't be accused of inciting counter-rebellion. Overlooking heretical tomes on Tibet, the Falun Gong bible and *The Tiananmen Papers*, Customs confiscated just one book: the English edition of Wei Jingsheng's prison letters, *The Courage to Stand Alone*. All versions of his writing were banned in China, although illicit copies often found their way onto a busy Beijing intersection where a diffident man on crutches once sold books from the back of his red motor-tricycle.

The father of Chinese dissidents looked delighted. 'Perhaps one of the customs officials wanted to read it,' he said. 'That's promising.'

COLONIAL CHOP SUEY

Going shopping with my mother in Hong Kong in the 1960s and seventies was an adventure, never a routine. While the expatriates in our apartment building ordered all their food from the Asia Provisions store and had the bags delivered in a big red van, my mum always did her own shopping. First we went to the steep lanes near the Central Market in the middle of the downtown area, which was known as Central. The lanes were crammed with vegetable stalls dripping with water that was sprayed over them to stop the lush greens wilting in the heat. We always went to the same lady with the deep tan and the big smile that revealed a gold tooth. This vegetable woman weighed the bok choy, spinach and tung choy (which has a hollow stem like a straw), all of which came from China. Her old-fashioned set of scales had a tin bowl at one end of a graded stick and a weight on the other. Everything was measured in catties, as it still is, not pounds; one catty equals 500 grams. After shopping at the street stalls we walked down the hill to Central Market, a place that both frightened and fascinated me. There was a mix of dead and live animals and a terrible, unforgettable, fresh meat smell. The cement floor of the market was always wet, so the stall-keepers walked on wooden clogs to keep their feet dry. Mum and I would pick our way past the hanging chickens (dead) and the jumping fish (very much alive) until we reached the pork man. From him, Mum purchased lean pork fillets to make stir-fries and butterfly pork chops that opened out so the bone could be easily removed. My brothers and I loved them. After the pork man we left the market and visited the dried food stalls a few streets away near the Communist-run department store called China Products. At the stalls we bought dehydrated mushrooms, scallops and little shrimps to flavour our meals. Mum would chat to the shopkeepers in Cantonese while I breathed in the pleasant but pungent aroma of dried dish and fungus. Finally, with our shopping almost done, we would trudge past the haberdashery stalls on Pottinger Street. This wasn't so much a street as a shallow stairway dating back to the nineteenth century, when sedan chairs were the only method of transportation between Central and the Mid-Levels, which were located higher up mountainous Hong Kong. The paving stones had been fashioned into a stairway so that the nimble feet of the rickshaw coolies could climb it more easily than a steep slope. These days the old ladder streets remain, but an 800-metre-long covered escalator stretching from Central to the Mid-Levels has replaced the fleet of sedan chairs. During morning rush-hour the escalator, built in 1993 and with sections so that it can be accessed at numerous points, moves downwards, taking wealthy Chinese and expatriates to work. In the afternoon it switches direction, returning them home. Long before the construction of the escalator, my mum and I took the tiny steps up Pottinger Street bound for Cochrane Street, where the China Tea Shop was located.

The tea shop and its smartly dressed merchants with their Brylcreemed hair and large spectacles scarcely changed over the years. They were always busy, and always polite. At the China Tea Shop you could find any type of tea except the stuff in tea-bags. (Mum always said that was the rubbish that was swept off the floor.) There were large jars crammed with specialty teas: diet teas, longevity teas, black, red and green teas. The more expensive varieties were moulded into pellets or patties and were usually out of reach on the upper shelves. Elsewhere, there were crates, barrels and tins, all full of tea, from different parts of China. I loved the smell of the tea shop, so fragrant and comforting. My mother was very particular about her tea and we always bought the same type: Lion Mountain Keemun Black Tea. Once the tea had been selected and weighed, it was placed in a brown paper bag, sealed and labelled. I liked carrying the square bricks of tea for Mum, and the old assistants, peering over their spectacles, would wave goodbye, making us feel like highly valued customers.

If it hadn't been for tea, my ancestors would never have travelled to the Far East. Or perhaps it would be more accurate to say that I owe my existence to tea and opium – for it was opium first and tea later that brought the British to China and eventually led to Britain's colonisation of Hong Kong.

Opium had been used for medicinal purposes in China since the Tang Dynasty (618–906), but when smoking opium became popular in the second half of the eighteenth century it grew into a national problem. The main supply came from India, and because of the British influence trade in the plant was dominated at first by the East India Company. China passed edicts against opium and in 1800 prohibited its importation, but the British smuggled it in regardless. From 5000 chests a year imported into China in the early 1800s, the trade grew to 40 000 chests by 1838–39. On the reverse side, the Chinese exported tea, which by the 1830s had become a nationwide addiction in Britain. The tea and opium trade drew adventurous Britons thousands of miles across the sea to the Orient. My ancestors were among them.

My great-great-grand-uncle Phineas Ryrie and my great-grandmother Josephine Ng Jo-shing, both on my mother's side of the family, are buried in the rambling colonial cemetery behind the Happy Valley racecourse in Hong Kong, together with hundreds of other colonial souls. Neither Phineas nor his two elder seafaring brothers, who also came to the China coast as tea-clipper captains, were involved in the opium trade. Phineas was born in Stornoway in the remote Scottish Hebrides, and came to Hong Kong in 1851 when he was twenty-one. He was a 'taipan' or big boss in the trading firm Turner and Company, and became a leading member of the Legislative Council. Phineas, who was large, eccentric and never gambled, was also the first chairman of the Hong Kong Jockey Club, founded in 1884. Phineas made Hong Kong his permanent home and became an extremely vociferous part of Hong Kong society, which was then completely dominated by the British. His frequent interjections during Legislative Council meetings earned him a place in the satirical magazine *China Punch* as a character called 'Funnyas Riley'.

Phineas' nephew, his sister Margaret's son, was Alexander Ryrie Greaves, my great-grandfather. Alexander was born in Lancaster, England, and moved East in the 1870s. He joined the prestigious trading firm Jardine Matheson and Company in Hong Kong as a tea-taster, and married a Chinese woman, Josephine Ng Jo-shing, who had come to Hong Kong from the Pearl River town of Zhongshan. The marriage didn't last, and when Alexander wanted to take their children back to Scotland, Josephine fought for custody and won. Josephine and Alexander's youngest of three surviving children was Cecil Keat Greaves. He married Elsie Mackenzie, the daughter of a Eurasian trader, and their fourth child was my mother, Bea.

As I mentioned in chapter 3, the Far East had also lured my paternal grandfather to its shores. Robert Rae Hutcheon was a marine engineer from Aberdeen who later took a job overseeing petroleum installations in China. In the 1920s when Shanghai was infamous as a city of sin and excess, home to thousands of foreigners and their legations, Robert met and married my grandmother, Ethel May, the daughter of an English military officer. In 1940, shortly before the outbreak of the Pacific war, the Hutcheon family left China, which was under attack from the Japanese, and decided it was safer to make the sea journey to Australia rather than attempt to sail for the United Kingdom. They landed in Sydney in January 1941. My father, Robin, returned to Hong Kong in 1953, aged twenty-five. There he met and married Bea Greaves.

The story of Hong Kong began very murkily with a war over opium or 'foreign mud', although from Britain's point of view, the real purpose of the Opium War (1839–1842) was to force the Chinese to engage in trade and diplomacy with the West. While there is no justification for the war, 'to say now that it was wrong,' Hong Kong scholar Solomon Bard points out, 'is not to appreciate the passage of history. The nineteenth century was a time of imperialism and colonialism. That was a fact.'

In the mid nineteenth century, China, with a population of 400 million people, was ruled by the last imperial dynasty of Qing emperors. Both Chinese and Western scholars agree that China, after achieving cultural and technological prowess in the previous dynasties, was inward-looking and in a state of decline by the Qing period. Chinese propaganda today boasts that the nation's 'four inventions' – the compass, gunpowder, paper and printing – transformed the world. But, ironically, gunpowder was unable to win any wars or concessions for its creators.

The 1839–42 Sino-British Opium War developed from a trade imbalance between Britain and China. The British East India Company purchased huge quantities of tea and silk from China during the nineteenth century, but the Chinese empire showed little inclination to purchase the cotton, wool and spices offered in return. Angered by the ever-increasing imbalance and the loss of its silver reserves to pay for the tea, the British government decided to use force to break down China's unwillingness to trade. The battering ram was opium, though what Britain really wanted was for China to buy its goods. Britain also wanted secure ports, governed by laws, from which its traders and ships could operate safely.

Arrogance was the reason behind China's refusal to trade. 'The

Chinese didn't call their country China,' says Hong Kong historian Dr Bard. 'To them it was the Middle Kingdom, the kingdom between heaven and earth; the Celestial Kingdom.' The famous quote by Emperor Qianlong (1736–1796) summed up China's mindset: 'The Celestial Empire possesses all things in prolific abundance and lacks no product within its borders, there is therefore no need to import manufactures of outside barbarians in exchange for our products.'

Despite imperial edicts banning the use of opium, the addictive habit had spread quickly in China. The emperor ordered Commissioner Lin Zexu to proceed to the south to physically destroy the trade. In Guangzhou, Commissioner Lin destroyed tonnes of the 'foreign mud' held in factories belonging to the British. The British responded with force, eventually defeating the once proud Celestial Kingdom, which, humiliated, was strongarmed into signing the first of three treaties. The Treaty of Nanjing invoked the establishment of five treaty ports – Guangzhou (Canton), Fuzhou, Xiamen (Amoy), Ningbo and Shanghai – which would be opened to foreign trade. Far more contentiously, the treaty ceded Hong Kong to the British.

Hong Kong had never been considered a prime piece of real estate by either Britain or China; Queen Victoria herself was less than impressed with the treaty outcome, as was her 'mortified and disappointed' foreign secretary, Lord Palmerston. The deal was done by Captain Charles Elliot, the British representative on the spot, following less than specific directions from Palmerston. Nonetheless, it brought wealth, opportunity and adventure to my ancestors and for me the chance to witness the final days in a chapter of history.

One hundred and fifty-six years later in July 1997, the sons of the Celestial Kingdom returned to take possession of the once muddy backwater which had been transformed into a wealthy economy, a millionaires' playground with the most expensive real estate in the world. In early 1997, the swimming pool at the British Forces Headquarters on Hong Kong's waterfront was said to have a land value of HK$1million (A$250 000) per square metre. On the eve of the Handover the 23 by 15-metre pool was worth around HK$350 million. For China, the Handover ended a 150-year period of 'national humiliation', the foreign occupation of Chinese soil. I joined the throngs of journalists covering Hong Kong's remaining years as a British colony. For me it was an extremely emotional event: I was watching my birthplace swap hands, not through independence, but through a change of sovereignty, and to an authoritarian one-party state at that. Today, Hong Kong is a shadow of its former self, plagued by downturns, bad government, a loss of direction and mysterious viruses.

My mother, Bea Greaves, arrived in Hong Kong at the age of nine in 1931. It had not been her choice to leave Shanghai; in fact, she thought she had boarded a boat to farewell her visiting Uncle Alf and Aunt Rose Greaves. Before she realised what was happening, the boat had set sail leaving the rest of her family in Shanghai. After her mother died when she was four, Bea had caught diphtheria, and the doctor persuaded her father that the warmer climate of the British colony might be better for her health. Keat Greaves' parting gift to his daughter Bea was a German-made Steiff teddy bear whose head twisted off to reveal a perfume bottle. Bea didn't return to Shanghai until she was an adult and though she wrote to her father frequently, she never saw him again.

In Hong Kong Bea lived with her aunt and uncle who, like my mum, were Eurasian. They lived in a big comfortable house opposite the Synagogue in Robinson Road on Hong Kong island, and Bea shared the rear part of the house with her blind Chinese grandmother. The grande dame of the house, Josephine Ng, recognised people by touching their faces. She had lost her sight following the advice of a quack doctor, who told her to bathe her eyes using water infused with a rusty nail.

In the 1930s Hong Kong was sparsely populated with low-rise colonial buildings hugging the foreshore while Victoria Peak rose dramatically in the background. Bea's school, Diocesan Girls School (DGS) in Kowloon, was where all the daughters of people with 'old' money went. She took the Star Ferry across the harbour and then a Kowloon Motor Bus right to the door of DGS, because the daughter of the bus company owner also went there.

Everybody lived in big houses in those days, because concubinage was still fairly common. In one house Bea and her friends found a secret room behind the wardrobe which tickled the young girls' imaginations. 'We used to say the Old Man would hide in there if he was caught!' she said.

Though there was a pecking order amongst wives and concubines, in Chinese families all lived in the same compound. However in Eurasian households, wives usually wouldn't consent to the arrangement and so the concubine, considered more of a mistress, was catered for in another home. 'Concubines were for life,' Bea recalls. 'They would be looked after with their own quarters, sedan chairs, cars and domestic helpers. My uncle had a concubine who lived on her own and he used to take me to visit her. I referred to her as Aunty and she was kind to me and often gave me money.' The concubine addressed my mother as a superior, calling her 'Honourable Miss Four' as my mother was the fourth child in her family.

In Hong Kong, having concubines was a sign of prosperity. Sometimes they came from brothels or were servants who'd earned the affection of their masters. It was an era when many marriages were arranged and women usually didn't work to support themselves. Securing a concubinage was a way to ensure a stable financial future. The practice wasn't outlawed until the early 1960s. Another somewhat feudalistic practice my mother recalls was the *mui tsai* set-up. A *mui tsai* (or young girl) was a slave girl, sold by her family because it was too poor to keep the youngest female child. My mother's aunt and uncle had a *mui tsai* called Ah Jun, who often played with Bea after she had finished the housework. In the end Ah Jun ran away after being frequently scolded by Aunt Rose Greaves. The *mui tsai* system was declared illegal in the 1950s after a 28-year battle instigated by Winston Churchill when he was Secretary of State for the Colonies in 1922.

When the Japanese invaded Hong Kong in December 1941, Bea's brother Stanley, who had fled the Japanese bombing of Shanghai in 1937, answered the call for able-bodied men to join the Volunteer Defence Corps. He died in a battle on the Lyemun Peninsula, one of the main access points to Hong Kong, six days before the fall of the colony on 18 December 1941. Stanley was just twenty-three years old. Bea's elder brother, John, had already migrated to Australia where he joined the Australian Imperial Force (AIF), fighting initially in Greece and later in the Middle East. Her sister Hilda, a staunch British supporter, chose to be interned in a Japanese camp for civilians in Hong Kong. Hilda always wanted to be considered Western, and civilians were not treated in the same harsh manner as prisoners of war. My mother escaped detention as she declared herself a 'third national', in other words, a Eurasian. For her, freedom was more important than her ethnicity. She was then a third-year university student and an auxiliary nurse.

To flee Hong Kong's brutal three-year occupation by the Japanese as well as the unwanted attentions of a Japanese business-man, Bea secured an exit permit, travelling to the Portuguese enclave of Macau, sitting on the open deck of a fishing junk which made the six-hour journey after nightfall. After spending the war years working as an auxiliary nurse in the British Consulate, looking after hundreds of émigré refugees, Bea returned to a very different Hong Kong. It was depopulated, destitute and eerily quiet, my mother recalls; the population had declined from 1.6 million to less than 600 000. As soon as the war was over, however, people who had fled to places like China and Macau because of the Japanese, started to return in what was the first postwar migration wave.

The 1949 Communist overthrow of the Nationalists in the civil war resulted in an exodus of mainland Chinese to Hong Kong, which created a base of workers that previously had been non-existent. As Hong Kong's prosperity grew the influx of refugees gathered pace year by year. Until 1981, the policy for mainland migrants was simple: anyone who touched base in Hong Kong was allowed to stay. While they adopted Hong Kong as their new home, their ambivalence toward the mainland made them even more determined to prosper. It's now estimated that nearly two-thirds of Hong Kong's 7 million people are descendants of post-1949 migrants.

Following her repatriation at the end of 1945, my mother, with the help of her journalist cousin Alec Greaves, became a court reporter on the *South China Morning Post*. She had learned shorthand in Macau, could type with two fingers and was fluent in English and Cantonese. One of her first assignments was to cover the war crimes trials against the Japanese. My father, Robin, meanwhile arrived in Hong Kong in 1953, after working as a reporter in Sydney and London. He was hired as a sub-editor on the *China Mail* (owned by the *South China Morning Post*) and on his arrival shared a flat with an eccentric colleague named Bill Smyly. Bill at one time kept as a pet a metre-high honey bear named Noodnik, and slept with the bear on the verandah every night. My dad enjoys telling the story of a stylishly dressed guest named Brenda who came to the flat one evening for dinner.

'On being asked whether she had met Noodnik, Brenda graciously extended a languid hand in the direction of the incoming guest. Her hand was grasped by a furry paw with two-inch-long extended claws, and the horror on her face when she set eyes on a one-metre-tall honey bear was unforgettable. That was Brenda's last visit to our house,' said Robin.

As Hong Kong continued its postwar recovery and the migrants continued to flood the colony, my parents met while working on the newspaper and were married in 1957.

'A steady trickle of refugees began crossing into Hong Kong

from China,' said Robin. 'They built huts and shacks on hillsides near the urban areas, many of them without access to water or sewage disposal. By 1953 these insalubrious shanty towns housed tens of thousands of people and Hong Kong faced a major crisis in trying to accommodate them.'

My mother recalls that the housing shortage signalled the end of Hong Kong's grand old houses with their sprawling gardens and servants' quarters. Owners were encouraged to redevelop, so up went high-rises and down came the magnificent mansions. With the influx of refugees came thousands of Chinese manufacturers and entrepreneurs, determined not to lose their life's earnings to Communism. The wealthier migrants put Hong Kong on the path to industrialisation while cheap labour continued to arrive in truck-loads by the day. The workshops produced mainly textiles, but also cheap toys and plastic flowers. Hong Kong became a magnates' breeding ground, a place where a man like Li Ka Shing could leave China with a polythene carry bag and a spare shirt. His education had been cut short by his father's death so he came to Hong Kong and worked in a factory. By the time he was twenty-two he owned his own plastics company and twenty years later controlled a global property empire.

Jimmy Lai was another former refugee who became a magnate. He founded the Giordano clothing group (Hong Kong's equivalent of Gap) and, later, the sensationalist newspaper, *Apple Daily*. The *Apple Daily* specialises in controversy, uncovering the seamier side of Hong Kong life and politics and is one of the top-selling news-papers in the territory. Unlike most of Hong Kong's entrepreneurs, Jimmy Lai is no friend of the present regime in China, even though it was the place of his birth. After the Tiananmen Massacre in 1989, he used his clothing company to print T-shirts for pro-democracy activists.

At his elegant home on The Peak, Jimmy Lai explained to me how he first heard of Hong Kong as a young boy. As he waited by a street in Guangdong province, a well-dressed man jumped off the back of a cart laden with bags and suitcases. The eleven-year-old Jimmy helped the man with his bags so the man tipped Jimmy with a chocolate bar. He had never tasted anything so good.

'What is it?' asked Jimmy.

'Chocolate,' said the man.

'Where are you from?' Jimmy asked him.

'Hong Kong.'

From that time the only thing in the young boy's mind was to get to Hong Kong. He eventually applied for a permit to travel to Macau, and from there he was smuggled in the bottom of a fishing boat into the colony. He began his career as an odd-job worker in a factory.

The colony's success, built on individuals like Li Ka Shing and Jimmy Lai, created a vibrancy that was unique to Hong Kong. On the mainland in the early 1960s, surviving often meant evading starvation or emerging intact after being 'exposed' by a family member. In Hong Kong thousands didn't simply survive, they became rich.

With China locked in its own political upheavals, Hong Kong consolidated its postwar growth under the laissez-faire business principles but firm foundations of British common law. Hong Kong's success in the 1960s ran absolutely counter to what was happening on the mainland: it was the exploitation of the working class by the industrial elite, and as in China today that created an ever-widening gap in living standards.

My earliest recollections of Hong Kong are a mixture of opulence and misery. Rising from the central business district is a dramatic mountain: Victoria Peak, or just The Peak. The lower section of the mountain, the Mid-Levels, was at that time dotted with apartment buildings, home to mainly foreigners and wealthy Chinese. This is where my family lived – my parents, Robin and Bea; brothers Stephen and Andrew; a large black dog named Huck; Ah Yi, a

Chinese amah or domestic helper, and me – in a block of flats on Bowen Road. At the top of the mountain were the homes of the extremely rich, both Chinese and foreigners, and Hong Kong government officials. Chinese people were only allowed to live on The Peak after the Pacific War. During the 1980s wealthy local Chinese began to buy up the more lavish properties on The Peak, for the dramatic view looking down on Hong Kong and across to the Nine Dragons (mountains) of Kowloon. I could never see the attraction of living in such an exalted location when for six months of the year extreme humidity put The Peak in fog and the interior walls of every home were damp to the touch.

I loved travelling in the car ferry to cross the harbour in the days before the tunnels were built, cutting the twenty-minute journey to four minutes. The sailors working for the Star Ferry and the Yaumati Ferry company wore blue and white outfits as sailors were supposed to, and there was usually a Popsy Man on board too. A popsy was an ice-lolly and Popsy Men belonging to the Dairy Farm Company hit the streets of Hong Kong on motorcycles mounted with refrigerated compartments. Choc-Frosts were my favourite. Throughout my childhood the same Popsy Man waited at the bottom of our driveway every afternoon. Years later he rode past me on a street and I impulsively shouted out, 'Popsy Man!' He turned and flashed a toothy grin at me, but by that stage I had grown out of Choc-Frosts.

In the 1960s downtown Hong Kong was just a few square kilometres in size and crammed with narrow streets and boxy cars. Back then there were few skyscrapers, the highest perhaps eight storeys tall. The downtown area was still filled with small-scale colonial architecture, a few statues and some grand public buildings like the glamorous General Post Office. The most eye-catching landmark was the old Hong Kong and Shanghai Banking Corporation at Number One Queen's Road, Central. Inside the banking hall, with its ornately tiled and artistically decorated dome, the tellers gave my brothers and me little red moneyboxes shaped just like the big bank. As a child I thought the building had been specially designed to resemble the piggy banks instead of the other way around.

On prime land in the centre of town across from a 1960s landmark, the Hilton Hotel, was Chater Gardens, formerly the grounds of the Hong Kong Cricket Club. On Saturday mornings the green cricket field was filled with dozens of children – both Chinese and expatriate – dressed in white shorts and T-shirts. We were part of Billy Tingle's Athletic Institute, a weekly supplement to the physical education pro-vided by schools attended by children of wealthier families. Billy Tingle was an Australian PE instructor who began life in prewar Shanghai where he taught boxing. His institute was a lot of fun until a little girl reached 'maturity'. Then we were no longer permitted to run flat races or roll around on the grass in obstacle or potato races. Mr Tingle was extremely conservative. He didn't consider it proper for 'ladies' to run around and get sweaty so at the age of ten we were forced indoors for square dancing, and Billy Tingle's lost its appeal.

That was the more privileged side of Hong Kong life. Just a few kilometres from the Hong Kong Club, on the south-western slopes where the mountains met the ocean's edge, teeming slums or squat-ter huts crammed the hillsides. On the Kowloon side, the squatter areas were even bigger and spread as far as the eye could see. This was Hong Kong's face of misery. I saw the huts every time we went out on the harbour or were taken by my parents to beaches on the south of the island. It wasn't until I became a reporter in the 1980s that I went into a squatter hut, onto a fishing boat and into the cage homes of the destitute elderly. Many people didn't associate Hong Kong with that kind of poverty.

The year I was born, 1962, became known as the Year of the Hungry Tiger. According to Chinese astrology it was the Year of the Tiger, but the refugee influx was so overwhelming – in one twenty-five day period 70 000 starving refugees from China flooded into Hong Kong – it became known as the Hungry Tiger. The calamity that caused so many to flee was Mao Zedong's Great Leap Forward, designed in 1958 to kick-start China's lagging industrial performance. The Communist Party mouthpiece, the *People's Daily*, first coined the famous phrase, calling on the population to reject conservative ideology to make way for 'a great leap forward on the production front'. Mao was so impressed with the slogan he suggested its inventor be awarded a PhD.

As the campaign went into full swing, output quotas were fixed higher and higher, in complete disregard of China's primitive technology and poor industrial foundation. This was the era of the 'backyard factories', when primitive iron foundries were set up to melt down scrap iron of all descriptions in an attempt to make steel. It was a complete failure. To compound problems, local officials were too afraid to contradict orders. And when they couldn't fulfil their quotas, they resorted to forging reports and lying. At about the same time the Great Leap Forward got under way, the first of a series of devastating famines struck the country.

The famines, the Great Leap Forward and the break-up of the Sino–Soviet friendship pushed China to the brink of economic collapse. Then, when he needed to change course to save the economy, Mao instead decided to launch another anti-rightist struggle. As mainland China became submerged in political and economic turmoil, it closed its rusting iron gates against the world, in much the same way as the Celestial Qing Empire had done against foreigners centuries before.

China's problems couldn't be isolated from Hong Kong by borders or fences. The ideological Great Proletarian Cultural Revolution spilled over into Hong Kong as an anti-establishment rebellion. It was, as the *New York Times* put it at the time, the collision between communism and capitalism that many had feared and believed would be Hong Kong's undoing. Would the Communists try to overrun Hong Kong? Would Britain's defence resources prove adequate? From 1966 to 1967 civil disorder reigned in the form of anti-British street protests, strikes, death threats and bombing campaigns, and made life in the colony a tense existence for both Chinese and expatriate.

The Maoists heaped scorn on the British as 'white-skinned pigs', Chinese who worked for them were 'yellow running dogs', and profiteering Communists were described as 'red fat cats'. From my family's apartment in the Mid-Levels, my brothers and I heard the protesters chanting slogans and the sound of tear gas being fired into the crowds. My father, by this time the assistant editor of the *South China Morning Post*, the main English language establishment newspaper, was working nights and was wakened each morning by a huge line of protesters marching up the hill to Government House to plaster it with anti-British slogans. He recalls they were led by a pro-Beijing Chinese newspaper proprietor who travelled up the hill in his air-conditioned Mercedes. Robin spent these months reporting the upheavals both in Hong Kong and across the border in China. The reports from China of leading officials paraded publicly wearing dunce's caps and big character posters denouncing their crimes were particularly alarming in Hong Kong.

'People in Hong Kong became increasingly apprehensive, not only because of the large Communist presence living in the territory but because we imported lots of our produce; one-third of our rice, most of our fruit and vegetables and almost all of our water from the mainland,' Robin said. 'If the increasingly xenophobic tone of the Cultural Revolution should turn against the British colony, its survival would be threatened.' So radical were the views of the Chinese authorities at that time that they even refused to accept a large order for carpets for a major Macau hotel because the carpets called for flamboyant imperial dragons in the design. Things imperial were completely frowned upon by the Communists, even at the expense of precious orders.

As a child, I heard a Chinese name mentioned frequently. I heard it as Mousey Tung, but of course it was Mao Zedong everyone spoke of. His vitriolic pronouncements and the power he wielded over thousands of hero-worshipping young Chinese who crammed Tiananmen Square waving their *Little Red Book* were discussed so fervidly in Hong Kong that I deduced he must be very important.

When I was given a gift of a toy mouse with pink fur, a wooden torso and black felt tail, I immediately named him Mousey Tung. Both Mao and Mousey disappeared sometime in the middle of the 1970s.

Meanwhile, big pro-Communist demonstrations rocked Hong Kong in 1966–67. The left-wing factions opposing the British administration were a coalition of trade unions and schools with many teenage children taking part in the frontline riots, braving tear gas and throwing stones and projectiles at the police. Communist newspapers hurled a barrage of invective and hatred against the government. The abuse was even broadcast through loudspeakers from the Bank of China building in Central, which the Hong Kong government tried to drown out with Chinese opera music played from a building behind the bank. The attitude of the majority of Chinese people was to stand behind the government, or at least take no action in support of the demonstrators. 'To have caved in to threats from China would have been to jeopardise all they had gained in escaping from the despised regime,' Robin said. The government forcefully put down the dissenters and by the end of 1967 the riots and bombings subsided.

In Hong Kong, the only contact I had with Communists was through China Products, Hong Kong's cheapest department store in the 1960s and 1970s. China Products, or the Commie Shop as the expatriate kids called it, was a no-frills store with a rather relaxed opening time of 11 am. In China Products, the shelves were stuffed with mass-produced mainland Chinese goods that were cheaper versions of Western products. They even stocked a copycat version of my favourite lollies, Maltesers. The red packaging was exactly the same except that the China Products version was called MyLikes. China Products service was brisk, often with the help of an overhead system of pulleys that transported cash to the register and delivered back change and a receipt. In 1986 in Beijing I went to the mainland equivalent, the Friendship Store, which took only foreign exchange certificates (like Monopoly money, and only used by foreigners), and I was shocked to find it dingy and so poorly stocked that goods were often spaced a foot apart. It was a very poor cousin to the 'Commie Shop' we had in Hong Kong.

Every morning I woke early enough to see my father's newspaper, the *South China Morning Post*, slide under the apartment door pronouncing the major news of the previous day. Television was still in its infancy, so it was bold newspaper headlines that made an impact on my mind: '6 Dead in Typhoon Rose'; 'Bruce Lee Dead'; 'I.I. [Illegal Immigrant] Survives Shark Attack'.

The story about the I.I. made a deep impression on me. He was swimming across the wide stretch of sea known as Mirs Bay, which separates Guangdong province from the part of British Hong Kong called the New Territories, when a shark bit off his leg. It wasn't the first time I'd heard of shark attacks in Hong Kong waters, but what struck me so much that I still think about it today was that he didn't *feel* his leg being bitten off by the shark and only realised it after seeing the water around him turn red and warm with blood. I never knew what happened to that young man but I often thought about him when I passed the one-legged shoeshine man outside the luxury Mandarin Hotel.

By the time I had finished studying journalism in Australia in the 1980s I returned to a very different Hong Kong. In line with soaring property prices, much higher skyscrapers now dwarfed our block of flats in Bowen Road so that we could barely see the magnificent harbour. Buses were air-conditioned and factories were disappearing. Hong Kong manufacturers had started to flood south China's Pearl River Delta to take advantage of cheaper manufacturing costs. Only higher end products such as electronics and fur coats continued to be produced in Hong Kong, though by that time it had evolved into the world's biggest container port.

As a radio reporter for Radio Television Hong Kong and then a television reporter and newsreader for Asia Television (ATV), I entered the world of journalism. My Cantonese improved exponentially after I joined ATV because the station only employed four English-speaking reporters and we were required to translate

154

stories reported by the Chinese channel. I found my early days as a television reporter completely exhilarating. The cameraman, Chinese reporter and I travelled around Hong Kong and the New Territories in a van with our logo on the side panel. It felt like being in an ambulance as we had two-way radio contact with our chief-of-staff, as well as being able to hear police radio. The only thing we didn't have was a siren. One moment we would be heading to a government news conference, the next we would be diverted to a squatter estate fire surrounded by sputtering wooden fixtures and exploding gas cylinders.

After a privileged and sheltered life, I finally saw how the under-privileged of Hong Kong lived and struggled. I covered everyday human tragedies: the plight of Hong Kong's boat-dwellers, a fisher-man delirious at the loss of his wife and three children after their rickety boat hit rough seas and sank. A mental patient at a halfway house located in a crowded housing estate ran amok with a knife at a kindergarten killing several children. A factory fire claimed more than twenty young men's lives after hazardous chemicals had been improperly stored and were then ignited by a discarded cigarette. I covered press conferences hosted by British Prime Minister Margaret Thatcher and a string of pompous British officials. They came to announce the creation of a new type of British nationality – British Nationals Overseas – so that more than five million Hong Kong people, unlike other former colonial subjects, wouldn't qual-ify for British passports assuring them residence in the United Kingdom. I also covered the influx of tens of thousands of Viet-namese boat people, for by the eighties refugees were not only pouring in from the mainland but from war-ravaged Vietnam.

Yet for all the excitement of being a new reporter in a world that was unfolding in her own backyard, the biggest preoccupation of the 1980s was Hong Kong's future. Through the 1842 Treaty of Nanjing, the island of Hong Kong had been ceded to Great Britain in perpetuity. However the much larger piece of land, the New Territories, which became part of Hong Kong at the end of the nineteenth century when the Western powers engaged in a so-called 'scramble for concessions' after China's defeat by Japan, was due to be returned after the expiry of a ninety-nine-year lease in 1997. The issue didn't come up for discussion between Britain and China until after Mao died in 1976, and by the early 1980s nervous businesspeople who wanted certainty over their leases helped kick-start talks between the two powers. To bolster confidence both locally and internationally, Hong Kong's currency was pegged to the US dollar at the rate of HK$7.8 to US$1.

By the time the terms of Hong Kong's handover had been agreed in the mid 1980s, the territory had risen in wealth and status to become China's main intermediary, handling about 40 per cent of the mainland's foreign trade. It had also become China's largest source of foreign investment, accounting for about half of China's foreign direct investment. In return, the mainland became the second largest source of inbound investment in Hong Kong and by 2000, Chinese companies had raised US$44 billion on the Hong Kong sharemarket. In the 1980s, more than 80 per cent of Hong Kong manufacturers established production facilities in China, due to rising costs in Hong Kong. One in six people were engaged in import and export trading.

When Chinese bureaucrats and businessmen began visiting the territory in the 1980s and 1990s, what they saw must have made their jaws drop. To see the turbo-powered launch boats or 'gin palaces' lining up at Queen's Pier on a Saturday afternoon for the weekly spin to the Clearwater Bay Golf and Country Club, a legalised gambling den called the 'stock market' and two luxurious racecourses, must have been like entering paradise.

Hong Kong people were truly different from mainland Chinese; they had been allowed to fulfil their human potential in a place that had established laws and regulations. Hong Kong wasn't a democracy; all the power was concentrated in the hands of a governor who was responsible to the British government. Yet the British government rarely exercised the full extent of its powers. In reality the inhabitants of Hong Kong enjoyed a high degree of individual freedom while the decision-making process was based on consultation with selected community leaders and a legislative council, which progressively became more representative and democratic.

I left Hong Kong at the start of 1989 and joined my parents in Sydney, where they had moved after my father's retirement. My brothers, too, were living in Sydney, having gone to boarding school there. I left because after covering the processes and committees deciding on Hong Kong's future, I felt the territory was going to substantially localise the media. After five years of reporting I felt ready for greater challenges, but the pool of jobs in English language television only seemed to get smaller. I decided then that if I worked overseas, I might be able to return to Hong Kong to report on the Handover for a foreign outlet and that became my professional goal. Six years later, I achieved it.

For all of Hong Kong's startling wealth, my barometer for the state of the territory was a simple roast meat shop in the busy Wanchai district. There, seven days a week behind a grimy glass counter, 53-year-old Shiu 'Fatty' Keung donned his plastic apron and hacked up ducks, crunchy roast pork and fillets of my favourite *char siew* or barbecued pork. Shiu Keung was a short, rotund man with a moon face often speckled with heat spots. He could appear quite fierce after treating his condition with gentian violet, which made the spots even more pronounced. Yet he always greeted the camera crew and me like long-lost friends when I began travelling regularly to Hong Kong in the mid 1990s after becoming the ABC's China correspondent. He was down-to-earth and never shy when talking in front of the camera, unlike thousands of his compatriots. The interview would always end with him vigorously shaking my hand. No trip to Hong Kong was ever complete without a plate of his barbecued pork on a bed of steaming rice, accompanied by a bowl of 'daily soup'. At Fatty's place, you could have your meal while discussing the finer points of finance and street philosophy.

Prior to the Handover, Fatty had done a roaring business, earning

HK$40 000 a month (A$10 000) and employing eleven staff. His small, no-nonsense shop, which seated about twenty people at a time, had been going strong for thirty years and was never short of customers. He served cheap but traditional Chinese fast food, much, much tastier than any Western equivalent. With just ten minutes to spare, a diner could sit down on a wobbly stool and share a table with a total stranger, relax, drink tea and have a satisfying local lunch.

After the Handover and even before the full effects of the Asian financial crisis had been felt in 1998 and 1999, Fatty's business, like the rest of Hong Kong's economy, took a turn for the worse. Fatty laid off four workers, convincing his son to return to work for him. His monthly earnings dropped to HK$15 000 (A$3750). He was only just breaking even. In October 1997, I returned to Hong Kong to report on one hundred days after the Handover. The new Special Administrative Region, as China called it, was in the grip of an unprecedented tourism slump. The crew, Sebastian Phua and Kate Wakeman, went off to film a tour run by the Hong Kong Tourist Association one Saturday morning while I wrote scripts. 'You won't believe this,' Kate said on returning. 'There was one guy on the tour bus, and he was a local resident.'

Week by week the news from Hong Kong got more depressing. 'Of course I'm happy that Hong Kong is now ruled again by Chinese,' a patriotic Fatty said during one of our discussions about the post-Handover environment. 'But times are very tough for the little people – compared with before, it's hard for them to make money so they cook at home and don't eat my food.'

The Asian financial crisis together with the post-Handover tourism slump hit Hong Kong hard. As if that wasn't bad enough the territory was struck by the avine or bird flu virus, taking chicken, duck and goose off the menu in every restaurant, including Fatty's, for several months. Apart from being a financial setback – the territory had to slaughter its entire flock of poultry – it was a psychological blow which continues to dog Hong Kong. Its poultry comes from Southern China, which can't assure a supply of untainted food, adding to the feeling of an ongoing decline.

Less than a week before the transition took place I began to feel a sense of numbness about the whole thing, although I knew returning Hong Kong to China was the right thing to do. In the few months before the Handover, the ABC's 'Foreign Correspondent' program had commissioned several stories about Hong Kong. One of them – originally my suggestion – concerned my upbringing in Hong Kong and my personal feelings about the Handover. I interviewed a childhood friend, a Eurasian named Lindzay Chan, who after leaving our secondary school, run by the English Schools Foundation, had become a dancer and actress and then moved into fashion design. Like most Hong Kong people, Lindzay's life was extremely frenetic, and between picking up her kids from an elite kindergarten, getting them to do their homework in the car between extracurricular activities and running her business, she summarised what I believe Hong Kong people are all about.

'Hong Kong people haven't really had an identity, they are very adaptable, they are very practical, and in the past it was a British colony, so they tried to adapt to the Western ways. And now that it's going back to China, things are going back the other way,' she said. I'm sure I'd thought that way when I was living in Hong Kong, but since I'd left the island and become 'Australianised' the sentiment now struck me as alien.

The end of an era – the last few days before the Handover – was strange and touching. It rained solidly before, during and after 1 July yet people braved the rainstorms to take photographs of the last vestiges of Empire: anything with the word 'royal', Her Majesty's red post boxes, the coat of arms outside the central government office building. The Empire was in vogue and I took photographs too. The old Kai-tak International Airport closed up shop much as the colony had done. Thousands of sentimental residents crammed the rooftops of Kowloon to watch the jets scream over them, almost close enough to touch, for the last time before the airport moved to its new location on Lantau Island. Finality was everywhere.

For the ABC's Handover coverage, we had hired two small windowless rooms within the BBC's massive studio facility located at the Academy for Performing Arts. I was to provide coverage for the news programs while producers, reporters and crews, editors and presenters arrived for other programs. There were 5000 international journalists present and the Hong Kong government and hotels exacted exorbitant fees from all of them. Although I had been involved in the planning of the ABC coverage, I still found it hard to believe that the closest I would get to the Handover ceremony – which took place in the Convention and Exhibition Centre a few hundred metres away – was through a 20-centimetre television monitor inside our windowless editing suite.

By the afternoon of 30 June, the rain was falling steadily so the chief producer cancelled plans for a live report into the main evening 7 pm news bulletin (5 pm Hong Kong time). I stood under a tarpaulin in my Chinese jacket, sweating profusely in the 100 per cent humidity while the rain sheeted down. It added to my feeling that the whole thing shouldn't be happening this way. Later, our Hong Kong-based producer, my former schoolmate Sally Round, joined me under the tarpaulin and offered consolation about the weather. I looked over to where the American networks had secured the best vantage points for their studios, at a cost of hundreds of thousands of dollars, and saw CBS's Dan Rather talking without autocue or notes to the camera. In a specially designed outdoor set, Dan was dressed in a crisp suit, had perfect make-up and was seemingly oblivious to the black rain.

'Look at that. No wonder he earns $16 million. He doesn't have a hair out of place,' I said as I pulled tissues from under my arms, placed there to stop sweat marks appearing on my silk jacket.

'That's because he has air-conditioning,' said Sally, pointing to the line of ducts aimed at Dan Rather's face. In an open-air studio like that, the air-conditioning bill alone would have paid my annual salary and superannuation.

The rain didn't stop for three days. It drummed sadly and steadily through the whole event, raining on everyone's parade – both the Chinese and British celebrations – without favour. Sebastian and Kate got used to being constantly soaked. Sebastian's camera gave up after yet another drenching on the morning of 1 July when he was out filming the arrival of the People's Liberation Army. At Government House an honour guard lowered the standard and presented it to a hunched Chris Patten, the last governor, his face dripping with rain and possibly tears.

Even squinting at my little TV in the booth, I found it difficult to contain my emotions. The British and Chinese sides had not been on particularly good terms. In the last few years, Chris Patten had attempted to quicken the pace of democratic elections to the Legislative Council, Hong Kong's law-making body. China promised to appoint an interim council and hold fresh elections in 1998. There were squabbles about the size of the PLA contingent to enter Hong Kong, fears about media freedom and the burgeoning problem of mainland migrants – since the closer economic integration between Hong Kong and China in the 1980s, Hong Kong citizens had married mainland residents. In theory, their children had the right to live in Hong Kong, but by the mid 1990s they were coming out of the woodwork and a method had to be devised to allow them to come in orderly numbers rather than a flood.

With his characteristic eloquence, Chris Patten uttered the most meaningful words of the occasion. He spoke of the British merchants who forced their opium upon China and accepted that 'from today's vantage point, at the end of the following century, none of us would wish or seek to condone'. Then he reminded China of its own upheavals over the years which had driven millions of Chinese to seek sanctuary in Hong Kong. 'Most of those who live in Hong Kong now do so because of events in our own century which would

161

today have few defenders . . . All that is a reminder that sometimes we should remember the past, the better to forget it.'

Because of the downpour, the midnight Handover ceremony took place indoors in the new and hurriedly completed Hong Kong Convention and Exhibition Centre on the Wanchai foreshore. The ceremony was stuffy and sterile. I wanted parades and Beefeaters, but all the audience got was a stiff march – reminiscent of goose-stepping – up the aisle. I felt that the end of 156 years of colonial rule deserved much better. As the Chinese and Hong Kong flags rose up the indoor flagpole, the sound of the wind machines that kept the flags taut filled the air. Then China began swearing in Hong Kong's new top officials. It seemed odd to hear Mandarin being used since the Cantonese – who make up the vast majority of Hong Kong's population – typically have a poor command of China's national language, preferring their own provincial dialect. Meanwhile, the rain stopped, providing a brief respite in time for the departure of the royal yacht, *Britannia*. My colleagues and I watched the Prince of Wales, Chris Patten, his wife, Lavender, and weeping daughters board the magnificent boat. We had a small television up on the roof with us so that we could see both the big picture as well as the detail. Then, slowly, Britain sailed out of the Fragrant Harbour for the final time.

Hong Kong's pro-democracy politicians – left out in the cold by Beijing's decision to institute a provisional legislation – appeared on the balcony of the Legislative Council Building in a show-stealing display of unity. The leader of the Democratic Party, Martin Lee, led the crowd in a chorus of shouts of 'Long live democracy! Fight for democracy!' Frontier Party member Emily Lau accompanied supporters in wrapping a yellow banner around the building. 'The yellow ribbon is a vow that we will return,' she told the crowd.

The next morning, 4000 People's Liberation Army soldiers arrived in a contingent by road, sea and air. Tanks and armoured cars rumbled across the same borders used by thousands of trucks and semitrailers each day in a booming cross-border trade. In the

New Territories, crowds lining the streets broke into applause as the new Hong Kong garrison stood on top of their vehicles, waving white-gloved hands in a ridiculously choreographed piece of propaganda and getting completely drenched. Those in Hong Kong who actually slept that night woke to an uncertain new world and the first currency shock of the Asian financial crisis. The 1997 bubble disappeared as quickly as the Handover champagne.

On the eve of the Handover, Hong Kong people feared that civil liberties, press freedom and the rule of law would be dismantled by China. Instead, the undoing of Hong Kong has been largely the post-Handover government's fault. The catchy phrases that were thrown about before the Handover, such as 'Hong Kong People Ruling Hong Kong' and Deng Xiaoping's creation, 'One Country Two Systems', have been proven lame. I remember an old television advertisement for a company making tennis paraphernalia. The message was, what would tennis be like if this brand didn't exist? To illustrate the point, the net disappeared, then the balls, the racquet and finally there was a woman in a tennis dress left standing on an empty court. The camera zoomed in on her dress as she pleaded, 'No, no!' before her dress was whisked away. Hong Kong reminds me of that ad, with all the good things rapidly disappearing.

Today, Hong Kong is in a state of economic turmoil and collective psychological depression. Since the Handover, property, once the pillar of the territory's economy, has seen prices plunge 65 per cent. Suicides are up, shares are down. Unemployment reached historic highs over 7.5 per cent, and in 2002 an estimated 20 000 people were expected to go bankrupt compared with 1400 in 1998. This bubble had its origins in the simple idea that because Hong Kong was a small place with a finite number of plots, land could only ever increase in value. This notion, together with the belief that a rising China would only improve Hong Kong's marketability, pushed property prices to levels that turned many of my friends into paper millionaires.

The symbol of Hong Kong's property demise was a luxury forty-room mansion on The Peak. Wong Kwan, the son of a poor southern

Chinese fishmonger, like thousands of others fled the horrors of the Cultural Revolution by swimming to Hong Kong in the 1970s. By the mid 1980s he had bought a rundown 'love' hotel (the kind that rents out rooms by the hour). By November 1996 his property company, the Oriental Pearl Group, had smashed the records by paying HK$540 million (A$135 million) for Genesis, an enormous, tacky mansion on Hong Kong's wealthy summit that was stuffed full of kitsch but had a magnificent view. Needless to say, after the property market collapse, the Oriental Pearl Group got into difficulties and slipped into receivership. Genesis went to a mainland Chinese billionaire in a fire sale for HK$230 million (A$57.5 million).

The unravelling of the property bubble went far beyond reducing the profits of Hong Kong's billionaires; it also wrought havoc for more than 200 000 middle-class residents, who, post-Handover, became known as the 'negative equity class'. Some unlucky investors, believing like the tycoons that property could never fail, ploughed life savings into apartments in the mid 1990s. After the property collapse, their precious homes were worth half of what they paid. Unable to sell, many of them will remain slaves to the mortgage for the rest of their lives.

'People are very depressed,' said Ian Perkin, chief economist for the Hong Kong General Chamber of Commerce. 'After thirty years of solid economic growth people were getting richer every year. Suddenly it comes to an end.'

Ian Perkin and many others in Hong Kong point the finger at the man at the helm of the Hong Kong government, Tung Chee-hwa. Like the last generation of Chinese leaders, Mr Tung is in his seventies, conservative and a former head of a traditional Chinese family business in the shipping industry. My mother recalls that Mr Tung's father was staunchly anti-Communist. However when the family company nearly went bankrupt in the late 1970s and was bailed out by a leading supporter of the Chinese government, the word was that the real price was Tung Chee-hwa's loyalty at a later stage.

Tung Chee-hwa isn't much of a people person; he's an awkward man in interviews – even when he chooses to give them, which is rare these days. He is not comfortable rubbing shoulders with the masses, something the last governor, Chris Patten, was fond of. Mr Tung governs Hong Kong by knee-jerk reactions to single events. For example, there's a tourism downturn; response: build a Disneyland in Hong Kong. Property prices are 65 per cent off their 1997 highs; response: halt land sales to support prices. The stock market tumbles; response: the government must buy shares. Yet Beijing trusts him because he is a patriot. Despite Mr Tung's initial promise to take the reins of Hong Kong for a single five-year term, he reneged on the undertaking and was 'elected' unopposed by 800 loyal-to-China stalwarts to serve as Chief Executive until 2007.

China's preferred form of election, both at home and in Hong Kong, is to gather a certain number of party faithful and to group them into an electoral college. The faithful must not have offered criticism in any form against Beijing. They must be respected community leaders, and usually wealthy business people. Every person in Hong Kong knows from the outset that the committee will select whichever candidate Beijing wants them to choose. As a result, a new climate has taken over Hong Kong, from the media through to charities: don't offend China in any way and, to be sure we don't offend, let's all second-guess what China wants us to do and be.

There are, however, a number of outspoken legislators who are elected directly by their constituents, and by 2004 half of the sixty legislators will be elected by the public. Emily Lau represents 1.6 million people in an electorate known as New Territories East. She's charismatic, feisty and a die-hard democrat, and for her sins she and others like her are banned from travelling to China. I asked to meet and interview her in her constituency, but somehow we ended up having lunch in the prestigious Hong Kong Club. I first knew Emily in the early 1980s when I was a young radio reporter and Emily, a seasoned television journalist, had Margaret Thatcher in a rage with her incisive questions about Britain's duty to the

Hong Kong people. As we ate a silver service lunch served by waiters in white and surrounded by very English oil paintings, Emily's
characteristic optimism was at work. Although the eight parties in
the Legislative Council represent very different philosophies, they
were learning about co-operation and how to form a coalition
against the government to achieve their varied aims.

'We can't just be the people who shout all the time,' said Emily.
'We have to seize the initiative.' Privately I got the feeling that the
days of having pro-democratic legislators are numbered. There is a
mechanism for elections in 2007 to be two-thirds elected. If that
doesn't happen then Hong Kong's dabble with democracy will be
over.

So far, Hong Kong post-Handover has been ruled by an aristocracy of money, to quote *Atlas Shrugged* author Ayn Rand, an
aristocracy consisting of a loose grouping of Hong Kong entrepreneurs, some of whom have made grand claims about their right
to be members of Hong Kong's 'shadow' government. The argument
wouldn't wash well in many countries, but some of Hong Kong's rich
believe that as they pay the bulk of taxation, they should also have
the greatest say in the conduct of political affairs. Sir Gordon Wu is
one of them. 'The trouble with Hong Kong would be because of the
inexperience of these 70 per cent of the people [who don't pay much
tax], they would vote in some radical people who would say, "We're
going to change the successful formula of Hong Kong,"' says the
property and construction magnate.

Sir Gordon's hair is grey and thinning, and he wears large, square-
shaped glasses. Although he is in his seventies, he is still passionate
about his work and about politics. I didn't agree with most of what he
said, but out of the magnates I approached, he was the only one who
agreed to be interviewed. (A faxed letter, requesting an interview
with the billionaire whom Hong Kong people call 'Superman', Li Ka
Shing, was responded to – in the negative – so quickly that I was still
standing at the fax machine.) Sir Gordon hadn't dispensed with
his British knighthood, unlike many of the more politically correct

Hong Kong identities. When the topic got around to democracy he told me he'd donated money to Princeton University in the United States, where a graduation hall bears his name. He named one of his sons after Jefferson to demonstrate his love of democracy. And yet, if Hong Kong had a one-person one-vote system, Sir Gordon could foresee nothing but anarchy. 'It certainly would change Hong Kong dramatically,' he said. 'Now suppose I am going [to stand] for elections, you know my tactics would be very simple: get elected at any cost. So I'll go and say, "Vote for me, I'll guarantee you free lunch, free dinner and free breakfast. And what else do you want? I'll give it to you – after all, it's not my money."'

Sir Gordon's office is on the top floor of Hong Kong's first circular office tower, Hopewell House, named after his firm Hopewell Holdings. In the comfortable, old-fashioned room stuffed with maps, plans, books and a worn leather lounge, the magnate works to the strains of Mahler while overlooking the city of skyscrapers. Sir Gordon's view is typical of the aristocracy of money: detached from street life but believing through wealth alone it has the right to rule.

Reflecting a diametrically opposed ambition, Christine Loh resigned after eight years as a legislator in 2000 and set herself up as the head of a community organisation called Civic Exchange. Christine had a British education, both in Hong Kong and the UK, and trained as a lawyer. She never practised, however, instead becoming a commodities trader before her skill and easy-going nature turned her in the direction of politics. As an elected legislator, her charisma and persuasiveness allowed her to tap into many ordinary public concerns ranging from rights and freedoms to Hong Kong's deteriorating environment. I always enjoyed interviewing Christine and was impressed when on one occasion we did some filming in a market and the faces of the stallkeepers lit up when they saw her. They felt she was speaking on their behalf. She is a tough, no-nonsense woman who, though attractive, has a slightly bookish appearance with short hair and round, severe-looking spectacles. While she can often come across as intense, with Christine you feel that you are in the presence of a humanist.

'In some sense, we are still the Third World,' she said as we stood in a pavilion overlooking a dramatic postcard vista of Hong Kong. Christine is a vocal environmentalist, and with environmental problems literally laid out before us we discussed more generally how the territory was slipping backwards. The harbour was polluted and in danger of shrinking because of reclamation plans. Air quality had declined and the food supply was also threatened as a result of the bird flu virus.

'I think the real difference between the First World and Third World isn't what you look like, isn't about how much money you have. It's really about human development: do you understand the consequences of your actions?' Christine fears that policies benefitting people overall are being trampled on by the wishes of Hong Kong's wealthy elite. As a result, their decisions seem to revolve around turning Hong Kong into an economic machine with no real concern for the lives of the individuals living there. 'The executive authorities here seem to listen to business more than everyone else. He [Hong Kong Chief Executive C.H. Tung] really has very little appetite, it seems, for building a new relationship with the people who have the people's mandate,' Christine said shortly before resigning as a legislator. 'Mr Tung doesn't seem to be able to get rid of the perception that the government favours certain businessmen. Now, I don't know whether he's deliberately favouring them, but that is the public perception. Politics is perception, people do not trust him.'

Christine was referring to the government's 1999 bid to spearhead a drive to become the Asian leader of the New Economy. The government signed a multi-billion-dollar deal to build a high-tech complex with luxury apartments in a development called Cyberport. But this was no ordinary deal. The usual land auction process was dispensed with and a multi-million-dollar piece of Hong Kong's disappearing waterfront was handed to Cyberport's developers. The company is Hong Kong's leading internet and telecom player, Pacific

Century CyberWorks, or PCCW, whose founder is Richard Li, son of billionaire 'Superman' Li Ka Shing.

'I thought Cyberport was the dumbest decision they could have made,' said Christine. 'Even if they couldn't actually have held a tender to avoid these allegations, I still don't know why they did it the way they did.'

Three years after the dotcom crash, Cyberport is searching for tenants to fill its high-tech galleries and Richard Li has taken a backseat, allowing PCCW to revert to its traditional role as a telecom provider after a prolonged sharemarket sell-off saw its valuation plunge from US$35 billion to around half a billion.

As the Chief Executive Officer of Civic Exchange, Christine Loh has turned her attention to Hong Kong's most pressing problem of late: a controversial government proposal to introduce subversion laws to the territory. Article 23 of Hong Kong's Basic Law requires the region to legislate to prohibit acts of treason, secession, subversion, sedition, theft of state secrets and links between local and foreign political organisations. Opponents of the proposal argue that there are existing laws covering these areas. Supporters of Article 23, mainly pro-Beijing individuals, say Hong Kong must bring its laws into line with the mainland.

These powerful laws have spooked journalists, human rights activists, lawyers, academics and even business leaders, who fear that the exchange of financial information may be targeted, obstructing the free flow of information vital to the business world. Even politicians in the European parliament and in the US have spoken out against them. 'The HKSAR Government's strategy on Article 23 seems to be to grit its teeth, generate semblance of support, and get new laws passed as soon as possible [by July 2003],' Christine said. 'It knows it has enough votes to get through the legislature. There is now an effort to round up the "united front" troops to show public support.'

For a dose of reality I accompanied social worker Sze Lai Shan of the Society for Community Organisations to the rooftop tenement buildings of Shamshuipo, home to Hong Kong's post-1997 immigration wave. Unlike those who arrived after World War II and during the Cultural Revolution, today's migrants are made up almost entirely of family reunion applicants – hundreds of thousands of Hong Kong men chose to marry across the boundary in China, and though their wives and children have the right to live in Hong Kong by virtue of being married to citizens, the One Way Permit system, which is open to corruption on the Chinese side of the boundary, controls the numbers allowed daily into Hong Kong. Since 1995, 155 mainlanders are allowed to 'emigrate' to Hong Kong every day; a total of around 56 000 new migrants each year. 'Madness' was how Mike Rowse, a British official in charge of encouraging foreign investment in Hong Kong, put it. Under the One Way Permit mechanism the government had no control over which immigrants could live in Hong Kong. Mr Rowse warned that the flow of low-skilled arrivals was contributing to Hong Kong's high jobless rate and putting a strain on education and welfare resources. Unlike the 1950s and 1960s, in the new millennium there are very few blue-collar jobs available for them.

Sze Lai Shan is a mainlander who came to Hong Kong at the age of fifteen. She has a gentle manner and understands the hardships confronting the new migrants. She guides me into the entrance of a rundown building, lit by a single naked bulb. We pass a set of mailboxes and continue up a dark concrete stairwell. There is no lift. We walk up eight storeys and then through a rusty gate onto the roof. Instead of emerging into the open, we step into a rooftop slum. I soon discover there are broken dreams either side of me. The Tsui family, though, are relatively well off. They have an air-conditioner.

Mrs Tsui has been living in her air-conditioned rooftop room for three years. Her husband, a construction worker who isn't at home, hasn't worked much in the last few months. The Tsui home is about 6 metres by 4 metres in size, crammed with three beds, drawers, wardrobe and a desk with a computer on it. The two boys, busy playing computer games, still attend school. Mrs Tsui had to leave her adopted daughter in the care of her parents in rural Guangdong and it upsets her to think about it. From a drawer, she takes out a photograph showing the whole family, including the sweet-faced nine-year-old girl, smiling in front of a studio backdrop of the Sydney Harbour Bridge.

'I never realised it was going to be so difficult in Hong Kong,' says Mrs Tsui. In 1997 when she and her husband decided to come to Hong Kong, they owned a house on the mainland which Mrs Tsui says 'was a five-star hotel' compared to the hovel they are now living in. They are in Hong Kong to give the teenage boys a better education and better career opportunities. 'Before, when we were in Guangdong, we saw people bringing back money from Hong Kong and building big houses. We thought we could make our fortune, but for the last three or four years business hasn't been easy,' she says sadly. 'Our bathroom was bigger than this room.'

Anyone familiar with the pre-Handover vibrancy of the city cannot help but be depressed by the continuing deterioration of the Special Administration Region's standard of living. Now, residents nervously anticipate a devaluation of the dollar because although it's currently pegged to the US currency at the rate of HK$7.8 to US$1, everyone knows that it is overvalued, its real value being closer to HK$10 or HK$12. Hong Kong is now something of a fool's paradise, and perhaps when that is accepted, the pizzazz that once fired its economy and the legendary get-up-and-go of the Hong Kong people might return. Under the terms of the 1984 Joint Declaration, Hong Kong was supposed to remain autonomous from China for fifty years. How ridiculous that now seems. It took just a few years for the reality to sink in that the former jewel in the British crown was always going to be reduced to just another Chinese city.

RENEGADE DUMPLINGS

On the internet recently, I found the following exchange: 'Why is China so silly about Taiwan? Is it greed or just the need for power or childish stubbornness? I can't seem to tell . . . time has come for China to grow up, let it [Taiwan] go, and move on to its own issues.'

'I am sorry that you don't understand what Chinese people think,' replied the mainland Chinese writer. 'Unification is important for this wounded country. It has root in our Chinese culture. We value so much about the get-together of a family. Taiwan is also part of our family. If we lose it, we will be heart broken. Almost everyone in mainland strongly surports [*sic*] Taiwan's coming back. If the government let Taiwan go away, the people will not agree.'

The Chinese response reflects the standard mainland view, that Taiwan is an indisputable part of China and unification is an unwavering goal. Like any good parent, China hopes the family will eventually be brought back together despite the difficulties. In an attempt to demonstrate the strength of the bond, several years ago former President Jiang Zemin told American interviewer Jim Lehrer that a delegation of 700 Taiwanese had once visited the mainland and the second name on the list of delegates was a former middle school classmate of the President. Mr Jiang said he instantly recognised the name. In his view, that was proof of the bond. The problem is the majority of Taiwanese don't share the affection.

Official Taiwanese history rejects the mainland claim that the island has long been under Chinese sovereignty. Taiwan, or *Ilha Formosa* (which means 'beautiful island', a remark made by a Portuguese sea captain in the early sixteenth century), was originally settled by people of Malay–Polynesian descent. In the seventeenth century it was a Dutch colony before being governed by China for 200 years. Then it was ceded to Japan in perpetuity after China was crushed in war in 1895. Japanese rule continued until its own defeat came in World War II in 1945. Yet while the island doesn't acknowledge Chinese sovereignty, with the exception of guest workers and half a million aborigines, Taiwan's largest ethnic group is Han Chinese, the predominant race on the mainland.

China's other problem child is Tibet. For long periods of history Tibet sat on the edge of imperial China and wasn't ruled by Chinese at all. However, Tibetans long sought the approval of the Chinese emperors, and later officials, in the choice of its spiritual leaders. Whatever history says, and it depends on whose version you believe, the vast majority of Taiwanese and Tibetans consider themselves to be independent of China.

'If you want to make friends with someone you can't bash the person and say, "Be my friend,"' observes Tenzin Choegyal, the Dalai Lama's younger brother. Yet China finds it difficult to 'love' without aggressive control. Though both regions – Taiwan and Tibet – have distinct characteristics that arguably put them outside the Chinese fold, despite half a century of turmoil China's obstinate desire to control them stands firm.

On a map, the island of Taiwan appears as a lone dumpling, floating off the coast of the motherland. This renegade dumpling, though compact in size, has a long list of achievements: a democratically elected government; a critical, vibrant media; an educated, hard-working population, and fantastic food. Despite this it suffers the international indignity of being 'the other China', shunned by the world community through a pact enforced by Beijing called the One China Policy. Taiwan's former ruling party, the Kuomintang (or Nationalists), claimed to be the true leaders of the whole of the mainland, but dropped the assertion in 1999. The mainland, however, has never relinquished *its* claim that it is the government of all of China – including Taiwan. Chinese school children are taught that Taiwan is like an absent family member who would return to the fold either with or without force. Until the 1980s Taiwanese school children were told that Mao Zedong stole China from Chiang Kai-shek and that the ousted Chinese living in Taiwan will one day go back and reclaim their property. These days the bit about going back has been dropped.

In 1949, four years after Taiwan reverted to Chinese rule, the Communist Party defeated the ruling Nationalists and their vanquished leader, Generalissimo Chiang Kai-shek, retreated to Taiwan. He took with him 800 000 followers as well as the nation's gold reserves and shiploads of treasures from the Forbidden City. Before mainland China could resolve the issue, in the 1950s it got caught up in the Korean War and its own ideological turmoil with the Cultural Revolution. Taiwan went its own way, establishing in the 1980s the seeds of a democracy, culminating in the first direct presidential election in 1996. By the second presidential poll in 2000, which brought Chen Shui-bian to power, the ruling Nationalist Party's 55-year hold on Taiwanese politics had finally been severed.

Though Taiwan's conversion to democracy is widely viewed as a success, since it lost the China seat at the United Nations to Beijing in 1971 its international status has been in free fall. Beijing insists that each of the more than 160 countries it has diplomatic ties with must acknowledge mainland China as the one and only China. Consequently, while Taiwan trades with every corner of the world, only twenty-seven countries, mainly Latin American, recognise it in preference to Beijing. In recent years Beijing and Taiwan have vied for diplomatic recognition from small nations by promising handsome aid packages, but not a single major power acknowledges Taiwan as an independent country.

The Chinese government, despite the enormous success it has

achieved, saves its outdated Communist rhetoric for the renegade province, complete with vitriolic asides about a 'so-called' president and 'sham' elections. Taiwan is even included on daily weather reports on state television, though curiously it is never mentioned on the airport departure board. There are no direct flights between the two territories, and there is no direct mail or even trade between the island and the mainland, on the insistence of the Taiwanese government. In 2001, a small step was taken to partially open links, with direct shipping restored between the Taiwanese islands of Quemoy and Matsu just off the Chinese coast, but everything else goes through a third party, usually Hong Kong. China uses every means to deride the 'no links' policy. In May 2002 a Taiwanese airliner carrying businesspeople bound for Hong Kong en route to China crashed, killing 206 people. The Chinese media unleashed an invective, lambasting the island government for contributing to 206 needless deaths due to 'political reasons'. The idea behind the broadside was that if Taiwan had allowed flights to travel directly to the mainland, the accident might never have happened. Despite the hurdles of cross-Strait travel, Taiwanese businesses are estimated to have pumped more than US$100 billion into mainland investments.

My first glimpse of Taiwan came when I was a high school student in Hong Kong. In 1979 visiting the mainland was out of the question for a pack of colonial schoolkids, but one of the teachers proposed a novel day trip that made me realise just how close we lived to a very complicated situation. The school organised an excursion to Taipei, the Taiwanese capital, just an hour's flight from Hong Kong.

Soon after touching down at Chiang Kai-shek Airport, I could see Taiwan was nothing like the China that was always in the news, but it was nothing like Hong Kong either. My classmates and I posed for photos beside the stone lions at the gate of the ornate Grand Hotel, and went for a hasty trip around the National Palace Museum which holds nearly a million antiquities, the largest collection of Chinese artefacts in the world, most of them removed from the Forbidden City in Beijing. In the 1930s, when it appeared that war with the Japanese was likely, the idea of having the entire Forbidden City collection fall into enemy hands became one of the Nationalist government's greatest preoccupations. The antiques were packed and transported by train to the southern city of Nanjing. They were shuttled to Shanghai and back to Nanjing, then taken to several parts of the country, even spending part of the war on a boat moored in the Yangtze River. When the Communist army began marching southwards in 1949, the Nationalists shipped the collection out to Taiwan, leaving behind 700 cases of treasures in their haste.

The Taipei daytrip was also memorable for a fabulous 'Mongolian' barbecue lunch followed by a shopping expedition for pirated records. Our tour guide took us to a street where a pirated vinyl record sold for a single Hong Kong dollar (less than twenty-five Australian cents). Not that Hong Kong was free of pirated goods then, but nothing could be bought as cheaply. My classmates and I bought the latest Bee Gees, Olivia Newton-John and Eagles recordings – I think I had at least twenty LPs in my bag, and without a second thought brought them through Hong Kong Customs. Ironically the centre of the counterfeit trade seems to have moved to the mainland now, but the day trip to Taipei made an excellent impression on me. Today, I still enjoy Taipei for its wonderful food and its intelligent, open and friendly people. Sadly, though, Taipei's environment leaves much to be desired. Attempts to add some greenery to the city have largely failed, and although it has plenty of monuments, few have an air of belonging to an old civilisation. Like many Asian cities there is a shortage of space and too many uninspiring buildings and flyovers. I find the most energetic part of the country is outside of the capital, where religious and street life flourish. Unlike China, where the Communist dislike of religion as a feudal practice has a restraining influence on popular religions today, in Taiwan popular religion is unfettered. On auspicious days the temples, particularly those dedicated to Taoist gods, become pulsating and chaotic. Joss sticks, fireworks, incense, musicians and devotees mingle together, spilling out onto the street. While in recent years Chinese officials have tried to shift indoors many outdoor activities they regard as unsightly – shopping, cooking and haircutting among them – the Taiwanese delight in taking their activities outdoors, from cleaning fish to washing clothes.

Often a sign of a vibrant society is its diversity of food and on Taiwan I discovered a food heaven, a place where cooking is on a completely different level to what it is on mainland China. There are all the usual regional Chinese cuisines such as Szechuan, Chiu Chow, Cantonese and Shanghainese, but there are also restaurants specialising in imperial dishes, food that the emperors would have eaten. There were snake meat and mushroom soups, made to warm the body, sweet lotus root dipped in fine batter and delicate noodles pulled apart by the master noodlemaker, topped with flavoursome pork.

My favourite restaurant was a humble dumpling shop which made the most succulent, delicious dumplings I've ever tasted. Though dumplings are a mainland invention, in this restaurant dozens of deft workers chopped, wrapped and steamed baskets full of the bite-sized delicacies, surpassing anything I've tasted in China. The restaurant did an exceptionally tasty version of my favourite dumpling, the *xiaolong bao*. Not only was the pork inside the dumpling particularly succulent, but the skin was exquisite, not too thick, not too thin. There were also vegetable dumplings shaped like an open clam, shrimp dumplings with sweet shrimp meat that melted in my mouth, and the dependable pot-stickers, tasty fried dumplings filled with pork and spring onion. I finished off with a bowl of silken wonton.

The manager, Mr Yang, is a second-generation mainlander whose father, a Nationalist sympathiser, founded the Shanghai-style dumpling restaurant in Taiwan. The eating house became so successful, with the average wait for a table around twenty minutes, that the Yangs decided to export the idea back to Shanghai. Despite the lure of a rapidly rising middle class keen to sample novelties such as delicate Taiwanese-made Shanghai dumplings, Mr Yang believes that China lags far behind Taiwan. 'People over there have a hard life,' he said, motioning for the waitress to bring yet another variety of dumplings to the table. 'When I go to Shanghai on vacation and visit my hometown in Shanxi, people seem to have a very rough life. They have no spare income left over and the social environment isn't good either; there are robberies and murders. It's all pretty bad.'

Unlike mainlanders who, because of visa restrictions, rarely visit Taiwan, many Taiwanese have had the opportunity to take a good look at what they've missed out on. The vast majority aren't sorry. From Taiwan's point of view, closer economic integration is not matched by a desire to reunify, a recent poll finding that 75 per cent of Taiwanese would be willing to defend the island if China attacked.

'I think the issue of Taiwan returning to China should be resolved slowly,' Mr Yang says. 'The difference between the two places is still too big. The political situation is also very different. We're democratic over here and they're not at all on the mainland. So we're completely different. I'd say, give it another ten or twenty years. Maybe that will be a better time.'

Though I wasn't aware of it at the time, my school day trip to Taipei took place during a tense period with Western embassies deserting the island in favour of the People's Republic. Among the deserters, Taiwan's biggest ally, the United States, was preparing to withdraw prior to the signing of the Taiwan Relations Act. The US legislation declared, ambiguously, that attempts to solve Taiwan's political future by anything other than peaceful means would result in US intervention. In the next ten years, however, the island's astounding political transformation lessened the likelihood of Taiwan invading China, although it increased the prospects of the reverse occurring. Taiwan's leader, Chiang Ching-kuo, the son of the Nationalist Generalissimo Chiang Kai-shek, who died in 1975, allowed the formation of Taiwan's first opposition party, the Democratic Progressive Party, and the publication of new newspapers. He also lifted martial law, which had been in place for almost a decade, giving military and intelligence agencies a role in perpetuating authoritarianism and extending control over citizens, and paved the way for Taiwanese to visit their relatives on the mainland.

During Taiwan's first direct presidential elections in 1996, I watched war clouds gathering in Beijing as the PLA test-fired missiles into the Taiwan Strait, close to the Taiwanese ports of Keelung and Kaohsiung. The Chinese military tests continued right up to polling day. Despite the fist-shaking, Beijing's nemesis, incumbent President Lee Teng-hui, won the vote, in a sign that the Taiwanese refused to be cowed by Beijing's military strength. Four years later in 2000, the ABC sent me across to Taipei to cover the second direct presidential elections. Just days out from the poll, Premier Zhu Rongji issued a stern warning at the news conference that marked the end of a 2000 National People's Congress meeting. His finger-wagging warning was broadcast live all over China, and naturally in Taiwan. Seeing it from the more vulnerable side of the Strait, it was somewhat chilling. 'Do not just act on impulse at this juncture,' Zhu Rongji cautioned Taiwanese voters, which was televised from a massive video wall near the Taipei railway station. 'Otherwise I'm afraid you won't get another opportunity to regret . . . Chinese people will sacrifice their lives and use all their blood to defend China's sovereignty and dignity.' In the convoluted language used by Chinese leaders he was telling voters not to choose the pro-independence candidate, Chen Shui-bian, or they could be blown to pieces.

Twenty-three million Taiwanese heard the warning and ignored it, voting for Chen, the most controversial candidate of them all. Thirty-nine per cent, enough to win a majority, chose charismatic lawyer Chen from the Democratic Progressive Party, which in the past had supported Taiwanese independence. This time round, Chen Shui-bian was taking a softly-softly approach: advocating closer economic ties but keeping the subject of independence safely on the backburner.

After the staid, intensely boring theatre of mainland politics, covering a Taiwanese election was like being struck with a bolt of electricity. It was loud, energetic and colourful and like nothing I had witnessed in Western politics. A typical rally usually began with a parade through the streets with the politician in one of the lead vehicles, followed by a convoy of cars and motorcycles, all painted or decorated in party colours. I short-sightedly chose to cover a KMT (or Nationalist Party) rally in the city of Kaohsiung, which was attended by only 100 000 people as opposed to the Democratic Progressive Party event, which had triple the number. Most of the supporters were from the grassroots and were probably paid in some way to attend, but that didn't stop them bringing the entire family and lapping up the Mando-pop singers and free junk food. Millions of dollars went into preparing street floats that snaked around the cities until they reached a stadium or giant square where the flotillas dissolved into an enormous party. There were speeches, pop singers, fireworks, food and the obligatory party campaign paraphernalia. As the ruling and richest party, the KMT had the most sophisticated handouts, from T-shirts to mugs to umbrellas. Unlike China, where foreign journalists and crews were tightly controlled and given the worst viewing positions at official events, in Taiwan the foreign media were treated like royalty. During rallies, residents would often make room for us, shouting, 'Let the foreign media through!' It was all a very new experience.

The rallies took place come rain or shine, which was lucky because it rains a lot in Taiwan. The rain arrives suddenly and politicians and citizens alike reach for the handy disposable raincoats handed out by the thousands. It was always a good idea to take two or three, because of the unpredictability of the weather.

When the presidential polls closed on Saturday, 18 March 2000, I watched the vote count with cameraman Sebastian Phua and bureau producer Cleo Leung in a high-tech hall. When it became clear that the Democratic Progressive Party candidate Chen Shui-bian was on his way to victory, we jumped into a taxi and headed for the DPP headquarters in downtown Taipei. On the street, the groundswell of emotion began to build as the final tally emerged. People began pouring out of apartment buildings, cheering and blowing plastic whistles. It was deafening, and highly emotional. I wondered whether such an event could ever happen in China. Taiwan had peacefully and democratically overturned fifty-five years of Nationalist Party domination by selecting the DPP team of Chen and Annette Lu, Taiwan's first female vice-president. The neighbourhood near the DPP headquarters erupted into a carnival with fireworks and blaring music. The celebrations were so loud that I got separated from Sebastian and Cleo and we couldn't hear ourselves talk over our mobile telephones. All over the island, thousands flooded onto the streets, waving Taiwanese flags and Chen Shui-bian dolls and paraphernalia. One family near me in the crowd had taken their wheelchair-bound son onto the street so that he, too, could absorb the euphoria and pride.

As I stood amid the revellers that night, filing my radio reports, I wondered how China's leaders would view the scenes or indeed whether they could comprehend the feelings of pride and freedom that spilled out in their renegade province. 'Tell China they should not bully us,' said one young man, speaking defiantly in English to Sebastian's camera. Did he worry about a Chinese invasion because of the result? I asked. 'Let them try [to attack]. They can't defeat the spirit of the Taiwanese people,' he replied.

Of all the people we spoke to that evening, not one feared the repercussions of a vote that flew in the face of Premier Zhu's dire warning. Many viewed the election as marking Taiwan's de facto independence. It must be extremely disappointing for the Taiwanese to be so proud of their achievements yet gain very little diplomatic recognition for them. I found it refreshing talking to people who felt free enough to criticise their government, rampant corruption and the Communist Party across the sea. In China, critical views could only be aired in private to select people. Many mainland Chinese also have a sense of powerlessness because of the lack of accountability in the Chinese government.

Because of his humble roots, the man chosen as president fired the imagination and compassion of the Taiwanese. Chen Shui-bian had been born into a poor farming family that had struggled to school him. Nonetheless he went to law school, became a supporter of the nascent democracy movement in the 1980s and eventually became the Mayor of Taipei and a DPP politician.

Television producer Wang Ben-hu, a passionate supporter of Taiwan's independence movement, decided to make a television series about the rise of Chen Shui-bian, but to make it even more appealing than the story of a poor boy made good, he turned it into a love story, *Ah Bian and Ah Jen* – the name of the president and his wife. 'Under the KMT [Nationalist] leadership, political figures were often mythologised, just like in the PRC [mainland China] with Communist leaders; they turn all their leaders into icons. This is a person who had a very poor social background who rises to success. By turning it into a love story it has real emotional impact with the Taiwanese people,' said the ebullient producer.

The series was filmed on location in the rural south of the island, close to the village where Chen Shui-bian grew up. Mr Wang told me that the villagers hadn't charged him for taking over their farmhouses because they were strong supporters of a president who was like a son to them. 'Chen Shui-bian winning the presidency was the happiest moment ever for me,' said a gentle, tiny old man, who had lived in the village from the day he was born. 'We all voted for him.' His wife was equally excited that their house was going to be on television. They spoke only Taiwanese, no Mandarin, so Mr Wang, the producer, translated for me. I asked whether they considered themselves Chinese or Taiwanese. 'My family has lived in these parts for nearly 300 years!' the woman said. 'Of course I'm Taiwanese.'

During a break in filming, Mr Wang took me for a walk around the narrow country lanes, only just wide enough for a car. Beside the roads were beautifully manicured rice-fields, lush from the rain that fell at regular intervals. In marked contrast to the Chinese countryside, rural Taiwan was tidy and well-off, despite the age of the farmhouses. They were like two different worlds. Why, I asked Mr Wang, couldn't the Chinese leadership accept this? 'The Chinese are stuck in the way of thinking of the emperors and dynasties established over 5000 years ago,' he replied. 'Beijing's leaders don't understand the way Tibetans think, the way Hong Kong people think, the way Uighurs [an ethnic Muslim minority in China's western Xinjiang province] think; it's part of the same problem.'

Mr Chen threw his weight behind the democracy movement after defending activists accused of igniting anti-government riots in the city of Kaohsiung. Soon after he became a politician, his wife Wu Shu-jen paid a heavy price for his anti-establishment views. Wu Shu-jen was born into a well-off family from Taipei. Her father was a doctor who initially opposed her marriage to Chen Shui-bian because he felt the young lawyer was too poor and from the wrong end of society. During a political rally in 1985, Wu Shu-jen was run over by a truck. It backed over her three times. Though the driver of the vehicle was arrested, no charges were laid over the incident, which Mr Chen and his supporters believe was politically motivated. Wu Shu-jen, paralysed from the waist down, accompanied her husband throughout his presidential campaign.

His supporters and the media call him by his nickname 'Ah Bian' (like calling someone Joe, for example, instead of Mr Joseph Brown), and he attracted a strong following among younger Taiwanese. The Democratic Progressive Party opened Ah Bian shops selling a line of hip-hop clothing, stationery, homewares and Ah Bian dolls, modelled on Mr Chen but replacing his heavily Brylcreemed hair, spectacles and immaculate suit with casual clothes and a beanie. The DPP even put out a compact disc with Ah Bian in rap mode. The marketing campaign and a web-site, again aimed at youth, set him apart from the staid campaigns of his opponents and eventually gave him just enough votes to win the election.

Ah Bian had already used gimmickry over the years, much to the delight of Taiwanese voters, turning up to political functions dressed as various super-heroes, including Zorro and Superman. In

person, Chen Shui-bian was nothing like the hip 'Ah Bian' character projected in the marketing, but he had undeniable charisma and
vision.

During an interview on the One China question, he was
unequivocal about Taiwan's status. 'How can it be that 23 million
people chose the President of the Republic of China [Taiwan] if we
are then to become a province or a regional government?' he said.
'I personally cannot accept that, nor can the majority of the 23 million Taiwanese. Taiwan is a democratic country. I must respect the
will of the people.' Then a hint of arrogance briefly appeared.
Referring to himself somewhat egotistically in the third person, he
intoned, 'If they force Ah Bian to accept the One China policy that
would be barbaric.'

Chen's running mate, Annette Lu, is a feminist and democracy
activist who spent nearly five and a half years in jail. She and the
president are the Odd Couple, rarely seen together after winning
the election while rumours fly of frequent disagreements and arguments, which they both deny. When Chen Shui-bian opted for the
softly-softly approach on the issue of independence so as not to
anger China so soon after coming to power, Annette Lu did not
tone down her pro-independence sentiments, which ran against the
wishes of Chen. 'This isn't simply a province or an island,' she told
me. 'Everyone agrees it's an independent state.'

Chinese leaders have described Annette Lu as a traitor, a lunatic
and scum of the earth. They don't even refer to Chen Shui-bian as
Taiwan's president, either using the title 'leader' or the more cum-
bersome description, 'the person in charge of Taiwan authority'.
Annette Lu brushes aside the name-calling. After our interview in
her palatial office in Taoyuan county, north of Taipei, she insisted on
showing me some of the souvenirs of her prison days. Ms Lu had
been the assistant publisher of *Formosa* magazine, a major opposition voice in the late 1970s. In 1979 she was arrested for making a
speech on human rights, charged with sedition and sentenced
under martial law to twelve years in prison. She served five years

My family in Hong Kong, circa 1982: me, Andrew, Stephen, and my parents, Bea and Robin.

On location at the 'handover ceremony' for the China Airlines cargo plane in May, 1986. This was one of the first incidents to pique my interest in the relationships between mainland China, Taiwan and Hong Kong.

THE RUPERT OF DEBATE.

A caricature of my great-great-grand-uncle, Phineas Ryrie. He arrived in Hong Kong in 1851, and frequently appeared in the Chinese edition of *Punch* as 'Funnyas Riley'. (*Courtesy of Arthur Hacker.*)

My maternal grandparents, Cecil Keat Greaves and Elsie Mackenzie, in Shanghai, circa 1920. Tragically, Elsie died when my mother, Bea, was four.

My paternal grandparents married in Hankow in 1924, three years after my grandfather, Robert Rae Hutcheon, arrived on the China coast. My grandmother, Ethel, was the daughter of a British officer sent to Shanghai to defend British citizens and property. I wonder where she got her fashionable wedding dress? Perhaps she had it made in Shanghai by one of the tailors on Nanjing Road.

Old Shanghai in the 1930s. This photograph was taken by my grandfather, Robert Rae Hutcheon. The buildings on the waterfront, which were in the French and International settlements, have barely changed. But these days there is noticeably more traffic on the river.

My grandmother, Ethel, on a rickshaw in Shanghai in the 1930s. Ethel would have hired the private rickshaw to visit friends and do the shopping.

From left to right, my mother's aunt, Mary Mackenzie; her stepsister, Frances; Lucy, a second aunt; their first cousin, Kate Anderson. Even though the women weren't fully Chinese, they probably enjoyed wearing the elaborate clothing. They would also have worn European outfits, depending on the occasion.

Shanghai, late 1920s. My grandmother Ethel (at the top of the table) and grandfather Rae (top left) enjoyed meals from every corner of the earth in this cosmopolitan city. Here they are eating Japanese food – obviously before anti-Japanese sentiment in the city reached its climax.

Shanghai, early 1930s. My father (left) and his brother Ian were looked after by an amah, who wears the traditional dress of a domestic helper: crisp white tunic, loose black pants and small leather shoes for her bound feet.

In the mid 1960s my father was the assistant editor of the *South China Morning Post*. He usually worked nights and slept in until late morning, starting work again at around midday. Despite his long hours, he always tried to eat dinner with us at home.

My mother, Bea (second from the right), was one of a handful of reporters in Hong Kong in the 1950s. She worked for the *South China Morning Post* and is seen here with colleagues from other newspapers covering the inaugural commercial Cathay Pacific flight between Hong Kong and Manila.

Hong Kong, 1986. Here I am with colleagues from Asia TV News after covering a story about border security, one of the issues discussed in the lead-up to the 1997 Handover.

Dinner at the Anhui village migrant ghetto in January 1996. Rubbish man Xiao Liangyu is on the right, and his cousin is on the left. When the crew and I travelled to Mr Xiao's hometown in Anhui province, we were detained by the local Foreign Affairs Office.

Xiao Cun, Anhui province. This is the farmhouse where I stayed with researcher Zhang Lijia and producer Madeleine O'Dea. To the right is the beautiful old bucket I bought from the family.

In May 1999 protests erupted in Beijing after US planes mistakenly bombed the Chinese embassy in Belgrade, killing three journalists. This photo was taken less than 100 metres from the compound where I lived and worked.

My ABC colleagues in Beijing, 2000. From left to right: Charles Li, Sebastian Phua and Cleo Leung.

This was the community in Chongwenmen, Beijing, that was dismantled in 2002 to reconstruct part of the ancient city wall. Demolition scenes are common all over China.

This photo was taken on the streets of Jinan, Shandong province, shortly before the 'showdown' about leeks with Jinan's traffic police chief. From left to right: traffic policewoman; sound-recordist Kate Wakeman; cameraman Sebastian Phua; researcher/translator Charles Li; the author.

My father's former home in Shanghai has been restored and is now an upmarket Vietnamese restaurant owned by businessman Jacky Cheung.

Early morning on The Bund. The walkway is taken over by exercise groups until about 8 am. Pudong, New Shanghai, is in the background.

The author with 'Fatty' Shiu Keung, the roast meat shop owner. Like many Hong Kong businesses, the shop closed in early 2002 after falling on hard times.

In Taiwan in March 2000, Chen Shui-bian won the presidential election, much to the joy of his supporters.

Tibetans in Qinghai province attend most activities in traditional dress.
These Tibetans were at the Ta'er temple, one of Buddhism's
most important temples.

Sebastian Phua teaches a Tibetan monk how to focus at Ganden monastery in Lhasa in 1998.

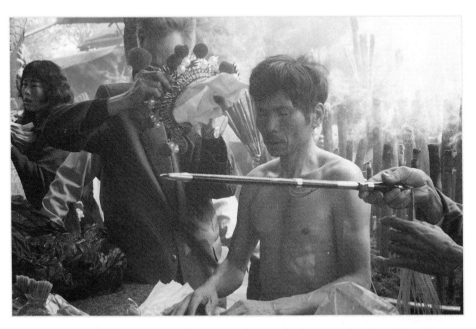

A devotee of the Taoist god, Heavenly Lord Zhao, at the Jiao Tian Jun temple in Fuzhou, southern China.

The entrance to the cave home of reservoir watchman Jiang Zuotao and his family in Shaanxi province.

Zhang Li Xin and his wife An Liping show off their rich woollen carpets. Mr Zhang left the state sector to start his own carpet business, which is now thriving.

Mr and Mrs Zheng, the 'Amway' couple.

This photo was taken in Hong Kong in the first few minutes of 1 July 1997,
the day of the Handover to China. I am with Sebastian Phua and
Kate Wakeman.

before she was freed on medical parole after being diagnosed with throat cancer.

Among the souvenirs, Ms Lu singled out a framed picture. It contained a few pages from a book written on toilet paper without the guards' knowledge. She wrote two novels while she was in jail, the feminist view of women's fate, *These Three Women*, and *Emotions*, about feelings for her country. She also passed her days in confinement crocheting dresses as a way of keeping herself occupied and alert. For my benefit she lifted a yellow dress up to her neck, full of pride for her work.

The Odd Couple's efforts to tackle the One China issue haven't met with success, though Beijing has wisely toned down the war rhetoric. Mainland leaders, however, sense the stopwatch is ticking and every second makes reunification more complicated and less likely. Instead, Beijing believes if it can persuade Taipei to open talks on re-establishing direct transport, trade and postal links, the island nation will eventually find itself held hostage to China's massive economy. In the meantime, China will become richer and more powerful and so will its military. Then, Beijing reckons, reunification will be inevitable.

In early 2003 Annette Lu accurately described the two biggest challenges facing Taiwan as economic sinicisation and the international marginalisation of Taiwan. By economic sinicisation she means the one-way flow of capital, technology and manpower from Taiwan to China. This is despite the many restrictions put in the way of Taiwanese businesspeople dealing with the mainland, from a cap on the size of their China investments to arduous travel impositions that make a two to three hour flight an all day affair because of the stopover in Hong Kong or Macau.

While the country puts on a brave face, attempting to do its part in international affairs, the bottom line is that because of China's coercive powers, Taiwan is a pariah without representation on world bodies like the United Nations and the World Health Organisation. It's little wonder that China has toned down its war-like rhetoric in the past twelve months; perhaps it only has to wait another ten years until the Taiwanese economy has been brought to its knees. Poor frustrated Taiwan; it deserves much better. President Chen may need that Superman outfit before long.

When Sunny Hu travels to China, via Hong Kong from Taipei, she puts away her Taiwanese or Republic of China passport and takes out her *Taibaozheng* or 'Taiwan Compatriot's Certificate'. The People's Republic of China – the mainland – doesn't recognise her passport. Even Sunny, an artist in her early thirties, refers to herself as a *Waishengren*, an 'out of province person', meaning her parents were born on the mainland. Local Taiwanese, like President Chen Shui-bian, whose families have lived on the island for generations, call themselves *Benshengren* or 'local province people'.

When the Nationalist Party fled to the island in 1949, Sunny's parents fled with them, but six of her father's twelve siblings remained in China, as did her paternal grandparents. 'When we were little, it was very clear we were Chinese, not Taiwanese,' she said as we sat across from each other eating Japanese food in a Beijing hotel. Sunny's chopsticks were like extensions of her long fingers, daintily scooping together the rice and pork. 'My dad worked for the Kuomintang government and all our neighbours had a similar background, coming from mainland China and working for the Taiwanese government,' she continued. 'I was always brought up to believe that we were Chinese and one day we would go back to reclaim our property.'

Sunny never realised the existence of what she now calls the 'arrogance' of 'out of province' people, who were at the top of the social pecking order in Taiwan until the late 1990s because of the Kuomintang's hold on power. She went to the best schools in Taiwan and finished her art studies in London and Italy. During an argument with a 'local province' friend who came to visit her in London, the visitor exclaimed that Sunny owed a lot to her parents because they had used their social advantage as part of the Kuomintang to obtain an international education for her.

It was a 1997 visit to the mainland as translator for an Italian company that really opened her eyes to China. She'd studied Chinese culture and history, but was otherwise ignorant about the country. 'We travelled to a lot of places in southern China looking at factories and talking to people, and I was really shocked at how backward it was,' she recalled.

Eventually the Italian company, which made batteries, chose a Chinese contractor over a Taiwanese factory. The company thought Taiwan's technology was superior, but China couldn't be beaten on price. The decision also made sense to Sunny, who found that life in Taipei was becoming too expensive for a single person. All her unmarried friends lived with their parents because they couldn't afford to live alone. It spurred Sunny into seeking employment on the mainland to realise new opportunities.

While thousands of Taiwanese now live on the mainland, curiously few discuss the issue that still divides them: reunification. Sunny doesn't discuss it with her mainland Chinese friends, and even with strangers she feels a barrier go up when someone discovers she is Taiwanese.

'People can be defensive, so sometimes I try to fake my pronunciation!' she said, laughing at her embarrassment.

On the question of Taiwan's status, she didn't hesitate. 'We are independent, but for our economic survival we have to go back to China,' she reasoned. 'All the same I don't like the politicians on both sides shouting about it and talking about war.'

Does she feel Taiwanese have anything in common with Tibetans? 'Some Tibetans look like Chinese, but I think they are different people,' she said. 'Chinese and Taiwanese people are much more alike.' Yet travelling around China she felt a sense of shame at what the Chinese have done to the ethnic minorities living in the People's Republic. 'I think the Han people have been too aggressive,' she stated firmly. 'You can see that many of these places have their own way of life, their own culture, but always there's some sign of Han domination. Like in a school ceremony, there always has to be one Han Chinese official present. The minorities must feel like they are always supervised.'

As the plane bounced in turbulence above a snow-speckled plateau four kilometres higher than the surrounding land, words written by British civil servant Charles Bell nearly one hundred years ago came to mind. 'Scoured by the wind, baked by the sun and crackled by the frost, these desolate uplands have a rugged grandeur of their own, set as they are in the cold, clear air high above the haunts of men.' Tibet is indeed the loftiest country in the world.

Since Bell's time, dozens of modern authors have attempted to capture the isolation, innocence and paradisiacal quality of the land. I, too, found myself anticipating what Tibet would be like and whether the rarefied mountain air would trouble me or the simplicity and goodness of the people affect me. Like almost everyone who has written about the place, I invented an imaginary Tibet, created over two years of asking for permission to visit and influenced by all the propaganda and stories I'd heard within China about the Chinese invasion and the exile of Tibet's leader, the Dalai Lama. When I first arrived in China in the mid 1990s, there were frequent disturbances in Tibet, particularly protests by monks and nuns rebelling against Chinese edicts, such as the ban on displaying photographs of the Dalai Lama. As a result of the frequent tensions there, the Chinese government allowed only small, select groups of journalists into the territory. In 1998 it was finally the ABC's turn.

Though Tibet today is much more accessible than it was one hundred years ago, I still felt as though I was penetrating a fortress because, surprisingly, there were no direct flights from Beijing to Lhasa. As journalists, my colleagues and I first had to obtain a special permit, stopping off in the city of Chengdu in neighbouring

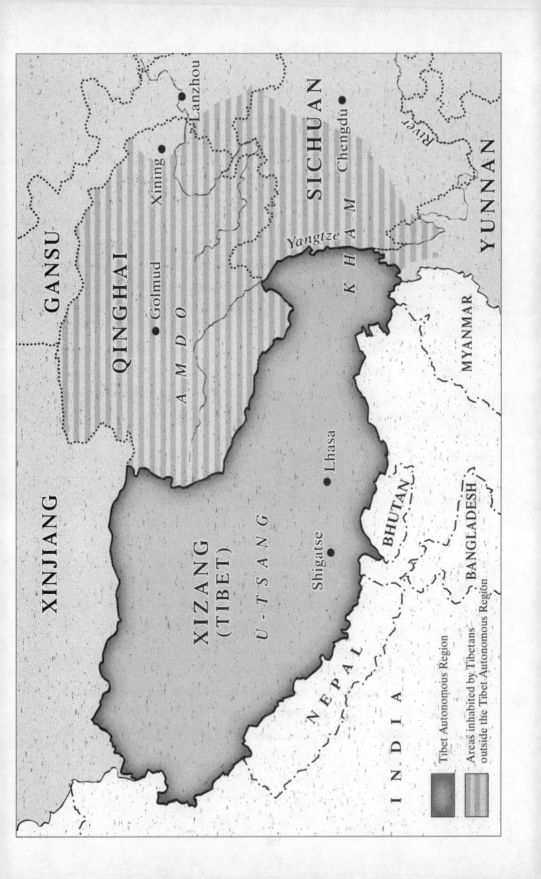

Sichuan province. After the plane from Chengdu arrived in Lhasa, from Gonggar Airport it was a two hour drive into the city, a distance of 90 kilometres. On the bumpy road into town you couldn't help but notice the Chinese military presence. Dotted along the route there were barracks and communication towers, and our van overtook several military convoys. If the presence was noticeable on the approach, it was even more obvious in the city. Military trucks roamed the streets and Chinese advertisements were plastered everywhere. It felt like occupied territory. My first impression of the city was one of disappointment. It was like a typical town in far western China: wide roads, rickety electricity poles, cars, karaoke bars and internet cafes.

Until I went to China in the mid 1990s, I didn't have a strong interest in the politics of Tibet. But the year I arrived in Beijing, 1995, had been a remarkable one in the ongoing tug of war between China and the exiled Tibetan lobby. Some months before my arrival, the exiled spiritual leader, the Dalai Lama, announced the results of a four-year search for a successor to the Panchen Lama, Buddhism's second-highest monk, who died in 1989. This was no ordinary search because, according to Tibetan tradition, the successor is believed to be a reincarnation of the deceased lama. No sooner had the Dalai Lama named his choice, which was also the choice of the official search committee, than Beijing discredited it, moving the six-year-old Gedhun Choekyi Nyima and his family to a remote region in China and placing them under permanent house arrest. Nothing is known of the whereabouts of this child, although his photograph is frequently published in the Western press, showing a little boy with wind-burned cheeks. It is a plaintive reminder that a boy, now in his teens, has lost his rights and freedom through no fault of his own. After deposing him, Beijing named its own candidate, installing him in the Panchen Lama's traditional seat at Tashilhunpo Monastery in the city of Shigatse. Entering China in the middle of this intrigue, I couldn't escape the politics of the Tibetan issue.

Outside China, Tibet is known mainly for its exiled spiritual leader and best-selling author of pop spirituality, the Dalai Lama. In virtually every country in the world his writings are prominent in bookshops – from international airports to small country towns. The Dalai Lama, whose title means Ocean of Wisdom, is responsible for the spread of accessible Buddhist teachings as well as being the living interlocutor of Eastern mysticism. Yet though his ideas are read by people of every race, religion and in every corner of the earth, they are shunned and in fact banned by the people he calls his own brothers, the Chinese. The government demonises him as a 'splittist', someone intent on smashing the unity of the motherland, and ordinary Chinese view him as a troublemaker.

The Dalai Lama's transgression, in Chinese eyes, is his outspoken condemnation during his globe-trotting tours, of the Chinese destruction of religious sites and culture in his homeland. In 1989 the Nobel Committee awarded him the coveted Peace Prize, for 'consistently opposing the use of violence' in the struggle for the liberation of Tibet. Rather, the Dalai Lama preaches the need for compassion in a changing world. By thrusting Tibet into the limelight, the Dalai Lama may have riled the Chinese beyond redemption. At sixty-eight, it is unlikely that Tenzin Gyatso (the Dalai Lama's given name) will ever see the land of his birth again. For a place that only entered the modern world in the last half-century, his country has achieved public attention beyond the capability of many nations.

When Tibetans speak of Tibet, they actually mean a much larger area encompassing the ethnographic spread of Tibetans, rather than the smaller Tibet Autonomous Region created by China in September 1965. Tibet, to the Tibetans, includes areas which are part of China's Sichuan, Qinghai and Gansu provinces. Apart from viewing the size of their nation differently to China, the Tibetan government-in-exile and its Western supporters vehemently reject China's historical claim to the territory. From the government-in-exile's point of view, Tibet was undeniably an independent nation in the forty years before Chinese troops brutally invaded it in 1950. Before that, the government-in-exile maintains, despite religious, cultural and sometimes political relationships between Tibet and China during imperial times, none of this amounted to China's sovereignty over Tibet. China, on the other hand, claims that political forces in Tibet had successively pledged allegiance with the Mongol Khanates as early as the 1240s, after which it became an administrative region under the control of the central government and remained so for the following 700 years. Both arguments contain elements of truth. However Tibet's defacto independence between 1911 and 1949 was never formalised and though weak and strife-torn, the Kuomintang or Nationalist government never gave up China's historic claim over Tibet. Then again, even Mao Zedong understood that Tibet in 1949 had a status that set it apart from China's other ethnic minorities. Mao told his generals, 'Tibet and Xinjiang are different. In Xinjiang in the old society there were 200 000 to 300 000 Chinese but in Tibet there was not even a single Chinese.'

After the 1951 Chinese invasion, which is consistently referred to as a 'liberation' by China, the Dalai Lama attempted co-existence. However his position as Tibet's political and spiritual ruler became untenable, and after massive demonstrations in Lhasa in March 1959 the Dalai Lama escaped with 80 000 followers to the other side of the Himalayas. In McLeod Ganj, the former British hill station in Dharamsala, the Indian government gave them refuge.

Dharamsala, the capital of 'Free Tibet' or the Tibetan government-in-exile, is approximately twelve hours by road from the Indian capital, New Delhi, or a six-week trek from Lhasa. In February 2000, Sebastian, Cleo Leung and I took a complicated route, flying from Beijing to Dhaka in Bangladesh and waiting in a retail-deprived departure lounge for four hours before flying to New Delhi, where we rented a four-wheel drive with a pleasant, careful driver named Ranu who drove us north until nightfall.

Eventually we reached the gentle slopes of Himachal Pradesh province. The road narrowed and curled towards the foothills of the Himalayas. On reaching Dharamsala, another narrow track stretched further up the mountain before it became so slim the vehicle could barely squeeze between the vegetable and cloth stalls. The town was packed with shoppers buying last-minute supplies before the onset of Losar, or Tibetan New Year. Only two days out of relatively orderly Beijing, I had a minor bout of India-shock: a feeling of being overwhelmed by the colour, stench and tiers of humanity clawing at my senses. We arrived in McLeod Ganj: an Australian correspondent, Chinese American producer, Singaporean cameraman and a New Delhi driver, feeling right at home in a cultural mish-mash of Tibetans, Indians and Westerners from every continent. McLeod Ganj was abuzz with the latest turn in the struggle with China. A few weeks earlier, the young Karmapa Lama, leader of the Black Hat sect, one of the four main traditions in Tibetan Buddhism, had escaped from Tibet to join the exiles.

The next morning I rose early because it was freezing. There was no heating in the room and water only came on for a few hours each evening. It could take ten minutes for the hot water to flow through the pipes, so the secret to falling asleep was to have a hot shower, allow the steam to heat the bedroom and then jump into bed wearing several layers of clothing. When I complained about the cold to the manager at the end of our stay, he said, 'You should have asked the staff for a heater!'

I took a short walk outside to discover that McLeod Ganj was so compact that our hotel was built on the side of a cliff. The view made up for the chaos: the surrounding mountains were sprinkled with snow like a scene from a Swiss chocolate wrapper. But remove the mountains and McLeod Ganj was a development nightmare, crammed with hotels, pizza restaurants, pashmina stalls and rickety backpacker hostels.

As it came to life, McLeod Ganj began to take on the appearance of a movie set, a Tibet full of oddly dressed actors. Heading for a new monastery beside the Dalai Lama's residence came a trail of claret-robed Tibetan monks, a few skinny dogs and Indian beggars. Next, clumps of foreign extras. It must have been their scene that day because there were plenty of them, dressed in traditional Tibetan clothes; 'wannabe' Tibetans who probably pasted 'Free Tibet' bumper stickers on their cars. The Dalai Lama's feisty younger brother Tenzin Choegyal believes the Tibetan cause has produced a characteristic among Westerners he calls 'Shangri-La syndrome': a yearning for the answers to life's questions through an immersion in the Tibetan cause.

Tenzin Choegyal, or 'T.C.', as he is known, fled Tibet at the age of twelve with the rest of his family. Like his elder brother, T.C. was also a *tulku* or reincarnate monk. At the age of three he was 'discovered' by a search team and taken from his home to be educated in Buddhist scriptures at the monastery of his predecessor, the Ngari Rinpoche. As a *tulku*, T.C. never felt special or spiritually gifted. It was tantamount to being taken hostage, he said. So at the age of twenty-five, he renounced the monkhood and married Rinchen Khando, who at the time of my visit was the government-in-exile's Education Minister. The couple lived in a beautiful Raj-era home named Kashmir Cottage overlooking the Dharamsala valley. They ran a guesthouse, closely guarded by fierce Tibetan mastiffs.

T.C. didn't become a particularly vocal member of the Dalai Lama's family until the late 1990s, by which time many Tibetan exiles had grown tired of the lack of progress of their cause. Shortly before the Tibetan New Year in 2000, T.C., in a newspaper interview, departed from the stance taken by his peace-loving brother and advocated the use of force to oust China from Tibet. 'The Chinese only understand the language of violence, so why not give it a shot?' he told a British newspaper. 'Of course, I would rather a peaceful solution is found, but if it isn't – and time is running out – then I am definitely in favour of a military approach.'

I visited T.C. on a glorious winter's day, when the mountain air was sharp but the sun beat down warmly. For once on this trip, my bones and my kidneys felt warm. I wanted to hear T.C.'s thoughts on the escape from Tibet of the fourteen-year-old Karmapa Lama, Ugyen Trinley Dorje, the leader of the Black Hat stream of Buddhism. The Black Hat or Kagyupa sect joins the Nyingma, Sakya and Gelug (the Yellow Hat lineage, to which the Dalai Lama and Panchen Lama belong) making up Tibetan Buddhism's main lineages. It is named the Black Hat sect because of the colour of the personal ceremonial cap of the Karmapa. Ugyen Trinley Dorje was the first reincarnation of a senior Tibetan lama recognised by both the Dalai Lama and the Beijing leadership. Since childhood he had trained at Tsurphu monastery outside Lhasa under Beijing's watchful eye and he was therefore crucial to China's attempt to realise legitimacy in Tibet. After the Karmapa's enthronement in 1992, which was attended by senior Chinese leaders, very little was heard of him. Then in January 2000 the young lama turned up in India, after a daring 1400 kilometre trek through the icy mountain passes of Tibet and Nepal.

Following the Karmapa's departure, China claimed the lama left a letter 'saying he was going to get black hats and musical instruments, not to betray the country, the monastery or his superiors' and that he planned to return to Tibet. Within a month, however, the young monk, ensconced in the sparkling new Gyuto monastery in the Dharamsala foothills, made his first public statement since his escape from China. He told followers that, 'the most important tenet of Tibetan Buddhist teaching is compassion. But to try to practise this, one has to be free.' He went on to say that 'with the blessings of His Holiness [the Dalai Lama] all the people of Tibet will soon be able to win their freedom'. The Tibetan government-in-exile celebrated while China responded with a witch-hunt at Tsurphu monastery.

T.C. didn't doubt that the Karmapa Lama's departure signified the failure of China's fifty years of effort to integrate Tibet. 'You see, I think the Chinese government never understood the problem of all minorities, particularly Tibetans. They haven't won the heart of the Tibetan people. If you treat a person well, have a certain amount of trust and faith in each other, then you might become friends. Just physically overpowering someone doesn't ensure the person's goodwill towards you.'

Government-in-exile officials and the Karmapa's senior teacher refused interviews on his behalf, but a government official said that he'd heard reports in recent years that the Karmapa had been unhappy with his studies under China's thumb. T.C. summarised the thoughts of the government-in-exile when he said that despite the status and authority given to the young monk while he was in Tibet, 'He didn't have freedom, because he felt he was being used as a puppet . . . he didn't want to be the chopping knife of the Chinese against the Tibetans.'

Disappointed at not being able to obtain an interview with the young monk, I decided to go along to the newly built monastery in Sidhbari, a short distance from Dharamsala, where the Karmapa had given blessings to small public gatherings. Inside the gates of the monastery, Indian construction workers were completing the building. Sari-clad women crossed the courtyard carrying baskets of sand on their heads. I waited with a group of Tibetans, foreign 'extras', tourists and dogs, which I'd learned by then are much loved by Tibetans. One of the Westerners told me to register with a man wearing a suit and sunglasses. When our names and passport numbers were called we were directed up a flight of stairs leading to a grand hall. At the top of the stairs Indian soldiers armed with automatic weapons guarded the entrance to the hall, emphasising the significance of the new guest. More soldiers, two male and two female, conducted body searches. In the calm of a Himalayan afternoon, the only noise coming from barking dogs and a lone crow, the security seemed excessive. But it did heighten my sense of expectation.

A soldier asked me to remove my shoes, socks, jacket and watch, then proceeded to search me. As her hands felt the front of my turtleneck sweater, her fingers got tangled in my underwire bra, deformed after months of abuse by a Chinese washing machine. Impulsively, we both giggled as she extricated herself.

The search over, the soldier indicated the way to the hall, and I stepped over a threshold onto an expanse of white marble in front of an altar and a throne bearing a large photograph of the Dalai Lama. It took more than an hour for the crowd to be searched and then seated in the hall. When all the devotees and hangers-on were finally inside, security guards closed the doors and spoke so urgently into their walkie-talkies it was as though we were about to witness the Second Coming. Moments later the awkward-looking, tall young lama walked in and took his place in a chair beside the Dalai Lama's throne, fidgeting.

The Karmapa Lama spoke for ten minutes, his speech interrupted by a monk interpreter. In essence he simply thanked the audience for coming to see him and then wished us peace. While the monk translated, the Karmapa tapped his foot on the marble and sniffed a little too loudly. He stifled a laugh when a baby in the audience began shrieking. Then without further ado the teenage lama rose from his chair and blessed a clump of red scarves, sprinkling imaginary water over them as if he was performing a magic trick. I had half a mind to crash tackle him and ask him some questions, but Sebastian and the camera had been made to stay outside. I also remembered the soldiers and their automatic weapons. The Karmapa then left through a side door while his attendants handed a blessed red scarf to each of us in the crowd.

Outside the monastery, Sebastian had set up his camera on a mound of construction sand. We had no interview and virtually no video of the young monk so we waited to see whether he would emerge to watch the disappearing crowds. I'd seen photographs of him on the roof of the monastery, so we waited like pathetic paparazzi for one little shot. Just as we were about to give up, a bright yellow robe suddenly appeared at a doorway. When the Karmapa saw the television camera pointed at him, even though we were 50 metres away, he retreated. I waved furiously at him and he returned the wave – and stayed on the roof for several minutes. I kept waving to the teenage monk until Sebastian had plenty of shots of him, waving, smiling and basking in the last of the day's light. The sun was dropping behind the mountains and the Karmapa turned to again retreat into the monastery. It was then I caught a glimpse of the hills behind the monastery. Rising over them was a rainbow. The Karmapa saw it too. Rainbows, apparently, follow him often and in Tibetan Buddhism are considered a good omen. Though I never spoke to him, I felt a sense of calm and satisfaction when we finally drove away.

The Karmapa was one of thousands of Tibetans who over the years have made their way across the Himalayas to India. Non-VIP arrivals who journey on foot across the mountains are given shelter at a reception centre in Dharamsala. Peak season for travel is mid winter, between January and March, when Chinese frontier guards withdraw from the Tibetan border, leaving the dangerous mountain route unpoliced. During that period, each week sees another batch of escapees. Sometimes the centre is so full that new arrivals sleep cheek to jowl. They arrive tired and hungry, their faces burned by the wind and sun. Occasionally someone in the party doesn't survive the arduous journey.

'We took a bus from Lhasa and travelled over 300 kilometres,' one young man told me. He spoke Mandarin and stood with his back to the camera, not wishing to be identified. 'Then we got off the bus and started to walk. We walked for fifteen days.'

Mr Zhang, as I'll call him, was tall and thin, dressed in a black leather jacket and jeans. He seemed street-wise and well educated. His group had survived the journey eating *tsampa* (roasted barley) and melted snow. The weather had been bleak, with freezing temperatures and heavy snowfalls.

Mr Zhang said that Tibetan youngsters came to Dharamsala for their education and often returned via the same mountain route. Others came to teach or exchange news. Mr Zhang, who looked around seventeen or eighteen, said that his family didn't have much money or influence so the chances of him getting into a good school in Tibet were slim. 'The Chinese government likes to talk about their investments in Tibet. All of these are designed for political reasons. They don't sincerely want to help us,' he said, repeating a view common among Tibetans.

Mr Zhang said he didn't plan to remain in Dharamsala permanently, but would return to Tibet to join the struggle for independence – hence he didn't want to reveal his identity.

'Here [in Dharamsala] I can meet countrymen who share my opinions and are concerned about the existence of our nation. On the surface, Tibet seems very stable. But look more deeply and it isn't so firm.'

A novice monk wearing a burgundy gown and a sweater came across the mountain pass with Mr Zhang. He had come to Dharamsala to further his religious study. His Chinese was poor, indicating that he'd had virtually no education, and so Mr Zhang translated for me. The monk said it was harder to enter a monastery in recent times. Monasteries had quotas fixed by the Chinese government to control the quality and political leanings of novices. If a family was too poor to afford schooling the traditional method of educating a young boy was by sending him to a monastery. Now this was less and less an option.

With money from its Western backers, Dharamsala has schools, hospitals specialising in Tibetan medicine and monasteries to train its people according to tradition. The exiled community may never return to Tibet, but even if it doesn't, it has developed and strengthened itself as a cultural bulwark in the event that the Tibetan language and traditions die out in Chinese Tibet.

The mirror image of self-determination in Dharamsala is grudging submission in Chinese Tibet. A report published in the major daily newspapers, CCTV and Chinese embassy web-sites stated that 'the majority of the 2.6 million [Tibetan] people . . . now have access to TV programs, radio services and electricity, and some of the Tibetans have bought their own cars, mobile phones and other modern telecommunications tools'. Another glowing report claimed that the average disposable income in Tibetan cities reached US$858 in 2001, above the national average of US$827. The reality is that the remodelling of Tibet from a backward, feudal state to a modern patriotic Chinese outpost is neither complete nor a success.

A massive building program is under way as part of the central government's 'Develop the West' strategy, launched in 1999 to narrow the gap between the affluent eastern provinces and the under-developed west. China's outer provinces are home to 23 per cent of the population – including most of the minorities – and cover 56 per cent of the country's land area. Yet the west's per capita gross domestic product is only 60 per cent of the national average. A second goal of the 'Go West' strategy is to develop the areas where ethnic minorities live to try to integrate them with the rest of China.

Through the 1990s, a major construction program aimed to replace – at a cost of several billion dollars – many of the monasteries that had existed before the decimation of Tibetan culture and religion during the Cultural Revolution. Those ten tumultuous years (1966–76) wiped out many of the traditional values inherited from pre-Communist society. Religion became a key target of the Red Guards, the majority of them Tibetans presumably believing they had no alternative except to destroy their culture. The practice of Buddhism was prohibited and effectively eliminated while temples and monasteries were torn down.

The rebuilding program couldn't and wasn't intended to replicate the pre-1966 number of monasteries. In 1951 there were approximately 2500 monasteries and 115 000 monks and nuns comprising 10–15 per cent of the Tibetan population, according to the state-run *Beijing Review* magazine. Now there are 46 000 monks and nuns and an estimated 1800 monasteries.

With the modernisation of Tibet proceeding according to plan, the Tibetan Autonomous Region government finally agreed in June 1998 – during a period of minimal political restlessness – that the Australian Broadcasting Corporation could visit Tibet, under certain conditions. The government insisted the ABC team, which included Sebastian, sound-recordist Kate Wakeman and researcher (Charles) Charles Li, travel with three other television networks – the American NBC, CBS and the international agency Worldwide Television News (now Associated Press Television News). Another condition was that we had to follow the government's itinerary. I didn't like the idea of travelling in a herd because it meant few opportunities to 'wander' and find the 'gold' that made a good story sparkle. However, I didn't have a choice. It was in a herd or not at all. And so we boarded the plane from Beijing to Chengdu, waited a few hours for our 'visa' to Tibet and the next morning took another flight to Lhasa, bouncing over the snow-covered plateau. As I stepped onto the tarmac, I noticed immediately it was harder to breathe; Lhasa is 3660 metres above sea level.

Under the watchful eye of our two Tibetan minders it was difficult to get a true sense of the place. The buildings, disappointingly, had the same bland architecture so familiar in towns across rural China, and Chinese signboards dominated anything written in Tibetan script. Lhasa, except for an old section around the Barkhor area, was very much a Chinese city with Tibetan characteristics. A pair of giant bronze yaks guard the entrance to downtown (a gift from China to celebrate the anniversary of the 'peaceful liberation of Tibet') while in front of a hill crowned with the Dalai Lama's former residence, the Potala Palace, spreads a giant Tiananmen-style people's square.

In every part of the city Han Chinese merchants, traders and hawkers dominate the shops and stalls while young Tibetans hang out in Made-in-China Western fashions – jeans and leather jackets. Older Tibetans wear traditional dress and clutch prayer wheels as they perform circumambulation, walking around an object of reverence to gain spiritual merit. During peak hour, police stopped traffic to give way to worshippers who knelt on the tarmac to per-form arduous prostrations. I wasn't sure if the police stopped the traffic because international cameras were filming them, but the religious Tibetans seemed out of place next to the cars and motor-bikes. Despite the diversity of Lhasa's population, it was more prosperous than I expected.

To demonstrate to the visiting foreign journalists that Tibetans have plainly benefited economically from Chinese rule, we were taken to a factory that made traditional Tibetan shoes for tourists. Our minders from the regional government said we could film freely in the workshops, where middle-aged women sat cross-legged on the floors, sewing pieces of felt and leather. A Tibetan entrepreneur owned the factory, and while I thought that might lead to an interesting segment in my story, the minder said he was out. Sebastian decided to shoot the low-tech production line and I wondered whether it was worth filming at all, until I noticed high above the heads of the women a photograph of the Dalai Lama. Even though he is so widely admired, it's forbidden to dis-play his image.

Researcher Charles Li made sure the minders were not in the room while Sebastian and Kate moved into place to record an impromptu interview with the women. They were very shy, but one of them answered in whispers. She said the lives of Tibetans had certainly improved economically since the Chinese had taken over Tibet, but now prosperity was under threat from the increas-ing numbers of Chinese moving into the region, and taking jobs from the locals. 'We don't have the right to say this,' said the woman timidly, 'but there are too many Han Chinese people here.'

I pointed to the picture of the Dalai Lama. Did they revere him enough to want him to return? At this, the forthcoming woman responded quietly but firmly. 'I want him to come back even if it's only in my dreams.'

With the camera still rolling, she took out a tissue and caught a tear slipping down her cheek. 'Why are you crying?' asked Charles. 'Do you miss the Dalai Lama?' 'Correct,' she replied.

Chinese writer Wang Lixiong, who has visited Tibet regularly since 1984, said that despite the region's growing prosperity, China had failed to gain the allegiance of the Tibetans. 'There have been no recent street riots, and things look peaceful on the surface. But there is no difficulty in sensing where their feelings lie. Virtually all Tibetans have the Dalai in their hearts.'

Wang Lixiong lives in Haidian, Beijing's university district. Like his lifestyle, which sees him travel around the country for two to three months of the year researching subjects of interest to him, his apartment is unusual, littered with ethnic artefacts from China's far west. Yak harnesses and skulls, stones and antlers were spread out between piles of books and papers. Wang disentangled himself from the state system. He used to work for one of China's biggest state enterprises, the Number Two Automobile Plant located in central Hubei province. But at the very start of the economic reforms in 1980, he left his work unit, to which all Chinese were once assigned, by keeping his position but relinquishing his salary. This was a widely practised method of circumventing the system since, to all intents and purposes, his personal dossier would still be in the hands of a work unit. People aren't allowed to disappear. Since leaving the work unit Wang Lixiong, who's in his early fifties, has pursued a writing career and without revealing his earnings says he makes just enough to live on.

Mr Wang's apartment belongs to his godfather, who has a special status as an 'old cadre' because he joined the party in 1937 and is now in his mid eighties. Relatives of old cadres like Mr Wang are often very outspoken, but their links to the old Communist regime and the fact that their parents or grandparents contributed to China's revolution mean that officials don't dare to give them any trouble. This may explain why Wang Lixiong has enjoyed comparative freedom in his work as a writer since leaving the Number Two Automobile Plant, although his subject matter is frequently controversial. In the early nineties he wrote a book called *Yellow Peril*, about a hypothetical civil war breaking out between north and south China. In the book, the south is backed by Taiwan and the war ends with nuclear conflict and thousands of refugees fleeing China.

In 1999, while researching a project on the restive Uighur population in western Xinjiang province, Mr Wang was detained on suspicion of revealing state secrets but was released without charge one month later. He has made more than ten trips to Tibet and spent more than two years living among Tibetans. His controversial book *Sky Burial: the Fate of Tibet*, published only in Chinese like *Yellow Peril*, is banned on the mainland. However he was more than willing to discuss his views on what he saw as Tibet's demise.

'I describe Tibet as a body lying in snow on the mountains. It is helpless; it has lost its ability to control its fate, and meanwhile forces from all different directions – Westerners, Beijing and the Dalai Lama – have torn Tibet apart according to their own needs,' he said in his measured way.

Wang's book is banned because he criticises China's attempt to modernise Tibet. While modernity and tradition may happily co-exist in some societies in the contemporary world, he said, they don't in Tibet.

As part of the ABC's authorised visit to Tibet, the regional government took us to a sprawling new traditional medicine factory, which appeared to be operating only in the section we were shown, where a few Tibetan workers packed processed herbs into boxes. Outside, more workshops were under construction within the complex. It seemed strange that the huge factory was so under-utilised, unless we'd been taken there well before it was operational.

Like the bulk of China's modernisation program, projects such as the medicine factory, said Wang Lixiong, served to demonstrate Beijing's political and military control over Tibet. He gave the example of another major construction, the expensive mountain highway between Qinghai and Tibet built by the Chinese in the 1950s. Wang said the road was mostly used to transport materials and supplies for the regular Chinese population and the military. The costly infrastructure had little to do with the rural Tibetans, some 80 per cent of the population, who lived widely scattered over the vast Tibetan plateau.

It would be wrong to believe that every Tibetan is opposed to the Chinese government's efforts at modernising Tibet. Tashi Tsering lives in the old Barkhor area of Lhasa near the historic Jokhang temple. Outside his home, in the Barkhor market, Chinese migrants sell T-shirts, sunglasses and Tibetan 'souvenirs', made in China or Nepal. Over the years Chinese cobblers have replaced Tibetan cobblers. Grimy-faced Tibetans have become beggars, hanging onto the sleeves of Chinese and Western tourists.

Tashi's wife, Sangyela, runs a cafe selling homemade *chang*, an alcoholic barley drink. To get to Tashi's apartment you have to walk through the cafe, always full of colourfully dressed, high-spirited Tibetans. Tashi, now in his seventies, raises money to fund his passion – educating rural Tibetans. He's built more than fifty no-frills primary schools in remote, underprivileged areas.

When I first heard of Tashi Tsering's work, I telephoned him and asked if he thought it would be possible to travel with him deep into rural Tibet to see his schools program. The Tibetan Autonomous Region Foreign Affairs Office didn't respond to my request. When the ABC trip was eventually approved more than a year later, the provincial government had scheduled a meeting with Tashi but no visit to the schools.

I explained to one of the minders that Tashi Tsering's school program would show a human side to the overall story and create a positive image of what was happening in Tibet. The minders had already shown themselves to be inflexible, and not surprisingly, my on-the-spot request was rejected. Our official time with Tashi was too short, so the crew and I sneaked out of the hotel to interview him again without the rest of the group. When I thought about it later, the government probably didn't want to have foreign journalists single Tashi out for special attention, as his schools were filling the gap in a massive shortfall in the education system.

Tashi's wife, Sangyela, is illiterate and he himself comes from a poor rural village, yet he became a passionate supporter of the changes China tried to introduce after 'liberating' Tibet in 1951. As a child and young adult, Tashi lived during the twilight years of traditional Tibetan society, which the Chinese melodramatically refer to as the 'dark ages'. Before the 1950s, monasteries and rich landlords ruled Tibet and common folk were treated like serfs; according to Chinese propaganda it had been that way since the Middle Ages. Tashi also feels Western backers of the Dalai Lama have a false impression of old Tibet. 'Western understanding on the whole is some kind of fantasy, some kind of Shangri-La story,' he said. 'This is the kind of dream that a great many Tibetans are hoping for, but I'm different from the majority of Tibetans.'

In 1939 when Tashi was ten years old, he was taken from his village, as a kind of human feudal tax payment, to perform in the Dalai Lama's *Gadrugba*, or dance troupe. Hundreds of kilometres from home, he lived with a foster family who treated him like a slave. Later, he became the homosexual partner of a monk official and went to live with him in his house. Tashi explains in his autobiography that none of this was unusual in traditional Tibetan society. In fact it was common practice for monks to have homosexual partners even though they took a vow of celibacy. In traditional society, celibacy meant abstaining from sex with a female or from sexual acts that involved penetration. Monks developed means to circumvent the law, for example by moving their penis between the crossed thighs of a partner.

As the sexual partner of a monk steward, Tashi was frequently pursued by other monks. On one occasion he was kidnapped by a monk from one of the monasteries and forced to have sex over a two-day period before being released. Despite the complexity of his role, the patronage and the connections he established helped him get a good education, something he'd longed for. Eventually, Tashi left the steward's home and went to study in the United States. This happened after China's 1950 invasion, but these were still peaceful, if uncertain, times in Tibet. By 1959, however, it was clear the agreement forged between China and Tibet after the invasion had gone sour. While Tashi was in the United States, the Dalai Lama's supporters staged an uprising and the Dalai Lama fled with his family to Dharamsala.

Tashi was faced with the choice of working for the Dalai Lama's government-in-exile or returning to Chinese Tibet. He chose the latter and arrived in time to witness the start of the Cultural Revolution. 'I ran into such a great disaster [with] the Cultural Revolution. I wanted to come back with my education to help Tibet and Tibetans; I particularly wanted to become a writer and teacher,' he said during one of our interviews in his Barkhor apartment. 'However, I also suspected that if I were to return to Tibet, I would be accused of being an American spy.'

He suspected correctly. The Communists pounced on Tashi, because of his time in the United States and because of his overseas contacts. He was jailed in a prison camp in Shaanxi province for five years. Years later, the Communist Party exonerated him. Tashi took me for a short walk through a narrow lane behind his home. He spoke sharply to a Tibetan woman and her child who came toward us, begging. In their defence, I suggested they might be victims of the Chinese migrant influx into Tibet.

'Why can't we Tibetans compete with the Chinese in the market system?' he said, pointing to a row of cobblers lined up on the pavement. 'Twenty years ago there were lots of Tibetan shoe menders around my house. But now there are none, it's full of Chinese because they are very hard-working people. Like myself,

I can compete with any Chinese. Why can't other Tibetans do that? [They are] very, very lazy, incredibly lazy.'

It was harsh criticism of his countrymen. After leaving Tashi, I thought long and hard about his words, including a five-page fax dogmatically supporting China's reforms he sent me after I returned to Beijing. Perhaps Tashi had always had superior strength of character and was able to work hard and excel, whether he was in Tibet or China or the United States. Perhaps this was not a trait shared by many Tibetans, who'd been dragged into the modern world by an invading and invasive power. Though I greatly admired Tashi for all he had been through, he had been taught to fend for himself. Most Tibetans under Chinese rule weren't so lucky. The Chinese had built schools in remote areas, but Tashi conceded that these were far from adequate, so he sold Tibetan crafts and raised money from Westerners to build his own schools in Tibet's harsh outback. I never got there.

With mountain ranges to its north, west and east, including the Himalayas, Tibet serves an overriding strategic purpose for China in that it acts as a natural fortress against attack. This is a key reason why China has always fought to keep hold of it. And yet China finds itself with a large, expensive and still hostile protectorate on its hands. Despite claims that Chinese policy has enhanced Tibet's economy, like the rest of China there's an enormous disparity in wealth in the region and that is only set to grow with the increasing influx of mainstream Han Chinese into Tibet. While officially there are 65 000 Chinese in Tibet, or 2.6 per cent of the region's population of 2.5 million, in the summer months their numbers swell to 300 000. China is constructing a controversial 26 billion yuan (US$3.2 billion) railway from the neighbouring province of Qinghai to Tibet, and though it's not scheduled to be completed until later this decade, there are already fears that the Tibetan minority will be swamped culturally, politically and economically.

China's response is that the construction of the railway will result in training and educational opportunities for over 1600 Tibetans within the next few years. But here's the rub: much-needed development to haul Tibetans out of poverty involves increased contact and integration with mainland Chinese, and the Qinghai–Tibet railway is an illustration of that dilemma. Writer Wang Lixiong fears the cost of the project will override its benefits. 'The true purpose of the railway is first and foremost that it's a landmark construction project for the government, like the Three Gorges Dam. It's the only railway constructed at such high altitude,' he told me via email. 'Its other purpose is that every government work unit or department will benefit from the project by corruption. That's the main reason I say the cost will exceed the benefits.'

A highlight of our 1998 trip was a visit to the Dalai Lama's former residence, the magnificent Potala Palace. Situated on top of a small hill and therefore propitious to Tibetans, it was built in the middle of the seventeenth century by the fifth Dalai Lama. An expensive renovation had just been completed.

Officials instigated a filming charge of between A$50–100 per chamber, although filming from the rooftop, we were told, was free. I thought the asking price was outrageous so I agreed to share some of the footage with another network, though this meant Potala goons watched Sebastian like a hawk to make sure he wasn't filming secretly.

Like other Tibetan monasteries I had visited, cameras were mounted in each chamber as a vivid reminder that the halls – emptied of the Dalai Lama's influence – were still potentially controversial. Then I stepped into a chamber where a young novice stood alone. I greeted him with the only Tibetan phrase I knew, '*Tashi Delek!*' and in English he replied, 'Hello, how are you? Which country are you from?'

Delighted that we could converse, but wary of Big Brother, I lowered my voice. 'How is the situation in here?'

He shook his head and replied quietly, 'Not good.'

I went to find Sebastian, who was still being tailed by two security guards. It seemed that an interview was out of the question. I found Kate and told her about the English-speaking monk. Then, to our annoyance, we saw one of the American television networks interviewing him in a dark corner.

When the American reporters had left, I walked toward the novice again, and this time he took my hand to shake it. As he did so, he pressed a piece of folded paper into my palm and quickly walked away. I took the note into another room where Kate was waiting and opened it up.

Tibet is not China's territory
Tibet needs assistance from your country to regain its freedom.
I love your good mood and your kindness.
Thank You
Ten Pell,
Potala Palace,
Lhasa, Tibet
~~China~~

Kate suggested that I return a note to the young monk by wrapping it in a banknote as a donation. Feeling like a pathetic secret agent, I wrote, 'Can you meet me at the west gate entrance to the palace at 6.00 pm?', folded it in a 5-yuan note, pressed it into his hand and hurried into the next room.

The entourage of foreign journalists moved through the darkened rooms while I nervously searched for the monk to see if he'd understood the message and was willing to meet. Kate and I calculated that if he agreed, we would have enough time to return to the hotel to fetch the small digital camera, pretending we were going out again to do some sightseeing.

I'd nearly given up hope when the monk suddenly appeared across the courtyard. He carried a large metal washing bowl and as he passed close to me he said in a loud whisper, 'Six o'clock, by the western gate.'

We took a few more legal shots in the palace and paid a quick visit to the Sera monastery before heading back to the hotel with the rest of the journalists. Sebastian, Kate and I took the small digital camera and then flagged down a taxi to take us to the western gate of the palace. On the stroke of six, I looked for a shaven-headed teenager wearing claret robes. There were lots of tourists, worshippers and hawkers, but no monks. He must have misunderstood. Then I felt a tap on my shoulder. It was Ten Pell, the novice. He had changed out of his robes and wore ordinary street clothes. He looked about fifteen.

We found a sheltered spot on a staircase beside a large stupa across the road from the palace. Ten Pell said he didn't have much time, so I began the interview by asking him about life in the Potala. In the past few years, he said, all the monks were forced to study patriotic education, to reinforce their loyalty to China. Monks were beaten if they didn't attend. His English was broken, but he insisted on using it, so I simplified my questions. I suddenly realised that he had no understanding of how television worked, so I told him for his own protection I wouldn't show his face or broadcast his real voice.

The interview continued. Only monks who pledged loyalty to the Chinese government could be stationed in the Potala Palace, he said.

'So if you oppose the Dalai Lama, you can stay in the palace forever?' I asked.

'Yes, that's right.'

'Do all Tibetans admire him?'

'Yes, we Tibetan people all love him. Many monks are afraid of the Chinese government. I am not afraid.'

Ten Pell had risked much to meet a foreign television crew and tell us, albeit briefly, of the harassment of monks and nuns who refused to renounce the Dalai Lama. I wanted to ask him many more questions: about his home, his family life, why he became a monk. But it was getting late and I didn't want to get him into trouble. Sebastian and Kate packed up the camera and I told Ten Pell that he should return to the palace quickly.

Before he left, he took several colourful objects from his cloth shoulder bag and presented one to each of us: wrapped parcels of some kind of medicinal herb probably grown by his family. I was touched by his thoughtfulness and yet in the rush to get there I hadn't brought anything to give him in return. Then I caught sight of my wristwatch: a freebie that was in the press pack for journalists covering the Hong Kong Handover.

I presented him with the watch, explaining the significance of the 'Hong Kong 1997' printed on the blue plastic dial. Ten Pell's face broke into a wide grin and he clutched the watch tightly as if it were his most valuable possession. Later it dawned on me that I had given this patriotic Tibetan monk a souvenir marking China's assimilation of yet another piece of territory.

After seeing both the real and the exiled Tibet, I felt uneasy about all the propaganda. Free Tibet didn't exist, not even in Dharamsala, because it was living on borrowed soil. But China was also labouring under the misapprehension that modernisation was winning over Tibetans. Our group was taken to the home of an elderly Tibetan lady named Pubu. The four camera crews and journalists squeezed into her modern, clean apartment to hear her views on life before and after Communism. Dorji, the Tibetan Foreign Affairs official, translated.

'My children, they have got jobs now, but in the old days it was impossible for them . . . It was such a dark society,' Dorji intoned.

For the sake of accuracy, after returning to Beijing I hired a Tibetan translator who picked up Pubu's hesitation at criticising the old days. Never did she utter the words 'dark society'. The translator took the tape back to the start of the interview and found that Dorji had done more than simply embellish the interview. 'Tell them what I've already told you,' he barked at the old lady from the back of the room.

During the interview I'd noticed a framed certificate on the wall of the apartment with a big red Communist star in the centre. Pubu, I discovered, had passed an advanced Marxism course and was a Communist Party member. Even with her certificate, she was unable to wax lyrical about a happy revolution under the Chinese.

SPIRITUAL DIM SIM

A glistening white cathedral rose from the grey earth in the middle of nowhere. Nothing too strange about that, except for the location. This was rural, supposedly atheist, China. The size of the cathedral and its startling position in a wheat field made me pause for too long.

'Come on,' said Lijia. 'We shouldn't stand out in the open like this.'

We were in a sensitive place at a sensitive time, investigating the underground Catholic Church in China, which rejects the state's control and instead pledges allegiance to Rome. Over the years, the region had undergone several major crackdowns.

Researcher Zhang Lijia and I had arrived in Baoding in rural Hebei province, three hours drive from Beijing. It was late May, the month traditionally dedicated to Mary, the Holy Mother, when thousands of underground Catholics made a pilgrimage to the township of Dong Lu to pray before the Holy Mary statue. Some estimates gave the number of arrivals over the month at more than 100 000. Dong Lu was the site of a shrine dedicated to Mary, and consecrated by Pope Pius XI in 1932. We had arrived after the first anniversary of what the locals describe as a miracle, which had taken place near by. The villagers here were surprisingly cold and unwelcoming; I sensed there must have been trouble with the authorities because their expressions told me that a foreign woman in their township could only spell more trouble.

The 'miracle' spoken of in hushed voices occurred in May 1995. Up to 30 000 devout Catholics gathered at a shrine in an open, dusty field to attend a mass being celebrated by four bishops and 110 priests from the underground church.

Several witnesses say they saw the sun suddenly go dark and then begin to change colour. Soon, different apparitions of a cross and Mary holding the baby Jesus were seen at the sun's core. The phenomenon continued for about twenty minutes before a curtain of white light brought the performance to a close.

In a narrow village lane close to the gleaming white cathedral, Lijia and I sat down in a makeshift restaurant, ordered tea and asked the locals to cook some simple dishes for us: vegetables, rice and the standard dish that can be made without any problem anywhere in China – scrambled eggs and chopped tomatoes.

I told the suspicious villagers I was a university researcher, while Lijia quizzed the farmers on the miracle at the shrine.

The information came slowly and painfully like a tap parting with its last drops of water. I later learned why the villagers were so hesitant. The police and army were preparing to tear down the statue and arrest the local priests, which they did some weeks after our departure. However, despite their concern we were told to seek out an old man residing in one village, which turned out to be another, at one point driving ten kilometres and then doubling back along the same bumpy route.

On that dull, dusty day driving in a bright blue Beijing Jeep with black number plates that screamed out 'FOREIGNER ABOARD', I lost my temper and Lijia and I had a brief shouting match.

It must have done us some good and our luck changed, for we soon turned into an isolated little village and parked the jeep along the orange walls of a farmhouse. On the front of every door in the village was a crucifix.

We had woken the old man whom we'd been told to look for. Aged in his seventies or perhaps early eighties, his home was dark. Did he not have electricity or was he saving on his bills? He spoke cautiously but with coaxing recounted the story of the day ten years ago when officials had come and dragged away the local priest. The priest, like the villagers, had been an adherent to the underground church, faithful not to the Chinese state but to the Pope.

From a trunk, the old man pulled out a roughly made frame with cracked glass and through it we saw a photograph of the bespectacled cleric. The old man said that long ago mass had been celebrated here in his home. But not since the priest had been taken away.

Did the priest ever return? I asked.

'Oh yes, he came back,' the old man said passively. 'They brought him back several years ago in a coffin.'

Religion and spiritualism have always been a bothersome force in the Middle Kingdom, most recently because the Communists regarded it as feudalistic superstition which ran counter to the Communist doctrine. Despite centuries of attempting to control or outlaw faith, emperors, warlords and bureaucrats have all failed.

In the Protestant house–church of Pastor Allan Yuan and his wife in inner west Beijing, a regular service can draw up to one hundred devotees, and frequently the crowd spills out into the lane, making it impassable. Allan Yuan is now about ninety, and for his faith spent twenty-two years in a labour camp. Security apparatchiks periodically attempt to close his house–church down, but he bides his time and opens the doors again, refusing to register or become part of the official 'Three-Self Patriotic Movement' – China's equivalent of the Protestant Church.

The Chinese state says there is religious freedom in China, and Allan Yuan is determined to preach. That is why the state fears spiritual belief. If a man's faith cannot be broken by brutality and harassment, how can state ideology triumph over the people? The struggle for China's soul is one of the most intriguing stories a correspondent can follow, whether it is the persecution of a bizarre meditation sect or those who claim they can talk to the spirits.

At midnight on the eve of the first and fifteenth day of each month, according to the lunar calendar, the Zhao Tianjun temple roars to life. Even at that hour, hundreds of worshippers flock to the temple for a type of worship that is familiar to hundreds of millions of Chinese all over the world: the lifelong pursuit of health, wealth and contentment in its varying proportions, with the help of Taoism's most esteemed deities.

A gong sounds and within minutes the temple has become a cocktail of humanity vigorously stirred with smoke and colour with a dash of music is sufficient to wake any deity. The acrid smoke from the joss sticks is so intense, many of the devout wear oversized goggles to shield their eyes, looking more like steel workers than devotees.

This is a modern temple, built since the end of the Cultural Revolution, in the southern city of Fuzhou in Fujian province. The temple edifice is small, consisting of three buildings wedged on the edge of a narrow canal, and constructed around a knobbly old tree standing in the middle of a courtyard. In this small space, worshippers come to seek the counsel of the Heavenly Lord Zhao, a minor but extremely popular local deity, who is said to protect and bring happiness to those who pray to him.

Here at the Zhao Tianjun temple, they gather for blessings, gratitude and wish-lists. A young mother prays to a brass statue of a cherubic boy, she even strokes it in the hope of conceiving a son. Beside the woman, a coiffed prostitute in pop socks and high-heels has her hands clasped together and her eyes closed in supplication. The very rich only come once a year, on Lunar New Year's day. Most of the time they worship in their private family shrines.

Whether it's Christians, Buddhists, Muslims or Taoists, scenes like this are proof of the revival of China's ancient traditional religions and beliefs. The problem is the boundary between what the state deems acceptable religious practice and what it sees as harmful superstition.

The religion of China's recent past was Maoism. Chairman Mao's maxim 'Serve the People' called on the masses to embrace a spirit of selflessness. Even today, twenty-seven years after his death, there are villages where Mao's portrait still takes pride of place in dingy family homes. Though his destructive policies may have killed millions of his people, many of those who survived to remember him revere him as a god.

Playing hide-and-seek with the Ministry of State Security wasn't my idea of a great night out. It began with a low-speed pursuit through Beijing's deserted streets. I had jumped into a taxi manned by a very grumpy driver who thankfully was oblivious to our tail. Behind the taxi were two black Audi cars, one with a bicycle hanging out of the boot in case of an attempted alley getaway by the person being pursued – namely me.

I asked the driver to turn into the Ta Yuan Diplomatic Compound about fifteen minutes from where I lived and indicated Building Number 5. By this time, the cabbie was livid about driving around in circles, so I gave him a good tip and took the lift up to the fifth floor.

It was March and still freezing. My breath fogged the windowpane as I pressed my face close to the glass and peered from the stairwell down to the driveway. My pursuers were still there: four men, two Audis, one bicycle.

Earlier that evening, I had received a crackly telephone call from Belinda Pang, the rotund Hong Kong-based spokesperson for the Falun Gong spiritual group. Though she had her own import–export business in China, she was not high on the state's list of preferred visitors, so I was surprised to hear she was in Beijing. She told me she was being followed and had been pursued for most of the day.

Chinese security agents want you to know that you are being pursued – at least that's what I assume, so obvious are their tactics. In Belinda's case, she had grown tired of the silly antics of the Ministry of State Security. Instead of trying to escape her tail, she invited the agents to join her in a Big Mac, her treat. Instead of a hot pursuit through Beijing, the three of them sat in silence licking special sauce off their lips, surrounded by dozens of little emperors and empresses (as spoiled kids, products of the One Child policy, are called) all doing the same thing.

When I caught up with Belinda after nightfall, she was sitting at a dimly lit table at the American chain restaurant called Thank God It's Friday. As I cast my eyes around the diners – most of them affluent young Chinese – I thought I could pinpoint the spies. There, that table, the two men in leather jackets! Or maybe it was the table to the left; that man with the women, wearing a leather jacket? Perhaps it was just a good night for leather jackets.

Belinda and I shared buffalo wings and pizza and discussed Falun Gong. When we left separately, both of us were followed, which was when I sought refuge in the Ta Yuan compound.

The rise, fall and persecution of Falun Gong dominated my journalistic life in China for nearly half of the five years I lived there. Belinda had been one of the key people who helped me understand what Falun Gong was all about. I had met her in Hong Kong in August 1999, four months after an incredibly provocative protest by approximately 15 000 Falun Gong practitioners in Beijing.

The day of the mass protest, Sunday, 25 April 1999, was a rare spring day in China: clear blue sky instead of oppressive grey, and a light breeze shaking the first leaves from the willow trees. As usual for spring, the air was full of pollen, a floating sea of feather-light cotton balls hanging in the air, creating a surreal atmosphere.

Word had gone around the correspondent circuit the previous day that Falun Gong practitioners were going to stage a protest. They were angered by what they said was biased coverage of Falun Gong by the state media. Local magazines and television stations had been critical, calling aspects of the group 'superstitious', a hint they might be declared illegal. I was highly sceptical of the news, as I didn't think it was possible that even one thousand people could gather, let alone 15 000. Surely the Beijing authorities would not allow any activity in the vicinity of one of the world's most secretive and well-guarded leadership compounds? I had to go along to see for myself.

At about 8.30 am my trusty Giant pushbike and I joined the flow of cyclists down Beijing's main thoroughfare, the Avenue of Eternal Peace. On my right, I passed the Beijing Hotel and the Grand Hotel and slowed down as I approached Tiananmen Square, covered in green scaffolding. So, too, was the Tiananmen Rostrum, the southern entrance to the Forbidden City which holds the Mao portrait and is where he proclaimed the birth of the People's Republic of China in 1949.

It was said the square and the rostrum were being spruced up for the fiftieth anniversary of the party's coming to power. The cynical believed authorities merely wanted the square out of operation for the sensitive period of the tenth anniversary of the bloody student crackdown.

At this point I decided that it was foolish for just me to check out the protest claim as I had no camera, so I telephoned Sebastian and asked him to meet me on an intersection close to the Forbidden City and to bring a small digital video camera with him. We hailed a taxi and asked the driver to take us to Beihai Park at the northern end of the old imperial city. Beihai, which means 'northern sea', is a vast lake fringed by weeping willows. From there it was a short walk to the north gate of Zhongnanhai, 'central and south seas', a compound built around a lake where China's top leaders live and work. It is surrounded by high vermilion walls and is off limits to the public. Unfortunately, the taxi wasn't able to take us very far because we ran into a massive traffic jam.

Concerned that we might miss the action, we paid the driver and hopped onto a *san lunche*, a tricycle with a loveseat on the back. The idea was for Sebastian and me to appear as if we were tourists. In hindsight, it was a ridiculous thought, as by this time we knew most of the Public Security Bureau officers in the 'foreigner' section by name (even by nickname – one was 'Mad Dog') and they knew us too.

The tricycle ride through the warm spring air was pleasant if slow and before too long we found the source of the traffic blockage: the road to the leaders' compound had been closed to everything but cycles and buses.

With the puffing tricycle driver standing on the pedals, we began to sail past the biggest protest vigil seen since the Tiananmen uprising in 1989, though it did not feel like a protest. A sea of people up to ten deep lined the wide pavements. It was as if they had been summoned to take part in one of those publicity-grabbing photo stunts – an aerial picture aiming to capture a portion of China's humanity.

They were mostly middle-aged and elderly, dressed in simple, comfortable clothing. Most were clearly visitors from out of town. There was neither anger nor defiance on their faces. Behind the high walls of Zhongnanhai, the central leadership privately and collectively went off its head. I have often wondered how, when I had known about the possibility of the protest at least twenty-four hours before it happened, the leadership had remained unaware and ill prepared.

Sebastian filmed the human sea by getting on a bus, using the height to give some sense of proportion to the size of the protest. I tried to talk to one of the practitioners. 'Are you from Beijing?' I asked a woman sitting cross-legged on a piece of newspaper on the ground. She looked up and put her finger to her lips, indicating her intention to remain silent. At that stage the practitioners did not talk to the media.

I proceeded further down the road and ducked into a small shop selling drinks. Looking back at the scene, I noticed a man near the doorway, dressed in black and talking into a mobile phone. 'Now I can't see him anymore,' he was saying into the mouthpiece. I looked around me in the little store and realised that none of the customers was doing anything other than looking out at the crowd; the place was literally packed with undercover police masquerading as thirsty passers-by.

New arrivals added to the already massive gathering and it continued to swell until just before nightfall. At about eight o'clock people began to disperse as if by order, picking up their newspapers, tea-jars, travelling bags and rubbish and melting away into the now still, smoggy night air.

That night many of the protesters slept outdoors or stayed with friends, relatives or fellow practitioners. Though thousands of police had been mobilised, outwardly the government seemed to take a relatively low-key approach to the protest. That changed in July 1999, when it outlawed the group and began arresting the protest leaders. For a few months following the ban, the city's subways, construction sites and pavements became open-air bedrooms for hundreds of practitioners from all over China. By September there were still scores of them camped around the city, hoping that their visibility and the attention they received might convince the central government to lift the ban. Instead the government cracked down harder, arresting practitioners lingering in Beijing. It wasn't difficult to find them. Because of a policy of honesty, when asked by police if they were members of Falun Gong, they would reply truthfully that they were.

Gradually, Falun Gong members were beginning to talk to the media – if they or the journalists weren't detained in the process. We had organised to interview a businessman named Mr Li, who agreed to come to Beijing from Harbin in North China. He seemed to be in contact with many of the out-of-town practitioners, and on a pre-dawn drive around the city we came across dozens of them asleep on plastic sheets out in the open. A favourite spot was the pavement in front of the Ministry of Construction. Mr Li and I watched as the first light of day touched the sleeping faces of the practitioners. They rose, meditated for a short while, then packed up their few belongings and left without a trace.

At the time of the mass protest, little was known about the group other than the fact it was one of a growing number of Qigong movements.

To witness the popularity of Qigong, position yourself at the gates of Ritan Park at 6.30 any morning, and let yourself flow with the chatty tide of snugly dressed retirees who pass through the park gates to begin their daily routine. They come alone and in groups, ready to seize the day. Some of them bellow to clear out musty morning breath, and the sound of 'Oh-Hooooooo!' – like someone making an amazing discovery – can be heard from every corner of the park. In the spacious centre of the park, you find the Qigong practitioners, up to twenty or more separate groups practising gentle exercises and having a good old natter in between.

Qigong began more than two thousand years ago, when Buddhism and its meditation methods spread from India to China. In 1122 BC the *I Ching*, or *Book of Changes*, introduced a concept of natural energies or powers, and studying the relationship of these powers became the first step in Qigong's development. *Qi* means life force, *Gong* means cultivation or work. So together they're the cultivation of the life force, the aim being to increase vital energy inside the body, lead it to the mind and direct it with intention.

Originally, Qigong was developed and practised among physicians, the elite, Taoist and Buddhist monks and martial arts masters. The theories and techniques were often kept a secret. It did not become a mass phenomenon until after the Cultural Revolution, when old traditions could be practised once again. But it was really in the 1980s and 1990s that Qigong became widespread. Since then, hundreds of Qigong masters have emerged to teach the public their techniques and have been allowed to form Qigong organisations. Today it's practised in the form of meditation, using a set of fluid movements like Tai Chi or shadow boxing. Often very little theoretical study is required.

But as many forms of Qigong go beyond exercise and involve philosophy, the Chinese government has had difficulty regulating Qigong's growth, underestimating the deep spiritual vacuum which opened up in Chinese society following the ideological demise of Communism. Groups like Falun Gong, according to a popular Chinese newspaper, the *Nangfang Zhoumo* ('Southern Weekend'), are multiplying like carp in a river. But far more worrying to the central leadership is the man at the helm of the group.

Born in 1952, Li Hongzhi rose to prominence in the early 1990s after spending most of his earlier life in Jilin province in China's north-east. According to his government files, he initially led a humble life as a worker at the Jilin Changchun Cereal and Oil Supply Company. Clearly though, he felt he was cut out for more than grain and oil, so he began secret studies, his practitioners say, of more than twenty Buddhist and Taoist sages. Master Li emerged in his own right and began teaching his brand of Qigong known as Falun Gong in 1992. By August 1993 Falun Gong had been accepted as a sect or branch under the official China Qigong Science Research Association. The Chinese government claims Li Hongzhi changed his date of birth to coincide with Buddha's on a second set of identity papers, to convince his followers he possessed special, mystical qualities.

These days, Changchun is widely known for its rustbelt status, and is crammed with decaying state factories. The province is a place of extremes where summers are short and winters harsh, and the people, as viewed by Chinese further south, are physically strong and often belligerent. Li Hongzhi possesses many of the hardy physical attributes of a north-easterner, but instead of finding him belligerent, many Chinese see him as a messiah.

The Communist Party believes there are two million Falun Gong practitioners, but the movement says it has 100 million followers. The real figure is almost impossible to estimate, but clearly Li Hongzhi and his teachings have attracted a great number of people from all walks of life and from every corner of the country, as well as overseas. With so many Qigong groups offering their own brand of exercise-cum-belief systems, it's difficult to know what makes it the preference of so many practitioners. Li Hongzhi's writings are widely available and because of the informal, cell-type structure of the organisation, practitioners find a ready community of like-minded people.

Li Hongzhi now commands his 'empire' via the internet from his base in Queens, New York. Despite repeated requests for an interview, I have never seen or met Li Hongzhi. But over the years I have spoken with dozens of practitioners of Falun Gong, though many of them have now disappeared off the face of the earth as a result of one of the most protracted and sweeping crackdowns in China's recent past.

The crackdown also brought unwelcome surveillance of the ABC bureau. In July 1999 we began to get practitioners contacting us almost every day. They had come from all over China to Beijing, to try to convince the leadership to ease its suppression of Falun Gong. But once they arrived in the capital they were usually arrested, rounded up and sent back to their own province. All of a sudden Beijing seemed full of police vehicles from other provinces, their localities clearly marked on their number plates. Many of the practitioners had the telephone numbers of foreign correspondents and called us before getting arrested. Heaven knows how they got our numbers, but as we were pursuing a story on the group I was at first keen to get as many interviews as possible.

One day, I received a call from a woman who spoke excellent English who said she was calling from Guangzhou. She said in a few days I would be contacted by some of her 'friends'. True enough, I received a call a few days later from a man who asked me to meet him across the road from our bureau at the Beijing Friendship Store, a busy department store catering mainly to tourists. Knowing that the call might be monitored, I didn't ask him any questions but said I would meet him at the main entrance of the store, beside one of the two stone lions.

Looking nervously around for undercover police, I saw a man standing beside the lions. I walked over, and gazing in the opposite direction said hello and asked whether he was the visitor from out of town. He replied that he was and said that he had others with him. I told him to take me to the others and that I would follow at a safe distance behind him.

The man led me into the Friendship Store and through to an exit where on a series of benches sat a total of nine people, including four small children.

My goodness, I thought. How was I going to get them all into the bureau? Interviewing them in the open would be foolhardy. We devised a plan to have some of them brought in by the office car and the others brought in through different gates of the compound. In the space of an hour we had ushered them all into our old office, which was often used as an interview room. My heart raced. Here I was with the crew and nine people who were members of a banned organisation. Any moment, the door of the office could be broken down and we would all be marched away by the cops.

That didn't happen. But we did get an incredible interview from a group of people who had been beaten and tortured and were ideologically lost and distressed. They wanted their faces and names used in the broadcast, and though I wasn't happy about it, I agreed. After they were ushered back to the Friendship Store in small groups, I never saw them again.

For anyone who believes that Falun Gong is an entirely harmless set of meditational exercises, the core text – the *Zhuan Falun* (which translates into 'The Wheel of Law') – quickly dispels that notion. Master Li's 'scripture', as his practitioners call it, contains some mighty weird propositions. Belinda Pang told me that I couldn't understand many of these ideas unless I was a practitioner. I wasn't sure how you could contemplate becoming a practitioner if you read the scripture.

For example, Li Hongzhi writes that unique to his model of practice is the pursuit of enlightenment. One method of obtaining this is through the 'placement' of a *'falun'* or wheel in the lower abdominal area. 'I will personally install it for practitioners in the class,' Master Li says in *Zhuan Falun*. 'Some people can feel it while others cannot feel it. The majority of the people can feel it . . . It will forever rotate in your lower abdomen area. Once it is installed in your body, it will no longer stop and will forever rotate like this year in and year out.'

Conveniently, explains Master Li, when the wheel rotates clockwise it absorbs energy from the universe and spreads it all over the body. When it rotates anti-clockwise it releases waste material and energy.

There is a moralistic and elitist overtone in the writings of Master Li, in that the cultivation that is practised turns one into a better person with a higher level of *Xinxing* (spiritual health or outlook). Master Li dismisses mental illness as nothing more than a weakness of 'main consciousness'. 'How weak can it be? It is like one who cannot always be his own boss.' In rising to the higher level, practitioners are taught that homosexuality is wrong, aliens exist and that the more they cultivate the Great Law, the less they are likely to fall sick. If they do fall ill, they should be able to heal themselves and not seek medical assistance.

By the end of 1996, Li Hongzhi had fallen out of favour with the official Qigong Research Association and Falun Gong was removed as a subordinate Qigong group. In 1997, Li Hongzhi moved to the United States, where he's lived virtually in hiding ever since. His lectures and thoughts are frequently posted on a variety of Falun Gong web-sites, although these are blocked in China – the government expends unprecedented energy on conquering this group, not just within China but through its embassies abroad. In the eyes of the government, Falun Gong is a superstitious cult and therefore a potentially dangerous organisation. Though it may seem implausible in the new millennium that the Chinese leadership is fearful of society losing its cohesion, Chinese history is riddled with examples of unusual spiritual beliefs threatening the social order. For example, the White Lotus Sect, which mixed aspects of Taoism and Buddhism and promised a new social order, existed under the Tang Dynasty (618–906) but re-emerged several times, attempting to overthrow the Mongol Yuan dynasty (1276–1368) and later the Qing dynasty (1644–1911). Persecution by the Qing government led to a widespread uprising by the White Lotus in the eighteenth century, and though it was suppressed by the beginning of the nineteenth century, some of their ideas lived on and found expression in the Boxer movement years later.

Another reason the government wants Falun Gong stamped out is that it has no control over Li Hongzhi or the material that he releases to his practitioners. In China, the five approved religions – Taoism, Buddhism, Islam, Protestantism and Catholicism – are all regulated by the state's religious affairs bureau. According to the constitution there can be no foreign domination of any religious or spiritual organisation. Yet to the annoyance of the Communist government, the group succeeded on several occasions in 2002 in breaking into China's satellite transmissions and domestic cable channels, beaming programs in support of Falun Gong into ordinary Chinese homes.

At first glance, Belinda Pang seemed different from the other practitioners I'd met. Born in mainland China, she had come to Hong Kong in the early 1990s. We first spoke at a dawn exercise session in Hong Kong's Kowloon Park. There amidst the drone of early traffic, I watched her move through a series of exercises that were habitual to the practitioners. Belinda was then thirty-seven years old and ran a fashion accessories company. Her business was successful, but she had spent less time running it since taking up Falun Gong.

I liked Belinda's quietly spoken manner. Unlike other practitioners who tried to talk me into a stupor about the lifelong benefits of Falun Gong, Belinda responded to my questions slowly and thoughtfully.

She had become interested in Falun Gong for spiritual reasons. '[At that time] I ran into a lot of tribulations, a lot of problems. You know, doing business by yourself isn't an easy thing. If I hadn't understood *Falun Dafa* [the 'universal law of falun gong'], I probably would have taken [my problems] in a very depressing way, and felt my life so miserable.'

After a short time as a practitioner, her life changed for the better. 'Before, I used to complain, like why am I facing all these problems, why am I having all these tribulations. And it's like, everyone else is better than I am. But I see tribulation, I see problems as a good thing now.'

I spent two full days filming with Belinda on that occasion and remained in email contact with her. In December 1999 I went to Hong Kong to cover an international Falun Gong convention that she had helped to organise. The convention concluded with an orderly march through the streets of Hong Kong, finishing in a public park at Admiralty, near Wanchai.

I found Belinda walking by herself, her face streaked with tears.

'What's the matter?' I asked.

'Can you believe this? These practitioners came from all over the world to be here. We *did* it!' she said ardently, wiping her eyes.

As I looked around at the protesters, I noticed that most of them seemed to be families, ordinary middle-class people you would rub shoulders with in the supermarket or see dining at a busy Yum-cha restaurant. While I don't believe the group represents itself accurately – its practitioners often claim that they only practise meditation, but a belief system is clearly involved too – the Chinese government's harsh treatment of Falun Gong seemed excessive. Recalling the many practitioners who streamed through our bureau – most of them now behind bars – I feel sad. The Chinese government saw them as disciples to a false god, namely Li Hongzhi, but I saw no evidence that they were different or more dangerous than most of the more eccentric religious groups around the world.

They were certainly persistent, however, sending emails virtually every day and trying to encourage me to file stories on the group for years after the crackdown. To me, Falun Gong's tenacity was symptomatic of a deep dissatisfaction with Chinese society, which was felt by a wide cross-section of the Chinese-speaking world. Many adherents are overseas Chinese who feel alienated from their former homeland. Tens of thousands within China also feel a sense of alienation.

How else could you explain the thousands who flock to Tiananmen Square for small demonstrations which end in them being bashed on the concrete and dragged, often by the hair, into waiting paddy wagons, kicked and punched all the way? Why do they continue to protest more than four years after the group was banned? These people are able to practise the exercises in their own homes and could obtain copies of the *Zhuan Falun* easily enough. Why do they need to go further? Ordinary people from towns or counties far from Beijing and Shanghai must be driven by feelings of hopelessness to travel to the capital via circuitous routes to avoid the security organs stationed at every airport, train station and bus terminal, sometimes sleeping on the streets, all for a 30-second demonstration that ends in a police cell or a soulless re-education camp.

Full of salty chicken wings and bad pizza on that cold Beijing evening, Belinda and I began to organise a meeting with a family whose two daughters, Li Xiaomei and Li Xiaobing, had been sentenced to five and seven years in jail. The family had good legal connections and had prepared a well-argued and well-written petition that they planned to send to the President of China as well as other key government and judicial officials.

As I believed my phones could be tapped, I insisted that all the arrangements be made face to face. I met with the family of the Li sisters over broiled catfish in the private room of a busy restaurant in Beijing. In case there was surveillance at the compound gates, I wore a black wig and spectacles, one of a number of disguises that I donned to cause confusion. They weren't particularly elaborate disguises, mainly hats and the wig to cover up my light brown hair. I didn't want to chance revealing my contacts.

During one 'hot' period, as my local colleagues used to call these times, I watched the bureau researcher Charles Li being followed along a stretch of Beijing's Chang'an Avenue. A man propped on a bicycle, reading a newspaper, suddenly looked up and seemed to speak into his jacket collar. Twenty metres further down the footpath, a second man with a big bag of fake CDs did a similar thing. So did a third man standing by a public phone booth. A few weeks later I was telling this story to my friend Dave Rae, a Canadian Broadcasting Corporation cameraman. He laughed but had a better story to tell.

One afternoon beside Beijing's self-proclaimed six-star hotel, the St Regis, Dave had come across a group of men practising 'secret filming'. Dave watched them place small cameras in their ubiquitous 'male' handbags – complete with custom-made mini-cam holes in the sides of the bags. Tucking the bags under their arms, the men perfected steady turning and tracking movements. Years later, on my last assignment in Shanghai when we had been told to leave the city, just such a human steady-cam tailed me. I began waving to his bag, which did not amuse the agent–cameraman.

The bone-filled flesh of the broiled catfish, which was Charles Li's idea of adventurous food, was getting stuck in my teeth and on my nerves, so I asked the family to tell me about their daughters' case.

Li Xiaomei and Li Xiaobing, like their mother, had been ordinary Falun Gong practitioners. They had operated a bookstore selling Falun Gong literature. The Chinese media described it as 'a base for spreading the fallacies of Falun Gong'. According to Xinhua News Agency, investigators had uncovered publications valued at more than 5 million yuan (A$1.25 million), at the bookstore and the sisters' homes, and described the sisters as practitioners who had profiteered from Falun Gong publications.

None of the dollar amounts are verifiable, but what can be confirmed through the dates of the Xinhua articles is that the investigations took place and the sisters were arrested even before

Falun Gong had been banned. The sisters had been held without trial for nearly three months until a retroactive anti-cult law was enacted. In other words, at the time the women were taken into custody, their 'crimes' hadn't even existed.

To tell the story I needed a member of the family to speak to me on camera. They were not willing to do so. I said if we arranged the interview carefully, we need not attract any attention, but that I couldn't vouch for their safety after the story went to air.

The family said they would think about it. A few days later I got a message that the mother, Nie Zhen, had agreed to be interviewed. She herself had been detained and then released by the police because she was nearly seventy. With her two daughters behind bars for five and seven years, she felt it unlikely she herself would be detained again. I had offered her anonymity, but she preferred to have her face shown and her name published.

The night of the filming I organised for our team to meet in a KFC outlet. We sat at separate tables and to kill some of the tension I ordered a chilli chicken burger while the others were separately chaperoned across the road to an apartment belonging to a Falun Gong practitioner whom I had never met. I was the last to be led to the apartment, after my escort checked carefully that we weren't being followed.

We politely declined food and tea. For secretive interviews like this, the plan was always to stay for as short a time as possible. The longer you linger, the more chance there is of attracting attention.

The interview over, we left the apartment quickly and separately. The next day we shipped the story on tape to Sydney, labelling it 'Jane's Birthday Party'. The tape went missing. So we sent another the following day. Mysteriously, the first tape turned up a day late. I believe it had been held back for a private viewing.

The day after the story went to air on ABC News in Australia, I noticed that the 'spy room' at the gate of the compound where I lived and worked became alive with activity. Every time I left the compound I was tailed by a black Audi. A fat man in a raincoat had been stationed at the entrance to my apartment building. Goons were also stationed outside our office building and at one stage lingered in the stairwell outside the ABC bureau.

This event coincided with the visit of my cousin Stanley from Australia. I had arranged to meet him and his Chinese fiancée, ABC bookkeeper Elaine Sun, at the Omar Khayyam Indian restaurant. The goons followed me into the restaurant, sitting down at a table opposite me and ordering beer and peanuts. One and a half hours later we were still munching on biryani and butter chicken when a mobile phone belonging to one of the goons rang.

'*Wei?*' 'Hello,' he said. 'Yeah, they are still here, but they've just paid the bill so they shouldn't be long now,' he continued loudly in Chinese. 'If I were you I would start the car.'

My first really close brush with Chinese surveillance left me gobsmacked. Either they needed serious work on their technique or this wasn't surveillance at all but very bad acting designed to harass me into submission. The story had already gone to air, after all.

That evening, I went back to the compound while agents played tag with my cousin and his fiancée. Stan and Elaine were chased into and out of a bar while one of the goons attempted to stop them getting into a taxi. My cousin was not impressed.

The following day, I received a rare call from the Foreign Ministry. The deputy spokesman, Mr Sun Yuxi, asked to speak with me at the ministry the next day.

Mr Sun is a quietly spoken man with excellent English and shiny hair swept back with gel or Brylcreem. He sat waiting for me in a large conference room. 'You may have noticed that you have been experiencing some different activities in recent days,' he said in calm understatement.

I complained about the harassment and pointed out that the action had gone further than troubling me, and had upset a visiting Australian who had nothing to do with journalism or Falun Gong. I suggested it might not leave my cousin with a good impression of China.

Mr Sun said I had conducted an illegal interview with members of a banned organisation. He reminded me that the laws of China prohibited correspondents from preparing reports of this nature.

I left promising nothing, but noting the Foreign Ministry's concern. Mr Sun suggested that avoiding such stories would release me, as well as the bureau, from future annoyances of this nature. It was not to be the last time our bureau was harassed for pursuing stories the Chinese government didn't want published.

Others fill the spiritual void in their own special way.

Madam Lin had recently abandoned her stall at the Zhao Tianjun temple in Fuzhou. The alleyway leading to the temple is lined with joss-stick stalls and fortune-tellers. Some call out to advertise their skills, others cannot be bothered, remaining asleep in their reclined bamboo chairs. Madam Lin left the alley to run her business from home. But she denies it is a business. 'It's just a hobby,' she says.

Madam Lin and her husband live in a brand-new five-storey home on the edge of the city. The house is two storeys taller than all the other brand-new homes in their district. Despite the family's protestations of simplicity, they show all the signs of having recently come into money – and plenty of it.

Entering the house through the front door I was hit by a wave of cool air rising from the marble floor. Above me hung a giant chandelier. At the far end of the room was a shrine to the Heavenly Lord Zhao. As we walked past the shrine, Madam Lin plucked handfuls of banknotes from a metal urn and stuffed them into her trouser pocket. The banknotes were offerings left by grateful worshippers. Madam Lin glanced at me sheepishly.

In a country where superstition is officially frowned upon, Madam Lin's business has to be conducted somewhat discreetly. In a small room at the back of the house an old lady, her daughter and some onlookers were waiting. Madam Lin, in her fifties with unkempt wiry hair, was dressed in simple trousers and shirt. She sat in front of another statue of Lord Zhao and a collection of brass urns stuffed full of joss sticks, ready for the ceremony to begin.

Her daughter-in-law began proceedings by lighting the joss sticks, and before long, thick plumes of incense stole through the dimly lit room.

Madam Lin's eyes were closed. She gulped in air and began belching loudly and uncontrollably. The belching became even more intense and soon she was convulsing and jumping out of her chair, first in small spasms, then leaping high so that the chair rocked and fell backward. Her daughter-in-law guided her back into the chair as Madam Lin began to twist her head and sing in a strange Chinese opera-style voice. Suddenly she stopped and with her eyes still shut called out, 'Yan!' or 'Cigarette!'

A packet of cheap local death sticks conveniently on hand, Madam Lin took one out and her daughter-in-law lit it. Now Madam Lin was moving her head like a Thunderbird puppet, and speaking in a strange voice. Her daughter-in-law whispered to me that the transformation was complete; Madam Lin the humble housewife and mother of four had become the spirit medium for the Heavenly Lord Zhao.

The small audience in the room remained silent and focused on the performance. After a quick gesture from the daughter-in-law, the old lady moved onto the bench beside Madam Lin, aka Heavenly Lord Zhao. Madam Lin began to knock on the wooden altar in front of her, singing a song in Fujianese which sounded like someone wailing painfully. Come the chorus, she again knocked on the wood, and squealing as if in pain, repeated the knocking sound over and over.

'Come here, let me talk to you face to face,' began Madam Lin's song.

The daughter-in-law explained that the Heavenly Lord Zhao was recounting the old lady's life story and it was a tale of hardship and strife. The old lady's husband who had long since died was telling the Heavenly Lord Zhao that he was sorry for the evil he had done and the sadness he had brought to his wife.

'I had a bad temper, and our relationship wasn't harmonious. To blame you would be wrong. I was so incapable. And you had to bring up my sons and daughters, you did everything on your own.'

The old lady began to sob as she listened to Madam Lin, still 'tek-tek'ing on the wooden desk and singing her strange song.

We sat transfixed for two hours, during which time more customers had slid onto the bench by Madam Lin's side to hear her interpretations of their lives. Then Madam Lin came out of her trance. By this time she had smoked two packets of cheap cigarettes and drunk several glasses of *Bai Jiu*, a strong white spirit made from a sorghum derivative. She came out of the trance in much the same way she had entered it: gulping air, belching and convulsing until she slumped back in her seat, exhausted. When she came to, her face had an ever-so-slight smile.

I asked her what had happened.

'I don't know,' she replied, shaking her head, still smiling. 'I can't remember anything.'

That evening, we sat down to a sumptuous meal prepared in a kitchen so tiny for such a large house that it was hard to conceive it produced more than tea and toast. Nothing but the best was brought out for us – meat, vegetables and fish cooked in a soupy, southern style without any chillies and plenty of see-through rice noodles which are common to this part of China. We sat in the brand-new parlour upstairs, complete with curtains made of Western fabric and fat sofas big enough for a giant. Over dinner, Madam Lin and her husband, a wiry army veteran in his late sixties named Yu Bizhi, told the story of their miraculous change of fortune.

For most of her married life, Madam Lin had been in constant pain, suffering from a sickness the doctors couldn't explain. In September 1998, divine intervention changed everything.

'I was asleep the first time the Lord arrived,' she said, referring to being possessed by the Heavenly Lord Zhao. '[From inside me], he suddenly spoke out his name. My fists were all cut and torn, the Lord jumped up this way, he jumped up and down, it probably lasted for about half an hour. I didn't know what happened to me.'

Madam Lin's husband was clearly delighted with the turn of events. So delighted he had chosen to build an extra two storeys on to his house. (Later, I learned, he and Madam Lin were forced to knock down the extra storeys.) 'Now it's very easy for us to do business,' he said. 'It's also easy for us to open shops. Whenever we meet problems, we consult Lord Zhao. Nothing bad has happened to our family. If we meet any trouble, he can come out and talk to us.'

But wasn't fortune-telling banned by the Communists? Wasn't this illegal superstition?

'We don't do it frequently,' Yu Bizhi said. 'We don't make a living by this, we only ask for protection. I don't support her doing this outside.'

Whether it's Taoism's pantheon of gods and goddesses, Qigong or spirit mediums, there is but a fine line separating what is legal and what is not.

Belief, be it in a mainstream god or in popular religion, is central to China's soul but it is not the image of modernity and progress that New China's rulers prefer to see and are now busy concocting. Spirituality, however, has its own strange force.

I am told that the temple to Heavenly Lord Zhao in Fuzhou was demolished about a year after I visited there. There were signs on the smashed walls reading 'Fight Evil Superstition'. Madam Lin still works from home.

As for Belinda Pang, the calm and loyal devotee of Master Li Hongzhi, after a time my emails went unanswered.

In May 2000, according to news reports emailed to me by one of Belinda's former Falun Gong friends, she apparently formed a break-away sect whose followers quickly proclaimed her 'the manifestation of the Lord of Buddhas in the human world'. They had all gone to live on Lantao Island, an island off Hong Kong where a large Buddha statue was erected in the 1990s and where the airport is located.

Over the internet, Master Li and Belinda traded blows to bolster their credibility. She claimed Master Li had left this world and that she, fashion accessories trader Belinda Pang, was the real McCoy. 'Several practitioners were enlightened,' according to Pang follower Mary Qian who was quoted in the press reports. 'We realised that [she] is the true master who created the entire universe.'

I felt privileged to have met and spent several days with the master of the universe, even if it hadn't been obvious at the time.

BIG RIVER, LITTLE FISH

Travelling down the Yangtze River on a commuter boat from the city of Chongqing in Sichuan province gives you a taste of another China. Chongqing is central-west China's Big Smoke: a mess of 30 million people living in a giant cauldron. It reminds me of one of my favourite meals, the Chongqing hotpot. A pot is filled with boiling stock, heated by a portable gas burner mounted on a table. Into the broth goes shaved raw meat, fish, frozen tofu and fresh vegetables. Then, after just a few seconds cooking, the ingredients are taken out and put into a bowl of sesame paste. Like the hotpot, the city gets so hot in summer it is often referred to as one of China's 'furnaces'. Staying true to its hometown reputation the boiling stock contains small but lethal chillies and handfuls of numbing pepper. Little wonder the Sichuanese have a reputation for robustness.

The city froths and bubbles with energy. It was the first place I visited in China where I felt culture shock, because it was just so different from the clean, wide avenues of Beijing and the thrusting skyscrapers of Shanghai. Situated in a basin on the confluence of the Jialing and Yangtze rivers, Chongqing overflows with rural Chinese who are much shorter and more dishevelled than their northern counterparts, and who can often be seen wearing brooding expressions and smoking a lot. They found me strange too. While I waited to cross a road one morning, in the time it took for the traffic lights to change, a crowd of about thirty people gathered just to stare at me. This was definitely another China.

Chongqing opened to foreign trade in 1890 and became a bustling industrial port crammed with junks sailing down from the interior. At one stage a significant opium trade grew from the south-west, but with the river's source in Tibet it became the equivalent of the Silk Road, carrying hides and furs, as well as hemp, salt, silk, rhubarb, copper and iron from the interior. Then from the Communist takeover until the mid 1990s, Chongqing deteriorated into a polluted backwater filled with sprawling state factories and rickety tenements. Yet it pulsed with life.

At first light, river traffic at the old Chaotianmen wharf was already bumper to bumper with boats of all size, origin and condition: passenger boats, cargo ferries and flat, pointed, Russian 'fast boats' that travelled to Yichang, near the site of the Three Gorges Dam, further downstream. The boats jostled for berths and when there weren't any they simply ploughed into the foreshore where a gangway splashed into the mud before a torrent of blue Mao suits, bamboo poles and brown cardboard crates spilled out. Merchants, delivery men and migrants duelled elbows in a mad rush to reach the long flight of stairs to take them up to the bus station and the big, smoky city.

Today, the chaos of the old wharf has been replaced by a steady, more orderly human flow on escalators encased within a gleaming new pier. Chongqing is again seeking to play a role as a major thoroughfare and central marketplace for China's vast interior, aided by the new Three Gorges Reservoir, which began filling up in 2002 and will reach its maximum height of 175 metres in 2009, able to bring large cargo vessels to Chongqing's door. Meanwhile, a decade-long, US$200 billion transformation is in full swing, remodelling the city from a scruffy inland hub to China's next Shanghai.

Bicycles are useless on Chongqing's steep streets. The best way to ascend the narrow stairways and winding roads is on a pair of legs. If the legs aren't up to it, there is always a sputtering minibus, and if your luggage is too heavy, you can call upon the foot soldiers of the *Bang-Bang Jun* or Bamboo Army.

The army's recruits are thousands of wiry men, who for a small price (around US$1) will carry your load, carefully tied and balanced on each end of a bamboo pole. The men are aged between sixteen and sixty, dressed in the Sichuan farmers' uniform of blue Mao jacket and rope sandals or rubber shoes. They usually chain-smoke but all are fit enough to run a marathon. The *Bang-Bang Jun* come from rural areas around Chongqing during the months when there are no crops to look after. If they are lucky, in the city they can make US$25 a week carrying luggage.

One night a mysterious sound like wind chimes wafted in through my hotel window together with the thick smell of coal. Days later, I discovered where the noise came from. A new highway was being built completely by human labour. The road had been cut into the side of a vast cliff by a brigade of workers, squatting in rows, holding hammers and chisels. There wasn't a machine in sight, or gloves, hard hats or safety goggles; only about one hundred or so men, wearing baggy Western suits, the other uniform of rural migrants in the city. Like the Bamboo Army, they were farmers or itinerant young men from other provinces, eager to earn a passage on the slow boat to wealth.

The camera crew, researcher and I boarded a Russian-made 'express' to take us part of the way down the Yangtze River. Though the locals called it a fast boat and we were travelling with the current rather than against it, it took about eleven hours, with stops, to reach the neck of the Three Gorges 450 kilometres downstream. Yet compared with other modes of river transportation, some of which should have been towed straight to the scrap-heap, the Russian boats seemed efficient and structurally safe, though they reeked of petrol. The three gorges – Xiling, Wuling and Qutang – are contained in a 240-kilometre passage. To accommodate the dam, the gorges will be flooded so that the canyons and sharp ravines will be less pronounced, making the scenery less dramatic. As an attraction, however, the pre-inundated gorges weren't particularly spectacular in my opinion, but they've inspired poets and artists for centuries and ancient history fleshes out their significance to the Chinese. Some diplomat friends of mine were delighted when they secured a special fare on a Chinese cruise boat. But they found the boat passed through the gorges at night so they didn't see any of the scenery. I was rather taken by a location near Yichang where some enterprising folk had erected a bungee rope over the river, and carved a cafe out of a cave. I doubt the bungee was accredited.

The Three Gorges Dam project has been a controversial one from the start. In March 1989 the State Council agreed to suspend the dam's construction for five years in the face of domestic and international pressure, but after the Tiananmen Square massacre in June 1989, the government clamped down on public debate about the dam. Throughout the 1980s a long list of leading international academics, engineers and environmentalists added their voices to the dam's critics inside China. They included the ageing but respected Sun Yueqi of the Economic Construction Group of the Chinese People's Political Consultative Conference and prominent journalist and activist Dai Qing, who was imprisoned for her opposition to the dam for ten months.

On the international front, the chairman of the Tennessee Valley Authority in the United States, David Freeman, headed a three week fact-finding mission to the dam site and on his return stated, 'In my opinion our delegation has killed the idea of a 700-foot dam that some Chinese engineers have been in love with for so long.' Environmental group Probe International has also spearheaded a long-running information campaign against the dam. However, despite the mountains of reports pointing out legitimate shortcomings in the engineering, as well as environmental and human issues involved in building such a large dam, the project was pushed through the National People's Congress in April 1992. Incredibly for China, an unprecedented one-third of the delegates either abstained or voted against the project.

On the fast boat downstream, our fellow passengers were a mixture of well-dressed merchants, couriers hauling heavy sacks of produce and a parade of other travellers in their odd inland fashions returning to their river-town homes. Outside the main cities, fashion is a mixed bag, to put it politely. While the shops stock a variety of modern garments, often people don't know how to put them together. For example, I once saw a young lady in make-up and high heels wearing pyjamas on the street. As the fast boat left the safety of the wharf at Chongqing, a woman sporting an elaborately curly, lacquered hair-do and wearing a frilly party dress (similar to one I owned when I was six) with anklet stockings and high-heeled shoes began an argument with a large, fierce-looking man who'd apparently taken her reserved seat. They shouted in sibilant Sichuanese, which I didn't understand. I couldn't decide who would win if it came to a stoush, but I admired the fiery woman for taking on someone twice her size. Eventually the express boat hostess, wearing a sash like a Miss Yangtze contestant, pacified them, showing the woman and her multiple sacks to another seat. Settling herself on the once-white seat cover, she began cracking sunflower seeds between her front teeth and sat back to watch a 1970s Hong Kong Kung Fu movie on the television at the front of the cabin. Everyone – including Kate, Sebastian, Charles and me – watched the movie. We had to, the volume was up so loud we had no choice. The express boat was what most inland travellers called luxury: it had entertainment, air-conditioning and reserved seats with covers.

As the cabin was quite small, anyone was welcome to stand by the open door of the craft as it sped downriver. Eager for fresh air, I positioned myself by the opening, borrowing a set of binoculars from a well-dressed man who said he was a salesman for a company that made woollen sweaters. Not surprisingly, our conversation turned to the Three Gorges Dam.

'Society is always changing; you can't hang onto history and still have development. For any country, development is much more important,' he said, expressing a common Chinese view on progress.

A few hours later, two foreigners boarded the fast boat. They were Italian film-makers searching for locations for a movie based on John Hersey's *A Single Pebble*, a novel about an American engineer sent to China to investigate the possibility of building a giant dam on the Yangtze in the 1920s. Amid the karate chops and flying bodies in the Kung Fu movie, I passed several hours chatting with Laura Panigadi, who spoke fluent English and Chinese, about why foreigners and Chinese viewed the construction of the Three Gorges Dam in such a different light. It seemed an overly ambitious project for a developing country and would require so much upheaval, not just for the more than one million people who had to move, but for a large and important farming region. Many Chinese, however, felt it was worth the disruption if people would benefit from it in the long term.

Surprisingly, socialist planners didn't dream up the idea of the dam. Dr Sun Yat-sen, the popular Nationalist Party leader, proposed it in 1919. The Nationalists, China's ruling party until 1949, then invited American dam expert John Lucian Savage to draw up a proposal in 1944 (inspiring John Hersey's novel), and two years later an agreement was signed with the US Bureau of Reclamation to design and build a dam on the Yangtze. Work on the proposal stopped in 1947 because of China's civil war. Yet the dream of taming China's longest and most powerful river didn't finish there.

Four years after the most devastating floods in China's history claimed at least 30 000 lives in 1954, a group of experts led by Premier Zhou Enlai inspected the most frequently flooded sections of the river. From there the influential Central Party Committee adopted a resolution calling for the 'active preparation' of the project. However the disastrous attempt to industrialise China during the Great Leap Forward (1958–60) once again delayed the work. Timing was still a problem later in the 1960s. Mao opposed construction of the dam at a time 'when the country is preparing for war', in reference to the ongoing tensions with the Soviet Union.

Mao at first was strongly influenced by the Vice-Minister of Electric Power, Li Rui, whom he made one of his political secretaries in the mid 1950s. Li Rui argued that smaller dams should be built first. Later, he believed that the dam should not go ahead as it would be too expensive as well as destroy many cities and fertile farmland. Though Mao initially sided with the outspoken young secretary, Li Rui lost Mao's favour because of his criticism of the Great Leap Forward. In 1959 he began an eighteen-year jail term.

From the time of its conception until 1992 when construction of the Three Gorges Dam was finally approved, it became one of the most researched and hotly debated issues in the country and one of the most controversial decisions ever taken by the leadership.

On board the Yangtze express boat, I asked to speak to the ship's captain. The crew and I were brought to the small bridge where Captain Peng Guofu held a cigarette in one hand and the ship's wheel in the other, never lifting his gaze from the river. There was a lot of traffic, from barges to fishing boats. Even in deeper parts of the river, according to Captain Peng, there was a danger of striking protruding rocks.

The towns along the Yangtze weren't particularly picturesque but they were somehow interesting. This was where some of China's heaviest state industry was located. Back in the 1960s Chairman Mao believed that if China ever came under attack, the industrial might of the nation – the so-called Third Front industries – would remain safe if buried deep in the country's interior. Today in Sichuan you can see the results of the policy. Sprawling Dickensian enterprises stain the landscape and spew chemicals into the sky, and nowhere more incongruously than on the banks of a scenic river.

Captain Peng, in his late forties, grew up on the river and was determined that he would be commanding vessels until the day he died. The thought of a giant reservoir, though it would be easy to navigate, filled Captain Peng with sadness. One day soon, he said, waving his cigarette at the window, the scene in front of us would disappear. 'It is a pity because we won't be able to see any of the relics in future. We will definitely lose a lot of precious things.'

The new reservoir, part of the US$28 billion Three Gorges project, has already begun to swallow up river towns. The river was dammed, according to China's official media, ahead of schedule at 9.48 am on Wednesday, 11 November 2002. By June 2003 the water level was expected to rise from approximately 70 metres to 135 metres. When the project is completed in 2009 the reservoir will be 175 metres deep and capable of generating enough electricity to match twenty-six nuclear plants. In the process the dam will drown thirteen cities, 140 towns, 1352 villages, 650 factories, 140 prehistoric and Stone Age sites, 570 burial sites and 300 buildings from the Ming (1368–1644) and Qing (1644–1911) dynasties.

US$40 million was allocated to protect Three Gorges relics and a number of the larger buildings, including the Zhang Fei Temple, across the river from the port of Yunyang, is to be relocated. The temple was originally built in AD 220–280, in honour of General Zhang Fei, a famous warrior during the Three Kingdoms period who was murdered by his officers. Zhang Fei's spirit is said to make itself felt through a wind that aids passing boats. The temple has been dismantled brick-by-brick and, if funds permit, is due to be relocated 32 kilometres away. Black wooden tablets with Tang poetry inscribed in gilt characters covered the inside walls of the temple and Mr Chen, a local official in charge of the temple's preservation, called me over to have a look at what was written on the reverse side of the tablets. There were slogans, written roughly in red paint.

'This is how local residents saved these priceless relics during the Cultural Revolution. They turned the tablets over and painted Mao's words on them. After that, the Red Guards never touched them,' he said proudly.

At Yunyang's main jetty, foreboding seemed etched into every stone. As the dam fills and the water level rises above the town within the next few years, it will swallow up narrow streets and all the houses and detritus left behind. I made my way up the steep stairs leading from the jetty, passing hawkers selling fresh vegetables, spices, live chickens and thousand-year-old eggs. Squashed between the tobacco sellers with their thick wads of pungent leaves and hawkers selling cigarette lighters and keychains, was a blind fortune-teller. My future was in the cards for just 1 yuan (A25 cents).

In Australia, I have never visited fortune-tellers or astrologers, but in China I did so on several occasions, all for work purposes when we needed to film a bit of colour. Though they were stamped out for many years, fortune-telling and *feng shui* are so much part of the Chinese psyche and society I found it difficult to ignore them. The blind fortune-teller asked me to select a card from a line in front of him. Someone in the crowd must have told him which card I picked; almost without hesitation he said 'Double happiness,' before launching into an obscure sort of poetry commonly employed by fortune-tellers. 'You have picked a lucky card. If you have a learned person in your home, a pair of magpies will bring good news. The learned one will become an intellectual, the pair of magpies will bring good news to you.'

There were no magpies visible in Yunyang, but later, whenever I saw them in Sydney I thought about the blind fortune-teller and decided that though his message was cryptic, the one yuan had been well spent because it made me remember the town. In the short walk from the pier to a decrepit guesthouse, painted marks on the walls indicated the levels of inundation, as if residents needed a constant reminder.

At the guesthouse, I struggled to find a rating that would match the three-storey building; half a star was too generous. At least there was a bed, a door and a toilet. There was also red carpet that had never been touched by a vacuum cleaner, a sink that let the waste-water splash directly onto the bathroom floor, and in the filthy shower recess the choice of scalding hot or cold water, but not both together.

Though the clock was ticking, Yunyang's narrow lanes were still crammed with industry: hawkers selling sizzling fried tofu and spicy chicken, watch-repairers, rope-makers, but the industriousness failed to mask the sense of resignation. It had been in mothballs for decades as China's leaders, hundreds of kilometres away, toyed with building the Great Dam. Any improvements to the town would have been pointless as there was always the likelihood that it would all be submerged one day, like dozens of other towns along the river.

Yunyang County is one of the districts that will be smack in the middle of the Three Gorges Reservoir. From the county 120 000 people were slated for relocation. In July 1999 the crew and I visited Yunyang a second time, after learning that 10 000 out of 15 329 villagers in one of its townships had supported a series of daring petitions to China's highest leaders, protesting against local officials who had cheated them out of resettlement money given by the central government.

Gaoyang township, part of Yunyang County, was inland from the river, about one and a half hours by car from the port of Yunyang. The trip was fraught with danger for a foreign television crew. I had not sought or been given permission to travel to this region, because I knew the request would either be turned down or we would be given an official tour of a happy and satisfied township, which had happened on other occasions. So without permission, Sebastian Phua, Charles Li and I travelled with a small tourist camera and went in search of the petitioners.

After staying the night at the half-star guesthouse in Yunyang town, the three of us boarded a taxi and asked the driver to take us to Gaoyang township. We selected a sturdy Volkswagen Santana for the long ride, but unfortunately didn't have time to check the driver's skills. As soon as he pulled out of Yunyang, he put his foot down and didn't take it off until we approached the township two hours away. It was a heart-stopping journey on a narrow, two-way road that wound around the edge of a jagged cliff, high above the Pengxi River, a tributary of the Yangtze. At any moment I expected a truck to come from the opposite direction and had visions of our Santana leaving the road, flying through the air and into the river.

Apart from the journey, the trip was nerve-racking because though we'd made contact with one of the farmers behind the petition, we had no idea whether officials had already found out about our visit and whether, on arrival, we would be greeted by a 'welcoming' committee. I wasn't worried so much about Sebastian and myself since we had foreign passports and if we got 'busted', in Sebastian's parlance, we would escape with a reprimand after some questioning. However I did worry about Charles the Chinese researcher. If caught, he could be blamed for letting the Chinese side down, and if the authorities felt it serious enough he could be sent to jail.

Hurtling towards Gaoyang, we passed the new township, a sprawling, half-built complex that looked like a city of white-tiled hospitals on top of a bluff. Beneath the new town, a giant banner proclaimed, 'Contribute to the Great Three Gorges to construct the new Gaoyang'. Then the taxi descended into a valley with lush banana trees and small thatched farmhouses. After nearly two hours of tension, it was a relief to stumble out of the taxi and into the foliage.

This is where we get ambushed, I thought pessimistically, knowing that a floppy blue sun-hat pulled down over my head would probably distinguish rather than disguise me. Sebastian, Charles and I clambered through the undergrowth until we found a track. Suddenly, standing in the middle of the path, clutching a bunch of giant fronds, was a short man with a crew cut. He was barefoot and wore shorts. We stood looking at each other for a while until he called out in a heavy Sichuanese accent, which I could just make out, 'Who are you?' Unsure of how officials looked and dressed in China's interior, but a little worried because of his crew cut, I replied with the same question. 'Who are *you*?'

'I,' he said proudly in his Sichuanese accent, puffing out his chest, 'am a local peasant.'

I was so relieved that I almost laughed, and indeed Mr Gan, the local peasant or farmer as they are now more commonly known, had been sent to look out for us to bring us to the home of Jiang Qingshan.

Mr Jiang, who appeared to be in his fifties, had a big grin which revealed rotting, tobacco-stained teeth. In the sweltering heat he wore a grubby white shirt and rope sandals, like the Bamboo Army in Chongqing. Fortunately, his house was surrounded by dense bush, and as the roof was being repaired, huge clumps of undergrowth had been hacked down and placed in his front yard. Though we were sheltered from roads and, with luck, the prying eyes of officials, every few minutes another person arrived just to have a look at the foreign television crew.

Though Mr Jiang and his friends were simple farmers, they had monitored the township government for some years. He was one of the representatives of two-thirds of the 15 000 residents who were to be moved due to the Three Gorges Dam who sent a petition to the central government in November 1997, asserting that they weren't receiving their fair share of compensation from the relocation funds. The petitioners believed they were due 20 000 yuan each, but the local government only allotted 10 800 yuan per person. Three months later a representative from the central government came to investigate their claim, and told the peasants that local officials were technically within their rights to withhold some of the resettlement budget to pay for infrastructure.

Gaoyang residents dropped their claim, until local resettlement officials began retaliatory action for the first petition. The residents decided to again look into matters and found numerous examples of corruption, including the creation of what Mr Jiang called 'fake migrants' to extract more funds from the central government.

'The central government distributed [money] to the local government. We only got a little bit and nothing else, so we feel desperate. They are cheating the people, deceiving their superiors and duping their subordinates,' said Mr Jiang. Some residents were also being forced into 'distant resettlement' in China's far western province of Xinjiang, which was tantamount to being banished. In their final petition in March 2001, residents wrote, 'We poorer people have insufficient funding to move. How can we maintain our current living standards with just 8500 yuan (US$1050) per head? We are even unable to build our new houses in the resettlement regions. How can we survive if displaced?'

Mr Jiang's family of five made a decent living in the order of 10000 yuan a year, because he occasionally worked in a brick factory as well as tending fields. However if his wife and children were expected to find urban factory jobs after being farmers all their lives, they stood little chance of finding decent work and Mr Jiang feared the family would slip into poverty.

After hearing the residents' grievances, I expected Mr Jiang to criticise the Three Gorges project. In fact he was proud of it. 'Of course I support it! I would even have given them some money out of my compensation because it's the most famous construction project in the world and we are proud of that. But what about the actions of the local government? For instance, say I'm an official. I take bribes here and then I just get transferred. And the people don't have any choice about moving.'

Then Mr Gan, the proud, short man with the crew cut joined in. 'If the right policies still can't be found we will have no choice but to move and to live in the local government building. If the party secretary goes out to eat, we will follow him. We will sleep wherever he sleeps. We are not even afraid of death.'

Added Mr Jiang, 'We are watching whether the leaders can save the party or not; if they can, it would be great! Otherwise the corrupt will still exist and the party will die.'

I didn't dare to linger in Gaoyang, despite the warm welcome from the farmers and the opportunity to learn about their lives. As soon as the interview was over, I stood up to go, thanking the men and women who had assembled to see the strange foreigners and their small camera. Each of them wanted to shake our hands and thank us for the opportunity of airing their story: the tale of one small township against their crooked government as mighty as a river.

We left Gaoyang and returned for one more night at the decrepit guesthouse before making our way down the uneven stairs leading to the Yangtze River's edge. On the ferry pier we sat and waited for the next fast boat to take us downstream to where the dam was being built. Feeling confident that we had filmed the interview and escaped without any problem, Sebastian and I took out small cameras to film some scenes from the pier. A few moments later, a cloud of khaki rolled down the gangway. The police had arrived.

The usual procedure was to play dumb and to insist we were merely on a tourist outing and that our small cameras couldn't possibly be used to film a television report. However, this time we were unsuccessful and a crowd gathered on the pontoon as a policeman took my passport and began leafing through it, showing it to the crowd. I grabbed it from him, telling him my passport was personal property and he had no right to show it to other people, even though it was unlikely they could have read English.

Poor Charles was left to argue with the police while Sebastian and I tried to move our luggage towards the edge of the pontoon, wondering whether, as soon as a ferry arrived, a quick departure might end the incident without further ado. Charles, however, shook his head at the suggestion. At that point, a fast boat pulled up and the pier attendant, in thick Coke-bottle glasses, held the ropes keeping the boat's gangway open. 'Just go,' he said quietly to me. 'Thank you, but it'll be too problematic,' I replied.

'Jane,' Charles said, looking concerned, 'this is bad. The police are going to call the *Waiban* [Foreign Affairs Office].' We had met the official from the Yunyang Foreign Affairs Office on the previous trip. That time, he had told us to come back any time, though he probably didn't mean uninvited. If the Foreign Affairs Office was to be involved, then the incident would have to be reported higher up.

We would probably miss the connecting tour boat we had planned to meet to continue filming our story on the dam.

Mr Zhang Banyun from the *Waiban* was a small, wiry man with a moustache and a very pleasant demeanour. At least, he had the previous time I met him. This time, he was like an angry bull charging down the gangway. He went straight for Charles, shouting and abusing him, hurt that old friends could behave like this. In the corners of his mouth were two spots of foamy white saliva that moved ever closer to his handlebar moustache. Charles tried to put his arm around Mr Zhang to console him, but he threw it off repeatedly. It took some time to pacify him, and all the while, fast boats and ferries came and went.

Mr Zhang made me write a self-confession about our illegal trip. I wrote it in English and Charles did a translation. We carefully avoided incriminating words like 'conducted an interview', using instead casual phrases like, 'I spoke to the residents'. Mr Zhang made us revise the treatise several times until he was satisfied it had completely let him off the hook. I prayed this would be the end of the matter, at least for now, and we would be able to continue our journey, even if a reprimand was waiting back in Beijing. After waiting on the pontoon for several hours and following numerous frantic phone calls to the senior Foreign Affairs Office in Chongqing, Mr Zhang permitted us to board a fast boat. He didn't look at or confiscate our tapes.

Though we had escaped intact and without a reprimand back in Beijing, the battle between the peasants of Gaoyang and local officials continued long after our departure. Several officials from Yunyang County were eventually charged and sacked for the abuse of resettlement funds. However, toothy Mr Jiang and three of his fellow petitioners (but not the friendly peasant, Mr Gan) were arrested in March 2001 in Beijing – two to three days travel for the farmers – as they were about to present another petition to the central government over alleged corruption by the officials of Gaoyang. In April 2001 they were sentenced to between two and three years jail for disturbing public order, leaking state secrets and maintaining illicit relations with a foreign country – in other words, the international media. I fear when they are released they will be forced to relocate to China's far-flung fringes to ensure they don't make trouble again.

Feeling deflated, Sebastian, Charles and I headed for the Great Dam, as the farmers called it, located 660 kilometres downstream from Chongqing. I joined a foreign tour group to hear what visitors to China were being told about the project and its human implications. Between 2003 and 2009 the area from Chongqing to Yichang will be inundated to form the Three Gorges Reservoir, 2309 metres long. By the time the dam is finished, its twenty-six turbines will provide one-third of the country's power supply. All-in-all it will have taken eighteen years to build at a cost of around US$30 billion, and displaced 1.3 million people.

Through the crackly microphone the tour guide told us that all of the Three Gorges migrants would be given jobs. Of the 40 per cent of migrants classified as rural, only 60 per cent of them would be allocated new farmland. The rest of the farmers would be retrained so that they could find factory work. Earlier, I had visited some of the towns that were due to be evacuated, accompanied by officials from the Chongqing and local Foreign Affairs Offices. The officials were surprisingly frank and didn't object to me stopping for impromptu interviews with residents. I took it as a measure of local people's dissatisfaction that they were openly critical even with the officials present.

One of the places we visited was the 'Ghost City' of Fengdu, so called because at the top of a hill which you could reach by a chairlift there was a temple dedicated to the god of the underworld. In the past, superstitious sailors refused to dock here for fear the ghosts would attach themselves to ships and haunt them through the gorges. I found that the residents of the Ghost City were battling with other demons, namely insufficient compensation.

'The local government only gives us, for instance, 10 000 yuan compensation, but the state has allocated 20 000. We can't buy a new house for this amount. What did they do with the money?' complained one woman. 'We hope that if you go to Beijing or somewhere else, please help our citizens to speak out about it. Please give us a little more compensation! We don't want to live in luxury; ordinary people will be satisfied with the houses they have.'

One hour away on a half finished road, the new city of Fengdu was taking shape. We parked on the main street where there were several completed buildings which even had their signage in place. There was a Bank of China and an office belonging to the tobacco company. The director of the local Foreign Affairs Office, Mr Wu, explained that certain companies had bought land and constructed their offices with compensation paid to them by the government.

'Rich work units came first and built their offices, but some of them bought lots of land, to build houses and then sell them,' explained Mr Wu. This wasn't according to regulation. Rich state entities were looking after themselves while ordinary residents found they couldn't relocate on their meagre allowance. I stopped two men walking down the street and they laid out a detailed list of grievances, from the low compensation to excessive fees and tolls charged by the local government. While Director Wu stood next to us, cringing, the older of the two men began laying into officials who coerced peasants into telling visiting journalists that their new package was a good one.

'They [the officials] put a carpet in one home, to create a false impression. Then they give a bonus to the peasant to say that their life is better than before they built the new city. In fact these are lies,' said the old man. Mr Wu told him to get lost. Mr Li, the Foreign Affairs official from Chongqing municipality and therefore senior to Mr Wu, had watched the whole incident. Sebastian, Charles and Mr Wu stayed on the street to take some extra shots while I got into the van. Mr Li, lanky and very forthright, said Mr Wu and the van driver privately agreed with everything the peasant had said.

'In their hearts, the driver and Mr Wu are not happy either. Mr Wu has to pay around 20 000 yuan of his own in order to move. Everyone feels sad,' he said quietly.

A few days later I was on the bed of the Yangtze River looking up at the Great Dam, two kilometres long and 180 metres high, still under construction. It was July 1999 and the river's flow had been diverted through a channel, yet it was a creepy feeling standing in front of what would one day be a great wall of water. Former Premier Zhu Rongji told dam officials that it must be built to last one hundred years, so thousands of workers swarmed over the site, like ants in a giant colony. I was told that international construction standards applied to the site, but many of the workers wore cloth shoes and no hard hat. Because of the deadline to finish the dam, there were three eight-hour shifts a day, and trucks brought lunch boxes down to the workers who sat on the hot, dry river bed, shovelling fuel into their tired, hungry bodies. The dam looked immense and impressive, but I remembered what China's leading Three Gorges critic, Dai Qing, had told me about the political motivation behind the dam. 'Chinese people always thought that foreigners were richer and stronger than us. Then after 1949 they thought that if they could do something to show the entire world that we were strong, we could build the best, whether it's the atom bomb or a giant dam, then it would show the world a kind of pride and honour.'

The dam is supposed to do many things: reduce disastrous summer flooding in the middle reaches of the river, produce electricity and bring large cargo ships to inland Chongqing. Every Chinese household pays a small Three Gorges surcharge on each electricity bill. Though the demand for electricity has increased more slowly than the forecasts, regions will be forced to buy Three Gorges power from 2003 to pay for the cost of the project. Either that or the government will subsidise the power and pass the cost on to taxpayers.

As for reducing floods, that remains to be seen. The worst floods of last century took place in 1954 when 30 000 people died, yet the population explosion between the 1950s and 1970s as well as modernisation in the form of widespread clear-felling of trees around the upper reaches of the river contribute to the Yangtze's flooding potential. In 1998 an extremely heavy season of rain over the Yangtze delta led to an incredible loss of life.

China's floods are destructive because the constant shortage of living space forces people to live right on the riverbanks and often in the catchment areas. The lack of foliage as well as massive soil erosion add a huge volume of water to the river. In addition, small lakes over the years have been reclaimed to provide land for housing and agriculture. As a result, the only way to ensure fewer deaths due to flooding is to stop the environmental degradation or force the relocation of millions of people. Given the Three Gorges relocation, any extra forced movement of people adds to the burden. The other problem is the strength – or lack of it – of China's extensive network of 85 000 dams.

By the end of September 1998, the raging torrent on the Yangtze had affected one-fifth of China's population, or 223 million people throughout 29 provinces. More than 3600 people died, 14 million were left homeless and the floods caused US$20 billion in damage. The disaster was so acute nearly 3 million people were forced to live in tents on the river's dykes, many of which were either badly damaged or in need of urgent repair.

More than a million soldiers were mobilised to help stricken communities along the lower reaches of the river in the biggest movement of the army since the 1949 revolution. The PLA provided great news fodder for the state media, which focused on the soldiers' heroism and basically glossed over the death toll. Every disaster has its most memorable image and on this occasion it was the rescue of a small girl, found clinging to a tree-trunk above the muddy swirl after the rest of her family had been swept away by the deluge. The TV cameras caught the entire rescue operation and played the story incessantly, accentuating the astonishing bravery of the soldier and the child. Apart from that incident, however, little else was heard of the personal tragedies of the thousands who died that summer. It was strange sitting in a perfectly dry Beijing, watching the nightmare of the floods unfold, almost as if they were happening in another country. That was how incongruent and unequal different parts of China seemed to be.

The Chinese government didn't approve of foreign journalists searching for stories emerging from small towns and villages along the Yangtze. As usual when a disaster or accident occurred, requests to visit the affected area were rejected or ignored until well after the event. Yet news trickling out from the floods was beginning to tell a bigger story than a clear-cut natural disaster. Man-made factors too contentious to ignore had surfaced, and many foreign journalists decided to head to disaster areas along the river to find out what was happening.

Our usual partners in crime on out-of-town excursions, the taxi-drivers, had been warned against guiding journalists to flood zones, and some unlucky correspondents didn't make it past police road-blocks before being ordered back to Beijing. However, I was given the telephone number of a reliable and apparently helpful driver who agreed to meet us away from the taxi rank at Wuhan airport which was being monitored for foreign journalists. After narrowly avoiding an argument with the taxi-rank supervisor over boarding an 'unauthorised' taxi because it wasn't in the queue, Sebastian, Charles and I were on our way to Jiayu County in Hubei province, where according to the Chinese media a major dyke had collapsed on the night of 1 August.

Our taxi-driver lived up to expectations and took us to Jiayu County, about 70 kilometres upstream from the city of Wuhan. After several hours in a barely roadworthy car driving on potholed roads, our destination, the small town of Hezhen, came into sight. So too did dozens of police cars and policemen guarding the entrance to the township.

Our taxi pulled over to the side of the road. I knew that as a foreigner, if I got out of the car and approached the dyke, I was likely to be detained and we would all be sent back without a story. Yet Sebastian and Charles, two Chinese men (though not ordinary in appearance as Sebastian had long hair in a pigtail), could pass as local or Hong Kong reporters, who were viewed as distant brothers rather than foreigners. I briefed Seb and Charles on the questions and with the small digital camera hidden in a common Chinese travel-agency bag, they got out of the taxi and went in search of some villagers.

While I waited in the taxi, I asked the driver about the town. To my surprise, he told me the dyke protecting Hezhen and the neighbouring township of Paizhou was about 40 kilometres long. More than 56 000 people were living in the townships when disaster struck. Witnesses told a Hong Kong human rights group that hundreds of villagers were swept away when the dam broke, with at least 1000 people initially declared missing. Another report, this one in a local newspaper, said 400 soldiers were also swept away. Despite these stories, the official death toll from the collapse of the dyke at Jiayu County was given as forty, while thousands of homeless villagers camped along the unbroken sections of the dyke for nearly four weeks after the disaster.

Nearly an hour later, after I had exhausted conversation with the driver and chewed off several fingernails, Seb and Charles returned. They had learned why the towns were crawling with police. The story was that the Paizhou dyke had broken at about 8.30 on the evening of 1 August while hundreds of officials, local residents and soldiers had been working to repair cracks in it. Thousands of others in the rural county thought they were safe in their homes and were preparing for bed.

'After the dyke broke no-one sounded an alarm. The news trickled down to us gradually,' said a middle-aged woman, speaking to the camera. 'According to our information at least a thousand people died. We don't know how many are still missing. Old ones can't find the young ones, the young can't find the old. They sent some of the children who'd been rescued to another town. I wanted to go back to fetch more things, but they told me that I'd better not go back, otherwise I would die. So I just grabbed this broken bed. We don't have clothes, we don't have anything at all. We borrowed this table. We borrowed everything. We don't even have food.'

It was six days after the dyke had broken and the woman and her family had been made destitute. Another villager explained that local flood-control officials initially found a thumb-size hole in the dyke. They informed the party secretary, an influential figure in local governments, who didn't believe there was a major problem. As time progressed, however, the hole grew to a crack which became wider and wider. In its final stages, it suddenly went from 10 metres in width to 300 metres as the dyke disintegrated. Two officials from the county, I later found out, were sacked for turning a blind eye to the problem.

After repeated requests from foreign journalists to pay an official visit to the flood scene, the Chinese government finally allowed a small group, including the ABC team, to see the aftermath in several devastated areas in Hubei and Henan provinces. Though the rain had long stopped and the dykes had broken three weeks before our visit, the scenes were still unsettling.

In Anxiang County, a breached dyke was being repaired by a contingent of PLA soldiers, who dashed into the water before impressively laying down hundreds of sandbags in a few minutes – I suspect for the benefit of the foreign TV cameras. However, the gaping hole in the earthen dyke gave some idea of the force of the flood water, which had gushed into small villages, filling them like swimming pools.

Officials took journalists down a tributary of the Yangtze River where the dyke was covered with tents for as far as the eye could see. The tents were made of red, white and blue plastic, a material used all over China for tarpaulins and large carry-bags. As it was mid-summer, most of the tent-dwellers sat in the open, in many cases just metres from their old homes. It was how I imagined a refugee camp might look. Curiously, electricity had been brought to the area and one family had their large television with them. Mirroring *The Truman Show*, they watched the coverage of the flood clean-up on their TV while it happened around them.

Premier Zhu Rongji toured the devastation in Jiujiang County in southern Jiangxi province. He couldn't hide his anger as a familiar pattern began to unfold. In the rush to make money, local officials had ignored the upkeep of the country's dykes and dams; some were so flimsy, he discovered, they might as well have been filled with bean curd.

Zhu Rongji's famous 'bean curd' denouncement unleashed a rare series of media investigations detailing the neglect – and in many cases corrupt behaviour – of officials who were supposed to maintain the dykes and safeguard the lives of citizens. In the town of Honghu between the cities of Yichang and Wuhan, one investigation found officials had contracted a company to repair a dyke at a cost of 9.4 yuan per cubic metre. One of the company's senior employees was the daughter of a local official, responsible for the maintenance of the town's dykes. Through the daughter's influence the company contracted out the repair of the dyke to a second company for 7.6 yuan per cubic metre, pocketing 1.8 yuan. The second company did the same thing, hiring a contractor for 5 yuan. For that amount, nearly half of the original price, the contractor couldn't afford sophisticated construction materials, so bricks and tree-roots were used instead. A subsequent study by the Ministry of Water Resources revealed that out of 84 800 dams, most of them built during Mao's era, 33 000 or more than one-third of them were in need of reinforcement.

In the years after the 1998 floods, the state media was given a controlled brief to investigate corrupt practices relating to China's biggest construction project – the Three Gorges Dam. It was designed as a kind of pressure valve, to allow ordinary people to express their frustrations as well as showing that the government was resolved to guarantee the quality of the dam. As part of the media's 'bean curd' witch-hunt, small local publications led the way, uncovering examples of official misconduct. One issue of the *Three Gorges Evening News* reported that on one 14-kilometre stretch of the Number 209 Trunk Road built for the Three Gorges project after the relocation of several townships, seventeen out of twenty bridges were found to be sub-standard and five had to be dynamited. One bridge in Badong County, about 100 kilometres upstream from the dam, collapsed and killed eleven people.

Badong County was a significant industrial area on the river. The only way to the off-limits Trunk Road high above the Yangtze, however, was through a cornfield, so Sebastian, Charles and I began trekking through the corn, trying not to trample someone's precious livelihood. We passed an old farmer working in the field who told Sebastian that no foreigners ever came to these parts and that we must be journalists. Although we were on an unauthorised trip, with no officials present, the farmer didn't seem particularly concerned about our presence so we continued making our way up through the tall stalks until we reached a row of simple farmhouses on the new highway which, due to the accident, was closed off. In the second house we found old Mrs Feng Guozhen whose brother and son had been working on the Jiaojia Bridge when it collapsed.

Mrs Feng's family could trace its roots in the area back five generations. She looked much older than her sixty-two years and wore the typical loose blue clothing of a working peasant and a blue head cloth. She was expecting us because we had called ahead. However, she seemed confused as she recalled the events of nearly five months earlier. Her son, Jiao Shilin, in his forties with a leathery brown face, came in from the fields to join us. Mr Jiao was a farmer, but to supplement the household income he occasionally worked on construction sites near his home. He was working for the Number Seven New East Construction Company and had been standing on the bridge when it collapsed.

'I heard a big noise and when I realised what was happening I ran towards one end, but I ended up falling off the bridge. Then they sent me to hospital,' he said.

His uncle and ten other workers hadn't been so lucky. They plummeted into the ravine. Mrs Feng's brother died in hospital a few hours later. Yet the family's misfortune didn't end there: a few months later, the shock of the incident, according to Mrs Feng, caused the death of her grieving 83-year-old mother.

I asked Mrs Feng if she knew why the bridge collapsed. She said people in the village said the construction company used sub-standard materials. Otherwise she wasn't clear. What she knew was that her family now survived on 200 yuan a month (US$24) compared to 800 yuan (US$97) before the accident. Jiao Shilin had made several visits to the county government to seek justice, and an official eventually visited Mrs Feng, but the total compensation the family was paid only came to 6600 yuan (US$800).

The indifference of local officials annoyed Mrs Feng. 'I told [the official] that the Communist Party should tell the truth. Until then, no-one came to visit us, no-one cared about us,' she said. Four officials were subsequently arrested, but her family still had not received an apology. Her son, Mr Jiao, who severely injured his leg in the fall and was unable to walk for several months, said the construction company had been short of funds so it used second-hand materials to erect the bridge.

'They built the bridge without any drawings,' said Mr Jiao. 'They didn't use steel screws and they used bad wood – there are many reasons why the bridge collapsed.' I asked him if corruption had been involved, but on this Mr Jiao didn't respond directly. 'I worked for them for fourteen months and was only paid 1200 yuan. I was supposed to get paid 450 yuan per month, instead all I got was 1200.'

In 2002 yet more reports were published, this time in the English language *China Daily*, detailing shoddy construction in the Three Gorges project. These reports concerned the dam itself and the appearance of large cracks in the cement work. A senior official ordered the cracks – measuring 1.25 millimetres in width and 2.5 metres in depth – to be 'repaired fastidiously'. Years ago, dam critic

Dai Qing warned that it was natural to expect corner-cutting construction to dog the project.

'The Three Gorges project is too wealthy,' he said. 'It's like a piece of meat with all the flies rushing to eat it. Most Communist Party cadres aren't promoted because of morality or because they are well educated. The first reason is political; they support the party. So it's extremely difficult for these kinds of people to resist the temptation of money. It's inevitable.'

Today with the dam a reality and the relocation virtually complete, some of the controversy surrounding its construction may die down. China claims more than 6000 foreign specialists have taken part in building the Three Gorges Dam. In 2002, American Ernest Mitchell was awarded a 'friendship award' for his contribution as the chief concrete quality supervisor. The award is the central government's highest recognition given to foreign experts working to help China's modernisation.

Yet the lack of transparency makes it impossible to know whether the cracks in the Great Dam have indeed been repaired fastidiously. The project's main supporter in the government, the former head of the National People's Congress, Li Peng, is no longer in office. If an enterprising Chinese journalist discovers another dam scandal, will his or her editors be brave enough to print it?

PORK BELLIES

In the mid 1990s a rural Chinese town came to embody what China's leadership regarded as a civilised society, in which people had aspirations to get rich as well as having a social conscience. This urban utopia was the city of Zhangjiagang in the Yangtze River basin, located a few hours drive from Shanghai on rich agricultural land the Chinese describe as a 'land of fish and rice'. Zhangjiagang's economic ascendancy began like the rest of southern China's in the early 1990s with an export boom from its township and village enterprises, then the construction of a container port. By 1995 it had built a dream town for its population of less than a million people, and boasted the cleanest, tidiest streets in China. The state-run media fell on Zhangjiagang as a socialist-market icon, and for its combination of economic and spiritual progress elder statesman Jiang Zemin bestowed on it the title of 'model city'. In most Western societies, wealth usually creeps up on a city gradually, but in China it often arrives overnight, and so it did in Zhangjiagang.

I had to see this utopia for myself, so in January 1996 I visited Zhangjiagang with the camera crew: Kate Wakeman, Sebastian Phua and Zhang Lijia. We were taken to see an 'urbanised farmer' Mr Ge, who earned 3000 yuan per month, which was then about six times the average worker's wage, and lived in a three-storey house with marble flooring and flushing toilets. We visited a shop where a large placard read, 'Our Five Guarantees: hygiene, pleasant environment, no bicycles parked untidily outside, no outdoor stalls erected without authority, safety and order'. Everywhere, I was told, riches replaced rags. Even the local steel mill which had started life as a small township enterprise had risen to become one of the top-twenty national corporations. Zhangjiagang's party secretary, Mr Qin, proudly extolled the city's progress.

'We set a standard and want people to reach that standard so that the whole city is orderly and people are civilised. Citizens live together peacefully and it is stable and economically prosperous, yet people are concerned about one another. This is the situation in Zhangjiagang.'

While a nationwide campaign called on all Chinese to 'Learn from Zhangjiagang', my suspicions were aroused when all the officials I met came late for their appointments and reeked of alcohol.

Zhangjiagang's Director of Foreign Affairs, Mr Zhang Jiliang, was large and affable. He arrived for one meeting dressed in a long black leather coat and carrying a brick phone and a man-bag, the male handbag popular amongst Chinese officials and plain-clothes police in the mid 1990s. Mr Zhang was a typical Zhangjiagang success story: he had risen from the ranks of a minor cadre in a nearby town before being promoted to Zhangjiagang's Foreign Affairs Office. He travelled abroad frequently to court foreign investors and met all the foreign journalists visiting Zhangjiagang. Yet like most of the senior party officials outside China's main cities, he had no background in media, investment or international affairs.

From his flamboyant appearance, I could tell Mr Zhang liked the good life. 'Do you like dolphin?' he asked me.

'Yes, I like dolphins,' I replied, wondering where the conversation was leading.

'We eat river dolphin here.'

I was unsure how to respond. Director Zhang was unfazed. 'There are dolphins in the Yangtze and they taste very good sashimi-ed, *hong shao-ed* [red-cooked, which is broiling in a sweet rich soy-based sauce], steamed or in a soup which is even more delicious. Making the soup is highly skilful work; it's all about heat and timing,' he said with the air and relish of a TV chef. 'Once you've tasted dolphin, it's hard to go back to eating regular fish.'

Taking my protestations for politeness, the director promised to let us sample dolphin during our visit, hastening to add that he would have to check his hectic schedule. In the meantime, he apologised for being too busy to accompany us during our filming of the city so he would send two of his subordinates to chaperone us.

In Zhangjiagang, each work unit or government organisation, whether factory, hospital, school or corner shop, was responsible for the patch of street in front of it. No-one was permitted to smoke in public and spitting was outlawed. (Not before time. Spitting in public places was only banned in Beijing in October 2002.) Throughout the day I was earbashed with examples of civilised behaviour, as I interviewed happy but wooden residents and walked on streets clean enough to eat off, but it was the director's comments about eating dolphin that kept haunting me. How could this be a model city when the Foreign Affairs director consumed an endangered species?

I told the team that in the evening we were going to waive dinner with Mr Zhang (and probably get out of sampling dolphin sashimi) in order to uncover 'dirt' – or in journalist speak, 'balance' – for our story about the civilised city. As usual, Zhang Lijia, the patriotic Chinese researcher now living in Britain with her Scottish husband and two children, berated me for my 'Western scepticism'. We flagged down a taxi on a street outside our hotel. The next moment the chatty driver was trying to rip us off.

'Normally in Zhangjiagang the taxi fare depends on where you're going, so how much are you going to pay me?' he asked. At that point Lijia conceded that the driver was maybe a little grasping. 'You are obviously well paid, but do any poor people live here?' she asked, searching for more evidence that things weren't quite right in this model town. The driver didn't bring up the money issue again. Instead, he dropped the pretence that everything in Zhangjiagang was always perfect. 'Oh yes. The poor people were pushed out of the centre of town when they started building all the fancy roads and buildings. The poor people were forced to move,' he replied.

Excited about our good fortune, journalistically speaking, Lijia completely forgot her comments about my Western scepticism and proceeded to do what she did best – sweet-talk the driver into taking us to where the poor villagers lived. He introduced himself as Yu Xingming, which means 'a surplus of bright apricots'. Though he owned an apartment in urban Zhangjiagang, his home town was just outside the city. 'If you like, I can take you to see the poorest person in our village,' he said. 'It's on the outskirts of town.'

It was not an enchanted evening. A pea-soup fog hung in the air. The bright streetlamps disappeared and the road became completely dark apart from the taxi headlights. The city seemed to end suddenly and then fields surrounded us. Half an hour later, Mr Yu stopped the car. The four of us stepped into the fog and the driver led the way through a soggy field holding his cigarette lighter in front of him. Sebastian did the same, but the light from two small flames was barely adequate. None of us had thought to bring a torch. As we stumbled after the taxi-driver, I felt mud squelching up over my shoes and onto the bottom of my jeans. I was scared we might drop the camera or another piece of equipment in the field.

Finally we reached firmer ground and I could just make out the silhouette of a farmhouse. It was no later than 8.30 pm but there wasn't a single light on inside. Mr Yu went ahead and banged on the glass window.

'Hey! Wake Up!' he shouted for the benefit of the entire village. 'Foreigners are here! You're going to be on TV!'

The house he had brought us to belonged to Mr Yang, a rice farmer. It was a large single storey house that looked as if it doubled as a warehouse, with sacks of grain piled about the entrance hall. Light came from several naked bulbs dangling from thick beams above us and wooden benches were brought out for us to sit on. From where I sat with my back to the door, I could see someone, probably Mr Yang's wife, sleeping in a room to my left, and to the right there was another room with an earthen oven in the centre. According to the driver, Mr Yang was so poor that none of the women in the village wanted to marry him. As a result he had to suffer the indignity of marrying a woman five years older than he was, and from another, poorer province. This is because the family of the male traditionally gives a bride payment, a type of compensation for the loss of a daughter. In Mr Yang's case, he couldn't offer enough to satisfy the families of the available women in his village. Mr Yu, the taxi driver who'd initially tried to rip us off, turned out to be worth his weight in rice.

Farmer Yang, tanned and looking older than his forty-six years, wore a brown woollen jumper covered in holes. His hair was dishevelled but he sounded remarkably alert for someone who'd been woken up five minutes before. He believed that his family, compared to others in the village, had fallen behind financially because they had sold most of their land to stay ahead. 'We get by, I suppose, but I'm not satisfied. China is supposed to be a socialist country, but on the surface it is capitalist. Poor people are really poor and the rich make a fortune,' he said, tugging uncomfortably at his jumper.

'This city looks good on the surface,' the taxi driver expanded, 'but underneath I don't think it's that good. Many enterprises are losing money. They rely on loans to pay salaries. They say this is a land of fish and rice, but that says nothing about the state of the economy.'

We left Farmer Yang, trudging again through the muddy fields, and took the taxi back to the hotel. Delighted at finding 'dirt' to balance the story of China's cleanest city, I paid the driver about 200 yuan (A$50) for his research and driving – or four times what he usually made in a day. Then, as Lijia, Sebastian, Kate and I sneaked back into the brightly lit hotel foyer, all pink wallpaper and chandeliers, we heard a familiar voice.

'Oh, *here* you are!' It was Foreign Affairs Director Zhang. We stood there, horrified, awkwardly clutching our various pieces of equipment. Lijia had told him we would eat dinner on our own that evening because I was suffering from 'female problems'. It didn't look as if we'd been eating, or I was suffering from anything other than acute guilt.

'We just returned from dinner and took the camera with us for safe-keeping,' I said to the smiling director.

'Oh, too bad! I wanted to invite you to dinner,' Director Zhang replied. 'Never mind. Maybe on your next visit. I hope you all have a good night's rest!'

The director didn't express suspicion or any other emotion apart from high spirits, so we shook hands and uttered pleasantries until he ushered us towards the lift.

When the lift doors shut, there was a collective sigh of relief. Then someone cried out, 'Look at our shoes!' All eyes dropped to the floor. The carpet was covered in mud; *our* mud falling from *our* shoes and trousers. No-one could have missed it as we trudged into the hotel tired and bedraggled from our expedition in search of 'dirt'. Director Zhang must have noticed, but in the civilised spirit of forgiveness, not a word was said.

Today Zhangjiagang has a thriving export trade and still basks in its status as a model city. But now there are Zhangjiagangs all over China: rice fields are turning into new cities filled with the more affluent people while the poor are banished to the edge of town. China has become one of the world's most stratified societies. The gap between rich and poor, according to an international bench-mark called the Gini Co-efficient, puts China in a state of 'absolute disparity', a wealth gap greater than the United States or Australia and one that continues to widen.

When Mao Zedong ruled China, his brand of Communism went beyond a straightforward doctrine of economic production; it was an all-encompassing ideology. Those who opposed it were purged. Yet for tens of millions of others, the Maoist ideology was also about human ideals such as the morality of the masses and selflessly serv-ing the socialist revolution as the path to modernisation. Even in a backward village in southern Guangxi province, I found several homes still kept dog-eared posters of old Mao tacked to their mud brick walls. Despite policy-induced starvation in the early 1960s, to millions in the countryside Mao was, and still is, viewed as a strong leader who stood for stability, equality and national pride. By the late 1980s when the reform era was in full swing, corruption, nepotism and bureaucratic ineptitude led to widespread dissatisfaction in a party seen as increasingly self-serving and out of touch with reality. Deng Xiaoping's era swept aside Mao's famous maxims such as 'Serve the People' in favour of an unofficial one, 'Help Yourself'.

China's leadership is extremely concerned, but in practical terms very little can be done about the disparity in wealth and living standards. By following Deng's dictum to let some people get rich first, the Third Generation leadership under Jiang Zemin raised the status of the private sector in the economy. It's a policy being continued by the Fourth Generation under Hu Jintao. But as capitalists are welcomed, the former vanguards of the Communist Revolution – workers and peasants – are slipping further and further behind.

In his contribution to China's still-supposedly socialist theory, the 'Three Represents', Jiang told cadres that the country's task was to turn people into citizens with lofty ideals, moral integrity, better education and a good sense of discipline. 'We must . . . instil into people's mind such ideas as self-reliance, competition efficiency, democracy, the legal system and the pioneering and innovative spirit,' he said. However, with the gap between haves and have-nots becoming more obvious in Chinese cities, towns and villages, the prevailing spirituality is money. In a Shanghai bookstore the most popular counter displayed Chinese translations of self-help and change-management books such as *Who Moved My Cheese?* and *Rich Dad Poor Dad*. Readers weren't the slightest bit interested in a self-acceptance manual called *How to Be Happy and Content on Your Income*.

Zheng Xinqing is typical of China's moneyed elite in that he went from earning a high 5000 yuan (A$1250) per month to what many would consider an astronomical sum – more than 10 000 yuan monthly – in the space of just two years. In the mid 1990s, like most Chinese, he dreamed of owning a mansion, a car and travelling abroad. Today he owns a luxurious split-level apartment, a prestige car and travels overseas frequently. To explain his success he tells a story about his first visit to the United States in 1997. He was captivated by Disneyworld in Orlando, Florida. He called the 'American creativity' of the Fantasyland castle, fireworks and Space Mountain a 'miracle'. Then, on a signboard, he saw the magic words that have become his life's motto: 'If we can dream it, we can do it.' For Mr Zheng, who grew up in a small town on the edge of Zhengzhou in central Henan province, it was a revolutionary concept that in modern China your dreams could determine your future.

Several years ago, Zheng Xinqing described his perfect home. It had to have a staircase and plenty of bedrooms in case people wanted to stay overnight. He wanted a separate study for himself and one for his wife, who works with him. The imagined home was far beyond what an ordinary Chinese dreams of visiting, let alone owning.

Zheng Xinqing and his wife, Zhou Fanyang, are both in their late thirties. In earlier years they spoke of wanting a child, but now there doesn't seem to be a place for one in their busy lives. I first met them at a motivational lecture they had organised in a large, rundown, socialist-style auditorium, but the lecture quickly dissolved into something more like an Academy Awards ceremony. Mr and Mrs Zheng were the stars walking arm in arm down the red carpet, smiling and waving. Then the beat of the 1990s dance hit 'Macarena' filled the hall as the crowd of more than a thousand middle-class aspirants danced and applauded the arrival of Mr and Mrs Zheng, leading distributors in the direct marketing organisation Amway – short for the American Way.

Five years later, Mr Zheng was giving me a guided tour of his brand-new apartment in Zhengzhou. Just as he had once imagined, it had lots of bedrooms (six in total), as well as three bathrooms, a staircase and a giant chandelier hanging over the living room. The Zhengs had a monstrous TV set which was the size of my dining table in Australia, a movie camera and a DVD player. We toured the kitchen, where Mr Zheng showed off his pride and joy – an American water filter. In his dining room he opened a drawer and took out a large flat plastic box filled with an array of pills, at least twelve to be consumed every day during breakfast. Seeing my concern, he quickly explained, 'They're not medicine, they are vitamin supplements.' Then we took the stairs to the master bedroom, which resembled a hotel suite, with ornate bedside lamps, walk-in wardrobes and a pull-out compartment containing coffee and tea-making facilities.

Mr Zheng loved showing off photographs and videos of his overseas trips like a newlywed anxious for another screening of the wedding video. Ms Zhou was too busy to watch as she was organising an afternoon sales session. So I was left with Mr Zheng who held me virtual hostage for two hours while he explained nearly 500 photographs of his travels since I'd seen him last, followed by a DVD of his latest trip to Malaysia. Then it was back to the relentless stack of photographs where he insisted on pointing out all the special people and attractions of each visit, for example his Taiwanese mentor and his wife, standing in front of their BMW and Mercedes.

When I first met Mr Zheng he had never travelled overseas. He described himself as previously being a 'bumpkin' who in 1991 had been so in awe of the luxury White Swan Hotel in the southern city of Guangzhou that he had asked the doorman's permission to go inside. Times have changed; these days when he stays at the White Swan he doesn't ask the doorman's permission, he goes straight to the lift and accesses the executive floors with a key-card. Since 1997 he has travelled overseas at least ten times, all courtesy of Amway, each time flying first class.

Mr Zheng joined Amway soon after its official opening in China in April 1995. Though he was earning a good income in the Hong Kong-based investment company he was working for, 'it would have taken me years to save up any money,' he said. After joining Amway, which he pronounces 'Amooway', he quickly rose to the rank of 'diamond distributor'. I wasn't entirely sure what that meant, but he always had a number of 'disciples' following close on his heels, taking notes whenever he spoke. He certainly has an ability to connect with people from all walks of life. In a shopping centre, I watched as he befriended a security guard and exchanged phone numbers with him in a matter of minutes. 'He comes from Zhengzhou too,' said Mr Zheng. 'I think I convinced him to become a distributor.'

Amway's early success suffered a major setback in 1998 after a series of scams unrelated to the group prompted the government to declare both foreign and domestic direct marketing firms illegal because they were seen to be preying on the poor and uneducated. The focus on the personal relationship between distributor and consumer, in the government's view, inspired superstition and the formation of cults. As direct marketing sales offices around the country were besieged, riots broke out in several cities and four people died. As a result of the ban, Amway was forced to reorganise itself into a retail-based operation. While at the end of 1997 it had 80 000 distributors, one year later the number had dropped to 50 000. After the reorganisation, Amway theoretically did away with distributors, as they were to be attached to retail outlets. However it created a 'privileged customer' category, in other words sales representatives, who could buy the product for on-selling at a discount.

The reorganisation initially dented the company's profitability but didn't appear to affect Mr Zheng's success. As well as the apartment, by 2002 he owned a luxury car, made by the Honda company in Guangzhou, and earned nearly US$10 000 a month, enough to ensure a secure and comfortable lifestyle for the entire family.

One of Mr Zheng's trusted lieutenants in 1997 was a vivacious woman named Su Lin. She had been in the PLA for sixteen years when she met Mr Zheng's wife, Zhou Fanyang, on a minibus. Su Lin had only just arrived in Guangzhou hoping to strike it rich after her long service in the army.

'When I worked for the army I earned just 500 yuan [A$125] a month, but I always dreamed of buying designer clothes. To be able to reach that goal is like gaining dignity,' she said. Today, like Mr Zheng, Su Lin is going from strength to strength. She hasn't looked back since leaving the PLA, even convincing her husband to throw in his job as a manager in a state enterprise to work for Amway. Now they travel the country and the world together.

The conventional way of doing business in China requires long-established networks and relationships. Mr Zheng, however, said he started out with no *guanxi* or status in society, yet was able to build up his own network through his family and ordinary people he met. He communicates using the internet. Most new apartment buildings in China, such as Zheng's, now come with broadband access. In many ways, his quality of life isn't far off that of an upper middle-class person in a Western country.

As the glamorous white Honda sped toward the airport where I would catch my return flight to Beijing, I took out a lipstick to moisten my dry lips. Ms Zhou tapped my arm. 'Our brand is better than that one,' she said. It seemed to me that Mr Zheng and Ms Zhou, for all their generosity, were sometimes a little too keen to impress, a common trait of the new rich. Perhaps they should have taken the advice they gave many of their clients in the days when they were door-to-door distributors: just a little bit goes a long way.

Who constitutes China's middle class? It's a very fashionable discussion in China these days. Is it the combined population of China's five richest cities or, as one US consultant says, people earning 150 000 yuan (A$37 500) before tax and having an apartment and secure assets of 1 000 000 yuan. The State Council Information

Centre believes that by 2005 China will have 200 million middle-income consumers, while China's chief World Trade Organisation negotiator believes that by 2010 there could be 400 to 500 million. A Chinese think tank, the Chinese Academy of Social Sciences, recently said China's middle 'stratum' amounted to about 110 million people. Perhaps they are all correct. Whatever definition is quoted, however, the Chinese government tries to avoid the term 'class'. The words 'middle class' conjure up images of 'capitalist roaders', 'bourgeois liberals' and 'running dogs'. Under Mao, all capitalists were condemned and citizens who emulated them were punished. Now the party fetes these people, while it searches for a more imaginative, less Mao-laden means of describing them. Using the word 'class' while disowning a socialist past can be tricky. So, party-speak for middle class is 'middle stratum' or better still, 'those with high incomes'.

He Qinglian, formerly a reporter with the *Shenzhen Legal Daily*, produced a highly credible breakdown of China's current class system which I believe is very accurate. In 1998, Ms He published a controversial book called *China's Pitfalls*. The book exposed in great detail the dark underbelly of Deng Xiaoping's reforms, specifically systemic and widespread corruption which helped tens of thousands of cadres and managers line their pockets with the state's assets and exacerbated China's growing, and potentially destabilising, wealth disparity. The highest levels of the party and government sought her theories until the middle of 2001, when sentiment turned against her. She believes her hard-hitting views had come to be regarded as potentially damaging to the government, so two weeks before she was due to travel to the United States, she quietly went to the airport without any luggage and boarded a plane. She remains there today, where she lectures on the Chinese economy to university students.

According to the Qinglian, China's labour force consists of five groups. At the top there's a political and economic elite of approximately 7 million 'very rich' people. Next is a middle class 'ladder', with 29.3 million 'rich' people on the upper rung, including employ-ees of state monopolies, white collar workers in foreign companies and private owners of small and medium-sized firms. Also on the ladder are 82 million 'middle rich' people – teachers, self-employed traders, state enterprise managers, lawyers, and employees within the arts and media. The next ranking down, without their feet on the ladder, are the marginalised working class of 120 million who work for state firms. The fourth group is comprised of China's 480 million peasants or rural–urban migrants. At the bottom of the labour force are the 100 million unemployed or off-post workers and the poorest peasants.

Whichever description of China's labour market is the most plau-sible, affluence abounds in China's coastal cities and has reignited the misguided dreams of foreign businesses that they may one day sell to a market of 1.3 billion people. In the space of ten to fifteen years China's once ubiquitous bicycles have been exchanged for BMWs, cloth shoes for Ferragamo, green tea sipped out of jars for Starbucks. China's middle class is hungry. It wants the good things in life: a home, a car, a package tour and a foreign education. And it wants them all now.

'Chinese people are born and then they go on a roller-coaster,' explained Chen Mei, a tall, attractive woman in her early thirties. I met her through colleagues several years ago but I find her insights so incisive that I seek her company on each visit back to China. Chen Mei trained in international trade at Shanghai's prestigious Fudan University. Now she's a management consultant. 'I worry that China is in too much of a hurry and that we'll end up like Argentina; that we're building a bubble and it could all collapse.'

Such pessimism emerged on a perfect late spring day in Beijing, with the warm sun beating down on our backs as we sat outside the Buddha Bar, Beijing's version of the slick Parisian establishment of the same name. Next to the Buddha Bar, *Ho Hai* or the 'Rear Sea', part of a complex of lakes in central Beijing, glistened in the sun-light. In winter, the lake freezes over and it's taken over by ice-skaters and winter swimmers who create a swimming pool by hacking away sections of ice. Come spring, the willows turn fluorescent green. On the lake, one-child families pedal away the Sunday afternoon in kitsch white boats shaped like giant ducks. This is where the working class comes to entertain itself; there are cheap sausages on sticks or Kentucky Fried Chicken and the duck-boats cost just a few cents to rent. Mother, father and one child are neatly dressed and can afford to eat well; judging from the growing number of fat kids, perhaps too well. The scene is a far cry from my first visit to Beijing in the 1980s when the people wore blue Mao suits and the markets only sold a very limited variety of vegetables. Until the early 1980s residents still used ration coupons to buy foodstuffs such as rice, sugar, flour and oil. The coupons were introduced before the Cultural Revolution when China's economy was centrally planned.

For urban residents much of the change has taken place within the last five years; it was only in the mid 1990s that Chinese workers were given the luxury of a five-day working week. (Even in wealthy Hong Kong the working week is five and a half days.) Now there are also three week-long public holidays for relaxation and spending hard-earned savings, important from the government's point of view to keep the economy growing strongly. To help consumers loosen their purses, interest rates have been progressively cut since the mid 1990s and a 20 per cent tax on interest income has been introduced to encourage people to spend rather than save. It wasn't progress that concerned Chen Mei that day by the lakeside – it was the speed at which it was occurring.

'The Chinese are always in a rush. If one person has three houses, then next he will want five. It's always short-term thinking. If people felt safe, they wouldn't have such a short-term mentality,' she said. The result is that many people, particularly those who have newly come into money, behave selfishly. For example, Mei explains, at the airline counters some passengers blatantly queue-jump, going straight to the front of the check-in counter. When a plane lands, passengers don't stay in their seats but get up to open overhead lockers seconds after the plane touches down. Chinese passengers notoriously carry armfuls of cabin baggage so that they don't have to check in their luggage. All this, Mei explained, is largely motivated by their 'can't wait' mentality.

Chen Mei's job entails explaining Chinese behaviour and business practices to leading international firms and institutions. She works for a foreign enterprise which runs training programs teaching foreign and Chinese organisations about teamwork. To explain the Chinese mindset to a delegation from a leading US university recently, she used an abseiling analogy. She had just taught the representatives to abseil down a wall on the outskirts of Beijing, controlling their descent with a rope. 'The Chinese don't have that rope,' she said, 'or at least they don't think they have that rope.'

Insecurity leads many Chinese to obtain a foreign passport or study overseas with the goal of securing one. An overseas education has become one of the most sought after commodities for China's new rich. At the end of 2000 there were 380 000 Chinese students studying in 103 countries, 24 per cent of all international students. In 2002 Australia gave out around 11 500 student visas to Chinese applicants, up from 8100 the previous year and just 1500 in 1996. Canada issued 11 700, up from 1733 in 1998. Better urban incomes and savings rates mean more and more families can afford to send a son or daughter abroad.

Between 1978 and 2001, 460 000 Chinese students studied abroad. Only 140 000 came back. Whereas promising Chinese who graduated overseas once chose to stay away, seeking jobs in Silicon Valley or on Wall Street, now increasingly stable political and economic conditions in China are enticing many of them to return. With her excellent English, fresh ideas and Cambridge credentials, returnees like Zhang Xin represent the changing face of the country. We are sitting in her ultra-modern office, eighteen floors up in SOHO New Town, the office and apartment complex built by SOHO China, the company she runs jointly with her developer husband, Pan Shiyi. Around Beijing, all the new apartment blocks built for the middle class have borrowed their names from landmarks of other cities, so there is a Central Park, The Riverside and Oriental Kenzo, to name a few. Like many in China's moneyed elite, Zhang Xin left a China broken after years of upheaval due to the Cultural Revolution before returning to immerse herself in its seemingly boundless opportunities fifteen years later.

She departed Beijing with her mother to live in Hong Kong in 1980, where she studied and did time on factory production lines for five years before studying economics at Sussex and Cambridge Universities. After that she worked on Wall Street and in Hong Kong with the investment bank Goldman Sachs. Her job was to find investment opportunities in China.

'I looked at hundreds of projects, selecting only the good ones, but in three and a half years I wasn't able to convince them. We didn't end up investing in one single project,' she said. Disillusioned with the negative perception of China's potential she decided to quit and looked into the opportunities for herself. In 1995 she and her new husband bought the piece of land where a rice wine factory stood and where SOHO New Town now rises. SOHO, which stands for Small Office Home Office, was a completely new concept in Beijing.

'When the whole of China was providing cement shells we built furnished apartments,' she said, referring to the usual Chinese practice of buying an undecorated unit. SOHO's apartments are between 108 and 315 square metres in size with broadband internet on tap. The interiors are designed to be 'movable', capable of serving home or office functions. At present 70 per cent of the apartments are used as offices and 30 per cent as homes ('That way you don't get a ghost town at night'). When SOHO New Town's colourful buildings came onto the market in 2000 they were presold for 9000 yuan (A$2000) per square metre. Now they sell for 13 000 yuan a metre.

It wasn't until Zhu Rongji's reforms to China's housing policy that private projects like SOHO were able to take off. In 1999 work units or government institutions and factories were ordered to sell all state housing to employees at cost price. This gave many workers the opportunity to acquire their usually old and run-down apartments for around one-quarter to one-fifth of the basic commercial price; in other words, purchase an entire apartment for a total of 20 000 yuan or US$2400. Other workers bought new homes as a result of old ones being demolished. If a new apartment cost 300 000 yuan, a worker would be expected to fund a 50 000 yuan down-payment from savings, obtain a 150 000 yuan mortgage and perhaps an additional low-cost 100 000 yuan loan from the enterprise. New apartments are almost always bought as empty shells off the plan. This in turn has fuelled a huge growth in lifestyle spending on furniture and bathroom accessories.

It was amazing to see the crowds at the Ikea stores in Shanghai and Beijing when the Swedish furniture chain opened in China in the late 1990s. The pent-up demand for foreign-designed, long-absent comforts often resulted in a stampede when the Beijing store opened its doors on the weekend. It was an exciting addition to shopping in the Chinese capital after decades of surly, state-run service. At Ikea, families could lie down on the display beds (which they frequently did, all three at the same time), relax on the plethora of lounges and browse around the innovative computer tables. The difference between Ikea and traditional domestic Chinese furniture was its simple modern look, which suited the new apartments that people had started to buy. Though Ikea was pricier than domestic stores, it rapidly became a prestige brand and that, in turn, spurned copycat companies producing modern homewares.

In the mid 1990s, housing took up just 3–4 per cent of a family's total income, which meant that state workers had collectively amassed huge savings. Not all workers, however, have the means to buy even cheap homes, and the policy of paying nominal rent to the state continues for many. My doctor, Zhou Daifu, once lamented that she turned down an offer to buy an apartment from a patient in the mid 1980s for around 4000 yuan (A$800). Though the amount was large at the time, Zhou Daifu kicked herself because the apartment, conveniently located on the Third Ring Road, close to the Jianguomen International Post Office, would today be worth a fortune. Like many state employees, she didn't see what was coming. With her household earning 3000 yuan monthly, including her husband's income, the only way a typical traditional Chinese medicine doctor like Dr Zhou will ever be able to afford to buy a home is if her present state-allocated compound is demolished and she is compensated. However, overall the home-ownership drive has been successful within a very short time.

Mortgage rates, which are set by the government, initially limited institutions to supplying 50 per cent of the cost of a home with a ten-year repayment period. Now banks can cover 80 per cent of the purchase price with repayments spread over thirty years. By 2001 consumer lending made up just over 5 per cent of the banks' total loan portfolio compared to 25–40 per cent in developed nations, but the total value of home-loans leapt an exponential six and a half times between 1997 and 2002 to 355 billion yuan (US$43 billion). The home-ownership revolution is in its early days; one in two people say they plan to buy or upgrade their home within the next two years.

Zhang Xin hopes to capitalise on the housing wave by being the first private Chinese company to list on the Hong Kong and New York stock exchanges in 2003. She enjoys the challenge of breaking new ground. Private companies in China have grown despite a systemic bias in the financial environment that has favoured state enterprises. Until recently state banks only lent money to state enterprises, because they were considered politically to be a safer bet. Even if the banks lost money, if it was to a state factory it was deemed acceptable.

'Everything we build, we sell to the Chinese consumer. A home is now a big chunk of a Chinese person's disposable income and this initial public offer [of shares] captures an essential part of China's economic growth. Why wouldn't a foreign investor want a hand in that?' she said. 'Everyone has been telling us not to go to New York [because of the current financial environment]. But I still believe that it will be such a milestone to be the first private Chinese company to be listed on the New York Stock Exchange, and we shouldn't be afraid.'

China's love affair with home ownership isn't just creating middle-class lifestyles, it's forging a new political awareness. The Wangjing (which means 'view of Beijing') New City development is an upmarket estate on the outskirts of Beijing, built by a state construction firm and named a model housing complex in the mid 1990s. In early 2002, however, hundreds of its residents held a series of noisy protests within the complex. When residents bought their apartments, the construction company had plans for a three-storey office building in the corner of the grounds. But the plans were ditched for a 33-storey complex that would stand three floors taller than the apartments, blocking the view of Beijing's skyline. After discovering the change, residents became outraged, blocking access to the construction site and initiating court proceedings against the developer. In early 2003 the case still hadn't been resolved and a white protest van, manned day and night, was parked at the entrance to the site.

Though it can't be surmised from just one incident that home ownership is going to lead to increased demands by the middle class for more representation in the government, the Wangjing incident could be the start of a slow march toward the middle class demanding their rights and rule by law to protect their investments.

In addition to home ownership, one of the biggest changes to Chinese society in the last five years has been the growth of the internet. Compared to what is offered via China's traditional media, the internet truly is another world and its capabilities are changing Chinese businesses and individuals.

Jack Ma, who is in his late thirties, established his Alibaba e-commerce portal in 1999. When I first met him in early 2000 I was surprised to find that one of the rising stars of China's late 1990s 'e' rage looked like a college student with an impish haircut, wide smile and an American accent. Alibaba operates as an online meeting place of suppliers and buyers, matching Chinese sellers with international buyers. For a US$5000 annual fee, Alibaba creates web-sites for small and medium-sized Chinese companies and runs two sites, one for international trade and one for domestic trade. Before the dot-com crash, he secured US$25 million in funding from venture capitalists. The site now has more than 1.2 million members, 800 000 of whom are in China, and attracts around 1500 new members every day.

I didn't realise the significance of a development like this until Kate Wakeman, our sound-recordist and tape editor in Beijing, returned to Australia and began a home-furnishings business based in Sydney. She was searching for a Chinese supplier who could manufacture high-quality silk-bound notebooks and found one using Alibaba. The supplier sent her digital photographs of his work and eventually custom-made a sample and posted it to Sydney. Orders followed and the transaction was a huge success. For someone who doesn't speak Chinese, finding a supplier would have been extremely time-consuming and costly before the advent of internet marketplaces.

'We have changed the way business people are doing work. Usually, if I am in export, I have to go all the way to another nation to attend trade fairs,' Jack told me as we sat in a beautiful tea-house in his home town of Hangzhou, a picturesque city about an hour and a half's drive down the expressway from Shanghai. 'What I do today is communicate with people over the internet. Everything is just through clicks. So life has changed.'

It's a change that is enabling a Chinese entrepreneur to create a global business from an apartment, something that would have been unthinkable five or six years ago.

'Establishing a company like Alibaba before China opened its doors to global trade might have once seemed like the riskiest of ventures,' he wrote in the *Asian Wall Street Journal*, after attending the World Economic Forum in Davos in 2001. 'But in fact, high-tech companies like ours are springing up all over China, invigorating local economies, creating jobs and bringing skills to workers in all regions.'

What is surprising about 39-year-old Jack Ma is that until the early 1990s he was an English teacher in Hangzhou. He hadn't touched a computer keyboard until a visit to the United States in the mid 1990s when he was appointed as an interpreter for a US–China joint venture. When he returned to China, he created a web-site for his translation agency, and on the first day it was up and running he received five email messages from the US, Japan and Germany.

Like Jack Ma, Xiao Meng's world has also been transformed. Xiao Meng is a homosexual. He lives in Guangzhou but I met him during a visit to Beijing where he was catching up with mutual friends. He has large expressive eyes and speaks slowly and thoughtfully. Though homosexuality isn't banned in China, it's still a social taboo in many parts of the country and Xiao Meng believes he would be stigmatised if he brought his sexuality into the open, so he hasn't told any of his colleagues at the technology company where he works.

'In traditional Chinese society, it's hard to find the sort of infor-mation that can help you figure out who you are, how you should live and that there are many people like you and that what you are is okay,' he said. 'So I started a web-page to help others like me.'

There are now hundreds of gay web-sites in China and as long as Xiao Meng doesn't display sexually explicit material, he has more freedom on the internet than he does in real life.

'If you take the issue of democracy and compare it with homo-sexuality, democracy would be the more important issue by far. So the government can exert a certain level of control over these "problem sites", but there's no way for them to impose absolute control over everything.'

When I first arrived in China in the mid 1990s, mobile magazine stands – basically a bicycle covered in newspapers, paperback books and magazines – stood on every street corner for commuters who were stuck on their bicycles at rush hour. There were plenty of domestic women's magazines promoting Chinese film and pop stars. Then gradually I noticed the faces on the magazines changed from Chinese to Western, and soon the foreign women's magazines arrived with cover stories about the lifestyles of 'Claudia', 'Cindy' and 'Kate'. Yet while glossy magazines have been one of the biggest publishing phenomena in recent years, which is directly related to the growth in the size of the middle class, their content is strictly controlled. Each issue of every foreign magazine title must submit story ideas for approval to a local partner, which is always a government-owned domestic magazine. For starters, there is an unpublished blacklist of both local and overseas Chinese personalities, judged by the Chinese government to have made unacceptable political or anti-Chinese statements. For example, Taiwanese pop idol A Mei, also one of the mainland's favourites, incurred a brief period of the government's wrath after singing at Taiwanese President Chen Shui-bian's inauguration. Her action was deemed to be in support of President Chen's pro-independence line. The Chinese-born actress Bai Ling, who appeared in *Red Corner* with Richard Gere, also fell from favour. The controversial film had Bai Ling playing a lawyer who defends an American entertainment attorney arrested in China for a murder he didn't commit. Together they uncover a conspiracy which leads to the highest levels of the Chinese government. As well as restrictions on topics, there are restrictions on the treatment of the content. Magazines cannot discuss homosexual love in the same way as love between heterosexuals. Nor can they promote extramarital sex in a favourable context or as acceptable Chinese behaviour, although in reality extramarital sex is widespread. A public furore erupted in the Chinese city of Nanjing in late 2002 after a young couple were fined 500 yuan (A$125) for sleeping together in a hotel and being unable to produce a marriage certificate.

'You can't report on politics so everyone just says it doesn't affect them. So lifestyle is flourishing because it can be talked about. The intellectual world is stunted. You still can't publish an opinion that really matters here,' said Beijing-based *Madame Figaro* executive, Korean American Saeri Ziebart.

The cover story on the Twenty Most Admired Chinese Women, however, was extremely revealing about what young upwardly mobile females aspire to. Apart from property developer Zhang Xin, the list included eleven actresses or entertainers, three high-flying entrepreneurs, two sports stars, two models and Wendi Deng, the wife of News Corporation Chairman, Rupert Murdoch. Young Chinese women today admire beauty, money – lots of it – and the freedom to choose their own direction in life. Olympic gold-medal diver Fu Mingxia made the list, but her sporting achievements were painted as inferior to her other 'achievement': marrying Hong Kong's Financial Secretary, Anthony Leung, 'who is twice her age', as the magazine points out.

With a flood of foreign magazine titles coming to China, including *Elle*, *Cosmopolitan* and *Marie Claire*, I was curious to discover what a 25–35-year-old reader seeks in her life in such a rapidly changing society. *Madame Figaro*'s managing editor, 29-year-old Zhu Yun, said that her readers believed that being pretty or attractive was important, but no longer good enough. One couldn't rely on looks alone as a ticket out of the everyday humdrum of life.

Zhu Yun is a focused, perceptive woman who wore a smart brown suit and had her hair up in a messy, fashionable style. She looked just as I expected an image-conscious editor of a Chinese fashion magazine should – until she smiled, revealing a set of crooked front teeth. She was comfortable with the way she looked, but some Chinese women go to extraordinary lengths to improve their physical attributes, including plastic surgery and a relatively new operation which adds inches to the person's height by stretching the bones in the leg.

Zhu Yun insists young Chinese women are concerned about

more than just looks. 'What matters to young women is what happens to them today. They are easygoing and are able to accept things moving quickly. I really admire this,' she said.

She often travels with young mainland models on fashion shoots in Hong Kong. 'When we come back through Hong Kong airport, the twenty-year-old models always buy the gossipy Hong Kong magazines, the ones that talk about who's screwing who or who's having an affair with someone else's wife,' she said smiling. 'Younger women want one of three things: to get married right away, to get a Sugar Daddy so they don't need to work, or to have three really great boyfriends and then get married!'

Apart from giving women quick, superficial information, fashion and lifestyle magazines are educating Chinese women about the wide world of brand euphoria, foreign designer labels and cosmetics waiting to break down the Gate of Heavenly Peace. *Madame Figaro* is pitched at women who earn approximately 4000 yuan a month. 'At that salary,' explained Saeri Ziebart, 'they might not be able to afford a designer lipstick, but they can dream of buying one. Wait until most women start wearing mascara. There definitely will be a point where the luxury items will take off.'

The magazine offers readers weekend seminars such as 'Maximize Yourself' which for 120 yuan (A$30) provide a series of sponsored lecturers teaching women new ways of dressing, applying make-up and doing their hair. Five years ago Chinese women had the option of perming or cutting their hair. Now, colour is the rage and easy fashionable styles using gels, mousses and spray. In the past women would have their hair 'done' in a salon.

There is a growing thirst for consumer goods taken for granted in the West. For example, the subscription base for *Madame Figaro's Pregnancy and Parenting* magazine jumped 200 per cent after a nappy bag giveaway. For a country which, according to China's 2000 Census, has 290 million children under the age of fourteen, most of them the sole child, China still isn't a baby-friendly place. That is slowly changing. Many children are now brought up on formula,

whereas once they were fed rice gruel. Foreign baby food companies not only sell food, but also new ideas about how to rear babies.
Parents wanting to give their one child the best are opting for
respectable foreign brands, but domestic brands have also entered
this competitive market as they can sell their products more cheaply.
The same will be true when parents and grandparents change a cultural habit of keeping infants indoors until they are at least one year
old. At the moment, it's rare to see strollers on the street, unless they
belong to foreigners. When the faster pace of life spreads right
through society, the stroller market is set to boom.

All kinds of toys for the adult market are booming too. I didn't
realise the pull of the car until I visited the north-eastern city of
Changchun, China's Detroit, for the launch of a new Audi. Families
gripped by car mania crammed into a giant showroom, nearly
knocking me down in their rush. Even for me, totally uninterested
in cars, it was hard to stay unaffected by the excitement. Spotlights
circled the room, splashing over the cars, while pouting models
wearing grey hotpants and holding giant red fans danced around
the Audis to thump-thumping music. It was mesmerising. One-
child families with aunts, uncles and grandparents in tow, pressed
fingers and faces against windscreens for the obligatory photographs, their eyes filled with happiness and longing. After fifty years
of first being banned from owning cars and then being unable to
afford them, Chinese are hungry for all that the car represents:
freedom, mobility and status.

In 1995 the types of vehicles available to ordinary people were
limited to a handful of brands and colours: joint-venture jeeps,
Xialis (a Chinese venture with Toyota) and Volkswagens in blue,
white or burgundy. In the mid 1990s fewer than 10 per cent of new
buyers were individuals. I was sceptical of the potential growth of
the private car market because traffic already seemed to be
snarled, despite there being few cars on the road. In addition the
price of a car was at least eight times what an ordinary worker
made in a lifetime. Times have changed. Now, at least half of all

vehicle buyers are individuals, while prices have dropped and the variety has greatly improved. One in every hundred Chinese now owns a car. A Volkswagen showroom in Shanghai each weekend fills with young couples ogling small, colourful Polos. Though cars are still expensive – in 2002 a Polo cost between 140 000–180 000 yuan (US$16 950–US$21 791) – nowadays with personal loans they are at least attainable.

While much of urban China seems intent on worshipping cars, rich women and rich husbands, consultant Chen Mei reminds me that a little contrition doesn't go astray when you examine the social upheaval China has been through in the last fifty years. No-one believes in the long-term so they grasp today what may disappear tomorrow. Modern-day concubinage, for example, is alive and well in China. Mistresses 'are so common that everyone is okay about them'. But when Mei attended university in Shanghai there was a girl in her class named Xian Feng who was known to be a prostitute. Mei's friends told her to stay clear of Xian Feng, but Mei liked her and befriended her even after university officials severely reprimanded the girl and threatened her with expulsion.

'Soon after that, Xian Feng told me that she had two brothers and her parents were laid-off workers in Liaoning [in northern China]. With her busy study schedule, she had no other way to make money to support them,' said Mei. 'You can't judge people as you might elsewhere. In China if someone engages in prostitution it's considered better than if they steal for themselves.'

Though Mei is only in her early thirties, the rapid change Chinese society has undergone in the past twenty-five years means that someone of her age already talks of a *dai gou* or generation gap when describing someone just five years younger than she is. Mei is old enough to remember the early years of reform when her family used coupons to buy daily necessities that were in short supply. She is old enough to remember how her parents once respected the Chinese Communist Party. Her father procured arms for the Chinese military throughout the 1980s, frequently travelling abroad to obtain weapons and ammunition as the PLA modernised. He refused to take his family overseas on his buying trips because his policy was never to waste a cent of the country's then meagre earnings. When his former boss, a leading general in the PLA's General Logistics Department, was executed in the mid 1990s for selling military secrets to Taiwan, Mei's father was devastated. Such high moral standards, she said, are rare in these times.

Many Chinese describe the loss of scruples as an honesty crisis which permeates every layer of society. A Chinese friend once explained why he quit his job working for a seafood importer, because he'd been told to inject water into shrimps to increase their size so that customers could be charged more money. Another acquaintance was reeling from a relationship in which his former fiancée left him, taking all his furniture and all but a few hundred dollars from his bank account. Everyone, it seems, wants money and everyone wants to get ahead.

For a few hundred yuan, you can obtain any type of bogus certificate, from diplomas – it's believed there are at least 600 000 fake diplomas in the country – to car-inspection stickers and even a marriage certificate. Then you can get a fake divorce certificate to void the fake marriage. The list of rorts, cons and deceits amused my Chinese staff and friends and after a short time they ceased to shock me either. Indeed, China's massive counterfeit industry has its pluses. The Chinese state controls the number of foreign movie blockbusters that can be screened in the country, yet many families can afford locally made DVD players, which cost only 1200 yuan (A$300) and can buy the latest pirated Hollywood films from DVD vendors on any main street in the country at one-quarter the price of a Western movie ticket. Few Chinese could afford Western DVD prices, yet this is one way – albeit illegal and morally wrong – that Chinese youth can become globally integrated.

The fakes industry also has its downside. A pitiful con job emerged one spring at the busy entrance to the popular outdoor 'silk market', itself a collection of every fake brand name ever created, near my apartment complex. A woman appeared with a basket of puppies. With rising incomes, pet ownership has taken off, but very few unusual breeds of dog are legally available in China because of size restrictions. The most common dogs are small white Pekingese. Outside the silk market, children took the puppies, which cost between 400–600 yuan, out of the basket to play with them. I picked up one of the dogs, which had Dalmatian-type spots over its face. Then I realised that the spots were too perfect and that they weren't natural at all, but some kind of paint or ink. Later I spoke with a Western vet who said vendors were trying to pass off puppies as some exotic breed, creating spots with toxic paint.

I had never before realised the kind of pressure ordinary people are under when they have to compete with thousands or even tens of thousands of people for a few hundred university places, where nine hundred might reply to an on-line job advertisement for a secretarial position, and where floods of images from Asia and the West show clean, modern homes, straight white teeth and foreign notions of fair play.

Chinese people certainly are on a roller-coaster, trying to reach that comfortable place where the middle class dwells. The only problem is, it's almost impossible to get off once the train has started its descent.

CRUMBLING RICE BOWL

Grandma Xu considers herself lucky. Every morning the retired worker and her husband rise early and take the number 717 bus to a park in the west of Beijing. There, come rain, shine or snow, she carefully lowers herself down a slippery flight of stairs into a lake, three to four times the size of an Olympic pool. With strong, slow movements, she breaststrokes around the lake while her husband practises Tai Chi until she has finished.

'We learned how to swim during the Cultural Revolution after watching Chairman Mao swim in the Yangtze River. I do it to stay healthy,' she said, referring to the famous event when an ageing Mao, according to the party propaganda, 'swam' nearly 15 kilometres in 65 minutes. The message had been that if the Chairman could conquer the mighty Yangtze, China's youth had the strength to overcome Mao's opponents. In reality, Mao hadn't conquered the river at all, but had floated downstream with the river's strong current.

Ms Xu, who is in her sixties, began working for the Railway Bureau as soon as she finished school. Together with her husband Mr Du their combined pension comes to 2650 yuan (A$663) per month, ample for a retired couple with few needs. They live in a rather soulless state apartment, its walls painted green on the lower half and white above. It appears that the last coat of paint was at least a decade ago. Because of Mr Du's status as a Revolutionary

Worker, a soldier before he joined the railway, he carries an Old Cadres pass which exempts him from paying for most public costs, including transportation, park entry fees and medical expenses. Yet while Ms Xu and Mr Du still rely on the 'iron rice bowl', the reality for tens of millions of workers is that the system of employment coupled with lifelong security instigated by Chairman Mao in the 1950s is in its dying days. Four million of Ms Xu and Mr Du's colleagues in the Railway Bureau have lost their jobs in recent years due to restructuring. Under China's accession to the World Trade Organisation, freight operations are to be gradually opened to foreign competition, signalling further upheaval in the industry. China today is no longer a workers' paradise and those who put the greatest faith in the state have paid the price. The constant uncertainty prompted a saying that goes: 'In the seventies we went *xiaxiang* [down to the countryside], in the early nineties we tried to *xiahai* [leap into the sea of business] and now we must *xiagang* [get laid-off from our jobs].'

In August 1966 Mao closed China's schools and unleashed the Red Guards to attack his enemies in the party. The Red Guards, so named because of their red armbands, came from urban high schools and colleges and were encouraged to 'make revolution', to take to the streets and 'clean up the filth and mire left over from the old society'. They launched a reign of terror in most major cities, destroying old culture by raiding houses, burning books and antiques, beating and shaming those with old ideas and killing those who tried to resist. By the spring of 1968 the country was in the grip of a Red Guard civil war and millions of urban youths roamed the lawless cities. When Mao saw that the situation had gotten out of hand, he ordered the Red Guards back to school to resume their lessons. Later he initiated the 'Up to the Mountains, Down to the Countryside' movement, which involved the mass migration of millions of high school students – including Red Guards – from the cities to the countryside. Many of the students had previously been considered privileged, born to good families in wealthier areas and educated in reputable schools until the outbreak of the Cultural Revolution.

Villages across the country soon became inundated with teenagers who shared the homes, food and work of the villagers, many of the students remaining until the end of the Cultural Revolution in the mid 1970s. They returned to their homes, having lost up to a decade of formal education, as well as career opportunities. On returning they were given preferential jobs as state workers, a reward for enduring years of manual labour in remote and often inhospitable places. The bulk of these workers continued to invest their hopes in the future of Chinese socialism and the promise of the iron rice bowl, despite many millions being laid off during the industrial restructuring of the 1980s and 1990s. They were known as Educated Youths in the 1960s, but by the 1990s they were considered China's lost generation.

Jiang Zuotao lives in a cave dug into the soft earth of Shaanxi province, close to where Mao set up his revolutionary base in Yan'an at the end of the Long March in 1936. Jiang Zuotao shares the cave with his wife, Chang Yulian, and two of his three children; the eldest son has moved to the city of Yan'an, nearly two hours away by minibus on a potholed road. When I first walked into the cave home, I was surprised to see that it had furniture: a sideboard, fold-up dining table, black and white television set and even a refrigerator. For the first and only time during my stay in China, I was served not tea, as I'd expected, but boiling water with sugar. I sat in the cave listening to Mr Jiang and Ms Chang talk about where their lives went wrong, but my mind was fixated on the sugar water.

When the conversation paused, I decided on a diplomatic ploy to probe the state of the family's finances. 'Which is more expensive, tea or sugar?' I asked.

'Tea, of course!' replied Ms Chang without hesitation. 'It's nearly twice the price.'

Then I learned that the furniture had been a gift from Mr Jiang's younger brother, a state-enterprise employee in Beijing. When Ms

Chang went over to the refrigerator to take out a plate of eggs, I noticed that it wasn't switched on. Ms Chang used it like a pantry to store food.

'Why don't you switch the refrigerator on?' I asked.

'Jiang's younger brother gave it to us with the other furniture. But electricity is too expensive, so we don't turn it on,' said Ms Chang. When she talked about the family's expenses, her lip began to tremble.

For someone born and raised in China's capital, Jiang Zuotao should have returned to his home, as most of the former students did. The 'Down to the Countryside' policy forced 17 million urban youths to live and work in rural areas. Mao said in 1968, 'It is necessary for the educated youth to go to the countryside and be re-educated by the poor peasants. We need to persuade cadres and others in urban areas to send their children who graduated from junior high, senior high and college to rural areas. Let us have a mobilisation. Comrades in rural areas should welcome them.' In 1979, three years after Mao died, the policy was denounced by the reformist leadership of Deng Xiaoping. The sent-down youths were allowed to return to their home cities, except for those who had married local residents or found jobs as workers in their rural areas.

Jiang Zuotao had been sent to the countryside because his father was a capitalist who made his living running an oil shop in Beijing. Officials told him he needed to spend only two years there. He arrived in Shaanxi with his *Little Red Book* of Mao's quotations and a wooden trunk for his belongings, given to all the Educated Youth and inscribed with Mao's own characters. Ten years later, however, he was still on the commune in the depths of Shaanxi province. When the Cultural Revolution ended no orders were issued for him to go home. Eventually he lost hope of ever returning to Beijing. Then one day he met Chang Yulian from a neighbouring village and they married and started a family. As a result he inadvertently cancelled his precious Beijing *hukou*, the residency permit which gave him the right to live in Beijing.

Tall, sinewy Jiang Zuotao looked much older than his forty-eight years. His cheeks were hollow and his chipped teeth stained with more than three decades of nicotine. His brow seemed permanently furrowed as he recounted the events of his life as if he still couldn't believe the hand fate had dealt him. The bureaucracy had somehow forgotten him, and by the time the Cultural Revolution ended both his parents had died, so he had no legal guardian to take up his case.

When his commune was dismantled, Mr Jiang first went to work for a factory before moving to his cave home beside the Victory Reservoir. On a walk around the reservoir he explained that the cave home, which isn't uncommon in rural Shaanxi because of the soft earth, came free with the job of looking after the reservoir. The reservoir had been a project devised during the disastrous Great Leap Forward in the late 1950s and had experienced such a severe silting problem it was rendered virtually useless. Due to corrupt officials and the sketchy accounting practices of the local Water Conservancy Bureau, Mr Jiang and his wife lived in their cave for free, but weren't paid a cent of their salary for ten years until 1996. The Victory Reservoir, like the historic events surrounding it, never lived up to its name.

In most Chinese homes these days a television set is an object of pride, but in this home it was bought to silence the neighbours in the caves next door who made fun of Mr Jiang's poor circumstances. He bought it in 1986, the family's first-ever electrical appliance. Every twist of his story was another pitiable thread of a life abused by those who should have looked after him, and yet he blamed his own naivety for his family's plight.

When I asked him why he didn't take his complaint to the provincial government he looked at me incredulously. 'I don't know anyone who works for the government, I have no power, no *guanxi* [relationship]! People say there is corruption in the Communist Party. If you want to do something about it, you need money. I don't even know how to *spend* money,' he said emphatically, holding his head in his hands.

For the man who brought calamity on the country he had no harsh words, and though I studied his face for a sign that he was being politically correct in front of a foreigner, I could find none. 'The Chairman is wise and great. I will always remember his words which are inscribed on my wooden trunk [the one given to every student to hold their belongings]: "It's necessary for the Educated Youth to go to the countryside to be re-educated by the peasants." I admire his words. I don't have any complaints about the Chairman,' he said. The trunk, which was tucked away in a small wardrobe beside a bed made of earth called a *kang*, is Mr Jiang's only memento from his time as an Educated Youth in the countryside.

Since 1996 the family's situation has improved a little. Their eldest son found work and sends them regular payments of A$165 a month or around 660 yuan. But the two younger children's education was being paid for with money borrowed from relatives. Though China has nine years of compulsory and supposedly free education, most schools have instigated fees and charges on a range of services from extra-curricular activities, study materials and even sanitation management. Ms Chang said she couldn't stop thinking about how different their lives could have been in Beijing. Then, amid all the talk of hardship and while her husband was busy chopping firewood for cooking lunch, Ms Chang quietly slipped a large silver coin into my palm.

'This is for you,' she whispered loudly in my ear. 'Put it away and don't tell anyone I gave it to you!' It was from pre-revolutionary days and worth around 50 yuan (A$12), I later discovered.

I protested and pressed it back into her nervous hands, but she thrust it back at me and stood up so that I couldn't hand it back to her. 'I already kept one for my daughter, for when she gets married,' Ms Chang said. 'I have no need for the other.'

Though I stayed in the cave for just one day it was difficult to leave. The family had invested such hope in the arrival of a foreign TV crew, believing that in some way we would be an omen of change. I insisted on giving Mr Jiang some money for the children's education, but I left with the large coin in my pocket feeling as if I had somehow robbed them. I turned to wave goodbye from the taxi and the entire family, including sinewy Mr Jiang, was weeping profusely.

If Mr Jiang had been sent back to the city all those years ago, he would probably have ended up working for a state-owned industrial enterprise. It's difficult to comprehend the scale of one of these until you get inside. They are not particularly imposing from the outside, with high concrete walls and an iron gate at the front, manned by a guard in a sloppy khaki uniform. In my first real look inside a state enterprise in the central city of Chongqing, I felt I had stepped onto the set of a Cecil B. De Mille epic. The 'factory' wasn't simply a conglomeration of workshops and endless production lines; it was more like a town. It had its own roads, schools, street markets and department stores. Some state-owned enterprises even have their own factories to make foodstuffs and consumer items to sell in their own department stores.

The duplication of work, though economically impractical, ensured a job for everyone after the Cultural Revolution. As a result, even today over-employment is blatantly obvious in virtually every sector of Chinese society. Each section of a department store may have at least ten to fifteen shop assistants, while another one or two operate the till. If there are two people, one collects and stamps the payment slip and issues the receipt while the other collects the money and returns the change. In Western countries it's mainly hotels and large stores that employ lift attendants, but in China, retired or injured workers operate dingy elevators in characterless concrete apartment blocks all over the country. Human button-pushers, stamping machines and excess attendants are everywhere; there is no shortage of people. This becomes clear when you visit a state concern: an entire town managed by a factory to support a workforce of anything from a few thousand to a few million.

Because of its location deep in China's hinterland, Chongqing had been a popular place to locate factories since the start of last century. Then, during the period of Soviet co-operation in the 1950s, more than 150 major industrial complexes were built with Russian aid. In the 1960s, as China became more isolated, Mao believed the country faced a serious threat of foreign attack. He called for the construction of the Third Front, a giant defence complex consisting of more than 1400 projects scattered within China's interior, supposedly safe from foreign bombs. (The First Front was the coastal areas, the Second was inland from the coast. From 1964, the government started sending soldiers and youngsters to the different fronts to construct infrastructure and facilities until the policy ended in the late 1970s.) Sichuan province, where Chongqing is located, received more than half of the Third Front factories and the city itself became a conventional arms production centre. My visit to the Three Gorges area revealed the results of Mao's Third Front call: hundreds of filth-belching Dickensian factories dotted incongruously along the slopes above the Yangtze River.

Until the 1980s, the Chinese state controlled the activities of its stable of factories through a bureaucracy in Beijing. The 300 000 enterprises, including 100 000 industrial concerns, churned out vast quantities of basic commodities like steel and cotton and consumer goods like bicycles and vacuum flasks, all with scant regard for quality.

At the Yangtze River Electronics Enterprise, vice-director Xiao Fuming told me that 11 000 workers produced more than a hundred different items in their workshops which had once formed part of an extensive military enterprise. The factory, which had a very old section (which we weren't allowed to see) and a more modern area, was desperately seeking foreign investment. Mr Xiao, who was in his forties and seemed quite open, said the factory manufactured many different products in order to keep all the workers in a job. Unlike businesses in capitalist countries where the returns or profits are the goal, Mr Xiao stressed that his first priority was to generate employment. 'To make the worker's life better and better is the factory's duty and society's as well,' he said. 'So we keep on developing new products to re-employ the laid-off workers.'

As a result, batch after batch of shoddy goods with no chance of ever seeing the market filled giant warehouses to the brim. We weren't allowed to see the warehouses, but instead Mr Xiao took us to a small new factory in the complex that made car radiators for one-third the price they could be manufactured in the United States. Then he presented me with one of the best souvenirs I ever received in China. It was a munitions shell converted into a ball-point pen. Mr Xiao said he had designed it himself to use as gifts for special visitors. Production of the bullet pen probably kept a few dozen workers in a job.

Throughout the 1990s various experiments began to convert China's centrally planned production into a market economy, albeit with state firms still playing a substantial role. In the early 1990s I interviewed Trade Minister Li Lanqing, who said he believed that converting loss-making enterprises into shareholding companies would turn their fortunes around.

'We're working on a way to build workers' enthusiasm,' he said, believing that if shareholders had partial control of these companies their performance would be significantly boosted. Success has come to a handful of the now 1200 firms listed on China's stock markets (of which about 1020 are state-owned and a further hundred are collectively owned by the workers but managed like private companies and eighty are privately owned). One such winner is the US$7.3 billion whitegoods maker Hai'er Group, the world's second largest refrigerator maker. Hai'er began life eighteen years ago in the port city of Qingdao when it was a loss-making state fridge factory. Now it's said to be collectively owned by workers (the chairman calls it a 'non-state owned industry', which means it's not totally divorced from the state). It has thirteen overseas factories and in 2002 bought a US$14.5 million building in Manhattan for its new American headquarters.

Few state or collective enterprises have reached Hai'er's heights. In fact experiments with shareholdings in the early 1990s should have sounded a low-key alarm to China's 110 million state workers. Within a few years the warnings grew louder as the central government made it clear that it was no longer willing to absorb the red ink from years of industrial inefficiency and mismanagement. In the mid 1990s, the state sector accounted for 40 per cent of China's gross domestic product and 60 per cent of state revenue. However one in three enterprises operated at a loss. Various measures had been taken to stop the haemorrhage: one of the first was allowing a profit split between the state and the enterprise. Later the emphasis switched to changing management techniques and introducing greater incentives to improve profitability. Hai'er's management system, for example, is known as 10/10. The top 10 per cent of employees in terms of performance are held up as models and get extra pay, while the bottom 10 per cent get demoted or sacked.

By the mid 1990s the red ink from state factories had turned to gushing rivers and it became clear that radical approaches were needed to prevent the country going bankrupt. Ownership experiments were one method of potentially slowing bankruptcies, but it was clear thousands of loss-making enterprises would have to be closed. The result was that millions of workers began to lose their cherished iron rice bowls, the cradle-to-grave employment and social security system that was once so sought after.

It had taken the ABC bureau several attempts to obtain permission to visit Chongqing. I wanted to shoot a story on the growing problem of unemployment and in my naivety I penned a letter proposing to cover several aspects of the issue, including a visit to both new and old factories, and interviews with both employed and laid-off workers. I also stressed that I intended to place equal emphasis on the successful and unsuccessful attempts at reform. The request was rejected. The timing was 'inconvenient', I was told, given the impending arrival of Chinese New Year. However after I probed the reason for the refusal, an official from the municipal Foreign Affairs Office, who was to act as our host and minder, helpfully suggested that a story on Chongqing's 'economy' rather than 'unemployment problem' might not meet with a negative response. It was one of the most helpful pieces of advice I was ever to receive from a *Waiban* official.

When Sebastian, Kate, Charles and I arrived in Chongqing, we found the Bamboo Army's footsoldiers, dressed in their blue Mao jackets, lurking on every street corner. They trudged up and down the city's long stairways carrying incredible loads dexterously tied to each end of their bamboo poles. Though it seemed inhumane to make them carry so much, it was their way of earning a living, so we did as others did and took on a 'soldier' to carry our camera equipment from the pier to the city, a distance of half a kilometre (about a twenty minute walk) for 20 yuan (A$5). The man left the rest of us puffing well behind and by the time we'd caught up to him at the top of the hill, he had untied the equipment, looped the rope around his shoulder and lit a cigarette. It was mid winter and the damp, cold air smelled of the coal spewing from 10 000 state factories, staffed by more than three million workers.

In 1997, Chongqing, like Shanghai in 1991, was given an imprimatur to develop. The central government awarded Chongqing special status as a provincial level city. This gave the local government a much greater area to control (some 31 million people) and the flexibility and autonomy to raise its own funds to position itself for a leading role in the post Three Gorges China. Two years later the city's status was further bolstered after the central government unveiled its 'Develop the West' policy, which aimed to raise living standards in China's poorer western regions by directing additional government funding and encouraging tax-friendly foreign investment.

The Jialing Motorcycle Company began its life as a military manufacturer in 1919 before turning to a popular consumer product, motorcycles, in the late 1970s. As part of one of China's largest state enterprises, it was converted to a limited company and then listed on the fledgling share market as a means to raise capital. Unlike many other factories, it wasn't insolvent. In fact by the mid 1990s it had produced more than 6 million motorcycles on modern production lines developed in conjunction with the Japanese Honda group. Despite its modernity, the production lines were still flanked by surplus workers standing idly by.

I requested an interview with a worker from the Jialing factory and the municipal government's Foreign Affairs Office contacted the factory to select one for us. Her name was Xie Daihua and like the socialist heroines cast in gushing Chinese propaganda films of the 1950s and 1960s, Ms Xie, aged forty-four, appeared from behind a Ned Kelly type safety helmet in the lathe workshop where she'd worked for twenty-six years. She went to change into her civvies and when she appeared, confident and well-dressed in pants and high-heeled shoes, it didn't take long to realise that she was no run-of-the-mill lathe operator. Ms Xie was a Model Worker, an award bestowed on her by the factory for her hard work and selfless dedication. It also meant she received more fringe benefits than other workers.

Ms Xie lived in a comfortable two-bedroom apartment with her husband, a Jialing motorcycle sales representative, and her son who was attending the Jialing factory middle school. She told me that apart from a salary of around 700 yuan (A$175) per month, the factory provided her family with its apartment (50 square metres in size), free water and electricity. The family paid just 10 per cent of its medical fees and a proportion of the tuition fees for the boy's schooling. When I asked Ms Xie whether she believed her family would be looked after by the factory forever, she looked at me quizzically.

'I don't think there'll be a problem,' she told me as her husband began to unravel the karaoke microphones in front of a giant television. 'My son will study in a university and we will pay the tuition fee on our own. After graduation, if the factory is looking for employees, my son could take the entrance examination and work for the factory.' On that note, Ms Xie's husband burst into song – a revolutionary anthem played on an organ and slowed down to sound like a Chinese version of Richard Clayderman. With the new karaoke machine, their tidy home and son's future taken care of, this was indeed a little piece of heaven, a healthy patch in the dying turf of the once great workers' paradise.

To venture into the world of the unlucky workers, I went with the crew to the outskirts of the city without our government hosts. A taxi-driver told us we would find a suburb with narrow alleys and low-rise concrete houses filled with laid-off workers. He knew because that was where he lived and he agreed to take us there. Walking down a rough concrete path, I saw a house with an open courtyard where a group of middle-aged men and women were playing mahjong. They laughed and cussed as their hands swept the small resin tiles around the table. It sounded like heavy rain on a tin roof.

They didn't mind us filming them and after a while they began to relax and talk among themselves. 'We have nothing else to do except play mahjong,' said one of the bystanders.

Beyond the mahjong table was the home of the Wu family. Mr Wu, in his early forties, had worked at the Chongqing Steel Processing Plant in the steel rolling workshop. In the mid 1990s when the factory went bankrupt and closed its mills, Mr Wu, who earned 800 yuan a month (nearly A$200), was laid off and paid a token wage of 40 yuan (or less than A$10), to stay at home.

Though Mr Wu had been laid off for three years, his name was still on the factory books and he was being paid a nominal wage, even if it was a pittance. An official dispatch from the Xinhua News Agency explained China's creative approach to calculating its level of unemployment. 'A displaced worker no longer has a job, but if conditions improve in the factory and the worker is needed again, his former post becomes available,' said the December 1996 report. 'In reality,' admitted Xinhua, 'this doesn't often happen.'

In the suburb on the outskirts of Chongqing the former state workers recounted their difficulties. Mr Wu's wife still had her job with a clothing factory, but was paid only 120 yuan (A$30) a month. Their child's school tuition fees came to five times that amount per term. Mr Wu sat on his lumpy bed beside his old mother, Madam Li, in the cold soulless bedroom, surrounded by a foreign television crew, going through each detail of his family's expenses without any hesitation. He knew how much he paid for electricity and the price of a load of coal briquettes to keep the house warm during Chongqing's damp winter.

'I'm willing to work,' said Mr Wu, 'even to clean toilets. But we are all middle aged, and no work unit wants to hire us.'

After sitting quietly listening to her son, Madam Li, without prompting, told us that after numerous approaches to the district government and the municipal government, both of which had failed to take care of them, some elderly people, including herself, had taken part in demonstrations earlier that month.

'We blocked the roads,' she said, describing the first protest. 'So someone from the municipal government took us to a reception room. We waited, but nobody came to talk to us, so we got angry and broke into the dining room and grabbed steamed buns and ate them. It was really funny! Then we went back to the reception room, but still no-one came to talk to us, so eventually we went home.'

It seemed extraordinary that this woman in her seventies had taken part in an act of civil disobedience. Off-post workers felt helpless, she said. The protests, however, came to naught.

As we left Mr Wu's home, an old lady who had been quietly watching the others play mahjong followed us out of the courtyard and into the lane. There she began tugging at my sleeve. She spoke with a thick Sichuan accent and I couldn't understand her. 'She wants to take you to see her home,' said researcher Charles Li. Away from the din of the clacking tiles, down broken concrete steps and beside what looked like a rubbish dump, she gestured towards the clay hut where she and her husband lived. Still hanging onto my arm, she led me inside the hut while Sebastian filmed us. There was a single derelict room with a bed, a few farm implements and a stove. The walls had been patched up with newspaper, a cheap alternative to insulation, and the floors were just dirt.

'What would Chairman Mao say if he saw this?' she said loudly, unable to contain her rage. She pointed to pieces of old newspaper peeling off the walls and flapping in the draught.

I asked how she felt to see her family in such hardship. Again she brought up Mao Zedong. Mao had been a saviour, she said. 'Some people are very rich now; some of them get up to a million yuan. But there are still those who cannot afford their food – like me. In Mao's era, it wasn't like this. There were no very rich or extremely poor people. I don't understand it.'

I wanted to stay longer in the off-post suburb, to talk more with the old woman and to meet other families, but a loud voice stopped us in our tracks. A neatly dressed man in an aubergine-coloured trench coat and with high, coiffed hair was walking towards us, shouting. I had noticed him soon after we emerged from the house with the mahjong players in the yard, and he had followed us to the old woman's crumbling home. When he saw Sebastian filming the mud hut surrounded by rubbish and filth, he began to shout at the crew and me, accusing us of wanting to portray China as a dirty and backward nation. The old woman shouted back at him; it was right for foreign television to show her disgraceful living standards. She didn't live like this in Mao's day, she repeated.

The angry man wasn't convinced. He said we were uninvited guests with a sinister goal of disparaging his country. He was going to call the police, he said, and took a mobile telephone from his pocket. It was time to leave. We walked as quickly as we could without running until we reached a busy food market. Two taxis approached and we flagged them down, greatly relieved.

Months later China's workers learned that far more sweeping plans were in store for the deconstruction of the state sector. President Jiang Zemin delivered a major blow to the slowly crumbling Chinese rice bowl during the five-yearly Party Congress in September 1997. In celebration of the Congress, Tiananmen Square had been temporarily remodelled into a carnival ground, filled with plastic palm trees which lit up at night, mounds of real grass and tinkling fountains. In the centre of the Square, close to the Monument to the People's Heroes depicting one hundred years of revolution, giant portraits of China's other revolutionary heroes – Marx, Lenin, Sun Yat-sen, Engels and Mao Zedong – had been erected. Binding the image together on all sides of the square and on the apex of the Great Hall of the People, red flags fluttered furiously.

Inside the Great Hall, President Jiang Zemin delivered a speech with the convoluted title of 'Hold High the Great Banner of Deng Xiaoping Theory for an All-Round Advancement of the Case of Building Socialism with Chinese Characteristics to the Twenty-First Century'. The contents, however, were much more direct. After years of experimenting with state-owned enterprise reform, Jiang took a bold step by enshrining the capitalist-style ideas of the late Paramount Leader Deng Xiaoping in the Chinese constitution. It meant no turning back from a bold restructuring program for the country's 118 000 industrial state-owned enterprises. He announced the 'Grasp the Large, Release the Small' policy, meaning the state would hold onto a strategic number of enterprises – 1000 of them – with the aim of merging, consolidating or converting them from socialist dinosaurs to world-class multinational conglomerates. As for the remaining 117 000 enterprises, President Jiang said they should be declared bankrupt, sold, or merged into new types of businesses like shareholding companies or co-operatives. So as not to completely alienate the leftists in the leadership, he carefully restated China's commitment to the dominance of public ownership. Yet he called for the definition of public ownership to be broadened, arguing that it shouldn't necessarily mean government ownership but could manifest itself in many forms. A co-operatively owned shareholding company like the refrigerator manufacturer Hai'er, for example, with a minority stake listed on China's fledgling exchanges could still be considered a company in the public domain.

Whatever title President Jiang gave to this transformation, the bottom line was that at least 1000 key enterprises would remain in the hands of the state and the rest would be privatised or closed down. It was also another way of saying that in addition to the millions who had already been made jobless during earlier waves of reform, tens of millions more state workers would be certain to lose their jobs. Despite the magnitude of the decision, in his speech at the Great Hall of the People, President Jiang dealt with the issue matter-of-factly.

'It will cause temporary difficulties to part of the workers,' he said, 'but fundamentally speaking, it is conducive to economic development, thus conforming to the long-term interests of the working class.' After calling on society to show concern for laid-off workers, he suggested that, 'All workers should change their ideas about employment and improve their own quality to meet the new requirements of reform and development.'

On leaving the Great Hall that day with hundreds of journalists and thousands of Communist Party delegates, I found it hard to contemplate the implications of the 'Grasp' speech. Going in or out of the Great Hall, where the entrance is two to three storeys high, I was always aware of a sense of insignificance, a feeling that I, like the rest of the people coming in and out of its doors, was like a lost ant. I wondered how a worker hundreds of kilometres away in China's north-east rustbelt, listening to the coverage of the Fifteenth Party Congress, would have understood the speech's significance. Months later in 1998 Premier Zhu Rongji said he would solve the problem of the enterprises within three years. Five years later many analysts quietly concede the 'Grasp the Large, Release the Small' policy has failed.

'Ninety per cent of the bankruptcies were shams,' a corporate lawyer told me. 'Money was moved out of the companies to somewhere else.' Another bankruptcy expert noted that a large number of enterprises practised a 'disappearing act from a complicated situation', dodging their liabilities by declaring bankruptcy but then shifting their assets, dividing their businesses and changing licences. In fact the practice had been happening for many years. One of the biggest bankruptcies to take place was at the Shanxi Textile Dyeing Plant, which in 1993 had been one of China's 500 largest enterprises employing 18 000 workers. In September 1996 it shut down with massive debts only to reopen a month later as the Taiyuan Xinkai Textile Printing & Dyeing Corporation Limited, a new textile company set up by the government to take over the factory. Its web-site lists the workforce as 4000 'without debt or redundant workforce'.

On the closing evening of the Fifteenth Party Congress, the socialist carnival around Tiananmen Square reached a climax. Coloured lasers darted across the night sky, piped music filled the air, while searchlights – which might have seemed ominous under ordinary circumstances – roamed the people-filled expanse. Mao's illuminated giant portrait gazed serenely down on the Square. Perhaps the portrait should have been dismantled and packed away with the fountains and grass and flashing plastic palm trees.

Following Jiang's dictate at the Party Congress, tens of thousands of state assets were sold, many of them for a song. Beijing businessman Wang Xiaodong recalls how he bought a small state-run printing factory which had been 'dead' for several years due to management problems. 'There were five companies bidding for the factory in an auction and we had to take over ten workers, but I still bid for the company,' he said. Mr Wang eventually succeeded, paying 4 million yuan in total, a price which also gave him all the production equipment. To his surprise, he found the three printing machines were only about six years old, so he called in engineers to service them. They were all in good working order and to buy them new would have cost 5 million yuan per machine. Mr Wang's bargain factory was the state's loss.

The state-owned sell-off continued as the Asian financial crisis deepened throughout 1997 while domestic concerns mounted. Growing discontent among laid-off workers as well as concerns over corruption and smuggling caused the central government to put the brakes on its much-lauded reform agenda. A slowdown in the sale of state assets was ordered to prevent a nationwide fire sale.

According to China's state media, Zhu Rongji's promise to turn around loss-making enterprises in three years achieved success. 'China has basically attained its goal of reforming the state-owned enterprises in three years and relevant figures provided by the government are authentic,' the *People's Daily* said, somewhat defensively. Between December 1997 and December 2000, state-owned enterprises registered a 185 per cent profit increase according to Sheng Huaren, the minister in charge of the State Economic and Trade Commission. Seventy per cent of 6599 enterprises were making a profit. However, not everyone accepted this reversal of fortune. A respected Chinese economist, Professor Wu Shuqing, told a Beijing newspaper that the rosy picture was temporary if not illusory, as many enterprises had managed to break even only because of privileges and the massive injection of funds to kick-start the reforms. 'Many enterprises take these privileges as the last supper. They were so scared they wouldn't get on this last train,' he told the newspaper.

From the mid 1990s worker protests became more common and grew larger in size. Chinese workers aren't particularly militant; they usually take to the streets only when they feel they've been unfairly treated and they have no other recourse. Even as Jiang Zemin's staff put the finishing touches to his address to the Fifteenth Party Congress, workers in the city of Zigong in Sichuan province clashed with police during a demonstration outside the state-run Number Two Radio Factory. Three hundred workers took part, complaining that they hadn't been paid several months of wages or benefits.

However the presence of riot police brought another 1500 people out onto the streets in sympathy with the workers. Though the police insisted they didn't end the action using violence, human rights groups have reported that witnesses contradict the claim. Two months later the city's pedicab operators protested for the second time in 1997. Most of the drivers were laid-off workers who had become self-employed. On the first occasion they took to the streets because the government tried to slap a 38 000 yuan (A$9500) licence fee on each driver, more than a year's earnings. On the second occasion later that year, between 4000 and 6000 drivers, along with several thousand sympathisers, protested against the city government's introduction of regulations banning the pedicabs from the city centre. The drivers and sympathisers blocked the streets and the railway station until late at night. In the space of fourteen months, Zigong workers protested at least five times.

Amid the unremarkable news items in the English-language *China Daily*, I found the perfect ruse to visit Zigong – and interview some restive state workers. January 1998 marked the start of what the paper claimed to be the 'world famous' Zigong Dinosaur Lantern Festival. Our application to film the Dinosaur Lantern Festival was approved by the local Foreign Affairs Office, and weeks later I arrived in Zigong via a new highway from Chengdu to find a city that had once serviced trade and merchants and still had relics of its ancient salt and banking industries. Zigong's immense public park had been festooned with a myriad of traditional lanterns as well as model dinosaurs (based on the city's discovery of dinosaur bones some years before) and lanterns in the shape of dinosaurs. The city officials, suspecting my ulterior motive, wanted the crew and me to leave as soon as we'd finished filming the festival. I took my time to become familiar with the local situation, learning that the local government spent 6 million yuan (A$1 500 000) hosting the festival, which was probably one reason they couldn't pay workers' salaries.

Despite our official approval to visit the city, workers and pedicab drivers told us it was too dangerous for them to talk. Disappointingly, I was left empty-handed. It wasn't until several weeks later that I made contact with a source who told me that one of the organisers of the Zigong protests was on the run and it might be possible to meet him and interview him in a city other than Zigong. The source suggested the bustling southern Chinese city of Guangzhou. Such a trip would be risky because we would be interviewing someone wanted by the police for attempting to organise workers into what effectively was an underground union. This was illegal as there was only one trade union permitted in China, the 100 million strong All China Federation of Trade Unions.

I decided that the best option was to book a room at one of Guangzhou's five-star hotels, which would be buzzing with foreign businesspeople and tourists. If Sebastian set up the camera inside the room and we got the worker to come to us, hopefully we wouldn't draw any attention to him. I wasn't sure what the man looked like, but I was worried he might stand out in the upmarket surroundings of the hotel, so through my contact I arranged for him to buy some new clothes, get a haircut and new spectacle frames so that he wouldn't look out of place walking into the foyer.

The plan worked well and at the appointed time Li Qiang (a pseudonym) walked into my room at the Guangzhou Garden Hotel. He was younger than I'd expected, in his late twenties, and slight. He had bought himself some inexpensive but stylish clothes from a Hong Kong clothing chain, and thankfully his arrival didn't attract unwanted attention. Li Qiang came from an ordinary working-class family in Zigong. His political awareness had been sparked during the Tiananmen student democracy movement in 1989. The movement wasn't confined to Beijing, and in the Zigong area Li Qiang's posters and speeches promoting democracy had earned him a summons from the police.

When his mother became seriously ill a year later, coughing up blood and losing her sight, the hospital stopped her treatment several times because of lack of payment. His mother's work unit, the

Second Construction Company of Zigong, did nothing to help her. Li Qiang believed that the only way to fight such injustice was to call for independent unions to protect workers' rights. His open protest letters posted on walls around the city again put him under the surveillance of local security agents. In 1997 when the municipal government threatened to slap a large licence fee on the city's taxi-drivers, he helped to organise them into an association and led them in a street blockade. He fled the city soon after that, fearing arrest.

In the comfort of Guangzhou's Garden Hotel that day, Li Qiang clung firmly to the belief that only independent workers' organisations would help to dispel the growing violence accompanying workers' protests. 'If this situation keeps going on like this, there'll be more large-scale upheavals. If our leaders don't confront reality to solve the problems, the government will probably be overthrown in the future and that would be a disaster for the whole of China,' he said.

For three more years, Li Qiang remained on the run, working in factories mainly in the south of the country and discussing the idea of free trade unions with fellow workers. To evade arrest he left China in 2000 and went to the United States. I never knew his name until I began writing this book and renewed my contact with him through a web-site devoted to Chinese labour issues, China Labour Watch, which he now runs from New York. His recent newsletters dealt with the poor treatment of workers at a southern China shoe factory with 50 000 workers under contract to leading international brands such as Nike and Adidas.

Today urban unemployment shows little signs of improvement, despite official predictions that the worst of the state redundancies would be over by 2000. In 2002 the official urban jobless rate stood at 3.6 per cent, or 6.8 million people. However within weeks of the publication of that figure (which has barely moved in five years) the respected Chinese Academy of Social Sciences' *Green Book on Population and Labour* claimed the urban jobless rate had already passed 7 per cent, or 13.4 million people, and is at the level considered by Chinese economists as the danger zone where dissatisfaction is rife and a potential exists for social instability. On top of that, there are officially 5.15 million 'laid-off workers' who are paid a minimal amount to stay at home. The real figures are anyone's guess. The Ministry of Agriculture estimated that China's December 2001 World Trade Organisation (WTO) accession would lead to the loss of 20 million farming jobs over the next few years, adding to the 160 million rural jobless. In the cities, China's World Trade Organisation accession is expected to create a net gain of only one million jobs (12 million jobs created versus 11 million lost). Also worrying, 12.4 million graduates will be looking for jobs each year between 2000 and 2005, but only 7 to 8 million new positions are due to be created.

Can China really support a workforce of 750 million? Perhaps in the thriving cities of Beijing, Shanghai, Shenzhen and Guangzhou new job opportunities will always be found. Not so in China's north-eastern rustbelt. In the city of Shenyang in Liaoning province, there are streets of factories where two out of three are closed, their heavy iron gates barred by chains and large rusting padlocks. In some cities like Chongqing, groups of workers gather in 'labour markets' advertising the work they can do and for how much. I saw dozens of painters, standing in paint-spattered blue uniforms holding paint rollers and trays. Yet laid-off workers are now becoming too numerous to stand on street corners advertising their skills.

To view the list of major protests taking place in China at any time, you need simply access the web-site run by former state worker Han Dongfang. Han lives with his wife and children in 'exile' in Hong Kong after convening the Beijing Autonomous Workers Federation in Tiananmen Square in 1989, the first independent labour organisation to be set up in China in fifty years. For his role, Han was jailed for twenty-two months without trial.

Now he runs the *China Labour Bulletin* and broadcasts interviews with Chinese workers over Radio Free Asia. Han is a tall,
gentle man who came from a poor working-class family. His goal is
to see the establishment of an independent trade union movement
in China. He said that when Chinese workers protest, it is usually
out of extreme desperation. The government system, said Han, has
broken down. 'Every government official from every level, there's
only one thing they want to do: let a few people get rich first. If they
have a small chance to make a little money . . . they will do it. The
radio listeners tell me in this country everybody is corrupt.'

Han believes worker unrest is like a time bomb that will explode
in the hands of the Chinese leadership. 'Now it's happening,' he told
me a few years ago, 'and nobody knows when it will explode.
Everybody will be hurt, including the Communist Party, including
workers and including everyone who has their interests in this
country.'

In March 2002 two major protests erupted in China's north-east.
One of them in Liaoyang simmered for weeks after the closure of
the Ferro Alloy Factory which left 4000 workers unemployed, without fair compensation and owed a year's wages. A factory official
was eventually arrested on corruption charges. The second protest
hit China's famous Daqing oilfields that until the 1980s had been
the model of Communist industrial prowess. 'Learn from Daqing'
went the motto in the 1960s, but by 2002 the lesson had changed:
industrial might must be achieved using fewer workers. Oilfield
managers wanted to retrench 80 000 workers, the latest round of
cuts since China's petroleum monopoly, the China National
Petroleum Corporation, launched a private subsidiary, PetroChina,
to compete against the world's top petroleum multinationals.
PetroChina made a US$3 billion debut on the Hong Kong and New
York stock exchanges in 2000 for about 10 per cent of its shares.
Now with a host of international investors, does PetroChina
respond to market demands or the political pressures of tens of
thousands of protesting workers?

Han Dongfang interviewed several Daqing workers as well as cadres during the protests which were covered in detail on the *China Labour Bulletin* web-site. I asked him to explain how he made contact with them, since a news black-out was placed on the event – it wasn't even covered by the *Workers' Daily*. Han said once he finds out the location of a protest he goes to the internet to find the web-sites of the residents' committees in the protest area.

'I'll pick the first five telephone numbers of the residents committee and change, say, the last two digits,' he said, smiling at his unscientific but highly successful methodology. He tells people he is from the *China Labour Bulletin* and is doing research on state enterprise reform. Using this method, he speaks to workers all over the country, querying them about their lifestyle, salary, how they are treated by the factory, what they can and cannot afford. A few days before we met in a Hong Kong coffee shop in May 2002, Han said he found and interviewed a retired worker in Liaoyang who received a small monthly pension of 380 yuan but no other benefits despite having problems with high blood pressure. Her son's employment contract had just one month to run and her daughter-in-law had already been laid off from a paper factory. By the end of their conversation the woman was in tears.

'My life is getting worse,' she told Han, 'but no-one asks me what I can afford. You've asked me about all the things that I've been wanting to talk about,' she said before breaking down into sobs. 'You see,' said Han, 'this isn't a revolution, it is a slow demise.'

This isn't a problem restricted to China's far-flung rustbelts. In 2002 I boarded a taxi in Shanghai and struck up a conversation with the driver about how wealthy the city appeared. 'Huh,' he replied, 'it's a rich person's Temple of Heaven.' The driver, Mr Li, was forty-six, and, I discovered, a state worker from the age of nineteen to thirty-nine. He and his wife had sold cigarettes and alcohol in a small government-owned corner shop. When he was laid off after twenty years of service, he received a salary for two years and then nothing.

The terminology he used to describe his previous status was *xiagang*, in other words, laid-off but still paid a nominal wage by his work unit. Then he decided to drop the pretence.

'I wasn't laid off,' he said, 'I was unemployed.'

For three years Mr Li searched for a job. One night while he was at home watching TV, he got a little drunk. He saw a program about how Shanghai successfully handled its unemployment problems and got its laid-off workers back into jobs. He had watched programs like this before and they were beginning to make him angry. He called up the station's newsroom and had a discussion with a young woman on the other end of the line.

'I'm unemployed and I can't find a job,' he told her. 'Why don't you come and interview me?' The woman said she would pass the suggestion on to her leader. But no-one from the TV station ever returned his call. Mr Li subsequently found work driving a taxi, which he'd been doing for more than a year, yet he still felt a strong sense of betrayal.

With the number of workers on the state payroll slashed from more than 100 million in the mid 1990s to 38 million by 2002, and the size of bureaucracy cut in half to 10 million, the government has turned its reformist zeal to another mainstay of the state workforce: employees of more than one million state-funded institutions such as hospitals, universities, publishing houses and think tanks. By the end of 2006, reported the Xinhua News Agency, 30 million people will exchange lifelong tenure for employment contracts, with some lay-offs expected. From worker to official to intellectual, socialism has well and truly been bled out of Chinese society, remaining only in the structure of the party and its infiltration of the government.

Protests against China's restructuring will certainly continue and some may significantly disrupt social order, as in the case of the large-scale Liaoyang protests in northern China, where the organisers have been charged with the serious political crime of subversion. Yet whether spasmodic protests will result in the activation of the time-bomb, as suggested by Hong Kong-based activist Han Dongfang, is somewhat doubtful. Han and numerous other dissidents and human rights activists haven't lived in China for many years. While there is widespread dissatisfaction, protests tend to be localised and over local issues. The Chinese government is aware of the growing discontent and has shown flexibility in dealing with protests by allowing people to vent their frustrations, which would have been unheard of decades ago. Besides, not all those who have been thrown on the jobless scrap heap are there for the term of their life. A year after I visited Jiang Zuotao and his family in their cave beside the Victory Reservoir, the local government finally responded to his plea for help. The family moved to the city of Yan'an, two hours away, where Mr Jiang has been placed in charge of a heating system at the Yan'an Water Conservancy Bureau, the same work unit which manages the Victory Reservoir. His elder son works for a large state enterprise, the Yan'an Iron and Steel Plant. Maybe a new Deng-style dictum should be invented: no matter what kind of rice bowl, cracked or otherwise, as long as Chinese people have rice to eat, it's a rice bowl.

NEW RICE

To explain how the Chinese economy works, a friend of mine who's a foreign businessman in China takes his visiting clients to a major Beijing intersection to watch the traffic. 'Think of what you're looking at as tomorrow's economic superpower,' he tells them. The roads are choked with players: cars, bicycles, carts and pedestrians, all trying to reach a destination. In highly developed economies all it takes is a traffic light to control the competing interests of the users, with police occasionally supplementing the lights when there's an accident or particularly heavy traffic. In Beijing, there isn't just one police officer at each intersection but four – one for each road feeding into the intersection. In fact, the police are not enough. Traffic 'monitors' armed with whistles control the pedestrians and cyclists, who tend to dart out into oncoming traffic with such abandon it seems they have a death wish. There is no rule about giving way to oncoming traffic and no-one stops at pedestrian crossings. Foreign drivers, particularly those belonging to the embassies, are among the worst at obeying road rules but are rarely stopped. From the motorist's point of view, only the threat of a fine or loss of points or their licence controls their driving behaviour.

It is only when the police officer and monitors vacate the intersection, or when a traffic light breaks down, that you see the true temperament of the traffic flow. It's chaos. Despite the unwieldy nature of China's traffic, with laws and direction, better quality cars and more driving experience, and after twenty-five years of market reforms, the traffic is slowly improving, despite the vast increase in the number of vehicles on the road. Many foreign businesses believe conditions are only now ready for foreign companies to make money, due to the country's accession to the World Trade Organisation in December 2001, and to the vast program of improvements China needs to undertake in order to hold the Beijing Olympics in 2008. Achieving the former took the Chinese fifteen years of complex negotiation, and saw them offer concessions on its tariffs, promise to open industries and agriculture to foreign competition and basically agree to reform its economy so that internal trade regulations comply with international trading rules. None of this will happen overnight, nor will it occur smoothly, according to optimistic foreign projections. Nonetheless, there will be change. The Chinese leadership is counting on it in order to keep the economy growing. So are thousands of multinational companies spending billions of dollars building the foundations of their China business on the expectation that this vast market will want their goods and services.

In a reception hall fitted out with chandeliers, gold leaf and flowery red carpet, the string quartet played Vivaldi while waiters filled tall glass flutes with champagne. Applause erupted as thirty-six graduates wearing gowns and mortarboards trimmed with beige filed in to take their seats in front of a small stage. One of the graduates, a tall woman with a mischievous face, suddenly caught sight of a colourful orange banner proclaiming, 'President Wu, May You Live for Ten Thousand Years!' The young woman, whose name is Shannon Wu, covered her mouth to stifle her laughter. Her fellow graduates didn't miss the joke either. The greeting, 'May You Live for Ten Thousand Years', was borrowed from the Cultural Revolution era when millions of Chinese repeated the phrase in reverence to Chairman Mao Zedong. The congratulatory banner was her friends' recognition of Shannon's hard work: after fourteen months of part-time study, Shannon was being awarded a coveted Executive Masters of Business Administration from the prestigious US business school at Rutgers University.

Like all of the graduates, Shannon is employed by a leading multinational in Beijing, in her case the second largest US software manufacturer, Oracle. Oracle makes software which helps to run the administrative side of businesses, helping Chinese businesses to improve their efficiencies and cut costs to meet the tough competitive pressures set by the World Trade Organisation.

Shannon already had a bachelor's degree in computer software design, was earning a handsome US$2000–3000 a month with life insurance, pension fund and housing supplied, but like thousands of working Chinese she wanted to obtain foreign management skills, both outside and inside China. 'In the long term, I think it will give me a leg-up,' said the 34-year-old human resources manager. 'It's important to get a foreign degree; it will help if I go to another country too.'

The guest speaker at Shannon's graduation ceremony was her boss, Oracle's managing director in China, Andrew Hu. He reminded graduates that they were entering a very competitive business environment and that if they didn't use their skills they would quickly lose them. 'There is no better time to be in China than over the next five years,' said the US-trained Taiwanese MD, but he cautioned graduates that, 'Only the paranoid survive.'

Like scores of multinational companies, Oracle has taken extraordinary steps to win business in China. It is the company's fastest growing market, expanding at a rate of 50 per cent annually. While just a few years ago China was the place to produce clothes and training shoes cheaply, it's now setting its sights on becoming a high technology supremo – in early January 2003 China successfully sent an unmanned rocket into space. Despite the progress, less lofty achievements such as software development, which requires highly trained engineers rather than cheap unskilled labour, has lagged behind. In 2001 China's software industry generated revenues of US$850 million compared with more than US$6 billion for India. Yet from this low base, Western software companies like Oracle believe they can one day make a killing in what is essentially a virgin market.

Oracle opened a representative office in Beijing in 1991, but its charismatic CEO, Larry Ellison – unlike many other China-struck CEOs – didn't visit the country until March 1995. He was impressed by what he saw, and when he made his second visit two years later described it as the fastest transformation he had witnessed in his life. Today, Oracle is still small by the standards of many multinationals, employing four hundred people, but it has set an ambitious target of being the leading business applications company in China.

In 2002 Oracle opened a development centre in the southern Shenzhen Special Economic Zone where more than one hundred software engineers take existing Oracle software and customise it for China. A second centre will open in Beijing in mid 2003. These development facilities, as well as other research and education partnerships that Oracle funds, also help to expand the country's technological capabilities. This is exactly what the Chinese government insists upon: it doesn't merely want foreign products but the know-how behind those products and their maintenance – or to be blunt, free staff training and plenty of staff benefits. Motorola, for example, claims to be the biggest foreign electronics enterprise in China with an investment of US$3.4 billion, employing 13 000 workers. Apart from a home ownership program for its staff, it contributes money to the education of poor rural children, provides more than 3000 university fellowships and has developed a management program to send selected managers abroad for months of training.

Global entrepreneurs have a soft spot for China. 'I think there's a much bigger risk in not investing in China than investing in China,' said Larry Ellison after flying into Beijing on his private jet to attend Oracle World, the company's first major conference in China, held in June 2002.

Media tycoon Rupert Murdoch would certainly concur. He first saw the potential of the China market as far back as the 1980s when he bought the English language newspaper my father had edited, the *South China Morning Post*. (Murdoch subsequently sold it in 1993.) In the early 1990s Murdoch bought a majority stake in Hong Kong-based STAR (an acronym for Satellite Television Asian Region), and a few months later angered China when he expounded on the virtues of satellite TV, declaring that it would be an 'unambiguous threat to totalitarian regimes everywhere'. After Beijing turned a cold shoulder towards the magnate, Murdoch realised the benefits of deferring to China. In 1994 the STAR network dropped the BBC, which had broadcast extensive coverage of the Tiananmen massacre as well as other uncomplimentary news items about China. Murdoch later admitted to his biographer, William Shawcross, that he did so to gain acceptance in China. His business and personal ties with the mainland grew – he met Chinese American Wendi Deng in 1998 and married her the following year. In 1998 HarperCollins, a subsidiary of his News Corporation, suddenly dumped *East and West*, the memoir of Hong Kong's last governor, Chris Patten. The book offers a negative assessment of the Chinese government.

Since Western companies started doing business with China in the 1980s they have become much smarter at learning how to work within the system. Many companies are now making a profit or close to breaking even. The soft-drink manufacturer Pepsi, which has had a presence since 1982, runs thirty businesses, holds total investments of US$800 million and employs 10000 people. Yet it only expects to turn its first profit in 2005. Despite Pepsi's history in China and success at establishing its brand when virtually every one of the country's 290 million children is familiar with *Ke Kou Ke Le* (the Chinese name for Coke, meaning 'tasty and good to drink'), Pepsi still has its problems. In August 2002 Pepsi submitted papers with an international arbitrator in Stockholm detailing a dispute with its joint venture partner, the Sichuan Radio and Television Industrial Development Company, a curious choice of partner for a soft-drink manufacturer. The disagreement centred on a bottling factory set up in the south-western city of Chengdu in 1993. According to the *Washington Post*, Pepsi accused the Chinese partners of looting the company, with the general manager of the venture helping himself to a Mercedes and a Toyota Land Cruiser and using company money to make frequent trips to New York where his wife and daughter live.

But shed no tears for Pepsi or other companies producing FMCGs, fast-moving consumer goods. With at least 100 million people able to afford their products and the number growing all the time, the profits – for some companies at least – will be forthcoming, but they will also have a life and death struggle on their hands. While foreign investors are fighting for a slice of the market, domestic firms are fighting for survival in the brave new post-WTO world.

While many commentators marvel at China's economic growth, which has averaged 7 per cent for the last few years and 10 per cent before that, it's growing because the government helps it along by spending money on infrastructure, which creates jobs and other economic spin-offs. The Chinese economy must continue to expand by at least the current rate of 7 per cent to keep its massive workforce – and around fourteen million new entrants each year – employed. Chinese leaders are gambling on two major developments to keep the country's economy expanding in this productive way: China's 2001 accession to the World Trade Organisation, and the dynamism of the emerging private sector. The odds on both races are far from guaranteed.

After the gradual abolition of private business following the Communist takeover in 1949, the private sector emerged on the fringes of the economy after the Cultural Revolution and took hold as a result of Deng Xiaoping's reforms after 1979. However it wasn't until 1988 that private companies were officially recognised. After the setback of the Tiananmen massacre in 1989, Deng's 1992 'southern tour' again provided the growth needed for the private sector to take off again, but its irrevocable licence wasn't confirmed until the Fifteenth Party Congress in 1997. According to official statistics, in 2002 the state sector produced approximately 37 per cent of all China's goods and services, and the private sector produced 33 per cent. The third category, the 'non-state sector', which as the name implies is an intermediate stage of ownership – neither fully private nor state-owned – accounted for the remaining 30 per cent. Many believe, however, that the private sector accounts for a higher proportion of the economy and that it could be as much as 50 or 60 per cent. Today, there are approximately four million registered private businesspeople, and 1.7 million private firms (defined as employing more than eight people) supporting twenty million private workers. Yet while private enterprise is seen as the lifeboat of China's economy, the government has been slow to create the conditions to truly let it flourish.

Jiang Jingxin is a former state factory worker who once worked for the Grain and Cereal Bureau, and who then found a niche in a new competitive industry springing up in China's major cities – fast food, Chinese-style. But his company isn't a Chinese McDonald's; it delivers hot Chinese meals in segmented cardboard cartons to more than 8000 office workers around Beijing. I visited one of the company's kitchens, where lunch for 2000 is prepared each day. The rudimentary kitchen space was rented from a state-owned chemical factory that went bankrupt in 1996. There were about a hundred workers in the kitchen, all busy with different tasks. A row of giant woks filled a corner of the small factory, with cooks dressed in blue doctors' coats and cloth hats using large ladles to stir the contents. The food looked like a rather non-descript stir-fry, with a little meat, plenty of vegetables and firm tofu – the smell struck me as soon as I parted the plastic sheets at the factory door. A line of workers removed vats of cooked rice from vast cookers while fried chicken drumsticks arrived from another corner. Then more workers formed a production line and divided the food into the cartons, clouds of steam rising from the meals. Once they had been served, the company's band of couriers – mostly laid-off state workers – set out on bicycles and vans to deliver meals throughout the city.

'When we started we were based in the suburbs, we had very little capital, poor location and no facilities like vehicles,' said manager Jiang, one of the four brothers who own the company. Beijing already had dozens of fast-food companies like Li Hua. Competition was fierce and customers demanding, but manager Jiang was aiming to grab a 10 per cent market share.

Though the business was sound, the main stumbling block to expanding it was lack of capital. In China there are very few venture capital firms and virtually no bond market because nobody trusts companies to pay back the bonds. It's extremely difficult for a private company to launch on the stock market, so often the only sources of funding are the state banks. Because of the small size of Mr Jiang's business, the state-owned banks didn't want to know him at first. When I visited the company in 1999, just 1 per cent of bank lending went to the private sector.

'We tried to get a loan when we were still small, but the bank wasn't interested. When we were expanding and became well-known, only then did the bank offer us a loan,' Mr Jiang said.

Despite years of reluctance to lend to the private sector, the government realised several years ago that upstart private businesses like Mr Jiang's could be the hope of China, soaking up the endless queues of unemployed. Li Hua's kitchens employ 600 people in six establishments, though all on a casual basis.

Robert Li is a big man in his late thirties with large eyes and thick hair that flops into his jovial, expressive face. It wasn't difficult imagining him as a child actor, chosen from among hundreds of twelve-year-olds to appear in the 'revolutionary' or propaganda genre of films made during the Cultural Revolution. In 1975 Robert starred in *Fishing Island in a Fury*, the story of a boy called Iron Egg who lives on an island and struggles against marauding Nationalists and their 'running dogs', according to the film blurb. Iron Egg joins the People's Liberation Army, which eventually defeats the Nationalists, and the boy becomes a hero. Robert had a privileged childhood, and later graduated from Beijing's film academy. But when the propaganda film genre began to wane in post-Mao China, Robert began to diversify his career by producing and selling cultural television programs and videos.

With the money he earned from his sideline, he set up a trading company and began importing luxury consumer goods into China through Hong Kong. It was now the early 1990s and Deng had added the word 'market' into the socialist economy equation. It was a heady time for entrepreneurs and savvy people like Robert Li didn't waste any time. 'The money was fast and easy,' he said. 'Things were opening up so quickly. We weren't even the earliest doing this, but it was still very easy to make money.'

From luxury goods, Robert's attention turned to real estate. He had always admired Beijing's traditional courtyard homes, situated in alleys or *hutong*s behind large red doors. He began buying up decrepit dwellings he felt weren't worthy of renovation. He paid around US$10 000 for each home, demolished them and in their place built new courtyards with modern facilities. To give the homes a traditional feel, he used his connections in the film industry to employ artisans – who also maintained the city's historic sites – to paint ancient scenes on the pillars and beams inside the courtyards. He then rented out the homes to foreigners for several thousand US dollars a month, a sum that most Chinese would consider eye-popping but by foreign standards was cheaper and more attractive than renting apartments or villas in compounds.

I met Robert Li through my colleague Cleo Leung, who lived in one of Robert's courtyards with her husband, consultant Josh

Brookhart, and another American consultant, James Leininger. The courtyard was situated near the Liulichang 'culture' street, in a *hutong* where no other foreigners lived. Old women sat on the railings outside the courtyard, gossiping the day away while men ferried coal, toilet paper and other necessities on carts, the perfect vehicle to pass through the narrow lanes.

Like many small business owners, Robert has a mixture of interests. When I first met him he owned a bar-cum-restaurant called the Iron Horse, a reference to his first movie role as the child hero, Iron Egg. The Iron Horse, like many locally-owned Beijing drinking establishments, had a curious decor: wallpaper made from counterfeit compact discs, with metal and mirrors everywhere. It had a large dance floor, room for a band, and dining tables in the restaurant section punctuated with mini-televisions screening Chinese music videos.

One evening Cleo and I, the token foreigners (even though Cleo is Chinese American), were invited to sample the food at the Iron Horse with the purpose of providing feedback and advice. Out came an array of 'Western food', including tuna sandwiches, fried cheese, crumbed chicken and a steak. With each bite we took, Robert's wife watched intently for our reactions. She very much wanted approval and so we pronounced the food a success. However, I pointed out that in my view a bar wasn't a bar without cocktails, like margaritas, for example. Mrs Li had been waiting for such a challenge and she snapped her fingers, summoning the single cocktail expert amongst the staff. Ten minutes later I had a small but drinkable margarita in front of me, stirred not frozen.

After our stint as food-tasters, the Iron Horse didn't last the course. There were just too many restaurants and bars clustered together in the same location. When I last saw Robert, the Iron Horse had disappeared, replaced by a restaurant on the west side of Beijing's Chaoyang Park. 'Everyone wants Chinese food now,' Robert said, trying to rationalise the failure. His latest idea is to open a traditional Chinese medicine clinic for foreigners – in a beautifully renovated Beijing courtyard. If that idea succeeds, the next stage is to open a similar clinic in the United States.

While he searches for investors, Robert's bread and butter is still the rental income from his modern courtyard homes. His business philosophy, shared by many Chinese as a result of the rapidly changing landscape, is to make the most of his opportunities while he can. 'I don't care if it's big or small, happiness depends on enjoying what you do,' he said, pouring Taiwanese Oolong tea into my cup at a teahouse near where the Iron Horse once stood. As an insurance policy and to safeguard his wealth, he's secured a coveted 'green card' and plans to educate his young son in the United States.

In the past, state enterprises, whether they were well managed or not, were given direct subsidies from the central government. These were later replaced with loans from state-owned commercial banks. State-owned enterprises (SOEs) consumed about 70 per cent of domestic lending. From the individual loan officer's point of view, lending to SOEs, even though they might never repay the loan, was a safer bet than lending to the private sector.

Chen Mei, the consultant I introduced in chapter 9, worked as a lending officer at the Bank of China for two years in the early 1990s. It was her first job after graduating from a prestigious Shanghai university, and apart from learning about the procedures in the central bank, she also got an insight into how the officers helped themselves before they helped others, through a complex system of fostering relationships and requesting bribes.

'If you weren't part of the "network",' she recalled, 'you didn't get pay rises, you didn't get training or anything. But it was your choice, join the "family" or not.'

A small private company making decorations approached Chen Mei for a half-million yuan loan so that it could expand sufficiently to seek foreign investment from the United States. Her boss wasn't keen on the idea, reminding her of the policy of 'responsibility to individuals' which made loan officers personally responsible for loans. Despite this onus, Chen Mei had faith in the small firm so she approved the loan. The company didn't disappoint her and repaid it within six months. Later she gave it another loan for 2 million yuan, which it also repaid.

'The first time I visited the company there were fifty women on very basic sewing machines, making decorations. The next time they had 300 women and they were on brand-new machines,' said Chen Mei. Normally to obtain the loan the company would have had to bribe the loan officer. The boss told her he didn't have the funds to bribe her. Chen Mei wasn't interested in bribes, she assured the boss. She also didn't want to join the Bank of China 'network', so she eventually left. 'I didn't want to lose the last shred of hope I had,' she said. Ten years on, the Bank of China and the other leading institutions are slowly increasing their lending to the private sector, though most of its growth has been achieved under difficult circumstances.

Apart from being hampered by poor access to external funds, the private sector is constrained by opacity and legal uncertainty. The concepts of management systems, delegating responsibility and employee trust are missing or dysfunctional and the country has a shortage of competent, trained business people. 'Business is a science,' a Western management consultant explained. 'There are complex principles that have to be learned. The way many Chinese managers run companies isn't scientific at all.'

Chinese offices are complex environments healthily dosed with intrigue, suspicion and one-upmanship. The Cultural Revolution taught most Chinese that they couldn't rely on anyone; that their neighbours, bosses and even family members were not to be trusted. Though decades have passed since then, the psychology has taken root in the way Chinese do business – by relying on relationships instead of building professional management systems. This works until a company grows too large, then efficient management may fall by the wayside.

James Leininger is an American human resources consultant who has lived in China on and off for more than ten years and who speaks fluent Chinese. James shared one of Robert Li's courtyard homes with my colleague Cleo and her husband, and over the years has become a good friend. In his mid thirties and an indefatigable optimist, James' work involves helping Chinese companies to set up viable staffing and salary structures, in response to the changes being forced on them by restructuring and the World Trade Organisation. Even after bad days, he always manages to find humour between the setbacks.

During one project, James worked for a private Chinese company headed by a businessman from the southern city of Wenzhou, famous for its entrepreneurs. 'Every Wenzhou kid wants to be a boss,' he said, and the entrepreneur he worked for was no exception. At the age of thirteen he was selling shoes on the street corner. By the age of twenty-eight he had one of the largest retail companies in the country with seventy-two shoe stores nationwide, employing more than 12 000 people.

Growing the company, however, came with its problems. In the space of five months, three human resources directors, two chief executives and two chief financial officers had been fired – James came on the scene shortly after the entrepreneur had fired the first CEO and human resources director. The entrepreneur's problems were typical of a family company structure that had grown too large, and where the selection criterion for senior management wasn't based on the ability to manage, but on the level of trust the entrepreneur could place in the employee. Most of his team were related to him in some way, and were therefore difficult or impossible to fire.

Though the entrepreneur had no political constraints because his wasn't a state enterprise, he had a different set of constraints in that he was using his own money, not state funds. Private businesspeople are always in need of political connections to get approvals and special treatment from government departments and the tax bureau. They are also often beholden to interest groups like family members or people from the same village who pressure them for jobs. Furthermore, unlike Western management which promotes delegation, because of the lack of transparency and proper regulations the Chinese way of doing business made the shoe entrepreneur responsible for virtually every decision, however major or minor.

As the shoe business grew larger, management problems multiplied. Eventually they began to affect the bottom line and the entrepreneur was unable to pay his bills. From an office behind a large glass door next to the shoe company's reception area, James witnessed the unfolding melodrama of the company's demise. One day an angry woman fronted up to reception, claiming the shoe firm owed her money. James later discovered she was a wholesaler who hadn't been paid in months. The exchange between the wholesaler and the receptionist became heated and eventually the wholesaler tried to force her way through the open glass door. The receptionist ran out from behind her desk to stop the woman. As the commotion raged just a few steps from James's office, a Chinese staff member came into his room, blocking the scene with her body, and nonchalantly told him to take no notice of the uproar.

By then, the angry wholesaler had proved herself a determined fighter and it took the combined strength of the receptionist and a security guard to stop her entering the back office. All of a sudden, she broke free and appeared in front of the glass partition holding a chair above her head. This time the nifty receptionist crash-tackled her and she fell to the floor, finally halted. All the while the Chinese staff member remained in James's office continuing her idle chatter in order to divert attention from the embarrassing incident. It was a vivid and dramatic finale to James's dealings with the entrepreneur. He completed his work with the company but the entrepreneur's problems didn't end. Two weeks after the incident with the wholesaler, the businessman's brother-in-law and father were murdered.

Apart from problems such as loose ownership structures, poor corporate governance and lax financial reporting standards, the legal system still falls short of providing guarantees to private business-people. Politically, private enterprise has been encouraged. After the 1997 Party Congress, Jiang Zemin elevated the private sector's status in the Constitution to an 'important part' of the socialist market economy, and foreshadowed further change after the Sixteenth Congress in November 2002: the need to enshrine the political rights of the 'new classes' of non-state entrepreneurs and professionals. In 2001 he invited entrepreneurs to join the ranks of the Communist Party, and in 2002 a dozen or so 'red bosses' were admitted to the Communist Party Congress of Guangdong province, the first time in the 82-year history of the party that private entrepreneurs had been selected as provincial congress delegates.

Despite the change of heart, vital laws which would guarantee the rights of private enterprises in China have yet to be enacted. In socialist China, the ostensible owner of all property was the people. However, it was the government and the Communist Party which controlled the property. Socialism held that it was unnecessary to distinguish property rights among different entities, since all property belonged to the people (the state). Consequently, property rights were vaguely defined and are still lacking.

This encourages the continuance of a pretty broad 'grey' area when it comes to business transactions. In Chinese there are three terms defining legality: there is *he fa* (legal), *fei fa* (illegal), and *wei-fa* (offends the regulations but not the law). Long-time Beijing-based analyst and journalist, Italian Francesco Sisci, explained over a cappuccino at the China World Trade Centre that within the government, opponents of a law that would secure private property believe it could lead to private capital acquired through shady deals being legalised. Such security could hamper future confiscations or reprisals. Mr Sisci has monitored the stages of China's political and economic development for fifteen years. He came to China in 1988 as the first foreign student admitted to the prestigious graduate school of the Chinese Academy of Social Sciences for field work on a PhD in ancient Chinese philosophy. He believes that the present insecurity of private entrepreneurs forces them to side with corrupt officials, who in return for favours and bribes protect the 'rights' of private business.

'Almost any official has the power to temporarily close down any business on the basis of almost any kind of suspicion,' said Mr Sisci. 'Such a temporary closure can deal a heavy, sometimes fatal blow to the company.' However leaving open the possibility of solving in the future a past crime, he believes, 'creates an environment in which crimes must be committed every day and where corruption thrives'.

It's difficult to tell whether the fall of high-profile businesspeople is the result of economic crime like corruption or tax evasion, or due to official jealousy. 'Show me a rich man and I'll show you a thief,' goes a popular saying. Yet during a crackdown on tax evasion in 2002 – a high-profile actress was dramatically ushered out of her Beijing villa in handcuffs – a report by the official Xinhua News Agency quoted tax officials saying only four of the richest fifty people in China had paid income tax the previous year. In addition, a survey among a small group of residents in China's three wealthiest cities – Beijing, Shanghai and Guangzhou – carried out by the ominous-sounding Prosperity Supervision Centre, found that one-third of the respondents admitted to paying only part of their tax while nearly 20 per cent said they didn't pay tax at all. Tax is levied on annual salaries over 10 000 yuan (A$2500).

'People think it's okay to cheat the system because otherwise their boss will gamble it away in Las Vegas or Macau,' said a young manager who asked to remain anonymous. He proceeded to explain the difference between good corruption and bad corruption. The good kind didn't hurt the people's or an individual's interest, it was about paying off some corrupt official so that, for example, the full tariffs weren't applied to imported homewares, and could be sold more cheaply to Chinese consumers. Bad corruption was defined as something that hurt the interests of others, for example factory cadres embezzling state funds so that workers went unpaid.

'People have so little respect for the system,' said the manager, 'we don't look at hurting state revenue as a bad thing.'

In 2002 a well-known and respected Beijing impresario, Qian Cheng, was arrested on suspicion of corruption. In 1993 he had taken over the management of the loss-making Beijing Concert Hall and made it profitable by increasing the number and calibre of performances. He also broke new ground by installing a computerised ticketing system, and – incredibly for China – banned mobile phones and pagers during concerts. A Chinese newspaper said the allegations against him concerned a private firm he had set up in 1996 into which he was said to have channelled money. However the murkiness of the system overall prevented an objective examination of the facts. If officials choose to go after someone, even if they are innocent, they are still doomed.

A report by the respected Hong Kong-based Political and Economic Risk Consultancy (PERC), which advises businesses on the risk profile of Asian countries, made some stinging conclusions about China: the reason many people in the public and private sectors are willing to risk quite draconian penalties for crime 'is a good indication that they do not feel particularly threatened about being caught or prosecuted'.

Though the report noted that China's corruption rating had improved in recent years, it slammed the judicial system in China as 'unreliable, vulnerable to corruption and difficult to deal with', maintaining that the ultimate authority in the country was the Communist Party and not the law. Furthermore, it was a misconception to believe that China's entry to the World Trade Organisation would somehow make its legal system compatible with WTO rules in the short term.

'It is not simply a matter of changing laws, however, but of training lawyers, judges and police and then making the systematic changes to remove the present systems' idiosyncrasies. This will take years, if not decades,' PERC's analysts concluded.

When the Chinese leadership goes on one of its periodic anti-corruption drives, it employs the full spectrum of its propaganda machine. One of the biggest anti-corruption displays I saw in Beijing was held during a steamy August in 2000. The Stalinesque Military Museum is a regular outing for school children because of its permanent collection of ageing armoury: tanks, big guns and small planes. When a 'Strike Hard' campaign decided to focus on corruption, the museum was transformed. 'You want to film our exhibition?' queried the Beijing Foreign Affairs Bureau official. 'Very welcome, how many people and what time will you arrive?'

After the traffic-snarled drive along Chang'an Avenue during which you pass the Who's Who of Beijing's Communist-era buildings, the crew and I were ushered into the grand hall where the corruption extravaganza was taking place. There we jostled with hundreds of school kids and honorary cadres, senior PLA soldiers, all of whom, like us, had been given free tickets to what was described by one newspaper as Beijing's 'best show on earth'. The highlight of the exhibition was the corner devoted to one of China's highest officials, the former vice-chairman of the National People's Congress standing committee, Cheng Kejie.

Chinese propaganda exhibitions can often be rather one-dimensional, relying on signboards, too many characters and big photographs. But this one surpassed itself. There were glass cases stuffed with stolen booty including watches, gold, diamond rings, pens, cash and even a life-size fashion mannequin of a short man with a grey wig (supposed to be Cheng Kejie) and sporting a designer watch, flashy suit and shiny leather shoes. All the people I interviewed at the exhibition were suitably horrified at the collection of luxury items accumulated by Cheng and other cohorts. No, they had no idea that their officials had amassed such wealth and yes, the government was doing a good job in bringing them before the law.

Cheng's downfall read like the plot of a seedy movie. His ambitious and financially astute mistress, Li Ping, was able to exploit the offices of the 66-year-old who, as well as being a former vice-chairman of China's parliament was also the governor of the province of Guangxi from 1990 to 1998. According to official media reports about the case, Cheng amassed US$4.9 million from graft. However, as Australian-based academic Hans Hendrischke points out, the case exemplifies the woeful inadequacy of China's attempts to tackle corruption because it fails to address a system that allows an extraordinary concentration of power and influence.

Professor Hendrischke says that although the case of Cheng and his lover lacked the conspicuous consumption and moral depravity that accompanied other major corruption trials, Cheng and Li Ping created an entire business empire through their networks. Incredibly for someone in such a senior public office, Cheng's corrupt activities continued for nearly a decade. He only came unstuck after his mistress attempted to secure two land deals that in essence trod on the toes of competing institutions.

The *People's Daily* blamed Cheng's actions on money worship, hedonism and 'extreme individualism'. The newspaper failed to mention the part played by China's reforms, instead blaming 'a small number of elements . . . who blindly hold western bourgeois values and way of life in high esteem'.

'The present government only thinks about money,' said my manager friend. 'Deng Xiaoping told us "white cat, black cat, as long as it catches mice it's a good cat". It's the guiding principle of the state.'

In a more celebrated incident in October 2002, Chinese officials detained a man known as the Orchid King, named by *Forbes* magazine in 2001 as China's second richest man, with wealth estimated at US$900 million. Yang Bin, aged thirty-nine, was born in China and moved to Holland in the 1980s. He became a student activist and after the Tiananmen uprising in 1989, applied to stay in Holland and was granted Dutch nationality. Business activities – horticulture

and property – took him back to northern China and to North Korea
in 1994. Days before his arrest he'd been appointed by the North
Koreans as the governor of Sinuiju, their new capitalist enclave.
Chinese authorities considered the appointment totally unacceptable as Mr Yang was a businessman – and a foreign national at
that – and held no official status in China. Yang Bin had already
admitted that he owed ten million yuan in taxes in the northern
Chinese city of Shenyang and was put under house arrest. One
month later he was charged with 'suspected . . . criminal activities
including running investment scams, using fraudulent contracts,
illegally occupying farmlands and offering bribes' according to the
People's Daily. The Chinese government said that though he was a
Dutch national, he would be dealt with under Chinese law as his
business dealings had taken place in China. The North Korean
government was forced to distance itself from Mr Yang.

Corruption was – and for the foreseeable future will be –
endemic both outside and within the state enterprise system,
despite efforts to clean up business and accounting procedures. The
reason corruption is so rampant is that, until recently, the heads of
many large and important SOEs employing hundreds of thousands
of workers only earned annual salaries in the ballpark of US$5000.
This was a remnant of the socialist system, under which, for example, the top person couldn't earn more than ten times the salary of
the person at the bottom. The CEO or enterprise chief didn't get
performance bonuses or stock options like his Western counterparts. As a result, he and his most trustworthy staff were given
side-benefits 'skimmed off the top' of the enterprise as a kind of
compensation for their low salaries. Often the value of the benefits
was more than fifty times the actual salary. It wasn't unusual for
a vice-president, for example, to have a large villa, an 'S' class
Mercedes Benz, servants, as well as lavish vacations all paid for by
the company. Was this corruption? Not necessarily, but it was, and
remains, a grey area. Such benefits don't appear on the company's
books and aren't subject to board control or shareholder scrutiny.

Like private enterprises, foreign businesses also face barriers and minefields. After I talked to one businessman in the upmarket Henderson Centre office complex in central Beijing, we took a lift down to the basement carpark. As we reached the lobby, the businessman indicated a row of empty lifts which appeared to be out of order. That day, the building management had summoned security guards to protect the tenants, including the chief executives of dozens of leading multinationals. Earlier in the week, the management had cut off the electricity and water supply to a popular Cantonese restaurant and nightclub because it owed 4 million yuan (A$1 000 000) in rent and fees. In response to the shutdown, the restaurant owner called on local thugs to blockade the lifts in an effort to arouse the sympathy and attention of the other tenants. This took place in a flashy Hong Kong-managed building. Clearly, the 'new' Beijing often struggles to keep up even the appearance of a modern Asian economy.

After China's December 2001 accession to the World Trade Organisation, the billboards around the capital displayed messages such as, 'WTO has arrived. Are you prepared?' The signs were talking to domestic Chinese companies, and in reality the answer was a resounding 'no', because the government was still working on the Chinese version of the bulky accession document for distribution to the nation's cadres.

WTO membership required all levels of the Chinese government to abide by the rules of transparency and fairness that govern international trading. Contrary to the perception given by both the Chinese and Western media that accession was the crowning achievement of a country striding toward developed nation status, membership of the trade organisation is far more complex. After its entry to the WTO, which represents more than 140 governments and 97 per cent of world trade, China embarked on a program of progressively lower tariffs and reduced barriers over several years, allowing foreign enterprises unprecedented access to the country's vast market.

There are several reasons why China wanted to join the World Trade Organisation. By doing so it put Chinese companies on a course of change – for example, increasing their efficiency and customer focus because of greater foreign competition and a decrease in protection for Chinese industries. The agreement also opens up foreign markets to a range of Chinese products that would previously have had restrictions placed on them. And finally, after centuries of perceived abuses by foreign powers and decades of self-induced isolationism, the Chinese people could say that they had finally 'made it' as a full and equal partner in the world community.

From the point of view of China's competitors, China's WTO membership will lower subsidies, enhance intellectual property rights, encourage the development of a respectable legal system and, best of all, provide new market access in dozens of industries. Software developer Oracle, for example, saw WTO membership as opening up the financial services sector, creating opportunities for its software in securities and capital markets. Oracle also hopes to benefit from the push to make Chinese companies more competitive, which again will create demand for its systems. On the negative side, the tariff reduction on agricultural products from 20 to 30 per cent in 2001, 15 per cent by 2004 and a maximum of 9 per cent by 2006 has the potential to exacerbate unemployment in the countryside. There is also a better than average chance that what the Chinese government wants for its economy may not be viewed as successful by those who are at the coalface.

Before 1981 carpets in the Gansu region had been woven in small workshops or on family looms. Officials then decided that to combine the small producers into factories would increase the region's profits, and the workforce of 3000 in 1981 was expanded so that by 1992 there were 50 000 workers in the carpet industry. Between 1981 and 1996 the Gansu Carpet Import Export Company borrowed a total of 550 million yuan before going broke and laying off 300 workers. Its bosses had invested the factory's money in cars, villas and apartments for themselves in the freewheeling economic zones of Shenzhen and Hainan. Zhang Lixin witnessed the rise and fall of his factory and began to look for opportunities outside the state enterprise. After the Cultural Revolution, he had studied to become a Japanese language expert at the foreign languages department at Lanzhou University. At night he studied classical Chinese. After he graduated, his job was to facilitate the sale of carpets to the Japanese market, and when the new economic impetus kicked in after the 1989 student movement he decided that he could make better carpets than the state factory and sell them on his own to the Japanese. He built a workshop in the western city of Lanzhou and began assembling workers who had once woven their own carpets. He lamented the decline of traditional Chinese carpet-making, which since being taken over by the state had descended to using dull patterns, poor quality fibre and chemical colouring. The same decline occurred with most of China's craft industries: the focus was on mass production with little emphasis on individuality or charm.

'My carpets couldn't be made by the state,' boasted Mr Zhang. 'Everything of mine is made by hand. I'm making old Chinese carpets for the new generation.' Mr Zhang doesn't simply make carpets; he lives for them. He relishes every aspect of the business, and despite being the company's executive director he personally sources natural dyes from remote regions of the country and checks the quality of the wool which comes from Ningxia province, as carpet wool did during the Ming and Qing dynasties. A recent trip took him to the south-western province of Guizhou where he travelled on a bus for six hours and then trekked three hours into the mountains to find indigo plants. His sells his high-quality carpets – the smallest piece costs about US$50 – to three Japanese galleries, and his hope is that as China gets richer the Chinese will learn to once again appreciate traditional craftsmanship. Mr Zhang's carpets are thick and luxuriant, with basic colours – from browns to blues and reds – and bold designs which include stylised flowers and geometric borders. My favourite design was one that looked like the profile of a small cream-coloured pine tree repeated in neat rows on a deep blue background.

After discussing carpets in their showroom in Beijing, Mr Zhang and his wife, An Liping, who is also the company's deputy general manager, suggested dinner at a hot-pot restaurant. As the broth bubbled away, we took turns dropping finely shaved lamb, slices of tofu, cabbage, thin 'needle' mushrooms and rice noodles into the pot, and when they were cooked, dipping them into a thick brown sesame paste before eating them. Chinese restaurants are extremely noisy and when the food has gone, it doesn't take long before you become mindful of the noise and the smoke from both cigarettes and hot-pots. So after the meal we went back to Mr Zhang's apartment for fruit and wine.

Mr Zhang took a bottle down from a display cabinet: it was Australian chardonnay. He poured it, unchilled, into tiny wine glasses and we sat around the dining table eating rockmelon and drinking tea and chardonnay from glasses the size of egg cups.

'You know, in 1989 [after the Tiananmen crackdown] I hated the Communist Party. It was grey, you couldn't see the blue sky. Now it's changed for the better. After 1989 I was given the opportunity to do what I loved and to do it well. The government hasn't given me any help or any loans, but its policies have softened.' Mr Zhang believes that if there hadn't been any international pressure after June the Fourth, China wouldn't have changed half as much.

'I think China's politicians will definitely change their world view and views on economic freedom within the next decade,' he said. 'Then if China gets half as much democracy as the West, I will be happy, and if that happens I won't emigrate!' He laughed.

I asked him why he felt the need to emigrate or obtain a foreign passport like virtually every other aspiring Chinese person I know. The simple reason is that travelling on a Chinese passport is highly restrictive. 'The only places we don't need visas for are Vietnam and

North Korea. I can't even travel to Hong Kong without a lot of trouble and I need an invitation to go to New York,' he said. There is no freedom for a Chinese businessman on a Chinese passport.

On the plus side Mr Zhang believes WTO will be good for China as it will result in the importation of hundreds of quality brands and labels. 'It's good from the quality perspective and hopefully WTO will make bad carpets disappear,' he said. However, Western businesses should remember that from the Chinese government's point of view, the cards are stacked in favour of the state-owned enterprises, and the opportunities supposed to flow to businesses as a whole will be directed first to state-controlled enterprises.

Mr Zhang believes one of the major problems facing business in China is the poor education standards of the middle and lower levels of the bureaucracy. In less wealthy regions such as his home province of Gansu in western China, this is especially so. 'In Gansu, the local government officials don't understand anything about WTO, they have a peasant's point of view!' he said disparagingly.

Yet from a Western business point of view, there's a feeling that the Chinese window won't remain open indefinitely. 'If you're not already in China, it's too late,' said one Western businessman. Most companies believe that China is too large a market to ignore over the long term. In mid 2002, the Singapore government paid a steep US$42.3 million for a piece of land in Pudong, Shanghai. It bought the land before it had any idea what to do with it and sought the advice of an international property consultant on how to develop it. Most companies, however, after twenty years of unrealistic optimism on China, have finally realised that it's a long hard road and nothing will happen quickly. 'I detect a huge resistance on the Chinese side,' said one China-based international lawyer, 'and they know there are all sorts of ways to passively resist their WTO obligations.'

This school believes the state is unlikely to assist in the destruction of any key domestic sector and will use WTO rules and non-tariff barriers to control foreign dominance without killing the competition it generates. 'It can't get any worse,' said one Canadian businessman, referring to the challenge of doing business in China. What is certain, according to a China-based management consultant, is that China hasn't embraced globalisation because of the leadership's altruism. 'They are willing to give foreigners a share of a bigger pie, but they are not willing to give them a bigger slice of the pie.' In other words, 'going global' is a survival strategy.

While the Chinese economy is unquestionably growing, so too are its myriad problems. China's growth has been achieved by running up debts. This isn't always a bad thing for a developing country if the debt has been used to build infrastructure that will help to grow the economy. However China's debt levels are significant. The government's budget deficit is close to US$40 billion as a result of infrastructure spending. In addition, international economists are increasingly concerned about the twin icebergs of non-performing bank loans that account for at least 25 per cent of the banks' portfolio and billions more in unfunded pension liabilities.

The problem of non-performing loans is a result of policy-oriented lending, mostly to badly run or mismanaged SOEs, totalling US$400–600 billion, or half of the country's annual Gross Domestic Product. Meanwhile the pension system is on the verge of bankruptcy largely due to a rapidly ageing population. By 2005 the government will face a US$15 billion shortfall which will increase to US$110 billion five years later. While these are very real problems that could potentially cause a financial meltdown, there are scores of other issues that threaten to deflate the benefits of joining an organisation like the World Trade Organisation, like China's customs regime, for example.

I knew that Customs regularly allowed an art dealer friend of mine to take antiques out of the country by virtue of a US$500 'payment' organised by a well-known Chinese dealer. Chinese Customs also applied its own charges to tens of thousands of parcels delivered to China via international courier companies. A businessman told me his wife had sent him from Britain ten packets of an inexpensive hypoallergenic soap for personal use. Customs had slapped a fee on the package which made it cheaper for the man to buy the most expensive imported soap available in China. The vice-director of Customs publicly promised that WTO membership would not affect his administration's revenue, which more than doubled to 220 billion yuan in 2000. Reading between the lines, I'm still not sure whether he meant that the volume of business will go up so sharply that it will offset reduced tariffs or that corruption and the 'back door' will ensure continued income flow.

Why does one in three foreign corporate executives cite China as their preferred destination for investment when there are such serious problems with the economy and a gaping lack of transparency? Why did foreign business pump in the region of US$40 billion into China in 2002 alone – and Chinese officials take a similar amount out of the country every year? 'Some [officials] have even bought luxurious houses in North America, Australia and Europe . . . given that their salaries are less than US$1000 a month, it is hard to see how they can legitimately afford school and university fees,' said the *China Daily*. Why – after twenty-five years of the reform process – has the Chinese government not sufficiently strengthened its institutions and moved to safeguard private property? Part of the problem lies with the attitude of foreign business.

In the mid 1990s scores of Australian companies tried to break in to the China market for the first time, investing funds in unproven Chinese ventures and recruiting smart, young but inexperienced executives to manage the projects. They poured out their woes at the Australian embassy bar every Friday night – I once heard that an

employee of an investment bank working on a housing project committed suicide three months after arriving in China. And I met an
Australian businessman who'd been given a one-way ticket to China
and told by his boss, 'don't come back until you make money'. Years
later, the businessman said the three years he spent in China were
the most difficult of his life because working there bore no relation
to how business is done in Australia. He was stuck in an office in a
small city with four Chinese staff including a secretary–interpreter
who tried to negotiate the demands of the company – which gave
him very little support – with the requirements of the partner, which
happened to be the local government and therefore extremely influential. 'My company wanted me to draw up some insurance for
buildings we were managing. "What do you mean, insurance?" my
counterpart would say. "This is China, if the building burns down, it
burns down."' The businessman, now based in Sydney, told me,
'What would be normal commercial terms in Australia seemed just
absurd to the Chinese.'

EPILOGUE · SLIPPERY NOODLES

My last visit to China at the end of 2002 was a time of much reflection. I was due to begin a new assignment in the Middle East in 2003 and part of me wondered whether my professional focus should instead stay on a part of the world I know so well. I contemplated becoming a 'lifer' in the Orient like my great-great-grand-uncle Phineas, who remained in Hong Kong until his death. I had seen rapid change in China over several decades, and yet there was much that stayed the same. Certainly, it remained a challenging destination for television journalists – controversial on-the-record comments are still accompanied by a quick glance over the shoulder to see who might be listening. Though curious about the unfolding story of China's economic change and the challenges posed by hosting the 2008 Olympics, I felt a break from China would do me no harm. Following the September 11 attacks, I wanted to know more about motivations in the Middle East. So I decided to close the China chapter of my life, leaving open the possibility of beginning a new chapter later on.

China today is a world away from the place it was in 1995. In five years it will be a different place again. As I report on events in the Middle East from my new base in Jerusalem, I watch China as an outsider with an insider's knowledge. So much of what is reported about Chinese politics involves visions of stiff politicians, spokespeople who deliver the government's line on everything from AIDS to UN Security Council vetoes. The po-faced people I see on television are a far cry from the real China, which is diverse, intense, desperate, cynical, forward-looking, humorous, distrustful of its leaders and sometimes bizarre.

The most significant transformation I witnessed during my posting was that China became richer. Despite my earlier, incorrect predictions that cars wouldn't be affordable, more and more vehicles appeared on the roads, clogging highways that were conceived, it seemed, in a long-gone era. The only way planners will be able to cope is if they make estimates based on their wildest expectations, and then double them. In what was once a low-rise country, high-rise apartments have sprung up everywhere as the apartment boom continues to spread across China. I also noticed that the quality of food improved greatly, and it's now possible to eat Korean, Japanese and French food in the major cities – if you can afford it. China's cities became cleaner and neater, with a growing emphasis on greenery and environmental concern. And whereas ten years ago you could pick out the mainlander from the crowds at Hong Kong Airport, it's less easy to do so today. China's youth, in particular, is well dressed and sports ultra-modern hairstyles, spectacles and accessories. Mobile telephones are a craze, not a utility, and it is not uncommon for young people to update their phone style every six or nine months.

Habits are changing too. In the mid 1990s coffee was a rare commodity. For one of my first stories in China, I went to an ordinary worker's house to see how he and his family lived. In honour of our visit, the couple had purchased a jar of Nescafé and coffee creamer because they'd heard that is what foreigners like. Not a fan of instant coffee, I turned it down until I realised how much trouble the couple had gone to in preparation for our visit.

When the crew and I went travelling, we resigned ourselves to drinking instant coffee and evaporated milk, or just sticking to tea, until we returned to Beijing. But in 1999, Super Coffee appeared and saved the day. Super Coffee was a Chinese-made instant cappuccino that came in a gold-coloured sachet. For some reason the 'Irish Coffee' flavour (which, unlike the original, was alcohol-free) turned out to be the best, and it was a thousand times better than any instant coffee we'd tasted. We travelled to far-western Qinghai armed with sachets of Super Coffee, safe in the knowledge that there was always a flask of boiling water nearby to bring it to life. By the late nineties, coffee drinking had caught on so quickly that we really didn't need Super Coffee anymore because there was a Starbucks on almost every street corner (except in the Taklamakan Desert, where no outlets have opened – yet). The success of Starbucks in China probably owes a lot to the fact that it provides a large sitting area where, for the price of a coffee, people can sit and talk all day in comfortable, temperature-controlled surroundings. This is the beginning of a new leisure phase for Chinese urbanites – people have time and money, but until recently there weren't many places to linger or simply 'hang out'. On my last visit I also noticed that private health clubs had moved out of the five-star hotels and into trendy new bar areas, another development catering to the increasing demand for leisure activities.

I also observed changes to China's leadership style, which became increasingly self-confident on the world stage. It plainly defined its national goals in opposing the war with Iraq and it did so with statesmanship. The leadership itself changed, too. When I arrived in China, the ailing Deng Xiaoping was China's patriarch and Jiang Zemin the president-in-waiting. Deng deleted the words 'planned economy' from the constitution; and he justified the introduction of the market economy, saying that the criteria for judging if something is capitalist or socialist should be whether it benefits productivity, enhances national strength and improves people's living standards. Now Jiang is the senior leader (not a patriarch in the way that Deng was) and Hu Jintao the president. Jiang Zemin's guiding principle, articulated in the uninspiring tome, *The Three Represents*, states that the Communist Party has evolved from being the party of the proletariat to a party that represents advanced productivity, advanced culture and, most importantly, the fundamental interests of the overwhelming majority of the Chinese people, not just the workers.

Despite this brave new age of user-pays capitalism, some things, such as shopping in department stores, didn't change. Cashmere sweaters are good value in China, and in department stores they are arranged by brand – King Deer in this corner, Snowflake in that one. To find a plain black cardigan you need to look at twenty separate counters, each one attended by three or four sales assistants. As you bend down to touch something that half-way resembles what you want, you hear breathing centimetres behind you. 'Are you going to take that one?' the shop assistant asks hopefully. 'No,' I reply, 'the neck is too high.' 'She says the neck is too high,' the shop assistant repeats. The assistants looking after competing brands mumble, 'She thinks the neck is too high!' 'Well, that's all we have!' says the assistant, virtually under my toes. No one bothers to help me search for what I'm after.

I am not qualified to predict anything about China's future and, as any analyst knows, China always defies prediction. It is not about to collapse. But if there's one thing that I would like to see change it is lack of transparency, in the financial system in particular. In March 2002, Chinese media reports confirmed that bank officials in southern Guangdong province embezzled US$500 million, siphoning it into overseas accounts over a ten-year period and laundering some of it in Macau and Las Vegas. In November 2002, the official Xinhua News Agency reported that a president of two major state banks had been expelled from the Communist Party and would face corruption charges. Wang Xuebing was accused of taking hundreds of thousands of dollars in bribes during his time at the Bank of China. In January 2002, the bank was fined US$20 million by United States and Chinese regulators for misconduct by the bank's New York branch, where Wang Xuebing was general manager from 1988 until 1993. The bank conceded that improper loans by its New York staff had cost the branch US$34 million.

Wang Xuebing wasn't a faceless banker but a respected international personality lauded by the likes of the chairman of the Standard Chartered Bank, Sir Patrick Gilliam, who once described him as part of 'a new breed of leadership in the major banks and regulatory authorities . . . they are modernisers and extremely impressive'. Wang Xuebing often attended international conferences, where he would outline the problems facing China's banking system. 'The subject I'm going to talk about is financial reform in China,' he told the Asia Society in May 2001 while he was president and CEO of the China Construction Bank. 'It's an old topic but still getting hotter. It's so hot that we see politicians worrying about political consequence and stability as a result of reform. We see the regulators blaming the bankers for their incompetence and mismanagement, undermining the stability of the banking system.' Now, he has become either a victim or a perpetrator of the very incompetence and mismanagement he once spoke against – because China's institutions are hidden behind a veil of secrecy, it's difficult to tell where the truth lies in the Wang Xuebing story. Today, new Bank of China staff are taken on a visit to a jail as part of their induction into the company.

And yet, while I was waiting in a queue at a Bank of China branch in the China World Trade Centre, the headquarters for dozens of multinational businesses in Beijing, I was approached by a woman offering to change my US dollars into yuan. She clearly wasn't a member of staff, but part of a 'black market' duo operating in the branch. Shortly after I refused her offer, the woman and her colleague sat down on a row of empty chairs inside the branch and proceeded to count a huge wad of US dollars. The bank staff ignored them. There must have been collusion with the branch for this to have taken place in such a prominent location, by such a prominent bank.

Foreigners are responsible for the other kind of secrecy I dislike. The conspiracy of silence isn't limited to businesses, but extends to governments and individuals who self-censor in order to avoid displeasing the Chinese government. Foreign governments fear being left out of the vast China market, and the fear is repeated down the chain so that nobody is prepared to tell it like it is. The conspiracy usually begins when a Western company makes a bid for a licence or contract for a Chinese project. During the application process, no-one dares rock the boat. (In the past five years, China has managed to silence most foreign critics of its human rights record, insisting on a bilateral 'dialogue' whereby each party – or nation – can criticise the other in private. The media is never invited.) The result is that Western governments hand over millions of dollars in aid to promote democratic institutions, but much of it amounts to little more than overseas holidays for a handful of Chinese who have good *guanxi*, or connections.

When I went to China as a correspondent I hoped to discover what the essence of 'being Chinese' was all about, to understand why my ancestors had been drawn to its shores more than one hundred and fifty years ago. Having grown up in Hong Kong and lived on the edge of China for years, I became disillusioned when the mainland turned out to be nothing like what I had expected. I suppose I had fallen in love with bygone eras – old Shanghai, colonial Hong Kong, and the romantic notion of getting on a boat to cross the world when such a journey was long and risky. Though the world is now a different, much more convenient place, I tried to live the adventures of my ancestors. Eventually, I began to love living in China for less deep-rooted reasons. It was like discovering a rare, antique carpet. The first time you look at it, it appears old and dusty. But after brushing off some of the dust, you notice amid the wear-and-tear the incredible colours that have stayed vibrant, despite the passage of time. After admiring the colours, you notice intricate patterns that tell a story about where the carpet was made, the life of its owner, and how it came to survive to the present day. Soon, the carpet doesn't look so old and dusty anymore; it becomes intriguing.

That's what living in China was like. As a child I felt I lived in the centre of the earth, a place where I could take a ferry ride across the breathtaking harbour and lose myself in a city of a million lights, where everything and everyone seemed to have energy and purpose. I came to have the same feeling in China. After work, I could step out into a world where migrant workers mingled with millionaires, and where energy and industry gave off a constant murmur, like a giant engine. It never stopped being a thrill to meet friends and venture down a narrow alley that had once been part of some century-old district, in search of my favourite restaurant, a nameless hole-in-the-wall serving five-spice duck pancakes, tofu pockets stuffed with pork and silken tofu and vermicelli soup. It was a ritual. My ritual. Each time I return to Beijing, I expect the restaurant to have disappeared, and each time I am surprised to find that it's still there.

Eventually the official restraints imposed on foreign journalists made work tiring after five years. But what kept me in China were the stories behind the people, from the rubbish man Xiao Liangyu, to Jiang Zuotao in his cave home beside the Victory Reservoir. I never tired of listening to their struggles and their successes, intimate vignettes of Chinese history. I lost touch with the rubbish man Xiao Liangyu, so I never found out whether he achieved his dream of becoming a chauffeur to the new rich. I'm sure that if I visit the village of Xiao Cun again, it will have a paved road instead of the dirt track I travelled down so many years ago. As for Jiang Zuotao, a few years ago he moved a few hours away from his cave home to the city of Yan'an, where the water conservancy bureau put him in charge of a heating system and began paying him a small salary again.

There have also been big changes for my colleagues. Sound-recordist Kate Wakeman, who worked in Beijing for four years, returned to Australia in 1998. She married my brother Stephen, who was the *Sydney Morning Herald* correspondent in Beijing from 1995 to 1997, and began a furnishings business inspired by Chinese fabrics and designs. She still works part-time as a video-tape editor at the ABC. Cleo Leung also married, and after a short stint in Sydney she moved to Shanghai in 2002 with her consultant husband, Josh Brookhart. Cleo, Josh and Kate are all now involved in the furnishings business. My cousin Stan Greaves married Elaine Sun, the ABC's bookkeeper, and they now live in Sydney. Intrepid researcher and loyal friend Charles Li moved to Sydney in mid 2001 to complete a Masters in Journalism. He graduated in May 2003 and returned to work in the Beijing bureau.

Sadly, the life and soul of the ABC Beijing bureau, cameraman Sebastian Phua – Sebas, as he was known – passed away in March 2003 at the far too young age of forty-six. Sebastian, a smoker, was diagnosed with stage four cancer in early 2002. He fought his illness bravely, never losing his optimism and his easy-going attitude. Survived by his wife Carol and their four-year-old son, Wesley, his death has left a void in my life, as I know it has in each person who ever met, befriended and worked with him. He was a rare breed and I thank him, wherever he is, for enriching me and making my television stories come to life with his beautiful eye. The world is poorer without you, Sebas.

When my plane finally took off from Beijing Airport, flying over brick farmhouses and dusty fields, I had flashbacks to some of the faces and places that had filled my life in China for the past five years. I knew that most of all I would miss sitting in roadside restaurants in remote, mountainous villages with a bowl and a pair of chopsticks in my hands, feeling that it was the most natural thing in the world.

ENDNOTES

Chapter 1 Pig's Face
Page
24. 'Dust will accumulate . . .': Mao Zedong, 'On Coalition Government', 24 April 1945, from *Selected Works*, vol. 3, pp. 316–17.

Chapter 2 Peking Ducks
Page
46. 'Walls within walls . . .': Tiziano Terzani, *The Forbidden Door*, p. 24.

Chapter 3 Shanghai Stir-fry
Page
82. 'The Shanghainese were inordinately . . .': Ling Pan, *In Search of Old Shanghai*, p. 53.
82. 'Not only because of its shops . . .': Ling Pan, *In Search of Old Shanghai*, p. 58.
86. Quotes by Dr Chengting T. Wang are taken from the *Shanghai Mercury*, 17 April 1929.

Chapter 4 Subversive Hotpot
Page
105. 'I believe that the sense of humanity . . .': student leader Li Lu, quoted in Ian Buruma, *Bad Elements: Chinese Rebels from Los Angeles to Beijing*, p. 101.
110. 'The Chinese government's . . .': Rod McGeoch and Glenda Korporaal, *The Bid: How Australia Won the 2000 Games*, p. 234.
117. 'A counter-revolutionary rebellion . . .': Deng Xiaoping's 9 June 1989 speech to Martial Law Units, quoted from <www.tsquare.TV/chronology/Deng.html>.
120. 'Slanderously referred to . . .': Indictment Beijing Procuratorate, Branch Office Criminal Indictment Document (1999) No. 141, 29 September 1999, from China Rights Forum Winter 2000, Human Rights in China website <www.hrichina.org>.

120. 'The future of China . . .': Jiang Qisheng, *My Final Statement*, 1 November 1999, Human Rights in China website <www.hrichina.org>.
122. 'I believe and the American people believe . . .': President Bill Clinton, quoted in the *Washington Post*, 27 June 1998.
123. 'Alas the old political system . . .': Wei Jingsheng, 'The Fifth Modernisation' from *The Courage to Stand Alone*, 1998, p. 201.
128. 'The fastest, largest . . .': 'China's High Technology Market' in *MFC Insight* e-magazine, 2002.

Chapter 5 Colonial Chop Suey
Page
141. 'To say now that . . .': Dr S. Bard, 'Tea and Opium', *RAS Journal*, vol. 40, 2000.
161. 'From today's vantage point . . .': Chris Patten's farewell speech, Hong Kong Handover, 30 June 1997.

Chapter 6 Renegade Dumplings
Page
188. 'Scoured by the wind . . .': Charles Bell, *The People of Tibet*, p. 2.
192. 'Tibet and Xinjiang . . .': Mao Zedong, quoted in Melvyn C. Goldstein, *The Snow Lion and the Dragon*, pp. 43–4.
194. 'The Chinese only . . .': *Sunday Times*, 21 November 1999, quoted on the World Tibet News Network website <www.tibet.ca>.
195. 'Saying he was going to get . . .': from a report quoting Tibet Autonomous Region Vice-Chairman Sun Qiwen, Xinhua News Agency, 20 January 2000.
195. 'The most important tenet of Tibetan . . .': Oliver August, 'Teenage Lama Backs Tibetan Cry for Freedom', *The Times*, 5 February 2000, p. 15.
200. 'The majority of 2.6 million . . .': 'Central Government Aids Boost Economy in Tibet', *People's Daily*, 25 May 2001.
200. Average disposable income: news release from the Permanent Mission of the PRC to the UN, 9 May 2002.
203. 'There have been no recent . . .': Wang Lixiong, 'Reflections on Tibet' in *New Left Review*, March–April 2002, p. 109.

Chapter 7 Spiritual Dim Sim
Page
223. The origins of Qigong: Yang Jwing-Ming, 'A brief history of Qigong' in *Qigong for Arthritis*, YMAA Publication Centre, Jamaica Plain.
224. Spread of Falun Gong: *Nangfang Zhoumo*, Guangzhou, 13 March 1998.
227. 'I will personally install . . .': Li Hongzhi, *Zhuan Falun*, pp. 40–1.
227. 'How weak can it be?': Li Hongzhi, *Zhuan Falun*, p. 215.
228. 'I ran into a lot of tribulations . . .': interview by Jane Hutcheon for *Foreign Correspondent*, Hong Kong, 7–8 August 1999.
231. Bookstore as a base for selling fallacies of Falun Gong: Xinhua News Agency report, 14 August 1999.
237. 'The manifestation . . .': from the Falun Dafa website <falundafa.org.hk>.

238. 'Several practitioners were enlightened . . .': article by Associated Press reporter Ginny Parker, 4 August 2000.

Chapter 8 Big River, Little Fish
Page
242. 'In my opinion our delegation . . .': David Freeman in Dai Qing, *Yangtze! Yangtze!* quoted on the Three Gorges Probe website <www.threegorgesprobe.org>.
245. 'When the country is preparing . . .': Mao Zedong, quoted in Dai Qing, *Yangtze! Yangtze!*, p. 268.
251. 'We poorer people . . .': letter from five migrants to Central Committee of the Communist Party, 22 March 2001, published on the Three Gorges Probe website <www.threegorgesprobe.org>.

Chapter 9 Pork Bellies
Page
271. 'We must instill . . .': former President Jiang Zemin, *Jiang Zemin on the Three Represents*', Foreign Languages Press, Beijing, 2002.
279. Chinese students abroad: Xinhua News Agency, 11 July 2002.
282. Home ownership revolution: Xinhua News Agency report, 13 August 2002.
284. 'Establishing a company . . .': Jack Ma, *Asian Wall Street Journal*, 20 February 2001.

Chapter 10 Crumbling Rice Bowl
Page
294. 'Clean up the filth . . .': 'Ode to Red Guards' in Kwok-sing Li (ed), *A Glossary of Political Terms of the People's Republic of China*, p. 157.
296. 'It is necessary for the educated youth': *ibid.*, p. 396.
302. Hai'er's management system: Dexter Roberts, 'Baby Steps for a Chinese Giant', *BusinessWeek Online*, 17 July 2002.
309. 'It will cause . . .': report by Jiang Zemin, 'Holding High the Great Banner of Deng Xiaoping Theory for an All-Round Advancement of the Cause of Building Socialism with Chinese Characteristics in the 21st Century', 12 September 1997, p. 25.
309. 'All workers should change . . .': *ibid.*, p. 26.
311. 'China has basically attained . . .': *People's Daily*, 1 January 2001.
311. 'Many enterprises take these . . .': Josephine Ma, 'Economist Warns of Complacency', *South China Morning Post*, 13 March 2000.

Chapter 11 New Rice
Page
323. China's software industry: Bruce Einhorn, 'High Tech in China', *BusinessWeek Online*, 28 October 2002, <www.businessweek.com>.
325. Pepsi dispute: Peter S. Goodman, 'Pepsi Seeks "Divorce" from China', *Washington Post Foreign Service*, 28 September 2002.

ENDNOTES

336. 'Is a good indication . . .': PERC report, 3 June 2002.
339. 'Suspected criminal activities including . . .': *People's Daily* online, 28 November 2002, <http://fpeng.peopledaily.com.cn>.
346. 'Some [officials] have even bought . . .': *China Daily*, 21 August 2002.

Epilogue
Page
352. 'A new breed of leadership . . .': 'A journey not a destination – the impact of China's WTO accession', from a speech made by Sir Patrick Gillam to Hong Kong General Chamber of Commerce, 140th Anniversary Distinguished Speakers Luncheon, 12 November 2001.

BIBLIOGRAPHY

Barmé, Geremie and Jaivin, Linda, *New Ghosts, Old Dreams: Chinese Rebel Voices*, Crown Publishing Group, New York, 1992

Bell, Charles, *The People of Tibet*, Motilal Banarsidass Publishers, New Dehli, 1994

Buruma, Ian, *Bad Elements: Chinese Rebels from Los Angeles to Beijing*, Random House, New York, 2001

Dai, Qing, *Yangtze! Yangtze!* Earthscan Publications, London, 1994

Dong, Stella, *Shanghai: The Rise and Fall of a Decadent City, 1842–1949*, Perennial, New York, 2001

Goldstein, Melvyn C., *The Snow Lion and the Dragon*, University of California Press, California, 1997

Hutchings, Graham, *Modern China: A Guide to a Century of Change*, Harvard University Press, Cambridge, Massachusetts, 2001

Li, Kwok-sing (ed), *A Glossary of Political Terms of the People's Republic of China*, Chinese University Press, Hong Kong, 1995

McGeoch, Rod and Korporaal, Glenda, *The Bid: How Australia Won the 2000 Games*, William Heinemann, Australia, 1994

Pan, Ling, *In Search of Old Shanghai*, Joint Publishing Co., Beijing, date unknown

Ryckmans, Pierre, *Chinese Shadows*, Viking Press, New York, 1977

BIBLIOGRAPHY

Studwell, Joe, *The China Dream: The Quest for the Last Great Untapped Market on Earth*, Grove Press, New York, 2003

Terzani, Tiziano, *Behind the Forbidden Door*, Henry Holt, New York, 1992

Wei, Jingsheng, *The Courage to Stand Alone: Letters from Prison and Other Writings*, Penguin Books, New York, 1998

Zedong, Mao, *Selected Works of Mao Zedong*, Foreign Languages Press, Beijing, 1967

Zemin, Jiang, *Jiang Zemin on the Three Represents*, Foreign Languages Press, Beijing, 2002

ACKNOWLEDGEMENTS

I received support and encouragement from so many, not to mention many of the people written about in the book. Without them this volume would have been much thinner! Whether it was brainstorming over the title or just discussing 'the book', I know I dominated far too many discussions. I thank you all for your patience and support.

I would like to single out a few people for a special thank you: Saeri and Geoffrey Ziebart for their hospitality and friendship; James Leininger, Chen Mei and Cleo and Josh Brookhart for their friendship, advice and feedback; my parents for their contributions and feedback and especially my mum, Bea, for coming up with the title over a caffe latte one day; my brother Stephen Hutcheon for his advice and help with the photographs; Manuel Panagiotopoulos for his encouragement and friendship; and Charles Li, for checking the facts and having an incredible memory and filing system.

Thank you also to Solomon Bard, Hans Hendrischke, Neil Cumine, Arthur Hacker, Mary Gu, Liu Dawei, David Murphy, Richard McGregor, Francesco Sisci, Martin Walsh, Michael Maher, John Tulloh for allowing me to stay in Sydney long enough to finish writing and, in ABC News and Current Affairs, Max Uechtritz, John Cameron and Walter Hamilton.

Finally, thanks to all my colleagues in the Beijing Bureau, and a

ACKNOWLEDGEMENTS

huge thanks to editor Amanda O'Connell, Fiona Inglis of Curtis Brown, and Bernadette Foley from Pan Macmillan. The next Yum-cha is definitely on me.

INDEX